THE POLITICS, SOCIOLOGY AND ECONOMICS OF EDUCATION

The Politics, Sociology and Economics of Education

Interdisciplinary and Comparative Perspectives

Edited by

Russell F. Farnen
Professor of Political Science
University of Connecticut, USA

and

Heinz Sünker
Professor of Social Pedagogics
University of Wuppertal, Germany

First published in Great Britain 1997 by
MACMILLAN PRESS LTD
Houndmills, Basingstoke, Hampshire RG21 6XS and London
Companies and representatives throughout the world

A catalogue record for this book is available from the British Library.

ISBN 0–333–68377–3

First published in the United States of America 1997 by
ST. MARTIN'S PRESS, INC.,
Scholarly and Reference Division,
175 Fifth Avenue, New York, N.Y. 10010

ISBN 0–312–17468–3

Library of Congress Cataloging-in-Publication Data
The politics, sociology, and economics of education :
interdisciplinary and comparative perspectives / edited by Russell
F. Farnen and Heinz Sünker.
p. cm.
Includes bibliographical references (p.   ) and indexes.
ISBN 0–312–17468–3 (cloth)
1. Education and state—Cross-cultural studies.   2. Politics and
education—Cross-cultural studies.   3. Education—Social aspects–
–Cross-cultural studies.   4. Education—Economic aspects—Cross
-cultural studies.   5. Educational change—Cross-cultural studies.
I. Farnen, Russell Francis, 1933–   . II. Sünker, Heinz.
LC71.P586 1997
379—dc21   97–5319
                                                                CIP

Selection and editorial matter © Russell F. Farnen and Heinz Sünker 1997
Chapters 1, 2 and 16 © Russell F. Farnen 1997
Chapters 7 (jointly) and 8 © Heinz Sünker 1997
Other chapters © Macmillan Press Ltd 1997

This book is printed on paper suitable for recycling and made from fully managed and
sustained forest sources.

10   9   8   7   6   5   4   3   2   1
06 05 04 03 02 01 00 99 98 97

Printed in Great Britain by
The Ipswich Book Company Ltd
Ipswich, Suffolk

Contents

Preface   vii

Notes on the Contributors   ix

Part I
Setting the Context

1   **The Present as Seen From the Past**   3
   Russell F. Farnen

Part II
Politics and/of Education

2   **Politics, Education, and Paradigmatic Reconceptualism:**
   US Critical Theory in the 1990s   15
   Russell F. Farnen

3   **Conservative Politics and National Curricula**   45
   Michael W. Apple

Part III
Education and Society

4   **Blaming the Victims: The Political Oppression of**
   Disabled People   63
   Len Barton

5   **The Repudiation of Criteriology: In Pursuit of Communities**
   of Democracy and Hope   73
   Siebren Miedema

6   **Socialization and Economic Reproduction in Pluralistic**
   Welfare Societies   85
   Stefan Hradil

7   **Inequality and Education: Changing Theoretical Conceptions**   101
   Fritz-Ulrich Kolbe, Heinz Sünker, Dieter Timmermann

8   Heydorn's Bildungs Theory and Content as Social Analysis   113
     Heinz Sünker

Part IV
Economics and Education

9   Educational Politics, Division of Labor, and Emancipation   129
     Peter Leisink

10   Corporatism and Identity   141
     Philip Wexler

11   Educational Reform and Politics in Israel: Change or
     Economic Reproduction?   153
     Ilana Felsenthal and Chaim Adler

12   Educational Policy as Technocratic Strategy: The
     Politics of Excellence   169
     Frank Fischer and Alan Mandell

13   Pedagogy in the Age of Predatory Culture   183
     Peter McLaren

Part V
Educational Reform

14   Recent Education Reform: Is It a Postmodern Phenomenon?   199
     Geoff Whitty

15   Educational Discourses and Creating a Democratic Public:
     A Critical Pragmatic View   211
     Tomas Englund

16   Summary/Conclusions: The Future as Seen from the Present   229
     Russell F. Farnen

References   249

Index of Names   285

Index of Subjects   291

Preface

From the start, this book has been a cooperative effort of many people, representing several educational organizations and institutions. The project began in late 1991 at the Center for Interdisciplinary Research (ZIF) at the University of Bielefeld, FRG. Then, nearly all of the present 17 contributors from seven different countries met to exchange papers and views on the conference theme of 'reproduction, social inequality, and resistance: new directions in the theory of education'. The results of these deliberations appeared in 1994 under the title of *Bildung, Gesellschaft, und Sozial Ungleichheit* (Education, Society, and Social Inequality), which Suhrkamp Verlag in Frankfurt am Main, FRG, published in 1994.

All of the contributors believed that we could enlarge the audience interested in these themes with an updated English language version of this book for a broader international group of readers, scholars, and teachers. Consequently, we assembled this latest version of our continuing joint efforts in the hope and expectation that such a book would provide a comparative, cross-national, and international dimension to our not very often cosmopolitan and more frequently provincial or domestically restricted courses in economics, society, and/or politics and educational policy making. In this respect, we earnestly hope our shared view about the worth of an interdisciplinary and international set of essays on a common theme will prove correct.

Both editors are specialists in politics and education cross-nationally as well as in the US and FRG; have authored or edited books in the field for publishers such as Peter Lang, Macmillian, St. Martin's, Transaction Books, Leske and Budrich, and Suhrkamp Verlag as well as University Presses in the FRG such as Bielefeld (ZIF), Oldenberg BIS, and Deutscher Studienverlag; are editors/contributors to major international journals such as *Politics, Groups, and the Individual* (formerly *Politics and the Individual*), *Social Science Review*, and *New Praxis*; are members of international professional organizations such as the International Political Science Association, the International Society for Political Psychology, International Studies Association, AERA, and the Comparative Education Association; and have spoken to UNESCO, German Political Science Association (DVPW), and other major conferences in the US and Western Europe. The 17 contributors to this volume are prominent scholars, well known for their work on the national as well as international social science and educational scene.

There would be an endless list of persons and organizations to thank were we to begin to name them all in expressing our appreciation for their help, guidance, advice, and support. We should single out for their special efforts in arranging our initial organizing conference and in producing the German language text, D. Timmermann and F. U. Kölbe, who joined H. Sünker in completing the prodigious tasks of editing financing, organizing, and completing this project in which we have all been participants. To these two colleagues, we all owe a debt of sincere gratitude.

We want like to take this opportunity to express our appreciation for financial support to the University of Connecticut Research Foundation and the German Research Foundation (DFG) as well as to Ms. Martha D. Bowman who performed the necessary editorial and word processing duties to turn our sometimes too vague ideas into tangible realities. In this same respect, the Macmillian editorial staff in London has also assisted us mightily from the beginning to the end of this arduous process.

An expression of thanks also goes to Erika and Christa who have provided the kind of essential support that defies description but without which little is accomplished. We should also acknowledge some members of the next couple of generations who could actually learn something useful from this volume. These include Monika and Michael, Mike and Erika, Tracy, Ted, and Allison to all of whom we confidently leave our future, certain that it is in their very capable hands.

Russell F. Farnen   and   Heinz Sünker
Farmington, CT   Wuppertal, FRG
April 1997

Notes on the Contributors

Chaim Adler served as Dean of the School of Education at Hebrew University, Jerusalem, Israel. His research interests are educational sociology, the relation between social structure and school system, and educational problems of disadvantaged youth. He wrote *Beyond the Dead End Alley of Mass Education* (with R. Sever, 1994, Boulder, CO: Westview Press).

Michael W. Apple is John Bascom Professor of Curriculum and Instruction and Educational Policy Studies at the University of Wisconsin, Madison, WI. He has written extensively on the relationship between knowledge and power. Recent works include *Official Knowledge* (1993, New York, NY: Routledge), *Education and Power* (second edition, 1995, New York, NY: Routledge), and *Cultural Politics and Education* (1996, New York, NY: Teachers College Press and London, UK: Open University Press).

Len Barton is Professor of Education in the Division of Education at the University of Sheffield, UK. He is interested in sociopolitical perspectives on disability and is currently engaged in a cross-national project on the idea of inclusive education. Recent volumes include *Disability and Society: Emerging Issues and Insights* (ed., 1996, London, UK: Longmans), *Making Difficulties, Research and the Construction of SEN* (ed. with P. Clough, 1995, London, UK: Paul Chapman Publishing). He is the founder and editor of the international journal, *Disability and Society*.

Tomas Englund is Professor of Education, Uppsala University, Sweden. His research interests include curriculum theory and history, political socialization, and political philosophy. Recent books include *The Education Policy Shift in Sweden* (1996, Stockholm, Sweden, HLS Forlag), *Curriculum as a Political Problem* (1986, Uppsala, Sweden: Uppsala Studies in Education; Stockholm, Sweden: Almqvist & Wiksell), "Citizenship Education in Swedish Schools" (1986, *Pedagogisk Forskning* [Pedagogical Research], vols. 65-6), and "Education for Public or Private Good" (1993, *Pedagogisk Forskning*, vol. 108).

Russell F. Farnen is Professor of Political Science, University of Connecticut, Storrs and Hartford, CT. His research interests include cross-national political socialization and education, mass media, authoritarianism and democracy, nationalism, cultural diversity, and civic education. Major publications include *Democracy, Socialization, and Conflicting Loyalties in East and West: Cross-National and Comparative Perspectives* (ed. with H. Dekker, D. German, R. Meyenberg, 1996, New York, NY: St. Martin's Press and London, UK: Macmillan), *Nationalism, Ethnicity, and Identity: Cross-National* *and Comparative Perspectives* (ed., 1994, London, UK and New Brunswick, NJ: Transaction Publishers), *Reconceptualizing Politics, Socialization, and Education: International Perspectives for the Next Century* (editor, 1993, Oldenburg, FRG: University of Oldenburg [BIS] Press), and *Integrating Political Science, Education, and Public Policy: International Perspectives on Decision Making, Systems Theory, and Socialization Research* (1990, Frankfurt am Main, FRG; New York, NY; Bern, Switzerland; and Paris, France: Verlag Peter Lang).

Ilana Felsenthal is Lecturer in the Division of Pedagogy and Teacher Training and is a research fellow of the NCJW Research Institute for Innovation in Education at the School of Education of the Hebrew University, Jerusalem, Israel. Her research interests include democratic education and justice in educational systems.

Frank Fischer is Professor of Political Science at Rutgers University, Newark, NJ. His research interests include the comparative study of environmental policy in Germany and the US. Recent publications include *Evaluating Public Policy* (1995, Chicago, IL: Nelson-Hall), *Greening Environmental Policy: The Politics of a Sustainable Future* (ed. with M. Black, 1995, London, UK: Paul Chapman and New York, NY: St. Martin's), *Technocracy and the Politics of Expertise* (1990, Newbury Park, CA: Sage Publications). He is the book review editor for *Organization and Environment*.

Stefan Hradil is Professor of Sociology and Dean of the Faculty of Social Sciences at the Johannes Gutenberg-University in Mainz, FRG. His research interests include modernization, social structure of modern societies, social inequality and stratification, social milieus and lifestyles, and power. Recent publications include *Sozialstrukturanalyse* (Social Structure Analysis, 8 volumes; series editor; 1996, Opladen, FRG: Leske & Budrich), *Die 'Single-Gesellschaft'* (The 'Single Society'; 1995, Munich, FRG: C. H. Beck), and *Die westeuropäischen Gesellschaften im Vergleich* (The Western-European Societies in Comparative Perspective; ed. with S. Immerfall, 1996, Opladen, FRG: Leske & Budrich)

Peter Leisink is Associate Professor of Social Sciences and Labor Studies at Utrecht University, the Netherlands. His research focus is on social inequality and labor relations. Recent publications include *Work and Citizenship in the New Europe* (ed. with H. Coenen, 1993, Aldershot, UK: Edward Elgar), *The Challenges to Trade Unions in Europe* (ed. with J. Van Leemput and J. Vilrokx; 1996, Aldershot, UK: Edgar Elgar), and 'Citizenship and Work in Europe' in M. Roche and R. Van Berkel, eds., *European Citizenship and Social Exclusion* (in press, Aldershot, UK: Avebury).

Fritz-Ulrich Kolbe is Educational Assistant at the University of Heidelberg, FRG. His research interests include school pedagogy, historical pedagogy, and educational theory. Recent publications include *Bildung und Aufklärung heute* (Education and Enlightenment Today; ed. with V. Lenhart, 1990, Bielefeld, FRG: KT-W), *Strukturwandel schulischen Handelns* (Structural Change in School Affairs; 1994, Weinheim, FRG: Deutscher Studienverlag), *Gewalt an Schule: Ausmaß, Bedingungen, Prävention* (Violence in the Schools: Proportion, Limits, Prevention; 1996, ed. with W. Schubarth and H. Willems), and *Reflexivität professionellen Könnens und Wissens* (Reflexivity of Professional Understanding and Knowledge; ed., 1996, Frankfurt am Main, FRG: Haag und Herchen).

Alan Mandell is Associate Dean and Director of the Metropolitan Center of the State University of New York/Empire State College, New York, NY. His research interests are adult education and the social and political contexts of contemporary schooling. Recent publications include *Portfolio Development and Adult Learning: Purposes and Strategies* (with E. Michelson, 1990, Chicago, IL: Council for Adult and Experiential Learning), 'The Authority of Uncertainty' (with L. Herman) in *Educational Foundations* (Vol. 10, No. 1, Winter 1996), 'From Teachers to Mentors: Acknowledging Openings in the Faculty Role' (in R. Mills and A. Tait, eds., *Supporting the Learner in Open and Distance Learning*, 1996, London, UK: Pitman Publishing). He is editor of *Kairos*, a journal of social and cultural criticism.

Peter McLaren is Professor, Graduate School of Education and Information Studies, University of California, Los Angeles, CA. His research interests include Marxist theory, postmodernism, critical pedagogy, and multiculturalism. Recent publications include *Critical Pedagogy and Predatory Culture: Oppositional Politics in a Postmodern Age* (1995, London, UK and New York, NY: Routledge), *Life in Schools* (second edition, 1993, New York, NY: Longman), and *Schooling as a Ritual Performance* (second edition, 1993 London, UK and New York, NY: Routledge.

Siebren Miedema is Associate Professor in the Department of Philosophy and History of Education at Leiden University and Hendrik Pierson Professor for Christian Education on the Faculty of Psychology and Education at the Free University of Amsterdam, the Netherlands. His research interests include critical pedagogy, hermeneutical pedagogy, early childhood education, philosophy of the social sciences, pragmatism, and religious education. His recent publications include *The Legacy of Pragmatism* (coeditor, forthcoming), *Opvoeding zoals het is* (Education As It Is; coeditor, 1995, Utrecht, the Netherlands: De Tijdstroom), and *The Politics of Human Science* (coeditor, 1994, Brussels, Belgium: VUB Press).

Heinz Sünker is Professor of Social Pedagogics, Department of Social Sciences, University of Wuppertal, FRG. His research interests include the theory and history of social work, social theory, and educational theory. Recent publications include *Bildung, Gesellschaft, Soziale Ungleichheit* (Education, Society, and Social Inequality; ed. with F. Kolbe and D. Timmermann, 1994, Frankfurt am Main, FRG: Suhrkamp), *Kindheitspolitik International* (Politics of Childhood, International Contributions; ed. with G. Neubauer, 1993, Opladen, FRG: Leske & Budrich), *Kritische Erziehungswissenschaft, Moderne, Postmoderne* (Critical Pedagogics, Modern, Postmodern; 2 vols., ed. with W. Marotzki, 1992/1993, Weinheim, FRG: Deutscher Studienverlag), *Education and Fascism* (ed. with H. Uwe Otto, 1997, London, UK and Washington, DC: Falmer Press), and 'The Politics of Childhood, Childrens' Rights, and the UN Convention' (in L. Chisholm et al., eds., 1995, *Growing Up in Europe: Contemporary Horizons in Childhood and Youth Studies*, Berlin, FRG and New York, NY: Walter de Gruyter).

Dieter Timmermann is Professor of Economics of Education and Educational Planning at the University of Bielefeld, FRG. His research interests are school finance, vocational education, transition from education to work, inequality, and quality of education. Recent books include *Vocational Education and the Labor Market in the 1990s* (ed. with F. Strikker, 1990, Frankfurt am Main, FRG: Verlag Peter Lang), *Financing Vocational Education* (2 vols., 1994/95, Hagen, FRG: Distance University Hagen), and *Managing Quality in Vocational Education and Training* (1996, Bielefeld, FRG: Bertelsmann).

Philip Wexler is Professor of Education and Sociology and Dean, Margaret Warner Graduate School of Education and Human Development, University of Rochester, NY. His research interests include sociology of education; social theory; sociology of knowledge, culture, and information; social psychology; and qualitative research methods. Recent publications include *Becoming Somebody: Toward a Social Psychology of School* (1992, London, UK, New York, NY, and Philadelphia, PA: Falmer Press), *After Postmodernism: Education, Politics and Identity* (ed. with R. Smith, 1995, London, UK and Washington, DC: Falmer Press), and *Holy Sparks: Social Theory, Education, and Religion* (1996, New York, NY: St. Martin's Press)..

Geoff Whitty is Karl Mannheim Professor of Sociology of Education and Director of the Health and Education Research Unit, Institute of Education, University of London, UK. His research interests include sociology of education, education policy, school reform, teacher education, and health education. Some of his publications are *Sociology and School Knowledge* (1985, London, UK: Methuen), *The State and Private Education* (1989, London, UK: Falmer Press), and *Specialisation and Choice in Urban Education* (with T. Edwards and S. Gewirtz, 1993, London, UK: Routledge).

Part I

Setting the Context

1   *The Present as Seen From the Past*

Russell F. Farnen

ABSTRACT

This chapter summarizes the salient features of each chapter and introduces the major themes dealing with the politics, sociology, and economics of education in Western Europe and North America. It introduces the reader to key concepts (such as critical theory), while discussing in a preliminary fashion international trends and prospects for educational and societal reform.

PART I: SETTING THE CONTEXT

This introductory chapter lays out the plan for the book, surveys some findings from each chapter, and identifies some common themes about politics, economics, and sociology of education (for example, critical theory is a major theme, including how it is addressed in similar/different ways in the US, UK, Germany, and Sweden). This book uses international and interdisciplinary approaches to comparatively study education's political, sociological, and economic dimensions. Major topics include critical theory, hegemony, postmodernism, oppression, disabilities, emancipation, corporatism, and meritocracy. We also discuss democracy, socialization, reproduction, pluralism, inequality, social analysis, postindustrialism, predatory culture, pragmatism, and 'subversion'. Distinguished international educators from the US, Canada, UK, Netherlands, FRG, Israel, and Sweden present a comprehensive picture of the current educational scene in the US and Western Europe, major policy debates, and possible solutions for current public policy dilemmas.

Our primary purpose in this book is to provide comparative, cross-national, and interdisciplinary views on major educational problems along with suggested approaches to educational decision and policy making in the US and Western Europe. The major topics of debate in the US and Europe deal with questions about privatization, education and the economy, equity, and equality of opportunity, as well as affirmative action, the conservative restoration versus social liberal/welfare approaches, pragmatism versus elite perspectives, discrimination on the basis of race, gender, disability, nationality, and ethnicity, and the major purposes of education in modern democratic, civil societies with mixed/market economics. Preparing youth to meet the challenges of the 21st century (with its new global, pluralistic, and technical/technological challenges) requires new roles and competencies for individuals, families, and governments at all levels (from local to EU and UNO). The book lays out the principal features of key debates over caste, class, elite, mass, multicultural, affirmative action, and other educational issues. These topics share certain ideological underpinnings such as authoritarianism versus democracy, elite versus mass, conservative versus (social) liberal, left versus right, national versus international, industrial versus postindustrial, and modern versus postmodern formulations. The views of critical education theorists in the US and Western Europe are thoroughly described and debated with the enlightenment of an international audience in mind.

PART II: POLITICS AND/OF EDUCATION

Farnen's discussion (Chapter 2) of US critical theory lays out the basic assumptions and criticisms from US reconceptualists, traces their recent changes, and assesses the current relevance of neo-Marxists in US educational circles today. He shows how some US critical theorists changed from a theory based on Marxism to one of social democratic liberalism, emphasizing democratic, nonrevolutionary reform. Other US/UK theorists (such as Bowles, Gintis, Giroux, McLaren, Apple, Willis, and Whitty) modified their arguments, moving from an economic basis to a philosophical, ideological, and social constructionist critique. Alternatively, they focused on more concrete topics such as civic education, science, or technical education. Although the neo-Marxists made positive contributions to past debates, with the bankruptcy of Marxist-Leninist systems, their views have less credibility today. They have either been prohibited from or are reluctant to engage in the 'culture wars' and contemporary public debates. These controversies are over liberal and conservative approaches to specific educational policies such as affirmative action, multiculturalism, diversity, and 'P.C. thinking'. Although the reconceptualists' argument on achieving equality in fact/condition is central to the debate, they remain peripheral because conservatives dominate both the definition of the new paradigm and command a popular following, unlike the old-fashioned (social) liberalism of the 1930s.

Apple (Chapter 3) discusses hegemony, ideology, equality, and the New Right. He differentiates between 'official' or legitimate knowledge and its political power and dominance over society. These issues involve race, gender, class, textbook publication, and the shape of the curriculum. How knowledge is estimated, organized, taught, and evaluated always gives preference to one elite over another. These curriculum debates involve economic and cultural capital, the reproductive and emancipatory roles of the schools, and school system organizational structures during this era of conservative restoration. These have implications for a national curriculum and national testing, both of which are ideological questions. Such a plan will harm those already most damaged in society and will advance the rightist agenda of privatization, 'choice', and a common culture (or literacy), based on the right's own set of meanings and values about grand narratives (such as the market) which now dominate our consciousness and lives.

Apple lays out the extent to which the US curriculum is already nationalized through its textbook and examination system in which 20 per cent of the population reap 80 per cent of the rewards. Or, looking at the UK example, the more advanced national trend there toward a national curriculum and examination system has not benefitted women, persons of color, or the working class, in particular. The neoliberal and neoconservative forces in the UK and the US defined the public good as pro-market and anti-state. They have done so without the benefit of an inclusive and genuine public debate about the diverse elements of a so-called common culture which reflect the basic elements of the millions of different people who populate these societies. Apple's personal answer to implementing these proposals comes from the Reagan era drug policy response; that is, 'Just say no'! to them.

PART III: EDUCATION AND SOCIETY

Barton (Chapter 4) holds that Britain's disabled have largely been marginalized in discussions of inequality and social reproduction plus in the society as a whole. The sociology of education treated them as a powerless, unorganized, invisible entity, rather than as a subject of professional inquiry. Special education has either been depoliticized, accepted as egalitarian, emotionally charged, or neutralized. The sociological analysis of special education raises questions about schooling, ideology, historical forces, group definition, and professionalism. The disabled have been systematically excluded or prevented from speaking for themselves. Medical definitions of disability lead to dehumanization, isolation, and oppression. The disabled can exercise options for choice, empowerment, new opportunities, and political pressure to overcome their low status, vulnerability, lack of choice, and absence of self-control over personal and public problems. Since they are not particularly socially or politically minded, the disabled are victims of learned helplessness. They focus more on meeting their needs than on advocating their own and the political rights of other oppressed persons. Disability is best seen as part of an equal opportunity perspective because it is a socially constructed concept. It provides a basis to link with other discriminated groups, a cause for social action, and the means to create a public issue and to define its integral importance. Disability must be transformed from a welfare to an equal opportunity and anti-oppression issue. So-called 'normalization' is nonproductive. It demeans the disabled since it is apolitical, individualistic, based on privileged professional judgments, uses false norms for comparison, and ignores power structures, poverty, and marginalization. It does not help to produce an open, democratic, and just society in which disability is treated as a public question, the disabled are organized politically, and their emancipation from oppression is part of the everyday political agenda.

Miedema (Chapter 5) describes the death of the 1970s pedagogical traditions of empiricism, hermeneutics, and critical-emancipatory goals. Four new educational approaches materialized in the 1990s to deal with curriculum reform, practical education, student motivation, and dropouts. These include new theoretical paradigms, historical research, pragmatism, and declarations about the end of pedagogy. Miedema also discusses the end of modernity, postmodernity, utopian thought, pragmatism, plurality, key Dutch pedagogical trends, and cosmopolitan citizenship. He mentions the different philosophical positions toward rationality, progress, and enlightenment. He discusses scholars' views on autonomy, independence, irony, *Bildung*, critique, solidarity, and democracy. The utopian pedagogical traditions of politics, rationality, progress, myth, and revolution are briefly reviewed. He features Habermas' and Dewey's ideas on democracy and education, public problem solving, creative experiences, pluralism, humanization, rationality, and liberal democracy. Rorty's and Bernstein's modern pragmatism is partially endorsed.

A case study of plurality and pedagogy in the Netherlands discusses the history of the denominational pillarization and social pluralism of that society and the tendency for the Dutch to import basic Western educational reforms, processes, and methods. Yet these views were accepted without the benefit of their philosophical underpinnings. The society also dealt with intra- and intercultural pluralism vis-á-vis ethnicity regarding guest laborers and immigrants. Dutch educational policy shifted from ethnic independence to monocultural dominance and assimilation in recent years. Miedema also describes different concepts of citizenship (for example, private and social) as well as how to integrate individuals' civic, social, and economic rights. With Habermas, Miedema lays the foundation for a liberal, universal, and cosmopolitan world concept of citizenship in which democratic educational practices play a leading role. John Dewey's previous work along this line is considered to be a useful model for developing shared interests and fruitful associations.

In Chapter 6, Hradil lays out the background of social change and pluralism in Germany and the West since the 1970s. He details certain parallel deficiencies in socialization research which empirical milieu research could rectify. In his discussion of socialization and reproduction in pluralistic welfare societies, Hradil examines concepts such as social inequality and vertical mobility using a milieu and class research framework. Socialization, biographies, mobility, and hierarchies make more sense in postindustrial societies if examined from a milieu perspective (using categories such as worker, bourgeois, technocrat, and hedonist). A case study of relevant milieus and life styles in western Germany increases the utility of this analysis.

Kolbe, Sünker, and Timmermann's contribution (Chapter 7) on the sociology of education asserts that educational policy is social policy and that a democratic society is based on an active, engaged, and politically involved citizenry. They discuss social inequality, education's class-based and economic reproduction role, contested issues in the 'new' German sociology of education debate in the 1980s, and a reexamination of reproduction theory. Concepts of the state, autonomy, subjectivity, resistance, and social structure are assessed. They recommend resisting the domination and overfunctionalization of education and implementing continual societal reform.

Sünker (Chapter 8) discusses Heydorn's educational philosophy as critical social theory, much as Adorno's analysis in the late 1950s would have done. He includes the concepts of autonomy, liberation, emancipation, Marxist praxis, critical theory, intersubjectivity, the dialectic, historicism, and interactions among power, economy, and culture. The theoretical contributions of representative neo-Marxists and other educational philosophers are integrated into the argument in a discussion of cultural revolution, contradiction, and the deconstruction of totality. Sünker discusses the theories, concepts, and reality of education using Heydorn's theoretical analysis as a baseline. Here, Sünker introduces contrasting and supporting ideas to reinforce his case against education as domination in a Western historical and philosophical setting. Alternatively, education as self-reflection, self-liberation, self-discovery, self-realization, and self-satisfaction in the process of historical acquisition and development replaces the traditional dominance of contradictory power relationships. In effect, this argument for educational humanism is based on a combination of Marxist theory and German idealism. The job of self-aware teachers in the Socratic tradition is to serve as leaders to liberate students (through hard work) from social/institutional oppression, repression, and 'subsumption' (that is, identity absorption).

PART IV: ECONOMICS AND EDUCATION

Leisink (Chapter 9) discusses education, labor markets, and social inequality in the Netherlands. He describes labor market trends, recent educational policy changes, social inequality, and emancipation. Believing that education, the economy, and the political system are closely interrelated, he asserts that espousing a reduction in social inequality without examining the labor market is doomed to failure. It does not matter if the object of such research is to support capitalist needs for educated workers or education for social empowerment and emancipation as alternative goals.

In the Netherlands, the utility of labor force statistics suffers from a barrage of changed job definitions, increases in low skill temporary jobs, changing female and minority (high) unemployment rates, new educational qualifications and requirements, significant manufacturing job losses, and increasing demands for computer literate, electronically skilled, and high tech workers. Now, there are more low-paying and dead-end jobs along with less job security and reduced career opportunities in the Netherlands. Formal education continues to perform new qualifications and credentialing functions as well as its traditional humanistic and instrumental roles. Because of 'overqualified' workers, gender and ethnic discrimination, and workforce segmentation, social inequality has increased in the 1980s and 1990s. In response to employer and state vocational training demands, the Dutch educational system has been modified considerably by using employer-provided job profiles, reorganizing the education system, implementing new apprenticeship programs, and increasing public-private cooperation. The reorganization of general secondary education and establishment of comprehensive schooling now more closely link education and work.

In Chapter 10, Wexler describes the fundamental corporatist reorganization of education as a partnership among progressive liberals, state bureaucrats, educators, and industry representatives. In the context of poststructuralism and postmodernism, we can observe the pursuit of identity production at the micro, and social control at the macro, levels of organization. Here, the ambivalent themes and demands of technology and morality are battling for intellectual control over educational settings.

School-corporate partnerships and the commodification and privatization of schooling are now *passé* since the 'Toyota School' objectives of standardized products, common outcomes, and quality control are the newly dominant imperatives. These requisites include performance-based, carefully designed, team efforts, with hands-on and 'real life' experiences being integral parts of both the new school and the emerging workplace. The post-Fordist educational system encourages capital accumulation and postindustrialism. Restructuring, vision, order, population management, productivity, innovation, elitism, assessment, and design are the key workplace and educational terms. Morality, choice, privatization, and readiness for the global marketplace are other basic ideas behind mass mobilization of efforts such as parental involvement, networking, flexibility, core learning, and cooperative teamwork - all representing the 'real' economic world. The new curriculum for this task is devoid of social studies and includes a superficial knowledge of history, elementary communication skills, personal morality, and basic reasoning. These are the objectives of external desocialization, not internal, social, or student-centered goals such as self-identity formation, personal reflection, and social responsibility. The new school is class-biased, performance-oriented, achievement-based, and divisive; exhibits no school spirit; and does not help with positive personality formation or personal moral development.

Postmodernism can be seen as the last gasp of modernity seeking to hold on to elements of the industrial and assembly line past. As such, its excesses (including unbridled consumerism) are understandable. It may also be evidence of widespread social anomie, conformism, license, overstimulation, media excesses, and the absence of a dialectic of differentiation. Imposing external authority to quash the supposed absence of self-reliance and self-regulation can be combined with religious fanaticism to prevent examining a constructive dialogue about reality-based 'otherness', identity, creativity, spiritualism, and grounding in the modern world.

In Chapter 11, Felsenthal and Adler question whether educational reform in Israel is based on real change or a reformulation of the reproduction basis of education as in most societies. They examine key elements (such as school integration) in the 'reform' process over the last 30 years. Besides being superficially a struggle between parents and educators, this is a symbol of the structural/cultural conflicts in Israeli society. For example, this issue represents the struggle between horizontal integration and vertical differentiation among Jews (that is, socialized or cultural differences versus class or group stratifications). Other recent 'reforms' (such as vocational education and the structure of matriculation exams) also accelerated 'legitimate' classifications and the resultant differentiation. These reforms restricted entry to higher education, increased selectivity, and excluded subordinate groups based on newly 'discovered knowledge' criteria. The groups most affected are the least knowledgeable about (and the most impotent to resist) such 'reforms', which do not benefit them. The integration process is appealing as a 'quick fix'. Allegedly costing nothing, these new practices are being implemented in a climate of increasing parental financial responsibility for education while promoting greater parental choice, increased school autonomy, and other competing narratives. Such initiatives may combine to scuttle Israel's overall social and educational egalitarian imperatives.

In Chapter 12, Fischer and Mandell deal with excellence, technology, and US educational policy. They discuss the long-range effects of *A Nation at Risk* (1983) with its technological imperatives and language of 'crisis'. They maintain that the language of 'excellence' for the last 20 years is based on consolidating elite power and its underlying meritocracy. Its advocates are high-tech, industrial power brokers who dominate the postindustrial transformation of American life and thought. Schools bear the burden and accept the blame for the present low-tech response to the new demands of an increasingly technocratic society. The realities of job growth are such that this new corporate imperative is largely mythical. That is, most recent US job growth is in the service sector, not in high-tech industries. Furthermore, schooling itself is less important than literacy and on-the-job training to increase productivity and develop new skills. The current testing controversy is also suspect because there have been no real declines in national scores (for example, in reading); other empirical indices of educational success are also favorable. In the past, US schools have not always been a force for democracy since they have promoted privilege, inequality, and class divisions. These trends will likely be repeated in the new postindustrial (also a contested concept) epoch when the educational sorting machine will still perform these socially divisive tasks.

Major groups and individual writers (such as the Trilateral Commission and Bell, Etzioni, and Reich) call for a nonpartisan industrial policy to replace interest-group politics and self-interested decision making. The new society envisioned will be based on education, knowledge, and intellect with symbolic analysts and professionals caring for the organization of science, which itself has become a new ideology. The pursuit of depoliticized merit and excellence is the new tocsin for the postindustrial revolution of professional service providers in the midst of a moral and ideological void. The real goal of this postindustrial master group is to use education to rationalize/ideologize the force of the emerging technology juggernaut and to ensure social acceptability for this new order. This will be done without actually preparing the next generation of students to fill (nonexistent) jobs in the 1990s class/elite system. However, this 'excellence' movement will likely soon play itself out. Thereafter, the real struggles in the schools over 'savage inequalities' and other educational realities will reemerge in our public debates. This will happen, however, only if informed communicators and critical intellectuals keep these important questions on the public agenda.

McLaren (Chapter 13) critiques contemporary pedagogy in today's predatory culture. In our era, democracy has been subverted. Institutionalized brutality, structured domination, and increasing marginalization of the powerless are the culprits responsible. As in Eastern Europe, the myth of modern democracy has been joined with media-generated impulses to buy, consume, produce, work, and to be either victims or stalkers in the predatory mode. His theme is that a 'structural unconscious' is shaping contemporary US culture. The role of critical pedagogy in this predatory cultural setting is to challenge its worst aspects. Critical educators can help to transform narrow visions of mainstream schooling and curriculum to produce historical transformation, radical democracy, 'critical cosmopolitanism', human liberation, social justice, and community (not communitarian) centered activities.

McLaren criticizes the New Right for its intellectual and ideological emptiness and basis in nothing but raw emotionalism (evident in its stress on so-called 'family values' and knee-jerk patriotic reaction to flag 'desecration'). For example, critical pedagogy can help students investigate everyday culture in all its sites, including electronic media with its 'perpetual pedagogy'. We need 'grounded aesthetics' in which power, privilege, and the self can be examined in light of a common culture and its negotiable imperatives. The goals of critical pedagogy include solidarity, praxis, liberation, and collective autonomy. Using alliances with other scholars, critical theorists can construct a new democratic social, economic, and political theory to produce a pedagogy of ethics, difference, 'otherness', and social justice.

PART V: EDUCATIONAL REFORM: SOME PROPOSALS

In Chapter 14 on educational reform and postmodernism, Whitty moves the educational policy debate beyond 'the market' or 'Thatcherism' to postmodern concepts of diversity, antibureaucracy, anti-assembly line ('post-Fordist') schooling, flexibility, differentiation, choice, localism, pluralism, and heterogeneity (for example, 'niche marketing' of differentiated, nonhierarchical, and decentralized schooling). This is in contrast and preference to the 'one best system' concept in the US which was part of modernism, industrialism, and the enlightenment projects. However, the market-based approach to school choice, local site management, magnet schools, and diversification goes beyond the proposals of those evidencing a New Right mentality. It is also popular (not only in the UK and US, but also in Australia, New Zealand, Japan, and Eastern Europe) even when minority, labor, and left governments are making such decisions. Feminists and minorities also seek pluralism, pragmatism, and local empowerment. These goals foster 'unprincipled alliances' of different economic classes which espouse heterogeneity, fragmentation, and difference. For example, some religious schools in Britain are based on non-Western, antisocial, undemocratic, and pre-enlightenment values, all part of worldwide religious revivals so characteristic of the 1990s. When combined with pro-market views, these values create a new master narrative which competes with social welfare, bureaucracy, and big government establishments in postcapitalist/postindustrial societies.

The first general conclusion Whitty reaches is that these market-oriented educational policies have not produced pluralism. Instead, they have reinforced traditional and structured inequality patterns. The new hierarchy of private, CTC, GMS, and LEA schools has not produced diversity and equality of educational opportunity in Britain. Indeed, a new educational underclass is emerging in Britain's inner cities. Historical class divisions are solidifying along lines of distinction and hierarchy, not difference and heterogeneity.

A second major conclusion is that the UK's national curriculum efforts have clearly targeted multiculturalism, liberal educational goals, and other threats to British and European culture as the enemies of 'conservative modernization'. However, both the left and right will have to consider the salience of yet another set of competing ideas which stress participatory, equity, and heterogeneity goals rather than merely promoting egalitarianism, comprehensive education, humanism, or individualism.

Englund's piece (Chapter 15) on educational discourses proposes creating a new public with a critical and pragmatic viewpoint. Pragmatism also requires the democratic goals of free inquiry, communication, imagination, and development of purposeful habits and conduct within an intellectual climate of fallibility and probabilism. Social science can play a constructive role in creating community and human solidarity. Alternatively, it may be used to solidify time-honored links between knowledge, power, and privilege.

Englund assesses the worth and relevance of two basic research traditions: the new and old sociology of education, including views on the state and society and the role of education in creating a democratic public. He proposes a new citizenship curriculum in which educational content is contingent on an expression of citizenship rights. In liberal democracies, these themes are subject to continual conflict, struggle, and public contest over the state and its apparatuses. He discusses the state, rationality, and evolution; policy determination; reproduction; forgotten aspects of citizenship (such as personal freedom, rights, and social justice); metadiscourses on education; and the creation of a critical polity. He details elements of three competing mass/metadiscourses: patriarchial (formal and organistic), scientific-rational (functional and market-oriented), and democratic (participatory and personal-rights-directed). These three modes are also, respectively, 1) idealistic, individualized, elitist, religious, and legalistic as versus 2) positivistic, technological, vocational, essentialistic, and apolitical as versus 3) communicative, pluralistic, community-based, reconstructionist, and critically literate.

Englund also discusses Habermasian theories of the public and private, the economic system, and the life world of mass communication as opposed to the private sphere of intimacy. He deals with pedagogical questions such as the proper interplay between teachers and textbooks in education's present scientific-rational-dominated world. The critically oriented teacher not only helps the student to question the text, but also to use the democratic mode of textual analysis which treats the textbook as a document, part of a conversation, and integral to a process in which meanings are determined. The teacher must balance his/her state bureaucratic and public servant/educator roles in deconstructing textual meanings. He/she must also promote the use of dialogue, talk, discourse, and judgment as a counter to authoritarian populism. Nonfoundationalism, community, democracy, and solidarity are the competing images useful for offsetting the dominance of New Right absolutism.

In Chapter 16, Farnen summarizes specific and general findings from the previous chapters as well as linking the text to current and probable future international trends in the politics, sociology, and economics of education. These include some of the particular and general features of critical pedagogy (this volume's major topic), common areas of agreement/disagreement, and important national and cross-national trends.

Part II

Politics and/of Education

2 Politics, Education, and Paradigmatic Reconceptualism: US Critical Theory in the 1990s

Russell F. Farnen

ABSTRACT

Within the general context of the US educational 'system', this contribution answers three questions: What are some recent and significant trends in critical social science or radical educational theory on social structure, culture, and individual or group behavior? Do these trends (such as ethnographic research and everyday politics) coincide with any current US developments in political science, socialization, and education? Is there any prospect that critical educational studies will have a significant impact on curriculum, research, or theoretical formulations in American political science, education, and/or socialization? We discuss such trends and draw relevant conclusions. In this chapter, 'critical' educational theory refers to a diverse group of radical democratic, New Left, neo-Marxist, and reconceptualist critics of both classic and social 'liberal' and 'neoconservative' concepts of schooling (that is, opposed to those espousing what Tomas Englund (chapter 15) describes as their 'patriarchal' and 'scientific/rational' discourses on education).

THE AMERICAN EDUCATIONAL SCENE: CURRENT CONTEXTS

Just how conservative is contemporary American political culture and how much influence does business have over US schools? Presently, the US is in the midst of yet another educational 'revolution', revolving around the development of a national curriculum (Smith, O'Day, and Cohen, Winter 1990). This effort will be enforced with a large measure of nationwide testing and performance 'report cards' (the original fear many of those involved had when the National Assessment of Educational Progress [NAEP] began work in the mid-1960s; Anderson et al., April 1990). However, this has been delayed by the relatively innocuous amounts (less than 1 per cent of total costs) regularly allocated for federal educational funding. The US also enjoyed the verbal beneficence of George Bush who had pledged to be the 'education President'. His aim was to make America 'number one' in science, math, and other business-directed processes, such as writing and reading skills. Luckily (or unfortunately, with respect to proper funding and public prominence) for political educators, he had not targeted the civic education curriculum for top-down reform. The administration focused on geography and history revisions, which it considered more 'solid' subjects than social studies and civics - a trend common to conservative regimes in the UK, Finland, Canada, and within several American states, such as California.

America's conservative climate is also illustrated in popular and administration views on education, achievement testing, and business' role in the schools. It is also evident in the current euphoria about history teaching and unitary notions about CIVITAS, the US Constitution, and calls for education for (historical, not contemporary) democracy. For example, President Bush's 'America 2000' educational reform proposals aimed for state and local implementation of conservative programs (such as 'core competencies', 'literacy', educational 'choice', 'flexibility', 'accountability', and 'uniform' national testing). Bush proposed to identify 535 'New American Schools' for reform; this was less than 1 per cent of the nation's 110,000 schools. He also wanted business to 'reinvent the American school' so he could 'unleash American genius' to redesign them. He also advised educational innovators to ignore 'all traditional assumptions about schooling and all the constraints that conventional schools work under'. However, this was not supposed to cost any more federal money. He hoped that 'By the year 2000, all children in America will start school ready to learn' (Tirozzi, 19 May 1991).

The elite's emphasis in US national educational goals is on science and mathematics achievement. Other competencies in more challenging subject matter (including English, history, and geography, emphasizing abilities 'to reason, solve problems, apply knowledge, write, and communicate effectively') are also targeted. The NAEP publishes 'content frameworks' and 'proficiency standards' in these areas. A national curriculum and testing program would be based on NAEP standards, with state-by-state 'report cards'. The current debate is about creating a national educational model (based on ones from Japan or France or states such as California). Even American Federation of Teachers (AFT) union leaders support a competency-based, confidence-producing, national curriculum. Important issues (such as whose goals, whose curriculum materials, accountable to whom, with what flexibility, with what implications for teaching, and under whose governance?) are being discussed.

At issue is the continuing existence of pluralistic (public and private) and democratic (local and state) control over educational decision making in the society. The need to dismantle certain existing educational bureaucracies in states and municipalities is being debated. New public agencies may have to be created to devise frameworks; to develop, revise, monitor, and coordinate standards; to produce models; and to both monitor and report findings. Also discussed is the fact that nationwide standards and tests will prompt teaching for them either directly or by rigid adherence to a curriculum blueprint.

Such blueprints endorse certain pedagogical and educational values plus descriptions of what is to be learned. For example, the California history/social science framework ignores the social studies perspective, favoring the historical approach, corresponding with the national trend. The role of exams in any new system will be critical. Paper and pencil, essay, and multiple-choice exams are not the only available options. Experience with more 'authentic' testing formats (in the UK, the Netherlands, and some US states) produced new evaluation formats. These tests measure abilities other than mere factual recall. Open-ended questions evaluate problem solving, data analysis, analytic writing, creative tasks, experimentation, and speaking proficiency. However, the old problems of how to make such tests, report results, and rank students, teachers, and systems on their results (plus built-in antiminority biases) are only a few examples of attendant, but seldom-debated, long-term testing conundrums. (For more on America's culture wars and reactionary educational climate, see Farnen, 1994a, 1996a and b.)

The Left/Right versus Center Debate

According to Aronowitz and Giroux (1985), these rightist critics have misdiagnosed America's ills, provided the wrong solutions, and wrongly blamed education for current social ills. Schools are not responsible for high unemployment, stagnant productivity, foreign competition, deficit financing, and the growing gap between rich and poor. Even the solutions proposed are irrelevant since the kind of polarized, service-oriented, and unskilled society of America-in-the-making has nothing to do with the conservative educational plan. With America near federal budgetary bankruptcy because of its deficit financing of huge and wasteful military expenditures ($3 trillion from 1980 to 1990), the current educational crisis is as much a cause of local and state impoverishment and shrinking resources as it is a result of philosophical and organizational confusion. The New Right's nostrums for business control of education belie the ethical and public mission of the school as a site for learning about civic participation, social reconstruction, and moral purpose. With their focus on economic goals, conservatives gloss over the schools as arenas for class conflict, sites for lower-class failure, and evidence of the shortcomings of consensus politics. Rightists thereby destroy the moral and political basis for public schooling. Without a democratizing mission, popular support and financing for public schools is at risk. A new public philosophy of education (based on a theory of democratic citizenship education for individual and group empowerment) is needed to provide the necessary antidote for rightist's poisoning of the American educational wells (Farnen, 1994a, pp. 201-6; 1996a, pp. 135-69; 1996b, pp. 39-105).

The Political Economy of Education: Carnoy's and Levin's Perspectives

Carnoy and Levin analyzed recent educational developments in the US along with changing national demographics and productive capacities. They assert that there are still strong conflicts between the capitalist/reproductive and the democratic/egalitarian dynamics in US society. One example of a social policy time bomb is the fact that more reproductive minority populations now constitute nearly half of the school population in certain states (such as California). At least one-third (a growing number) of the pre-collegiate school population is disadvantaged because of racial, recent immigration, or class factors. Such statistics indicate the existence of a new underclass that is ill-prepared for the demands of work life and a group which state and business interests cannot long ignore in terms of providing either more social justice, equity, and/or equal access to schooling (Carnoy and Levin, 1986, pp. 44-45).

Carnoy and Levin also categorize reconceptual analysts of schooling into autonomous and functionalist varieties which, respectively, assume that schools operate separately from the economy and society (for example, Dewey, Bourdieu, Apple, and Giroux) and those who stress education as producing 'human capital', thereby reproducing class relations in correspondence with society's economic and social needs (for example, Carnoy, Levin, Bowles, and Gintis). The critical autonomy analysts also see workplace culture reflected in the school curriculum and ideology; however, they insist that schooling is independent of economic production and, therefore, creates values apart from the rest of society. The critical functionalists stress correspondence and reproduction; yet, they differ over ideas (such as the nature and purpose of man, society, and government as well as the meaning of progress) and simultaneously dismiss observed differences between schooling and society as trivial. Carnoy and Levin claim a paradoxical relationship between schooling and work in that they are both alike and different. Schooling makes a difference because 'formal education is the principal source not only of values and norms among youth but also of skills and practices of production'. Yet 'neither the practices nor the outcomes of schooling correspond directly to the structures and practices of work' (Carnoy and Levin, 1986, p. 37).

The social conflict dynamic pits democratic forces operating through the state to increase the pace of social change, workplace equality, economic security, and participation in decision making. The same forces are at odds in the schools, where the power of competing groups determines which way the balance (capitalist or democratic) will swing. The influence of capitalist production and class conflict is expressed in the hegemonic bourgeois state. Yet, the modern state also plays an important interventionist role in the production process, just as it does in the schools. Education is 'responsible for justice and equity in an inherently unjust and inequitable system of production'. Education's role is to reproduce inequality while trying to produce equality, thereby creating ideological conflicts over status, property, and power. Since such institutional conflict is system-wide, education can influence (and be influenced by) other social institutions operating under the force of capital accumulation (Carnoy and Levin, 1986, pp. 38-40).

Although democratic schools must prepare citizens for their life roles, teaching students about equal opportunity, human rights, civil liberties, participation, and the law is in direct conflict with job-related 'skills and personality characteristics that enable them to function in an authoritarian work regime. This requires a negation of the very political rights that make for good citizens' (Carnoy and Levin, 1986, p. 41). Strong, social movements can influence the trend toward equal rights and opportunities; weak, business interests can predominate by stressing reproduction roles and inequalities. Periods of economic expansion and relative prosperity allow social groups to exert greater influence than do periods of contraction or retrenchment (such as during the 1990s). During the 1980s (and 1990s), education reforms proposed more competition, rigor, excellence, standards, and basic skills as well as improved teacher training, testing, merit pay, longer school schedules, homework, efficiency, and productivity. Gone were the previous emphases on 'equity, equality, and access' as well as compensatory education for the disadvantaged, learning-disabled, bilingual, or minority students. Vouchers, tax credits, market competition, aid to private schools, tax reductions, high-tech education, and computer skills were proposed to end previous democratic reforms. Efficiency, competition, discipline, skills, standards, and better management became the new watchwords during the Reagan and Bush years of educational retrenchment and attempted hegemonic and private control over public schooling (Carnoy and Levin, 1986, pp. 41-5).

The Need for a Theory of the State: Macpherson

Critical social scientists' continual emphasis on the state's key role in the production and education sectors led political scientists such as Macpherson (1977) to both raise the question of the need to go beyond the explanation of political processes to the question of the need for a revised theory of the state in the 'grand' classical tradition of great theorists like Bodin, Hobbes, or Hegel. Macpherson reported that the 1970s crop of liberal democrats and empirical and normative theorists said we do not, while social democrats and Marxists said we do. His earlier treatment of 'contemporary Marxist lessons for liberal-democratic theory' is still instructive. He proposed that 'there is a lot to learn from them. For they do see more clearly than most others that what has to be examined is the relation of the state to bourgeois society, and they are examining it in depth'. This is quite unlike liberal theory which unquestionably accepted both the bourgeois state and society as a single package (Macpherson, 1977, pp. 61-7). The complementary work of Offe and Ronge (1975), Carnoy (1984 and 1985), and Fischer (1990) are evidence of the significance of this trend.

SOME BASIC AND CONTRASTING PERSPECTIVES IN AMERICAN RECONCEPTUALISM: ANYON, APPLE, AND GIROUX

A New Civics and the Hidden Curriculum

In contrasting radical perspectives on schooling and society in the UK and the US, Arnot and Whitty (1982, pp. 93-103) delineate three characteristics of the American approach. These are a critique of schooling combined with educational intervention for social change, a commitment to 'intellectual and methodological pluralism', and an interactive relationship between theory and empirical research. These theoretical constructs are not only linked to, but depend on, European (including British) theoretical underpinnings. In this regard, the work of Anyon, Apple, and Giroux is exemplary.

Both Apple and Giroux criticize the 'monolithic' views of the strict correspondence theory. The mediating role of schools and the resistance to dominance practiced there illustrate the active contestation, struggle, and contradictions which emerge in both educational and workplace settings. The social transfunctional role of schooling allows the possibility of change and emancipatory reconstruction of both schooling and society.

Anyon, Apple, and others showed that school textbooks were designed to be conflict-free, legitimated the social order, and stressed stability and social harmony at the expense of 'sordid' reality. The distortions, 'silences', and misperceptions in textbooks are shaped by social realities in which the powerless play no important role in US history; this reinforces their impotence. School texts present an ideology which is designed to produce meanings and which, itself, must be deconstructed. The commodification process of the text production system involves publishers, textbook writers, readers, and other relevant interactions which are beyond mere reproduction theory (Arnot and Whitty, 1982, pp. 96-7; Anyon, 1979 and 1980)).

Similarly, the hidden curriculum as a socializing influence illustrates the implicit and covert transmission of values, beliefs, attitudes, norms, and behaviors through curriculum structures and the social relations of schooling. Once again, the simple economic correspondence model of Bowles and Gintis did not explain conflicts, contradictions, and discontinuities both within and between schools and the economy they were supposed to reproduce. Willis, Apple, Giroux, and others recognized that the very tensions and contradictions in schooling allowed school to be considered a potential site for both innovation, change, and transformation. This allowed Anyon et al. to develop the more complex theory of 'the reproduction of conflict rather than merely the maintenance of domination'. For instance, Anyon's study of classes in five US East Coast elementary schools shows the degree to which resistance and struggle to traditional schooling are both alike and different among students from various class backgrounds (Anyon, 1983).

Since a critical pedagogy to resolve such contradictions is still lacking, Giroux proposed moving beyond reproduction and critique to a transformational, liberation, and emancipatory emphasis (which the hidden curriculum concept promises). In this regard, he is joined by Apple, who also sees the possibility of intervention through schooling against the panoply of technical controls which restrict teachers and which are designed to produce professional consumers for the economic system. Anyon's studies of schooling also revealed the transformational possibilities of penetration, resistance, and counterhegemony. Like Apple, Anyon sees these possibilities may be limited to particular classrooms, teachers, schools, and sites since curricula, classes, and social expectations vary according to the 'curriculum in use' there. Moreover, gender, race, and class are also relevant when considering such transformational possibilities. These are mainly revealed through ethnographic educational research (Anyon, 1983, pp. 98-102).

Giroux's work tries to move beyond structural-functionalist and reproductive theory to 'a radical pedagogy that connects critical pedagogical theory with the need for social action in the interest of both individual freedom and social reconstruction' (Giroux, 1981a, pp. 7-8). Reproductive rationality is useful, but deficient, because of its 'one-sided determinism, its simplistic view of the mechanisms of social and cultural reproduction in schools, its ahistorical view of human agency and, finally, its profoundly anti-utopian stance toward radical social change' (Giroux, 1981a, p. 14). The correspondence or 'black box' model of schooling is too simplistic in that teachers and students produce as well as conserve knowledge. Resistance, the dialectic, human agency, contradictions, mediation, and opposition are part of the process for recreating and changing the social order, not merely mirroring it. Ideological hegemony can be linked to culture and resistance in schools to expose hegemonic practices to explore transformational possibilities, to disclose structural limits, to reveal contradictions in the lived lives of teachers and students, and to develop a radical pedagogy to allow students to explore the sources and limits of meaningful discourse. Giroux finds that modern pedagogy is 'atheoretic, ahistoric, and unproblematic' so that its positivistic outputs are technologically sound, but undemocratic and nonemancipatory. A new curriculum must be based on students' everyday lives and historical and societal dialectics. It should be reflective, critical, demystifying, transcendent, and reconstructive (Giroux, 1981a, pp. 37, 107, 123, 130-2, 143; Wood, Spring 1982, pp. 63-71; Popkewitz, May 1985, pp. 429, 436).

As Wood (Spring 1982, pp. 63-71) shows, part of the problem with Apple, Giroux, Anyon, and other radical critics is the communication and 'translatability' of theory into practical educational language and action. Thus, Apple proposes that teachers transform their work lives to regain control and autonomy over teaching and engage in direct political action against proposals, such as tax credits for educational 'choice' in schooling. Sponsoring revisions of the history curriculum, worker democracy, and feminist programs, and encountering 'possessive individualism' by tapping students' 'lived culture' are more reform possibilities to challenge 'the balance of forces within a specific arena' (Apple, 1982a, pp. 88-90, 130-4).

Apple also endorses the 'rediscovery' of the 'heuristic power' of history and puts the contemporary form of social relations in an historical context. Responding to classical, elitist, and conservative critics of schooling, he advocates considering 'critical literacy', understanding diverse traditions and histories (normally excluded from schooling), and fostering 'a democratic curriculum'. This includes using knowledge and skill to create and pursue one's own interests while being able 'to make informed personal and political decisions; and to work for the welfare of the community'. He proposes democratic reforms to insure site management of schooling, more local initiative and control, greater freedom and flexibility, decentralized examination and textbook selection, and less educational bureaucracy. More collective and cooperative teamwork among teachers, sabbaticals and study periods, and teacher control over teaching/learning innovations are other strategies he proposes. To develop a more democratic educational environment, he suggests salary increases, peer reviews, and greater school-university linkages, along with implementing a new assessment and evaluation plan and engaging students in challenging learning settings. Student empowerment, counter-hegemony, and demystification of inequality are still other features of this political awareness curriculum (Apple, 1988, pp. 11, 189-95).

OTHER TRENDS IN CRITICAL SOCIAL SCIENCE AND EDUCATIONAL THEORY

Some General Observations

Critical educational, radical reconceptualist, and neo-Marxian theories of schooling in the US, Sweden, the UK, France, Germany, and elsewhere represent a serious and useful attempt to intellectually disaggregate what schools do in modern industrial and postindustrial societies. While these theorists disagree on details of the economic-political-cultural-educational nexus, certain basic concepts frequently appear and reappear in their writings. These include terms, processes, and concepts such as social reproduction, qualitative and ethnographic methods, correspondence theory, the hidden curriculum, discourses, contradictions, resistance, and institutional sites. Also included are human agency, penetration, limitations, ideological hegemony, social and cultural capital, deskilling, the critique of modernism, postindustrialism, positivism, structuralism and functionalism, inequality and oppression. They also discuss the utility of dialectical tensions, enlightenment, liberation, transformational praxis, and the critical importance of community, class, gender, and race as criteria for identifying social oppression in different cultural sites and social practices.

Three major schools of thought use the economic, cultural, and hegemonic-state reproductive models. The political economy model (Bowles and Gintis, 1976, 1986, and 1988) is the dominant one for the 'hidden curriculum', educational policy, and ethnographic research studies. Bowles and Gintis use correspondence theory to equate school classroom practices with workplace needs and demands. The social division of labor and the class structure are mirrored in schools. The 'hidden curriculum' in schools legitimizes the workplace's authority, rules, values, rationality, and power relationships. Intellectual, hierarchical, and competitive tasks are valued more than manual, democratic, or group/shared processes. Students learn to read, write, and add for productive work, to behave properly to meet job expectations, and to respect the rules and hierarchy imposed by the capitalist order. To this analysis, Althusser (1971) adds an ideological dimension. The day-to-day 'culture' of the school is one aspect of this ideology. Its 'unconscious' dimension is found in the 'meanings, representations, and values' underlying school practices, shared images, structures, and concepts. Christian Baudelot and Roger Establet see schools as sites of ideological conflict, stemming from external sources. Class culture is seen as the primary source for such resistance; yet, ideology actively involves both dominant and oppositional strains. These contradictions may impede both self- and collective-liberation.

Bourdieu's (1973, 1977, 1984, and with Passeron, 1977 and 1979) cultural-reproductive model posits the dominant culture of the ruling class as the hidden basis for maintaining class interests, hierarchy, and domination. Since schools are relatively autonomous, they are perceived as being 'neutral' in transmitting cultural capital and rejecting less-valued, lower-class culture. The school's curriculum, language, and positive behaviors are actually those of the dominant culture (that is, the ruling class). The historical conditions ('habitat') and deliberately cultivated, durable, individual dispositions ('habitus') of persons enable schools to dominate the 'unconscious' of young workers so completely that they willingly accept their predetermined lot in society. Structural conflict is possible in Bourdieu's theory, but it is rather mechanistic, just as his views of class are overly homogeneous. His rejecting conflict, struggle, and resistance within different classes and his ignoring both the active reconstruction of ideologies and resistance to their imposition through counterideologies are other shortcomings in his analysis, according to Aronowitz and Giroux (1985, pp. 85-6). He is also ignorant of the oppressive burdens of material conditions and other economic constraints which impede the growth of working-class students and, at the same time, limit their possibilities for critical thinking and emancipation (Shirley, 1986).

If the nexus between the state and capitalism was illuminated in Antonio Gramsci's writings, that between the state and schooling is explained by Apple (Spring 1979, Spring 1980, 1982b, 1983, and with King, 1983, and with Weiss, 1983). They use the state hegemony model to explain the process of class domination over the political and educational system as well as the economy and its cultural superstructure. Gramsci saw hegemony as primarily the expression of the ruling class's and their allies' world view and, then, as the forceful imposition of a dominant ruling ideology over the consciousness, everyday lives, knowledge, and culture of subordinate groups. The state itself consists of both a political and civil society, which use 'official' ideology to eliminate opposing views. Ideological hegemony must be continuously maintained by force, consensus, and/or domination. This is true even if it meets resistance from those refusing to be incorporated or unwilling to give 'active consent' to the rulers. The state represents class, power, interests, rule, struggle, domination, and divisions, all masquerading as 'normality' and 'nature'. Different ruling class factions may quarrel over specific public policies, but not over fundamental power and economic relationships. These remain unquestionably supportive of the capitalist order. State rulers defend the economic and moral order and engineer the consent of the ruled through false promises of opportunity, democracy, and happiness. They also 'rewrite history' and destroy class opponents amidst obvious ideological contradictions found in everyday reality (Aronowitz and Giroux, 1985, pp. 87-92).

Schooling is used to reinforce society's dominant ideology, culture, and economic practices. Schooling highly values positivism, science, mathematics, basic research, competence, credentials, vocational education, national history, and other production-related output products which support economic efficiency and allow for 'capital accumulation'. Planning, bureaucracy, and rationality keep children in school and off the streets and label 'deviants' (or 'victims') responsible for their own mistakes. This is the alternative to illuminating the social and economic causes of 'failure' or allowing the masses to share in decision and policy making. The capitalist state allows a liberal democratic ethic of individual rights and responsibilities to operate in schools. This philosophy assumes that the state is neutral. Conflict is rationalized at the individual (rather than the more-threatening class) level and is, thus, made more impotent. Laws undergird the school system, force change, ensure conformity and compliance, and indirectly quash resistance. However, such an analysis may also be a bit abstract while ignoring the role of resistance to domination through counterhegemonic practices (Aronowitz and Giroux, 1985, pp. 92-8; Giroux, 1981a, pp. 91-109).

Aronowitz and Giroux (1991) also appropriated elements of the postmodern critique into their explication of class, race, gender, and sexual preference questions in contemporary American and Western societies. For example, Giroux (1991, pp. 1-59 and 217-56) looks to a synthesis of liberal freedom, postmodern particularism, feminist everyday politics, and democratic socialist solidarity and civism into a new unity in diversity. This 'difference within unity' goes beyond radical critique, intellectual redefinition, and democratic pedagogy to a new form of democratic 'cultural politics' devoid of any master narrative and focuses on resistance and the democratic struggle to achieve 'justice, freedom, and equality' (Giroux, 1991, pp. 56-9).

A 'border pedagogy' of antiracism is needed to empower students to decode knowledge and power relationships within different cultural settings using historical and cultural analysis, lived experiences, democratic authority, justice, and power interrelationships along with redefining constructs such as 'the other' and 'otherness' both in and out of schools (Giroux, 1991, pp. 247-56). In this setting, schooling becomes one form of 'cultural politics' and is linked to democratic public life; teachers become 'engaged intellectuals and border crossers' who develop '. . . forms of pedagogy that incorporate difference, plurality, and the language of the everyday as central to the production and legitimation of learning' (Aronowitz and Giroux, 1991, p. 187). However, this postmodernist view of the radical reform project comes under severe criticism for its fashionable amalgam of several popular discourses as well as for its confusing call to politicize teachers in the absence of a well-argued and principled case for redemptive justice, 'self-enlightenment', equality, and an ideologically sound conception of 'utopian universalism' which will have meaning for many teachers in the US and Canada.

The US: Bowles' and Gintis' Dynamic Views

With Ivan Illich's (1970) notion of deschooling society, Marxist reproduction theorists created a dismal portrait without any hope for reforming schools, either from within or without. As Willis (1981, p. 63) notes, the new convention deals with those proposing radical educational change within the classroom as being optimistic proponents of liberation, praxis, and enlightenment. By contrast, those pessimists adhering to reproduction theory eschew any possibility for educational change in the absence of economic and social reconstruction along truly egalitarian lines. For example, Wood (Spring 1982, pp. 56 and 63) labels the reproductive school of Marxism as the philosophy of 'paralysis' and 'cynicism'. As examples of reproductionists, Bowles and Gintis (1976) accept Althusser's (1971) characterization of schools as 'ideological state apparatuses'. There, oppressed students accept their fate as products of the 'false consciousness' developed through capitalistic schooling. While liberal theories of development, integration, and democracy are content to justify schooling as preparation for later life, reproduction theorists claim that cognitive skills learned in school have little relation to the actual requirements of work life. Capitalistic society uses a hegemonic ideology which persuades students that their job roles are ethical, necessary, 'natural', or right. Schools legitimate this nonparticipatory, undemocratic, and hierarchical order while developing a consenting consciousness among their pupils. The schools both reflect and are modeled on the workplace, with its 'hierarchical division of labor'. This is the 'structural correspondence' theory in operation. It promotes 'subordination', 'powerlessness', inequality, and hegemony. Bowles and Gintis (1976, p. 224) originally perceived 'a strong *prima facie* case for the causal importance of economic structure as a major determinant of educational structure'. Economic reform was, consequently, a prior condition for any educational transformation.

Schooling in capitalist societies diverts attention from the need for equality and liberation by imposing a 'false consciousness' and ideology of hegemony on students, rather than addressing the need for 'a revolutionary transformation of economic life'. However, 'revolutionary educators' can serve as a vanguard of the proletariat role by pressing for educational democracy, dissolving the workplace-education correspondence, rejecting 'simple anti-authoritarianism and spontaneity' as principles, creating 'class consciousness', and practicing transformational 'political work' for short- and long-run change (Bowles and Gintis, 1976, pp. 127-34, 265, and 286-7; Wood, Spring 1982, pp. 55-63).

Wood's analysis of Bowles' and Gintis' and Althusser's work subscribes to Bernstein's (1978) earlier critique of the latter's neo-Marxism by labeling the lot with terms such as structuralist, positivist, economic determinist, empiricist, and being advocates of pseudo-scientific 'laws'. As the dominant 'educational ideological apparatus', schools join the police and military as a 'repressive state apparatus' to ensure capitalist domination and hegemony. Liberal social humanists mistakenly underwrite repressive testing, ordering, and empirical social science positivism, as well as cultural reproduction, according to these radical educators of the American left. In Wood's (Spring 1982, pp. 61-3) view, this verdict encourages 'paralysis', cynicism, negativism, disillusionment, and silence among other educational practitioners. It also ignores the democratic, egalitarian, liberating, and social transformation mission of American schooling, as well as the possibility for resistance to hegemonic forces. To fill this gap (between the 'authoritarian' impetus of reproduction theory and the realities of schooling), a second group of radical critics (for example, Apple, Giarelli, Aronowitz, and Giroux) has evolved, providing a message of hope, possibility, and social reconstruction.

In fact, Gintis and Bowles (1981, pp. 45-59) restated and re-evaluated the correspondence principle. They also answered charges of alleged radical functionalism and 'missionary pessimism', ascribed to their lack of appreciation for the systemic contradictions within education and between it and capitalistic economic processes and social relations. Moreover, with Dewey, they recognize liberalism's egalitarian, developmental, and integrative educational principles, rather than its merely being unequal and repressive schooling which, in the process, produces 'good citizens' for an undemocratic capitalist society - without democratic power, participation, cooperation, emancipation, and social and economic relations. However, they still maintain that the correspondence principle has explanatory value, point to the need for systemic reform through democratic socialism, explain school outputs as products of structural social relations (not just content), and identify control over (rather than ownership of) schools as the route to follow for progressive educational reform. Inherent contradictions between education's legitimizing and reproducing roles and advanced capitalism's accumulating and restructuring processes places these two systems 'out of synch' with one other. American higher education previously reflected this contrast between the post-1945 needs of the growing white-collar/service economy and the older, liberal, elite education designed for a managerial class on the one hand and the emerging vocationalism and anti-intellectualism on the other. The growing incongruence between inert, 'old' schools and the dynamic, 'new' service economy established the groundwork for 'back to basics' claims which were founded on the apparent cultural lag between less-responsive higher education and the demands of the capitalist economic order.

The social relations (or forms, rather than contents) of liberal education produced and legitimated institutions and communications discourses which are the products of interclass 'accords'. Therefore, schools remain both progressive and reproductive. These tensions can only be resolved by democratizing both the school curriculum and its social relations. This could fulfill the liberal promise of equality, democracy, liberty, and emancipation, but without (or with lessened) propertied/accumulative/capitalist hegemony, dominance, and subordination (Gintis and Bowles, 1981, pp. 45-59).

The US: Carnoy and Colleagues on the Political Economy of Education

Between 1977 and 1990, Martin Carnoy (with various coauthors) studied education and employment, educational reform, the political economy of education, economic democracy, and the state and political theory. Much of this work is on third-world countries (such as China, Cuba, Nicaragua, Mozambique, and Tanzania). Its focus is on cross-national and comparative analysis of the politics and/of education.

Carnoy and Levin (1985 and 1986) also examined the topic of schooling and work in the democratic state. This includes relationships between theories of the state and education, social conflict, reproduction, and contradictions in schooling and educational reform. They posit that schools and workplaces are both alike and different. Both are 'large, bureaucratic, impersonal, hierarchical, and routinized'; both use external rewards as motivators (grades and wages) and allow experts, authority, regulations, and schedules to dominate the same minorities and classes which fail in both sites. Yet, American schools 'more than any other major social institution' also 'provide equal opportunities for participation and rewards'. Workplace gender inequities are not reflected in education nor are the vast differences in societal wealth mirrored in the more-equalized level of educational investment in the society.

Educators and students also have more rights and freedoms than do workers (as a result of forces such as politics, law, and democratic 'mobilization').

While US schools prepare students for inequality, they are more equal and participatory than offices and factories. The correspondence principle must be qualified since there is a clear conflict between the economic reproduction function and the dynamic for rights, equality, and participation. Schooling reflects the struggles underway in the society at large (that is, between democratic egalitarianism and the demands of capital). This historical 'struggle' occurs within the state and is reflected in the schools. In effect, educational change is based on a new theory of politics and the state. The latter is seen as 'the condensation of conflictual class and social relations' and both as 'product and shaper of such relations'. The state has tried to 'move class and social conflict' into politics by declassifying and redefining workers, farmers, women, and blacks as 'citizens' with equal rights and responsibilities. This thrust for democratic egalitarianism produced social conflict since politics could 'drastically alter the conditions of capitalist accumulation'. The school is 'situated in the heart of sociopolitical conflict', reflecting these 'tensions'. Educational change is a product of internal conflicts within the state. At different historical periods (partly depending on the strength of social reform movements), either the democratic or reproductive capitalist ethos dominates. Dominated groups can make 'authentic' changes and gains. In turn, they produce changes in the basic rules of the political and educational 'game', despite the prevailing influence of the capitalist class. In effect, they conclude that 'school struggles and outcomes have an impact on the workplace and force change in civil society as well as in political society' (Carnoy and Levin, 1986, pp. 528-41).

Carnoy and Levin (1985) also analyze the relative utility of the progressive (Dewey), critical progressive (Goodman, Holt, Kozol), functionalist (Inkeles), critical functionalist (Althusser and Bowles and Gintis), critical autonomy (Apple, Giroux, and Willis), and their own model of educational change via social conflict. They counterpoise utilitarian, pluralist ('common good'), 'class-perspective' (Marxist), structuralist, bureaucratic 'third force', and their own 'social conflict' theories of the state. For example, Carnoy and Levin summarize Offe's (with Ronge, 1975) views on state autonomy and the 'representative' role bureaucracy plays. Bureaucrats must satisfy the interests of the capitalist class. Yet, bureaucrats simultaneously increase labor's power via educational programs while legitimizing themselves by meeting certain demands of labor while ensuring profitability and a smooth-functioning economy. For Offe, the bureaucracy actually coalesces the interests of the capitalist class and serves as an 'independent' mediator for struggles over capital accumulation. But the 'crisis of legitimation' resulting from performing these bureaucratic roles makes the state a battleground for conflict resolution. Education allows the state to be legitimate, reproduce capitalism, and ensure employability for labor. Carnoy and Levin, however, claim that Offe's and Ronge's analysis of education is too unidimensional, neglects other 'ideological apparatuses' (such as mass media), and underestimates the important role of social movements in ideological formation and in setting the state's agenda, rewards, and policies (Carnoy and Levin, 1985, pp. 15-45).

Carnoy's (1985) analysis of the political economy of education 'treats education as a factor shaped by the power relations between different economic, political, and social groups'. As he says, 'how much education an individual gets, what education is obtained and the role of education in economic growth and income distribution are part and parcel of these power relations'. Thus, his analysis requires a clear perspective on the governmental sector, the political system, and a functional 'theory of the state'. As he sees it, the state must mediate between employers and workers as well as between voters and capitalists, using education to provide a skilled workforce, to socialize workers, and to inculcate the appropriate ideology. Sometimes, these contradictory goals can overproduce educated workers or encourage workplace democracy, whether as intended or unintended outcomes of schooling (Carnoy, 1985, pp. 157-8; Carnoy and Levin, Winter 1986).

Critiques of the Reconceptualist Critics from the UK and the US: Cole and Liston

There is no uniformity in critical social science or pedagogical approaches, 'schools' of thought, or even in personal theoretical or philosophical consistency over the years. This poses difficulties for the uninitiated reader's understanding of the broad dimensions of critical educational theory. For example, Cole (1988a and 1988b) examines the changing political philosophy of Bowles and Gintis. He makes a convincing case that these two authors' basic orientation in *Schooling in Capitalist America* (1976) agreed with reductionist Marxism (that is, base/superstructure and economic determinism) and revolutionary socialism. In their later article on 'Contradiction and Reproduction in Educational Theory' (1981), they moved away from this position by tempering Marxism in their theory of sites (state, family, and capital production) and the practices which support personal, group, or class 'interventions' to maintain or transform certain social realities. They also humanized and pluralized their definition of the state while simultaneously distancing themselves from a neo-Marxist stance, moving toward a liberal democratic formulation of the state as primarily a governmental institution.

Cole claims that Bowles and Gintis (1986) moved even further away from their original position to embrace 'postliberal democracy' with its expanded personal economic rights (property) as well as political rights for citizens with 'equal' rights, regardless of race, gender, or class. This shift proposes the revision, reconstruction, or destruction of current capitalist institutions through 'workplace democracy', 'democratic economic planning' through increased power and worker control, 'community access to capital', reduced ('equitable') economic inequality, socially directed ('collective') capital 'investment decisions', and 'democratic accountability'. However, these authors identify the most significant flaws in classic liberal theory. These include ignorance of exploitation and oppression, its application of principles (such as liberty and equality) to the state (but only liberty to the economy), its false distinction between a 'private' economy and 'public' state, and liberals' allowance for private exploitation, dominance, and/or oppression of 'learners' in school, of the incarcerated, 'uncivilized' races, and of 'irrational' wives in the family (Cole, 1988b, pp. 459-60).

This critique, itself, consistently applies neo-Marxian analysis of key concepts (such as state domination and oppression, antipluralism and liberalism, class, gender, racial exploitation, hegemony, labor solidarity, and discourse analysis) to Bowles' and Gintis' writings, theory, and philosophy. As such, Cole may well be more faithful to the British or European school of Marxist analysis, just as Bowles and Gintis are both products of, and are reacting to, the perhaps stronger liberal (both individual and especially social) tradition in American political culture (also see Cole, 1989).

Liston (May 1988, pp. 323-50) analyzes some changing contexts and neo-Marxist positions on schooling and social reproduction theories. For the latter, he says 'little reliable empirical knowledge has been ascertained' to support their functional/logical explanations. These are often stated in tautological terms. Often, Liston maintains, the arguments of Bowles and Gintis (1976), Apple (1982a, 1982b, and 1983) and Carnoy and Levin (1985) employ 'weak' functional explanations. Thus, effects are noted, institutional or agency functions are attributed, and this course of reasoning is considered equal to (or sufficient for) an explanation for the described social phenomenon. By comparison, 'real' functional explanations clearly identify real effects, then prove a practice or institution exists because of, to maintain, and/or as a cause of this given effect (for example, schools exist to maintain the society as it is; or school tracking systems exist to minimize economic crises or legitimize the capitalist order in capitalist societies). Such 'facile' functional explanations are also applied to other assertions. These propose that, while schools exist to maintain the capitalist system, they also conflict with this order. This happens because their capital accumulation and meritocratic or legitimating roles may clash with the social order if those who 'strive' in schools do not find jobs and 'thrive' later in the economic world. Such explanations would be more soundly based, Liston maintains, if they could show how school affects 'products' or if outcomes explain why schools are as they are (causation), not merely their either sustaining or contradicting capitalism and its related effects (Liston, May 1988, pp. 328-30).

Liston also describes the variety of philosophical underpinnings in various neo-Marxist analyses of schooling. Bowles and Gintis are responsible for shared insights, such as 'historical correspondence'. This theory shows that when major economic transformations occurred, power and class structures and relationships changed and the educational (cultural) superstructure mirrored these altered economic conditions. There is also the more specific phenomenon of school-work-life correspondence where the social division of labor is reinforced in schools by maintaining class structures and cultivating relevant parental expectations. Consequently, professional parents expect self-motivation and a free-wheeling or open woɪk/school atmosphere. The working class 'prefers' a restrictive and controlling educational climate because it reflects their personal modes of routinized, meaningless, and orderly work life. Correspondence (Bowles and Gintis, 1976) is also based on an economic determinist model. That is, the forces and relations of production determine the forms, meanings, structures, and processes of schooling as well as other social institutions (superstructures). This model also accounts for contradictions and conflicts (sometimes 'muted') in the economic sphere, which are responsible for subsequent educational conflicts and changes as well. Schools also require students to compete, rather than cooperate, with one another for grades and 'honors'. Since students lack self-motivation, they only respond to external rewards. The credentialing system, the top-down organization of school hierarchy, and the deskilling of teachers (via prepackaged curricula and diminished professionalism) lead to the legitimation of prevailing social norms and rules for work life management.

Because schools reflect the class, race, and gender structures of the general society, they try to respond to a multiplicity of competing demands from employers, workers, educators, parents, and politicians. All help to influence tracking, hierarchy, curriculum, teachers, resource allocation, and other aspects of schooling. Schooling may also be considered a democratic 'right' of all citizens. Consequently, a certain amount of excellence and equality through democratic schooling (if properly understood) may be possible. It can result in social transformation through theoretically informed action (praxis), along with an informed understanding of the close connections between capitalism and schooling (Liston, May 1988, pp. 334-42).

Tracking must be examined through empirical and qualitative studies of differential, class-based curricula, which subsequently result in higher social status as well as greater social and economic power. Informed studies (with a proper theoretical base) can produce findings which will help to meet functionalist criticisms as well as to provide grounded underpinnings for the theoretical construct being examined. Historical studies (with case studies of tracking controversies at the urban level) can show the influence and interest of business classes in a tracking system and a differential class-based curriculum. In this way, Liston contends, a structure or procedure can be shown to produce interactive effects which feed back into its maintenance based on these supporting effects (Liston, May 1988, pp. 344-8).

A Comparative (Swedish) Perspective: Englund

Englund (see Chapter 15) provides a useful comparison among patriarchal, scientific-rational, and democratic conceptions of democracy, equality, the good society, rationality, science, individualism, schooling, literacy, and politics. While the neoconservative position is based on the patriarchal conception and includes formal, elite, organic, idealistic, atomistic, private, nationalistic, reformist, religious and legalistic values, the scientific-rational (or what Fischer [1990] calls the 'technocratic rationality') model is based on funtionalism, equal opportunity, the market, positivism, individualism, choice, private values, vocationalism, progressivism, empiricism, political neutrality, and utility. He prefers the democratic conception, which is participatory, results- and human-rights-oriented, pluralistic, neopragmatic, communitarian, comprehensive, public-welfare-minded, critical reconstructionist, and devoted to popular political and social education for conflict resolution.

Perceiving civic education as an example of both the politics of education and a case of politics and education allows for an analysis of curriculum as a political problem in Sweden and other countries. Englund (1986) analyzes criticisms of Freeman Butts' unitary approach to American citizenship as historical study by detailing his stress on *unum* over *pluribus* in social studies education. Butts' critics affirm that no social consensus exists on unitary values. The educator should reflect social tensions and conflicts (not just some artificial consensus) and increase the public's capacity for civic discussion and the formation of new publics, not parrot state or media-sponsored official ideology. Along with Giroux, he sees the civic educator helping create a new public philosophy of education, learning, and citizenship (apart from the state), raising citizenship to a complete ethical, moral, and social (not merely political) philosophy for 'developing democratic and just communities' self-governed via ethical public leadership principles (Englund, 1986, pp. 328-30).

Englund shares English and American views of civic education as political involvement, activity, and participation. The goals of citizen 'awareness' and 'responsibility for political decisions' are highly valued. He agrees with Giroux (1984) and Giarelli (1983) that the civic educator should lead public discussions. There, the public can discharge their civic purposes by exercising the 'office' of citizen to form new publics. We need new 'public spheres' where people can learn and apply their skills to 'the wider political, social, and cultural processes'. Citizenship should not be viewed as a function of the state, as Giroux maintains, but as a 'quality' that applies to all of social life. As Giroux says, the goals of this type of citizenship are 'critical literacy', 'social empowerment', and 'developing democratic and just communities' through an informed citizenry that is 'capable of exercising political and ethical leadership in the public sphere' (Englund, 1986, pp. 329-30; Giarelli, 1983, p. 35; and Giroux, 1984, pp. 190 and 192).

ETHNOGRAPHY, CRITICAL STUDIES, AND POLITICS

Certain 'interpretive approaches' also contribute to the study of education and schooling from a comparative perspective on micro systems or 'the world of everyday life'. This ethnographic perspective focuses on social reality in the schools, observations there, and social interactions, while using videotaped or audio-recorded documentaries (Tobin, 1989, pp. 173-7). 'Critical approaches' to the ethnography of schooling 'emphasize class conflict, the dissimilar interests of various classes, and their differing relationship to (and benefits from) the workings of the educational system' (Masemann, February 1982, p. 9). 'Conflict approaches' also have social (and structural) theoretical underpinnings, but are less compatible with functionalist approaches. These approaches see schools as agents for the 'reproduction of society', where personality trait reinforcement prepares different classes for economic roles as workers or managers. They posit a 'theory of correspondence', in which 'social relations of production are mirrored in the social relations of education'. For example, some theorize that schools stratify and produce the 'cultural capital' (ideas, ideology, etc.) the dominant class needs. Teachers, like workers, are becoming 'deskilled' professionals with ready-made, prepackaged curriculum. Key research topics include student alienation, curriculum packaging, credentialing, required courses, norms of prediction, social control mechanisms, socialization practices, and miscommunication. Student 'resistance' to such manipulations include cheating, distancing, absenteeism, mindlessness, inattention, avoidance, or rebellion. Praxis is avoided since schooling, knowledge, and credentials are not usefully applied, only 'banked' for future use (Masemann, February 1982, pp. 5-14).

Specific ethnographic research on school socialization and desegregation policy produced much harsher conclusions about democratic socialization and racial equality practices in public schools (Wilcox 1982a and 1982b; Hanna, 1982). Wilcox (1982a) asserts that schools transmit culture and socialize children for 'available' adult work roles. Adult work roles are highly differentiated and stratified. Therefore, while US schools are supposed to encourage equal opportunity, they also stratify persons for future jobs by teaching and evaluating those cognitive skills, learning abilities, and technical skills ('human capital') deemed useful for later work life. They also develop appropriate roles for workers and managers through 'self-preparation' for the work hierarchy. Personality factors which are appropriate for relating to authority differ from one job role to another, with some being 'externally' (assembly line workers) and others 'internally' (managers) motivated. These critiques of multidimensional sources and self-image development (anticipatory socialization) have major implications for schooling, the social context of the classroom, the teachers' interactions with students and parents, and vice versa (Wilcox, 1982a, pp. 268-309).

Micro- and macro-level perspectives on schooling and change also interest ethnographers. Teachers often use closed control systems and restricted language, even in 'open' classrooms where they monopolize some class time for management. Merely having (or paying lip service to) learning centers and individualized learning practices does not necessarily reduce 'authoritarian teacher control mechanisms', which are used more harshly against lower-SES students. Black children in white-dominated classrooms are resegregated by achievement levels, even without tracking. Administrative ignorance and unwillingness to help teachers experiencing difficulty in newly integrated schools was also observed. No conjoint, multicultural curricula developments were supported, nor was outreach to minority parents attempted. (Parents are systematically excluded from schools, as a rule.) Different class members learn similar roles in the schools. But the values of success in the general society predominate when school/societal discontinuities occur. By detailing such relations, ethnography helps us compile a more dynamic view of what happens to whom, and with what lasting effects, in schools (Wilcox, 1982b, pp. 462-78).

DO CURRENT TRENDS IN CRITICAL EDUCATIONAL THEORY PARALLEL AND REINFORCE OR CONTRADICT RECENT DEVELOPMENTS IN US POLITICAL SCIENCE, SOCIALIZATION RESEARCH, AND/OR CIVIC EDUCATIONAL REFORMS?

Political Science and Decision Making

American political science is still searching for a disciplinary core by discussing methods, processes, and the role of different subfields and concepts. Some relevant and useful unifying concepts include power, influence, authority, political 'values', the state, politics, and government. Appropriate accepted research methods and political processes are behavioral, neo-Marxist, statistical, postbehavioral, qualitative, philosophical, psychological, public or rational choice, pluralism, and decision/policy making approaches. Certain subfields of analysis identify political theory, public policy, or the general study of politics or governments as key elements in such a core. While political science remains undisciplined, political scientists intuitively recognize and embrace something or someone as their own and reject that (or someone's work) which is not. In many respects, what is left of a diffuse political science core is merely a shared focus on the process of policy analysis or decision making or a common vocabulary which allows comprehensible discourse to occur in a continuous metadiscourse with colleagues in the same field or subfield (Monroe et al., March 1990, pp. 34-43; Farnen, 1990, pp. 29-48; Almond, Fall 1988, pp. 828-42).

The 'Discipline' of Political Science as an Undisciplined Field of Study

The relevance and applicability of critical social science and radical educational theories to US political science, socialization, and education research and writing are still unclear, undeveloped, tangential, and weak. There are neo-Marxist, radical, or New Left political analysts in the academy; but they mainly prod, arouse, or act as scapegoats for centrist-oriented colleagues. Mainstreamers often treat them in a condescending way, much like carnival freaks - something human and alive, but bizarrely deformed and sometimes repulsive. Only in certain conceptual areas, political topics, or cultural sites do political scientists and critical social and educational theorists have opportunities to come together. Instances such as discussions about the politics of education, collective union negotiations, social or cultural 'capital', civic education, or the 'hidden curriculum' provide occasions for mainline political scientists to discuss relevant 'left-wing' theoretical and evidentiary constructs. These marginal intersections 'mainstream' these ideas into the continuing public discourse about the relevance of political questions to learning, schooling, civic education, and public educational policy.

In this regard, Dryzek and Leonard maintain there is no exclusive tradition in American political science, saying that 'disciplinary pluralism is the norm, and the existence of skepticism itself accentuates that pluralism'. They claim that the profession has often been involved in 'real politics' and just at the right time as well. As they observe, recent currents of disciplinary skepticism very aptly reflect present political realities and 'the context of a polity and a discipline that have lost their bearings' (Dryzek and Leonard, December 1988, pp. 1256-7; Dryzek, May 1986).

Critical Pedagogy, Political Science, and Political Education: Some Developmental Parallels, Clashes, and Collisions

Most recent discussions on core values and appropriate methods in contemporary US political science seem singularly unenlightened about many questions which have motivated political study. These involve the nature and purpose of human beings, society, the state, and government as well as contrasting views about the good society and paths or policy choices which might be taken to achieve the public good either today or tomorrow. Instead, US political scientists are overly concerned about conversational themes such as pluralism, objectivity, political neutrality, and the primacy of classic democratic political theory in their intradisciplinary discussions.

But which themes of critical educational theory appear most useful for both enlightening and 'liberating' American political science, citizenship education, and political socialization research? Critical educational theorists and social scientists add to our knowledge about politics, education, and socialization in several areas. Nevertheless, there are several other areas where conspicuous 'silences' in their texts provide few satisfactory answers to still other pressing current problems. A review of these contrasting contributions may help answer this question.

A Workable Theory of the State

The first productive area stemming from trends in critical social science resurrects discussions about a current and viable theory of the modern state. Much of political science, civic education, and socialization research has no clear concept of what the state, government, or civil authority is supposed to do, what it does, or why it does what it does. Vague formulations of popular sovereignty are combined with a penchant for participation to achieve abstract notions of democratic fulfillment. In this regard, critical social scientists clearly oppose the liberal/capitalist state's basic values and manifestations (Offe and Ronge, 1977). These challenges are both radical and essential to an appreciation of the central questions of power, authority, bureaucracy, legitimacy, justice, freedom, solidarity, and equity (Carnoy, 1984 and 1985).

Radical theorists clarify this aspect of their political and educational philosophy while challenging their detractors to debate alternative views with appropriate evidence, knowledge, and value claims. Therefore, as Macpherson (1977) and Finkelstein (November 1984) observed, radical philosophical critics helped raise basic political and teleological questions about the nature, nurture, and purpose of human beings, society, and government. Alternatively, their self-satisfied liberal and conservative opponents prefer to ignore such questions or assume answers to them as part of the conventional wisdom. But little in the contemporary debate about the nature of political science is concerned with a viable theory of the modern democratic state. In fact, when the right proposes statist ideas, the left (not the center) has felt most compelled to respond to their undemocratic elitism, self-serving economic and class-based motivations and their reduction of human interaction to self-interest, exchange relationships, and moral/ethical anarchy or conformity.

Using critical social science perspectives to analyze US public policy making, some American scholars questioned the normative, ethical, political, and philosophical basis for neoconservative and liberal notions of efficiency, 'the market', and cost benefit analysis (Fischer and Forester, 1987). Fischer's (1990) analysis (see Chapter 12) identifies links between the postindustrial economy and the new administrative state. Within a nonpositivist and democratic framework, Fischer proposes redesigning bureaucratic institutions to counter their 'managerial bias' by encouraging 'participatory expertise' in community cooperatives, democratized work settings, 'alternative technology projects', 'new social movements', and achieving social reconstruction via a form of 'political ergonomics' in policy making (Fischer, 1990, pp. 7-11, 13-35). This analysis has implications for across-the-board educational reform.

Liberal Culture and Everyday Politics

A second useful area is radical theory's emphasis on practical political culture as 'lived culture', the politics of everyday life, and schooling as an actual experience. While often argued in abstract terms (for example, resistance, cultural reproduction, and correspondence theory), the basic point of the struggles, commonplace, agony and ecstasy of everyday work, school life, and community interactions is that they are real experiences. These accounts enlighten readers, evoking empathy, understanding, and compassion for those whose daily lives are very different from political science textbooks or televised soap-opera myths. Thus, there is some congruence with the subfield of political science/behavior which studies political 'patterns in everyday life'. Peterson (1990) summarized research on 'ordinary people' and politics, including the politics of sex, family, workplace, clubs, religion, and media. For example, the person on the street thinks of politics as the government (state), power, and influence; as functions and evaluations; and as political actors. Ordinary people see politics as part of church, family, work, and club life.

In terms of decision making, the family had the greatest effect on participation and efficacy levels and the church the least influence. This study corroborated the powerful effects of education and income on influencing decision making and decision makers, whether in interest groups, clubs, or traditional forms of political participation. Merely acknowledging that politics happens in everyday life translates into greater influence over decision making in such group settings. Peterson concludes that while SES, education, and gender influence civic orientations and political decision-making participation, it is equally true that greater political efficacy and participation in decision making in everyday institutions also influence formal political decision making and increased participation (Peterson, 1990, pp. 39-55).

Politics and/of Education

Also interesting is the concept of politics and education and the politics of education. Reconceptualists propose that politics is an educational process, while schooling is infused with political content, meanings, processes, and structures. Recognizing the state's role in schooling, the correspondence and reproduction theories, and the schools as independent sites for transformative democratic practices and principles all point to the unity of politics and education as well as the politics of the educational process. The formal and informal, overt and hidden, political and social curriculum is just one aspect of this unity in a democratic political polity between politics and education.

Furthermore, as Richard Merelman (June 1980, pp. 319-20) said when criticizing the hidden curriculum's alleged socially harmful effects, the problematic role of the schools in teaching democracy 'is not just an educational problem, for education is a major arena of public policy. Educational failures are, *ipso facto,* policy failures'. The failures of democratic education are also those of American politics.

Class, Gender, and 'Minority' Status

Political science is also interested in the critical perspective on class, gender, race, and minority status in schools and the society. Though less developed than the class perspective on schooling, the emerging critique of patriarchy, the socially and individually destructive nature of racial and minority discrimination, and the related treatment of the powerless by the economically and politically privileged (in supposedly democratic societies) inform the field of political science. This should influence its professional agenda, obligations, and acceptable topics for research and analysis. For example, political socialization studies must not only deal with majoritarian values, processes, and knowledge, but also with alternative perspectives. Moreover, the pattern of social, economic, and political discrimination and the public's knowledge, feelings, and behaviors on this topic are necessary components of any new research on political socialization, especially from a cross-national perspective.

The Social Dimension of Schooling

A related area of critical educational thought involves educational systems and developmental patterns. Certain radically oriented researchers examined patterns of educational growth, development, and experimentation in third-world and developing socialist systems. For example, these studies focused on the collective, group, and social dimensions of schooling as contrasted with the individualized mission of American and capitalist schooling. These findings not only show the degree to which changes in basic educational skills (such as literacy) are possible, but also the extent to which a social dimension to schooling can be successfully planned and developed. Teaching cooperation, teamwork, and group creativity is important. 'Team' control over the work, standard setting, problem solving, or decision making tasks and other aspects of schooling (beyond individualism, olympic-style competition, and discriminatory grading practices) is important for both postindustrial capitalistic and developing countries (Carnoy and Werthein, 1977).

Democratic Personalities in Their Social Contexts

Critical pedagogical theory's resurrection and appropriation of the Frankfurt School's and the American social reconstructionist philosophical traditions is significant to political science's renewed interest in pro-democratic and antiauthoritarian personality characteristics as well as their social and cultural manifestations, interactions, and reinforcements. For example, the earlier work of Fromm, Adorno, and Marcuse on empirical-theoretical links, the authoritarian personality's 'escape from freedom', and the process of dialectical interrogation across the cultural spectrum (for example, media, politics, aesthetics, and education) is valuable in creating 'the sane society'. This is especially true with the end of the cold war because the nationalistic imperatives engendered for over 40 years in the West impacted authoritarianism and its cultural correlates (such as antiauthoritarianism and democracy) in the US and other countries. Farnen (1993a, b, and 1994 a, b, c), Meloen (1994), and Hagendoorn (November 1991) discussed the relevance of authoritarianism, militarism, nationalism, cultural hegemony, ethnocentrism, and dogmatism to the study of democracy and education.

Ethnography (Cultural Studies)

The progress which radical ethnographers, critical educational theorists, or English practitioners of cultural studies (such as Willis and Anyon) made in combining cultural studies and theoretical constructs with the ethnographic method shows the power of this qualitative approach to 'thickly descriptive' analysis of 'lived lives' and school 'cultures'. To unravel the mysteries underlying significant questions (such as 'Do schools really make any difference?'), critical ethnographers uncovered the basic outlines of hierarchy, cultural dominance, and class hegemony which operate in capitalist schools. In schools today, the correspondence and reproduction principles function along with strains of resistance and transformative possibility.

Policy Making and Political Socialization

Critical social science research in public/educational policy making and for political socialization research is also valuable. While many critical educational theorists dismiss much of the work on political socialization and educational politics and decision making as theoretically uninformed, liberally biased, and counterproductive for depicting both the reality of schooling and the possibility for reform, they offer few constructive alternatives, models, or actual case studies as a more viable approach. However, the work of Willis et al. (1988) on the social conditions of youth in Wolverhampton, England provides some insight. This radical policy research and cultural studies project focused on a local economy, youth unemployment, relevant survey findings, and a 'qualitative' picture of youth culture and local youth services. Its goal was development of 'a policy and institutional framework capable of grasping the full range of needs of young adults and empowered to respond to them in a coordinated and integrated way' (Willis et al., 1988, p. 3).

Policy proposals based on this research study include coordinating local policy, structuring (not individualizing) concepts of unemployment, combating redundancy and victimization approaches, establishing empowerment through problem self-definition, developing a collective focus on a 'policy/services/resources' package, and trying 'riskier' and more liberating policies than now exist. Even more specific policy proposals for a local council, enlightened policy statement, bureaucratic restructuring, and a town 'youth site' are proposed in accordance with a youth-developed 'charter' (Willis et al., 1988, pp. 231-43). This type of action-oriented and theoretically informed research could be applied to political socialization, multicultural education, and civic education curriculum projects in other research settings.

The Hidden and Explicit Curricula

New Left and neo-Marxist discussions of the 'hidden curriculum' (as versus the formal curriculum) not only interest political scientists and educators, but they actually provoked a heated debate in *American Political Science Review* during 1980 and 1981. At that time, two prominent political scientists (Richard Merelman and M. Kent Jennings) engaged in a spirited exchange. Merelman (June 1980) claimed that democratic schooling did not seem to make much difference, whereas Jennings (June 1980) held that it did. (For an evaluation of this exchange, see Farnen, 1990, pp. 54-61; also see Merelman, March 1981, and Jennings, March 1981, for their final views on this subject.)

When this debate continued the following year, it mainly devolved into an argument about which scholar could provide more statistics supporting the influence of education on democratic values. More to the point is Giroux's perspective on the Merelman argument, which he terms part of 'the liberal problematic'. Giroux (in Giroux and Purpel, 1983) faults Merelman (ignoring Jennings) for not seeing that the intraschool division he describes 'may have its roots in the dominant society' (that is, in 'the very nature of capitalist society' which restricts democracy to politics and inequality to economics). Instead, Giroux attributes to Merelman characteristics that typify 'the liberal perspective in general' (that is, 'little or no understanding' of how social conditions create 'oppressive features of schooling', as well as 'the ideological texture of school life'). There is no room in the liberal view for evaluating 'contradictory knowledge claims' or explaining both how such a 'reality' emerged or how it may be successfully resisted through 'critical thinking or constructive dialogue'. The alternative, radical approach to the hidden curriculum does not merely dismiss the phenomenon as a 'structural constraint' or consensus-producing techniques, but rather uses it as a 'focus on conflict' and 'on social structures and the construction of meaning' (that is, it questions reproduction, 'dominance', 'exploitation', and class 'inequality') (Giroux and Purpel, 1983, pp. 54-6; Giroux and Penna, 1981, pp. 209-30).

These three perspectives show that there is both a pluralism in (and division among) political science views about the hidden curriculum. It is also relevant to current disciplinary discourse and its modernistic 'great conversation'. But radical critics obviously hit a very sore spot by attacking present formulations of democratic schooling. This discussion illustrates the lack of engagement and what Giroux called 'constructive dialogue' between the radical and traditional political science communities. The Merelman-Jennings debate lost sight of the radical critique, posed an alternative model, quarreled over the democratic relevance of schooling, and heaped statistical evidence (minus any theoretical underpinnings) on one another without a real debate over the radical critique summed up by the phrase 'the hidden curriculum'. None of the information in the American political socialization and ethnographic literature on class and racial divisions (the work of Litt, Jaros, Greenberg et al., reprinted in Bell, 1973, pp. 91-128 and 189-299; Anyon, 1979 and 1980) was discussed. Nor were the radical critics asked to reply to the terms of this debate. This left a huge silence instead of useful answers. Such deficiencies surely need correction in future encounters of this sort.

Political Education

Finally, we focus on civic education, citizenship, and political education. The utility of the radical critique in this respect is its formulations of both the 'hidden curriculum' and other useful constructs (such as resistance and the possibility of transforming schools which may exert a liberating and emancipatory influence on students, teachers, and the society itself). This critique is holistic in its approach because schooling is placed in the context of the home, media, job, and across all groups, institutional, individual, internal, and external agents and levels in a lifelong perspective.

Since the radical critique has mostly been at the theoretical level (because of its roots in classic and neo-Marxist, Gramsci, Friere, Dewey, and Frankfurt School analysis), the details of how one creates a radical curriculum (that is, educational praxis) have not been superabundant. But we now have some indications of what this more mundane aspect of schooling actually means.

As an alternative to traditional models, Apple and King want schools to move beyond mere reproduction of work and rhetorical humanistic models to a Gramscian analysis of the school site as an ideological setting by asking: Whose interests do the schools serve? How are cultural and economic capital distributed? Can institutions 'enhance meaning and lessen control'? What are these social interests? But they expect no consensual or monolithic answers (Apple and King, 1983, pp. 82-99). Giroux's 'new sociology of curriculum' is also based on the answers to questions about the curriculum, such as: What is such knowledge? How is it produced? How does the classroom reproduce the workplace? Where does its legitimacy come from? In whose interests? How are 'contradictions and tensions' over knowledge mediated? And, what legitimizing role does evaluation play? (Giroux, 1981b, p. 104). Giroux's view of citizenship education as evoking civic courage among an active, involved, public-minded citizenry to produce just and democratic communities also sets a context for such interrogations. Still other radical political economists applaud Piagetian active cognitive formulations and reject Kohlberg's moral stages as an irrelevant discourse about moral development without a basis in 'the coordinates of social action' (Huebner, 1981, p. 134). Yet, Giroux and Purpel (1983, pp. 61-81) think enough of Kohlberg to accept his piece on 'the moral atmosphere of the school'.

Radical democratic educators have not yet come to terms with stage, developmental, moral, or structural/functional cognitive theory or with decision making, problem solving, or cross-national political socialization findings. An entire generation of recent research in these areas remains beyond the pale of the reconceptualists (Farnen, 1993a and b). While these findings might benefit from post-hoc critical pedagogical scrutiny, it might be more fruitful for radical educationists to join such cross-national research projects to influence the questions asked of whom as well as when, where, and why we should ask them. In this respect, the more culture-bound Anglo-Saxon theoretical constructs which inform critical social science and educational study in the US, UK, and Germany (for example, the liberal and neoconservative critique) may be quite inappropriate in a former state-socialist-command economic/political system (such as Hungary), whereas the correspondence, resistance, and implicit curriculum concepts may fare better. An Hungarian listening to a neo-Marxian analyze schooling might think these missionaries of the left had arrived 50 years too late since they have only just begun to develop the market, democracy, civil society, or opportunities for choice among competing public philosophies and policies.

CONCLUSIONS

In assessing the relevance of reconceptualism to political science, political education, and political socialization, the great virtue of this diverse school of thought (which is united only through a common political economy, social justice, and transformational nexus) is its dialectical and interrogatory approach to schooling, the state, politics, social traditions, and the economy. In performing this controversial and often negative critique, the uninitiated reader has no secure curriculum, evaluation, or teaching technique safety net. Although the neophyte reader is exposed to a myriad of 'what's wrongs and what not to dos', there are 'silences' about what will work and why. For example, critical pedagogy does not enlighten us about developmental stages or stances or about cognitive psychology, schema theory, and/or whether these ideas can be radicalized, reconceptualized, or made to withstand rigorous interrogation. While not differing much from humanistic evaluators, radical critics often focus on teacher training rather than on the teachers of teachers and/or students, curriculum, and instruction (that is, the latter is perhaps the actual 'stuff' of schooling). While an educational philosophy is admirable and an enlightened theory may emancipate us all, there is also a danger of orthodoxy, intolerance, and conformity to one theoretical principle: that espoused by the political economists of schooling. Consequently, the reader must keep track of who is up and who is down on the list of acceptable reconceptualists or 'right thinkers'. Adding to the confusion, radical theorists score their hits and errors differently.

There is also a potentially dogmatic strain in the radical critique, which must be offset via a commitment to honest dialogue and debate. This purpose is not well served when the opposition is demonized as the 'enemy', using schools and other 'ideological state apparatuses' to spread reproduction-based 'myths' of pluralism and liberalism. Excoriating the conservative philosophy of schooling as essentially undemocratic is one thing, but linking the 'misguided' liberal *innocenti* as fellow travelers of the right wing is quite another. While conservatives may be as economically deterministic as the most radical neo-Marxists, 20th century social liberals have merely to reorganize their political views along more social democratic and critical educational lines to reach a working consensus with the critical left.

And so it might go with other topics on the US national agenda. These include the probable critical stand on individuals and teachers determining what both learn in school, the need for commonality in theory, but an appreciation of multiculturalism while working to offset race/class/gender oppression in both schools and society, and opposing values 'transmission' in favor of their mutual development through a liberating curriculum process.

These are just a few of the primary issues in the American educational debate in addition to those previously mentioned, such as parental educational vouchers ('choice'), merit pay, antidiversity, competition, and the America 2000 educational policy agenda (Klein, 25 August 1991, pp. 4-7). To be more effective, the radical critique could be deployed for or against such conservative policy proposals (or partially in favor of certain social liberal alternatives). Not to be more fully involved in this debate is to allow the strong forces of resurgent traditionalism and phoney individualism to go unchallenged and uninterrogated. After all, radical pedagogy and social science are both internally and externally controversial - as both its fundamental nature and developmental designs oblige reconceptualism to be.

3 *Conservative Politics and National Curricula*

Michael W. Apple

ABSTRACT

Education is deeply implicated in the politics of culture. The curriculum is
never simply a neutral assemblage of knowledge, somehow appearing in a
nation's texts and classrooms. It is always part of a selective tradition, someone's selection, some group's vision of legitimate knowledge. It is produced
from cultural, political, and economic conflicts, tensions, and compromises
that organize and disorganize a people. As I argue in *Ideology and Curriculum* and *Official Knowledge*, the decision to define some groups' knowledge
as the most legitimate and official while the other groups' hardly surfaces
says something important about society (Apple, 1990 and 1993).

Think of social studies texts that refer to the 'Dark Ages' rather than the
historically more accurate, less racist 'age of African and Asian Ascendancy'
or books that treat Rosa Parks as a naive African American woman too tired
to go to the back of the bus, rather than discussing her training in organized
civil disobedience at Highlander Folk School. Realizing that teaching, especially at the elementary school level, has largely been defined as women's
work (with its accompanying struggles over autonomy, pay, respect, and
deskilling) documents the connections between curriculum and teaching plus
the history of gender politics (Apple, 1988). Thus, differential power intrudes
into the heart of curriculum, teaching, and evaluation. What counts as knowledge, how it is organized, who is empowered to teach it, what is an appropriate display of having learned it, and who is allowed to ask and answer these
questions constitutes how dominance and subordination are reproduced and
altered in this society (Bernstein, 1977; Apple, Spring 1988, pp. 191-201).

INTRODUCTION

There is always a politics of official knowledge, embodying conflict over
what some regard as neutral descriptions of the world and others call elite
conceptions that empower some groups while disempowering others.

Speaking of how elite culture, habits, and 'tastes' function, Pierre Bourdieu said:

> The denial of lower, coarse, vulgar, venal, servile - in a word, natu-
> ral - enjoyment, which constitutes the sacred sphere of culture,
> implies an affirmation of the superiority of those who can be satis-
> fied with the sublimated, refined, disinterested, gratuitous, distin-

guished pleasures forever closed to the profane. That is why art and cultural consumption are predisposed, consciously and deliberatively or not, to fulfill a social function of legitimating social difference(Bourdieu, 1984, p. 7).

These cultural forms, 'through the economic and social conditions which they presuppose, . . . are bound up with the systems of dispositions (habitus) characteristic of different classes and class fractions' (Bourdieu, 1984, pp. 5-6). Thus, cultural form and content function as class markers (Bourdieu, 1984, p. 2). Granting sole legitimacy to such a cultural system by incorporating it in the official centralized curriculum creates a situation in which the markers of 'taste' become those of the people. The school becomes a class school.

The tradition of scholarship and activism that formed me was based on these insights: the complex relationships between economic and cultural capital, the role of the school in reproducing and challenging the many unequal power relations (which go well beyond class), and how the content and organization of the curriculum, pedagogy, and evaluation function in this.

Now, these kinds of issues must be taken most seriously. During this conservative restoration period, when a group of conservative Republicans took control of Congress in 1994, conflicts over the politics of official knowledge are severe. The very idea of public education and a curriculum that responds to the cultures and histories of large, growing segments of the American population is at stake. Even after a 'moderate' Democratic administration was re-elected in 1996, many of its own commitments embodied these tendencies. While more 'moderate' forces are in power, we need to consider what can happen when the government is pulled (for political reasons) in increasingly conservative directions.

To understand the proposals for a national curriculum and testing program, we must connect them to the larger conservative restoration movement. I believe a very dangerous ideological attack is behind the educational justifications for a national curriculum and testing. Its effects will damage those who already have the most to lose in this society. I will present a few interpretive cautions, analyze the general project of the rightist agenda, show the connections between national curricula and testing and the increasing focus on privatization and 'choice' plans, and, finally, discuss the patterns of differential benefits that will likely result from all this.

THE QUESTION OF A NATIONAL CURRICULUM

Where should those who are part of the long progressive tradition in education stand in relationship to the call for a national curriculum?

In principle, I am not opposed to a national curriculum nor to the idea or activity of testing. Rather, I provide a more conjunctural set of arguments that (based on today's balance of social forces) there are very real dangers we must consider. I largely confine myself to the negative case here. My task is to raise enough serious questions to make us think about the implications of moving in this direction in a time of conservative triumph.

We are not the only nation where a largely rightist coalition has put such proposals on the educational agenda. In England, a national curriculum (created by a Thatcher government) is now essentially in place. It consists of 'core and foundation subjects' such as mathematics, science, technology, history, art, music, physical education, and a modern foreign language. Working groups determine the standard goals, 'attainment targets', and content in each subject. This is accompanied by an expensive and time-consuming national system of achievement testing for all students (at ages 7, 11, 14, and 16) in state-run schools (Whitty, 1992, p. 292).

In the US, many assume we must follow those nations (such as Britain and Japan) or fall behind. Yet, we must understand that we already have a national curriculum determined by the complicated nexus of state textbook adoption policies and the market in text publishing (Apple, 1990; Apple and Christian-Smith, 1990). Thus, we have to ask if a national curriculum (linked to a system of national goals and nationally standardized tests) is better than an equally widespread but somewhat more hidden national curriculum established by state textbook adoption. States such as California and Texas control 20 to 30 per cent of the market in textbooks (Apple, 1990; Apple and Christian-Smith, 1990). Whether or not such a hidden national curriculum already exists, there is a growing feeling that a standardized set of national curricular goals and guidelines is essential to 'raise standards' and to hold schools accountable for their students' achievement or lack of it.

Granted many people from an array of educational and political positions call for higher standards, more rigorous curricula at a national level, and a system of national testing. Yet, we must ask: What group leads these reform efforts? This brings up a broader question: Given our answer to the former, who will benefit and who will lose as a result of all this? I contend that rightist groups set the political agenda in education and will generally reproduce the same pattern of benefits that characterize nearly all areas of social policy (in which the top 20 per cent of the population reap 80 per cent of the benefits) (Apple, 1989, pp. 205-23; Burtless, 1990).

We should not assume that because a policy or practice originates within a distasteful position, all aspects of it are fundamentally determined by that tradition. For example, Thorndike's often repugnant social beliefs (including participation in the popular eugenics movement and his notions of racial, gender, and class hierarchies) do not necessarily destroy the value of his research on learning. While I do not support this research paradigm (whose epistemological and social implications need major criticism) (Gould, 1981; Haraway, 1989; Harding and Barr, 1987; Tuana, 1989; Harding, 1991), it requires a different kind of argument than that based on origination. (Indeed, some progressive educators turn to Thorndike to support their claims about what needs to be transformed in our curriculum and pedagogy).

Not just those identified with the rightist project argue for a national curriculum. Others historically identified with a more liberal agenda have attempted to make a case (Smith, O'Day, and Cohen, 1990, pp. 10-7, 40-7). Smith, O'Day, and Cohen suggest a positive (if cautionary vision) for a national curriculum. It would involve inventing new examinations (technically, conceptually, and politically difficult) teaching more rigorous content, thus asking teachers to do more demanding and exciting work. Teachers and administrators would have to 'deepen their knowledge of academic subjects and change their conceptions of knowledge itself'. Teaching and learning would have to be seen as 'more active and inventive'. Teachers, administrators, and students would need 'to become more thoughtful, collaborative, and participatory' (Smith, O'Day, and Cohen, 1990, p.46).

> Conversion to a national curriculum could only succeed if the work of conversion were conceived and undertaken as a grand, cooperative learning venture. Such an enterprise would fail miserably if it were conceived and organized chiefly as a technical process of developing new exams and materials and then 'disseminating' or implementing them. . . . A worthwhile, effective national curriculum would also require the creation of much new social and intellectual connective tissue. For instance, the content and pedagogy of teacher education would have to be closely related to the content of and pedagogy of the schools' curriculum. The content and pedagogy of examinations would have to be tied to those of the curriculum and teacher education. Such connections do not now exist (Smith, O'Day, and Cohen, 1990, p.46).

They conclude that such a revitalized system, which includes such coordination, 'will not be easy, quick, or cheap,' especially if it is to preserve variety and initiative. 'If Americans continue to want educational reform on the cheap, a national curriculum would be a mistake' (Smith, O'Day, and Cohen, 1990, p.46). Yet, they do not sufficiently recognize that much of what they fear is already going on in the very linkage they want. More importantly, it is what they do not pay sufficient attention to (the connections between a national curriculum and national testing and the larger rightist agenda) that constitutes an even greater danger.

BETWEEN NEOCONSERVATISM AND NEOLIBERALISM

The name 'conservatism' announces one interpretation of its agenda: it conserves. But other interpretations are possible. One could say conservatism believes nothing should be done for the first time (Honderich, 1990, p. 1). Yet often in the current situation, this is deceptive. For with the Right now rising in many nations, we are witnessing a much more activist project. Conservative politics now frequently involve alteration. Clearly, the idea of 'Do nothing for the first time' is not a sufficient explanation of what is going on either in education or elsewhere (Honderich, 1990, p. 4).

Conservatism has meant different things at different times and places. At times, it involves defensive actions; at others, taking initiative against the status quo (Honderich, 1990, p. 15). Today, we see both. Because of this, we must consider the larger social context in which the current politics of official knowledge operates. There has been a breakdown in the accord that guided a good deal of educational policy since World War II. Powerful groups within government and the economy, and within 'authoritarian populist' (Apple, 1993) social movements, have redefined (often retrogressively) the terms of debate in education, social welfare, and other areas of the common good. What education is for is being transformed. No longer is education seen as part of a social alliance which combined many 'minority' (the majority of the world's population is composed of persons of color) groups, women, teachers, community activists, progressive legislators and government officials, and others who together proposed (limited) social democratic policies for schools (for example, expanding educational opportunities, equalizing outcomes, and developing special programs in bilingual and multicultural education). A new alliance with increasing power in educational and social policy has been formed. It combines business with the New Right and neoconservative intellectuals. It wants to provide the educational conditions believed necessary both for increasing international competitiveness, profit, and discipline and for returning to a romanticized past of the 'ideal' home, family, and school (Apple, 1993).

The power of this alliance can be seen in several educational policies and proposals: 1) programs for 'choice' such as voucher plans and tax credits to make schools like the thoroughly idealized free-market economy; 2) the movement at national and state levels to 'raise standards' and mandate both teacher and student competencies and basic curricular goals and knowledge by implementing statewide and national testing; 3) the increasingly effective attacks on the school curriculum for its antifamily and anti-free-enterprise 'bias,' secular humanism, lack of patriotism, and supposed neglect of the knowledge and values of the 'western tradition' and 'real knowledge'; and 4) the growing pressure to make the perceived needs of business and industry into the primary goals of the school (Apple, 1988 and 1993).

In essence, the new alliance favoring the conservative restoration integrates education objectives into a wider set of economic and societal ideological commitments. These objectives include expanding the 'free market', drastically reducing government responsibility for social needs, reinforcing intensely competitive structures of mobility, lowering people's expectations for economic security, and popularizing a form of Social Darwinist thinking (Bastian et al., 1986).

The political right in the US has successfully mobilized support against the educational system and its employees, often exporting the crisis in the economy onto the schools. Thus, one of its major achievements has been to shift the blame for unemployment and underemployment, for the loss of economic competitiveness, and for the supposed breakdown of 'traditional' values and standards in the family, education, and paid and unpaid work-places from the economic, cultural, and social policies and effects of dominant groups to the school and other public agencies. 'Public' now is the center of all evil; 'private' is the center of all good (Apple, 1985).

Essentially, four trends characterize the conservative restoration both in the US and Britain: privatization, centralization, vocationalization, and differentiation (Green, 1991, p. 27). These largely result from differences within the powerful neoliberal and neoconservative wings of this alliance.

Neoliberalism envisions the weak state. A society that lets the 'invisible hand' of the free market guide all aspects of social interaction is seen as both efficient and democratic. On the other hand, neoconservatism is guided by a vision of the strong state in certain areas (especially over the politics of the body and gender and race relations, over standards, values, and conduct, and over what knowledge should be passed on to future generations) (Hunter, 1988). Neoliberalism actually does not ignore the idea of a strong state, but it wants to limit it to specific areas, such as defense of markets. Those two positions do not easily coexist in the conservative coalition.

Thus, the rightist movement is contradictory. Is it not paradoxical to link all of the feelings of loss and nostalgia to the unpredictability of the market, 'in replacing loss by sheer flux' (Johnson, 1991, p. 40)?

The contradiction between the rightist coalition's neoconservative and neoliberal elements are 'solved' through what Roger Dale called 'conservative modernization' (Edwards et al., 1992, p. 156). This policy is engaged in

> simultaneously 'freeing' individuals for economic purposes while controlling them for social purposes; indeed, in so far as economic 'freedom' increases inequalities, it is likely to increase the need for social control. A 'small, strong state' limits the range of its activities by transferring to the market, which it defends and legitimizes, as much welfare [and other activities] as possible. In education, the new reliance on competition and choice is not all pervasive; instead, 'what is intended is a dual system, polarized between...market schools and minimum schools' (Dale quoted in Edwards et al., 1992, pp. 156-7).

That is, there will be a relatively less regulated and increasingly privatized sector for the children of the better off. For the rest (the economic status and racial composition of many urban people attending these minimum schools is predictable), the schools will be tightly controlled and policed and will continue to be underfunded and unlinked to decent paid employment.

One of the major effects of combining marketization and a strong state is 'to remove educational policies from public debate'. Thus, individual parents must make a choice while 'the hidden hand of unintended consequences does the rest'. In the process, the very idea of education being part of a public political sphere in which its means and ends are publicly debated atrophies (Education Group II, 1991, p. 268).

There are major differences between democratic attempts to enhance people's rights over schooling policies and practices and the neoliberal emphasis on marketization and privatization. The former want to extend politics, to 'revivify democratic practice by devising ways of enhancing public discussion, debate, and negotiation'. It is based on a vision of democracy as an educative practice. The latter seeks to contain politics. It wants to reduce all politics to economics, to an ethic of 'choice' and 'consumption' (Johnson, 1991, p. 68). In essence, the world becomes a vast supermarket.

Enlarging the private sector so that buying and selling (competition) is society's dominant ethic involves a set of closely related propositions. It assumes that more individuals are motivated to work harder under these conditions. (We 'already know' that public agencies are inefficient and slothful while private enterprises are efficient and energetic.) It assumes that self-interest and competitiveness foster creativity. More knowledge and experimentation is created and used to alter what we have now. In the process, less waste is created. Supply and demand stay in a kind of equilibrium. This creates a more efficient machine which minimizes administrative costs and ultimately distributes resources more widely (Honderich, 1990, p.104).

This is not meant simply to privilege the few. However, it is the equivalent of saying that everyone has the right to scale Mount Everest, providing that you are very good at mountain climbing and have the institutional and financial resources to do it (Honderich, 1990, pp. 99-100). Thus, in a conservative society, access to a society's private resources (and the goal is to make most of society's resources private) largely depends on one's ability to pay. And this depends on one's being entrepreneurial or efficiently acquisitive. Alternatively, society's public resources (the more rapidly decreasing segment) depend on need (Honderich, 1990, p. 89). In a conservative society, the former is to be maximized and the latter minimized.

The conservatism of the conservative alliance does not merely depend on a particular view of human nature as primarily self-interested. It has gone further; it has set out to degrade human nature, to force all people to conform to what at first could only be pretended to be true. Unfortunately, it has succeeded. Perhaps blinded by their own absolutist and reductive vision of what it means to be human, many of our political 'leaders' seem unable to recognize what they have done. They have dragged down the character of a people (Honderich, 1990, p. 81), while simultaneously attacking the poor and disenfranchised for their supposed lack of values and character.

CURRICULUM, TESTING, AND A COMMON CULTURE

As Whitty reminds us, what is striking about the rightist coalition's policies is its capacity to connect the neoconservatives' emphasis on traditional knowledge and values, authority, standards, and national identity with the neoliberals' emphasis on extending market-driven principles into all areas of our society (Whitty, 1992, p. 294). Thus, a national curriculum (coupled with rigorous national standards and a performance-driven system of testing) is simultaneously able to aim at 'modernization' of the curriculum and the efficient 'production' of better 'human capital'. It also represents a nostalgic yearning for a romanticized past (Whitty, 1992, p. 294). When tied to a program of market driven-policies (for example, voucher and choice plans), such a national system of standards, testing, and curricula, while perhaps internally inconsistent, is an ideal compromise within the rightist coalition.

But does not a national curriculum coupled with a system of national achievement testing contradict the concomitant emphasis on privatization and school choice? Can one simultaneously do both? This apparent contradiction may not be as substantial as one might expect. One long-term aim of powerful elements in the conservative coalition is not necessarily to transfer power from the local level to the center (though this may be true for some neoconservatives who favor a strong state when it comes to morality, values, and standards). Rather, they prefer to decenter such power altogether, redistribute it according to market forces, and thus tacitly disempower those who already have less power while claiming to empower the 'consumer'. In part, both a national curriculum and national testing can be seen as 'necessary concessions in pursuit of this long-term aim' (Green, 1991, p. 29).

With the current loss of government legitimacy and crisis in educational authority relations, the government must be seen as doing something to raise educational standards. After all, this is exactly what it promises to education 'consumers'. A national curriculum is crucial here. Its major value does not lie in encouraging standardized goals and content and boosting achievement levels in what are considered the most important subject areas. Although this should not be totally dismissed, its major role is to provide the framework within which national testing can function. It enables the establishment of a procedure that supposedly gives consumers 'quality tags' on schools so that 'free market forces' can operate to the fullest extent possible. If we are to have a free market in education, giving the consumer an attractive range of 'choice', both a national curriculum and more particularly national testing essentially act as a 'state watchdog committee' to control the market's overall performance. (This is a 'functional', not necessarily an 'intentional', explanation. See Liston, 1988. For a discussion of how such testing programs may actually work against more democratic school reform efforts, see Darling-Hammond, 1992, p. 18.)

However, even with some people supposedly emphasizing portfolios and other more flexible evaluation forms, there is no evidence to support the hope that something other than a system of mass standardized paper and pencil tests will be installed. Yet, we must be clear about the social function of such a proposal. A national curriculum may be seen as a device for accountability, to help us establish benchmarks for parents to evaluate schools. But it also establishes a system in which children will be ranked and ordered as never before. One of its primary roles will be to act as 'a mechanism for differentiating children more rigidly against fixed norms the social meanings and derivation of which are not available for scrutiny' (Johnson, 1991, p. 79).

While national curriculum advocates may see it as a means to create social cohesion and to enable us to improve our schools by measuring them against 'objective' criteria, the effects will be the opposite. The criteria may seem objective; but the results will not be, given existing differences in resources and in class and race segregation. Rather than cultural and social cohesion, differences between 'we' and the 'others' will be socially produced even more strongly, worsening the attendant social antagonisms and cultural and economic destruction. (This will also be true with the current outcomes-based education, a new term for older versions of educational stratification).

Richard Johnson (1991, pp. 79-80) helps us understand the social processes at work when he calls for all curricula to explain themselves. In complex societies, the only 'cohesion' possible is one in which we overtly recognize differences and inequalities. The curriculum should not be presented as 'objective', but rather must constantly subjectify itself. That is, it must 'acknowledge its own roots' in the culture, history, and social interests out of which it arose. Accordingly, it will homogenize neither this culture, history and social interest, nor the students. The 'same treatment' by sex, race and ethnicity, or class is not the same at all. A democratic curriculum and pedagogy must begin by recognizingn 'the different social positionings and cultural repertoires in the classrooms, and the power relations between them'. If we are concerned with 'really equal treatment', we must base a curriculum on a recognition of those differences that empower and depower our students in identifiable ways (Johnson, 1991, p. 79-80; Ellsworth, 1989, pp. 297-324).

To understand how power works, Foucault recommends looking at the margins, knowledge, self-understandings, and struggles of those who society's powerful groups have cast off as 'the other' (Best and Kellner, 1991, pp. 34-75). The New Right and its allies created entire groups of 'others' (people of color, women who refuse to accept external control of their lives and bodies, gays and lesbians, the poor, and the vibrant working class). By recognizing these differences, curriculum dialogue can go on. This national dialogue begins with the concrete and public exploration of 'how we are differently positioned in society and culture'. What the New Right embargoes (the knowledge of the margins, of how culture and power are indissolubly linked) becomes a set of indispensable resources here (Johnson, 1991, p. 320).

The proposed national curriculum would recognize some of these differences. But, as Linda Christian-Smith and I argue in *The Politics of the Textbook*, the national curriculum serves to both partly acknowledge difference and, at the same time, recuperate it within the supposed consensus that exists about what we should teach (Apple and Christian-Smith, 1990; Apple, 1993; Whitty, 1992, p. 290; Whitty, 1997). It is part of an attempt to recreate hegemonic power that has been partly fractured by social movements.

The neoconservatives' idea of a common culture for building a national curriculum is a form of cultural politics. Despite the immense linguistic, cultural, and religious diversity that generates today's constant creativity and flux, the Right's cultural policy is to 'override' such diversity. By supposedly reinstituting a common culture, it is instead inventing one much like Hirsch tried to do in his self-parody of what it means to be literate (Johnson, 1991, p. 319; Hirsch, 1986). A uniform culture never truly existed in the US, only a selective version, an invented tradition that is reinstalled (though in different forms) in times of economic upheaval and a crisis in authority relations, both of which threaten the hegemony of the culturally and economically dominant.

The expansion of voices in the curriculum and the Right's vehement responses are crucial. Multicultural and antiracist curricula challenge the core of the New Right's program. In a largely monocultural national curriculum (which deals with diversity by centering the always ideological 'we' and usually simply mentioning 'the contributions' of people of color, women, and 'others'), a threat to maintaining existing hierarchies of what counts as official knowledge, revivifying traditional 'Western' standards and values, returning to a 'disciplined' (and largely masculinist) pedagogy, and so on also threatens the Right's entire world view (Johnson, 1991, p. 51; Rose, 1988).

The idea of a 'common culture' (in the guise of neoconservatives' romanticized Western tradition or some socialists' longings) does not recognize the immense heterogeneity of a society that draws its cultural traditions from all over the world. The task of defending public education as public, as deserving widespread support 'across an extremely diverse and deeply divided people, involves a lot more than restoration' (Education Group II, 1991, p. x).

The debate in England is similar. The Right sees a national curriculum as essential to prevent relativism. For most of its proponents, a common curriculum must basically transmit both the 'common culture' and the high culture that grew out of it. Anything else will result in incoherence, no culture, a mere 'void'. Thus, a national culture is 'defined in exclusive, nostalgic, and frequently racist terms' (Johnson, 1991, p. 11).

One thing is perfectly clear: the national curriculum is a mechanism for the political control of knowledge (Johnson, 1991, p. 82). Once established, there will be little chance of turning back. It may be modified by the conflicts that its content generates, but it is in its very establishment that its politics lies. Only by recognizing its ultimate logic of false consensus and, especially, its undoubted hardening in the future as it becomes linked to a massive system of national testing can we fully understand this. When this is connected to the other parts of the rightist agenda (marketization and privatization), there is sufficient reason to give us pause, especially given the increasingly powerful conservative gains at local, regional, and state levels.

WHO BENEFITS?

Since leadership in such efforts to 'reform' our educational system and its curriculum, teaching, and evaluative policies and practices is largely exercised by the rightist coalition, we must always ask: Whose reforms are these? and Who benefits?

This is reform on the cheap. A system of national curricula and national testing cannot help but ratify and exacerbate gender, race, and class differences in the absence of sufficient human and material resources. Thus, when the fiscal crisis in most of our urban areas is so severe that classes are being held in gymnasiums and hallways, when many schools cannot afford to stay open for the full 180 days a year, when buildings are literally disintegrating before our very eyes (Apple, 1993), when in some cities three classrooms must share one set of textbooks at the elementary level (Kozol, 1991), it is simply a flight of fantasy to assume that more standardized testing and national curriculum guidelines are the answer. With the destruction of the economic infrastructure of these same cities through capital flight, with youth unemployment at nearly 75 per cent in many of them, with almost nonexistent health care, with lives that are often devoid of hope for meaningful mobility because of the pornography of poverty, to assume that establishing curricular benchmarks based on problematic cultural visions and more rigorous testing will do more than label poor students in a seemingly more neutral way is also to totally misunderstand the situation. It will lead to more blame for students and poor parents and especially the schools they attend. It will also be very expensive to institute. Enter voucher and 'choice' plans with even wider public approval.

Basil Bernstein's analysis of the complexities of this situation and its ultimate results is useful here. As he says, 'the pedagogic practices of the new vocationalism [neoliberalism] and those of the old autonomy of knowledge [neoconservatism] represent a conflict between different elitist ideologies, one based on the class hierarchy of the market and the other based on the hierarchy of knowledge and its class supports' (Bernstein, 1990, p. 63). Whatever the oppositions between market- and knowledge-oriented pedagogic and curricular practices, present racial, gender, and class-based inequalities are likely to be reproduced (Bernstein, 1990, p. 64).

What he calls an 'autonomous visible pedagogy' (one that relies on overt standards and highly structured models of teaching and evaluation) justifies itself by referring to its intrinsic worthiness. The value of the acquisition of the 'Western tradition' lies in its foundational status for 'all we hold dear' and by the norms and dispositions that it instills in the students.

> Its arrogance lies in its claim to moral high ground and to the superiority of its culture, its indifference to its own stratification consequences, its conceit in its lack of relation to anything other than itself, its self-referential abstracted autonomy (Bernstein, 1990, p. 87).

Its supposed opposite (one based on the knowledge, skills, and dispositions 'required' by business and industry and one that seeks to transform schooling around market principles) is actually a much more complex ideological construction.

> It incorporates some of the criticism of the autonomous visible pedagogy . . . criticism of the failure of the urban school, of the passivity and inferior status [given to] parents, of the boredom of . . . pupils and their consequent disruptions of and resistance to irrelevant curricula, of assessment procedures which itemize relative failure rather than the positive strength of the acquirer. But it assimilates these criticisms into a new discourse: a new pedagogic Janus. . . . The explicit commitment to greater choice by parents . . . is not a celebration of participatory democracy, but a thin cover for the old stratification of schools and curricula (Bernstein, 1990, p. 87).

Are Bernstein's conclusions correct? Will the combination of national curricula, testing, and privatization actually lead away from democratic processes and outcomes? Here we must look not to Japan (where many people unfortunately have urged us to look) but to Great Britain, where this combination of proposals is much more advanced. In Great Britain, there is now considerable evidence that the overall effects of the various market-oriented policies introduced by the rightist government are not genuine pluralism or the 'interrupting [of] traditional modes of social reproduction'. Instead, they may largely provide 'a legitimating gloss for the perpetuation of long-standing forms of structured inequality' (Whitty, 1991, pp. 20-1). The fact that one of its major effects has been the disempowering and deskilling of large numbers of teachers is also not inconsequential. (Compare this to the US experience in Apple and Jungck, 1990, pp. 227-51.)

Going even further, Edwards, Gewirtz, and Whitty have come to similar conclusions. In essence, the rightist preoccupation with 'escape routes' diverts attention from the effects of such policies on those (probably the majority) who will be left behind (Edwards, Gewirtz, and Whitty, 1992, p. 151). Thus, it is indeed possible (actually probable) that market-oriented approaches in education (even when coupled with a strong state system of national curriculum and testing) will exacerbate already existing and widespread class and race divisions. 'Freedom' and 'choice' in the educational market will be for those who can afford them. 'Diversity' in schooling will simply mean the condition of educational apartheid (Green, 1991, p. 30). (For further discussion of the ideological, social, and economic effects of such 'choice' plans, see Karp, 1992, p. 4; Lowe, 1992, pp. 1, 21-3).

AFTERTHOUGHTS BY WAY OF A CONCLUSION

I have been more than a little negative in my appraisal. I argued that the politics of official knowledge (in this case, surrounding proposals for a national curriculum and for national testing) cannot be fully understood in an isolated way. All of this needs to be situated directly back into larger ideological dynamics in which we see a new hegemonic bloc attempting to transform our very ideas of what education is for. This transformation involves a major shift (which would have made Dewey shudder) in which democracy becomes an economic, not a political, concept and where the idea of the public good withers at its very roots.

But perhaps I have been too negative. Perhaps there are good reasons to support national curricula and national testing, even as currently constituted precisely because of the power of the rightist coalition. Furthermore, it is possible to argue that only by establishing a national curriculum and national testing can we stop the fragmentation that will accompany the neoliberal portion of the rightist project. Only such a system would protect the very idea of a public school, protect teachers' unions (which would lose much of their power in a privatized, marketized system), and protect the poor and children of color from the vicissitudes of the market. After all, it is the 'free market' that created the poverty and destruction of community that they are experiencing in the first place.

It is also possible to argue, as Whitty has in the British case, that the very fact of a national curriculum encourages both the formation of intense public debate about whose knowledge is declared official and the creation of progressive coalitions across a variety of differences against such state-sponsored definitions of legitimate knowledge. For example, Andy Green, in the English context, also sees merit in having a broadly defined national curriculum. Yet, he thinks this makes it even more essential that individual schools seriously control its implementation, 'not least so that it provides a check against the use of education by the state as a means of promoting a particular ideology'. (See Green, 1991, p. 22.) The fact that a large portion of the teachers in England have essentially gone on strike, refusing to give the prescribed national test, also supports Whitty's arguments. It could be the vehicle for the return of the political which the Right wants to evacuate from our public discourse and which the efficiency experts want to make into merely a technical concern.

Thus, it is quite possible that establishing a national curriculum could unify oppositional and oppressed groups. Given the fragmented nature of today's progressive educational movements today and a school financing and governance system that forces groups to focus largely on the local or state level, one function of a national curriculum could be the coalescence of groups around a common agenda. A national movement for a more democratic vision of school reform could be the result.

In many ways, we owe principled conservatives (and there are many) a debt of gratitude. It is their realization that curriculum issues are not only about techniques that helped stimulate the current debate. When many women, people of color, and labor organizations (groups not mutually exclusive) fought for decades to have this society recognize the selective tradition in official knowledge, these movements were often silenced, ignored, or absorbed into the dominant discourses (Apple and Christian-Smith, 1990). The power of the Right (in its contradictory attempt to establish a national common culture, to challenge what is now taught, and to make that culture part of a vast supermarket of choices and thus to purge cultural politics from our sensibilities) has now made it impossible for the politics of official knowledge to be ignored. Should we then support a national curriculum and national testing to keep total privatization and marketization at bay? Under current conditions, I do not think it is worth the risk, not only because of its extensive destructive potential, but because I think it misconstrues and reifies the issues of a common curriculum and a common culture.

Here I must repeat the arguments I made in the second edition of *Ideology and Curriculum* (Apple, 1990). The current call to 'return' to a 'common culture' in which all students are to be given the values of a specific (usually dominant) group does not concern a common culture at all. Such an approach hardly scratches the surface of the political and educational issues involved. A common culture can never be the general extension to everyone of what a minority mean and believe. Rather, and crucially, it requires not the stipulation of the facts, concepts, skills, and values that make us all 'culturally literate', but the creation of the conditions necessary for all people to participate in the creation and recreation of meaning and values. It requires a democratic process in which all people (not just those who are the intellectual guardians of the 'Western tradition') can be involved in the deliberation over what is important. This necessitates removing the very real material obstacles (unequal power, wealth, time for reflection) that prevent such participation (Williams, 1989, pp. 35-6).

In speaking of a common culture, we should not talk about something uniform to which we all conform. Instead, we should seek to participate in the common process while creating meanings and values. Blocking that process in our institutions must concern all of us. Our current language speaks to how this process is being defined during the conservative restoration. Instead of people who participate in the struggle to build and rebuild our educational, cultural, political, and economic relations, we are defined as consumers (of that 'particularly acquisitive class type'). This is truly an extraordinary concept for it sees people as either stomachs or furnaces. We use and use up. We do not create. Someone else does that. This is disturbing enough in general, but in education it is truly disabling. Leave it to the guardians of tradition, the efficiency and accountability experts, the holders of 'real knowledge,' or to the Whittles of this world who will build us franchised 'schools of choice' for the generation of profit (Apple, 1993). Yet, we leave it to these people at great risk, especially to those students who are already economically and culturally disenfranchised by our dominant institutions. As I initially noted, our society has identifiable winners and losers. In the future, we may say that the losers made poor 'consumer choices', which is how the markets operate. But is this society really only one vast market?

As Whitty reminds us, when so many people have discovered via their daily experiences that the supposed 'grand narratives' of progress are deeply flawed, is it appropriate to return to yet another grand narrative, the market (Whitty, 1992, p. 290)? The results of this 'narrative' are visible every day in the destruction of our communities and environment, in increased racism, in the faces and bodies of our children, who see the future and turn away.

Many people can disassociate themselves from these realities. There is almost a pathological distancing among the affluent (Kozol, 1991). Yet, how can one not be morally outraged at the growing gap between rich and poor, the persistence of hunger and homelessness, the deadly absence of medical care, the degradations of poverty. If this were the (always self-critical and constantly subjectifying) centerpiece of a national curriculum (but how could it be tested cheaply and efficiently and how could the Right control its ends and means?), perhaps it would be worthwhile after all. But until then, we can take a rightist slogan made popular in another context and apply it to their educational agenda. What is that slogan? 'Just say no'.

ACKNOWLEDGMENTS

This chapter was originally presented as the John Dewey Lecture, jointly sponsored by the John Dewey Society and AERA, San Francisco, April 1992. I would like to thank Geoff Whitty, Roger Dale, James Beane, and the Friday Seminar at the University of Wisconsin, Madison for their important suggestions and criticisms.

Part III

Education and Society

4 Blaming the Victims: The Political Oppression of Disabled People

Len Barton

ABSTRACT

As Raymond Williams said, it is hard to seriously consider major issues of human existence in a society which provides so many distractions (Williams, 1983, p. 18). With regard to disability, the distractions have been powerful. In the sociology of education, this subject has been largely neglected. In other areas of study, professional values and objectives have been significant. These have defined needs, policy, and practice in relation to disabled people. This legitimated marginalizing the position and perspectives of disabled people. Thus, discussions of inequality and social reproduction fail to adequately consider this aspect of social differentiation and discrimination.

SOCIOLOGY OF EDUCATION

Sociological analysis of education applied different perspectives to a range of topics, covering structural and interactional features of the educational system (Barton and Meighan, 1978; Barton and Walker, 1978; Karabel and Halsey, 1977; Robinson, 1981; Reid, 1978). Research, under structural functionalist influence, helped develop the discipline (Floud et al., 1956; Glass, 1954; Banks, 1955). This was restricted to a specific set of concerns, including achievement and social mobility. Investigations examined input-output measures; findings supported the view that working-class ability was seriously wasted (Jackson and Marsden, 1962; Jackson, 1964; Douglas, 1964).

Interest in the social determinants of educability highlighted the extent and stubbornness of inequalities in terms of access, duration, and outcomes of educational opportunity and experience. These inequalities were both unjust and provided via an inefficient system. Recent work confirmed inequality as socially divisive and identified how race and gender factors compounded these divisions (Arnot, 1981; Davies, 1984; Weiner, 1986; Carrington, 1986). These analyses encouraged interest in the politics of social reproduction and equal opportunities. Antisexism and antiracism became crucial issues. New research topics, questions, and explanations were established (Williams, 1986; David, 1986; Gillborn, 1988; Demaine, 1989).

In debates on sociology of education, there is little reference to disabled people or special educational needs. By focusing on 'brightness' or 'ability', education sociologists hardly considered the relationship between the ordinary and special school system, especially regarding transferring pupils from one system to another based on 'special need' (Tomlinson, 1982). They assumed that children in special school settings were politically insignificant. Therefore, the nature and functions of the special educational system has been essentially invisible as far as sociological analysis is concerned.

What are the grounds for and difficulties of making a sociological analysis? Special education lives under a reductionist form of dominance which stresses individualistic explanations. Within-the-child factors portray 'special needs' as personal, not public, issues (Mills, 1970) and depoliticizes them. Because of this restrictive viewpoint, introducing complex questions of class, gender, and race into the analysis seems unnecessary and unhelpful (particularly where the 'special' quality is justified on the grounds that all children be treated equally). The strong tradition that 'special needs' professionals are caring, patient, and loving makes it hard to raise questions about low expectations, patronizing and overprotective practices, and stigmatizing labels. However, sociologists are concerned with how society deals with objectionable groups or individuals. Where discrimination and oppression exist, sociologists focus on how and under what conditions this occurs (Carrier, 1990).

DEVELOPING INTERESTS

Within Britain, sociological analysis of special education is fairly new. Understanding the plight of marginalized groups gives us insights into the nature of society. Growing sociological interest focused on identifying and critiquing individualistic and deficit views of disability (Barton and Tomlinson, 1981 and 1984; Barton, 1986). This involved examining how legislation, policy, and practice contributed to the legitimation of key assumptions and categories. Analysis focused on the centrality of power, control, and vested interests to understand the complex issues involved (Barton and Smith, 1989; Tomlinson, 1982, 1985, and 1988).

New topics which need to be examined include the social construction of categories, how economic and political factors shape definitions, the role of professional groups in developing and legitimating disability practices, the relationship between 'normal' and special schooling, and the role of ideology and how disabled people make sense of their world. Historical and comparative material stimulated sociological imagination in this field of study (SCU11, 1982; Ford et al., 1982; Fulcher, 1989; Barton, 1989).

A QUESTION OF DEFINITION

The issue of disability lets us question the nature of the existing and ideal society. The complex and contentious nature of discourse and practice often results in intense struggles, with participants adhering to competing objectives and operating from unequal power relations (Fulcher, 1989). The struggles include disputes over the meaning of 'disability'. Our values influence how we interpret this activity. Multiple (and often antagonistic) discourses exist. Ball maintains that these discourses are

> . . . about what can be said, and thought, but also about who can speak, when, where and with what authority. . . . Words and propositions will change their meaning according to their use and the positions held by those who use them (Ball, 1990, p. 17).

These ideas, which Foucault (1977) shares, are part of a wider interest in the relationship between knowledge and power. This perspective lets us highlight the nature and intensity of the struggles involved over disability definitions, effective policy, and practice. It also offers a way to explore these relationships between actors in different arenas and levels of the system.

Neither official nor academic discourses about disability include the voices or writings of disabled people themselves. Micheline Mason, a writer who happens to be disabled, describes the results as follows:

> Where are the studies asking disabled people what they think of their education so far? Where is the consultative mechanism to improve the service according to the needs and aspirations of its consumers? You won't find them. Why not? Because disabled people are still the victims of a deeply held prejudice which essentially says that we are incapable of knowing what is best for us (Mason, 1990, p. 363).

They are explicitly prevented from speaking. This is related to how disability is defined and to associated expectations and practices. It is about unequal social relations and conditions and how power is exercised in our society. This both shapes and legitimates the marginalization and exclusion of disabled people. Whose definition is significant, why, and with what effects are questions of fundamental importance in this context.

DISABILITY AS A FORM OF OPPRESSION

Disability is a complex issue. Definitions are crucial since the presuppositions informing them can be the basis of stereotyping and stigmatization. One of the dominant influences shaping policies and practices has been the medical model which emphasizes an individual's inabilities or deficiencies. 'Able-bodiness' is the acceptable criterion of 'normality'. According to Hahn (1985, p. 89), a medical model 'imposes a presumption of biological or physiological inferiority upon disabled persons'. Terms such as 'cripple' or 'spastic' reinforce this individualized medical definition based on mainly functional limitations. Brisenden, a disabled person, critiqued the medical model.

> We are seen as 'abnormal' because we are different; we are problem people, lacking the equipment for social integration. But the truth is, like everybody else, we have a range of things we *can and cannot* do, a range of abilities both mental and physical that are unique to us as individuals. The only difference between us and other people is that we are viewed through spectacles that only focus on our inabilities, and which suffer an automatic blindness - a sort of medicalized social reflex - regarding our abilities (Brisenden, 1986, p. 3).

This perspective provides a variety of individualized responses to disabled people. For example, they are often viewed in heroic terms, as brave and courageous. Their position is constantly compared with an assumed notion of 'normality'. Indeed, pursuing this 'leads to neurosis and is the cause of much guilt and suffering' (Brisenden, 1986, p. 3) on their part. This perspective does not seriously consider a sociopolitical dimension. It provides a very different understanding of disability and the issues involved; it entails an alternative set of assumptions, priorities, and explanations.

> . . . [D]isability stems from the failure of a structured social environment to adjust to the needs and aspirations of citizens with disabilities rather than from the inability of a disabled individual to adapt to the demands of society (Hahn, 1986, p. 128).

This unadaptive, unhelpful, and unfriendly environment must be examined and changed. Being interested in how disabled people suffer requires examining the material conditions and social relations which contribute to their dehumanization and isolationism. Advocating the social nature of oppression implies that disabled people are viewed as inferior because they are disabled. Abberley also notes that

> It is also to argue that these disadvantages are dialectically related to an ideology or group of ideologies which justify and perpetuate this situation. Beyond that it is to make the claim that such disadvantages and their supporting ideologies are neither natural nor inevitable. Finally, it involves the identification of some beneficiary of this state of affairs (Abberley, 1987, p. 7).

Exploring the origins of differences in the lives of disabled people compared to the rest of the community is a fundamental element in a social theory of disability. Capitalism is significant in this process via its emphasis on and distinction between productive and nonproductive people. This legitimates a form of social relations in which disabled people are viewed in terms of what they cannot do. The problem is thus individualized.

Participation in society is not contingent on merely the individual limitations of disabled people, but rather the physical and social restrictions of an essentially hostile environment. Writing on the politics of disability, Oliver summarized the essential features of this alternative position.

All disabled people experience disability as social restriction, whether those restrictions occur as a consequence of inaccessible built environments, questionable notions of intelligence and social competence, the inability of the general public to use sign language, the lack of reading material in braille or hostile public attitudes to people with nonvisible disabilities (Oliver, 1990, p. xiv).

Oliver (1989) maintained that disabled people are involved in a difficult struggle and must strengthen their endeavors as a political pressure group. Disability is a social and political category in that it entails regulation and struggles for choice, empowerment, and opportunities.

For some disabled analysts, merely defining disability as social restriction is inadequate. The issue is not that society ignores the disabled but how it takes them into account. We must examine why society treats this group differently at specific times (Findlay, 1991). Both ideological and material conditions must be considered to identify and challenge discriminatory policies and practices at different levels of the social system.

In a society organized and administered by and for able-bodied people, the position of disabled people in relation to education, work, housing, and welfare services is a matter of grave concern (Abberley, 1987; Oliver, 1991). In many ways, it reflects their marginalization, low status, and vulnerability. Since relationships with various professional agencies are often difficult, disabled people have argued for a range of changes. These include greater choice in the nature and amount of services provided, more control over the allocation of resources (especially for independent living), and new forms of accountability of service providers to disabled people (particularly handling disagreements) (Brisenden, 1986; Oliver and Hasler, 1987; Oliver, 1988). Glendinning claims social policy matters have actually gotten worse and that

The economic and social policies of the last decade have done little to enhance, and much to damage, the quality of life of disabled people. Despite the rhetoric of 'protecting' the most 'deserving', 'vulnerable', or 'needy', much of this 'protection' has been illusory (Glendinning, 1991, p. 16).

Such events resulted in reduced autonomy and choice for the disabled but an increase and intensification of 'scrutiny and control by professionals and others' (Glendinning, 1991, p. 16). These handicapping conditions and relations encourage passivity and dependency on the part of disabled people (Bishop, 1987). It is integral to the process of learned helplessness which depicts problems as personal troubles rather than public issues (Mills, 1970).

Disability is a form of oppression. Being disabled entails social and economic hardships plus assaults on self-identity and emotional well being. But disabled people are not a homogeneous group. Terms such as 'the disabled' imply a sameness. But the difficulties of and responses to being disabled are influenced by class, race, and age. These can cushion or compound the experience of discrimination and oppression. For example,

> . . . women with disabilities are perennial outsiders; their oppression and exclusion renders them one of the most powerless groups in society. The personal care situation encapsulates so many different dynamics that for many women with disabilities it becomes the arena where their oppression becomes so clearly magnified and distilled. (Begum, 1990, p. 79).

Supporting this perspective, Morris (1989) illustrates from the lives (including hers) of some disabled women that privacy, body image, and sexuality cause tension and difficulties in relation to care. She relates the disadvantages disabled mothers experience in bringing up their children, running their homes, and working outside the home. Socioeconomic circumstances play a major role; the more they can afford, the greater the chances of coping. Since few disabled people are in this position, the overall situation is bleak. Many disabled people are 'located at the bottom of the income ladder, or out of work and dependent upon social security benefits' (Borsay, 1986, p. 184).

Since political discourse largely concerns the market and policies 'have grown up in an ad hoc fashion, without a coherent framework to guide policy development' (Borsay, 1986, p. 183), inequalities of provision and opportunity are intensified. Questions of social justice and equality are marginalized in this socioeconomic climate. Struggling for empowerment, disabled people and able-bodied colleagues must increase interest in rights, rather than needs (Hudson, 1988). Critical attention can focus on structural and institutional factors which constrain and serve the interests of the more powerful (Oliver, 1989). Oppression is more than a denial of access and opportunity, it is about being powerless and worthless in an alien society. The disabled cannot learn self-pride and dignity (Findlay, 1991). Oppression takes many forms and is experienced through differential treatment.

Being disabled does not mean automatically understanding and accepting other disabled people. This is part of a learning process leading to a collective identity. Not all disabled people are political. Some are prepared to work within the system and seek minimal changes. We must recognize the complex factors involved in subordinate relations, including how disabled people maintain their learned helplessness. Much must be done to base the struggle on critical awareness and an agreed set of values and agendas.

EQUAL OPPORTUNITIES

Political action is necessary if disabled people are to control their lives and set their own agendas in relation to fully participating in society. This is both a serious and urgent task. To implement equal opportunities, Leach contends:

> Disabled people's issues are still seen, across much of the political spectrum, as largely non-political. Paternalism and the exclusion of disabled people from participation in decision-making, is still largely the norm (Leach, 1989, p. 75).

We must perceive disability as an integral part of equal opportunities for several reasons. First, it is part of the wider issue of prejudice and economic inequality in which ideologies play a socially divisive role. This framework helps establish connections between other discriminated groups. Second, it is a basis for identifying features of the existing society, policy, and practice that are unacceptable, offensive, and need to be challenged and changed. Third, it helps us critique individualized and deficit models and interpretations, changing the emphasis from personal to public issues. Finally, it redresses the extent to which disability has been excluded from them, or merely attached as a token gesture (Leach, 1989 and Rieser and Mason, 1990).

'Equal opportunities' means different things to different people. It is not about gaining access or being able to compete against able-bodied people on equal terms; the stakes are much higher. It means challenging the status quo. The struggle for equal opportunities is one of disabled people setting their own agendas, defining their needs, and having real choices and rights. Breaking down structures and their ideological supports (which exclude, debilitate, and control disabled people) must be part of a process which ultimately seeks liberation and empowerment (Findlay, 1991).

Various analysts challenged some equal opportunity interpretations, especially its inability to provide alternative values and concepts of socialist education (Lauder, 1988). Others said some reforms (in the name of equal opportunity) helped the state prevent more radical, revolutionary changes (Hall, 1988). Feminists highlighted theoretical weaknesses, including simplistic notions of learning, forming gender identity, and stereotyping. Too often the outcome emphasized changing the pupil rather than the oppressive structures. This focus justified operating within existing structures, not removing them (Arnot, 1991). Given these limitations, the argument for considering disability an integral component of equal opportunities must both recognize and struggle against crude reformism, unwitting complicity, or the softening of endeavors required to empower disabled people. On this basis, the demand for equal opportunities is transitional (Branson and Miller, 1989).

NORMALIZATION - AN INADEQUATE AGENDA

Some writers advocate normalization. This takes various forms in the litera- ture, but some of the essential presuppositions have strongly structured defini- tions of, and debates about, the quality of life for people with learning diffi- culties. Influenced by Scandinavian and American ideas and practices, nor- malization advocates tried to convince policy makers and practitioners of its benefits (Ayer and Alaszewski, 1984; Alaszewski and Ong, 1990). The anti- institutional debates of the 1960s and the following processes of deinstitutionization and community care strengthened their motivation.

This approach emphasized reducing stigma and providing quality ser- vices and support so people with learning difficulties will be able to enjoy fairly regular lives in society. One objective of normalization is 'to create or support socially valued roles for people in their society' (Wolfenberger and Thomas, 1983, p. 23).

Normalization theory assumes a consensus between providers and users. Any power differentials between providers and users can be ameliorated if the latter act out the normalization principle. The position and role of values and attitudes is emphasized in this ameliorative process. Staff training includes identifying unacceptable, disabilist attitudes and substituting enabling ones.

Some have criticized normalization theory. A feminist critique drew analogies between the women's movement and the marginalization and vulnerability of disabled people, maintaining that normalization is both apolitical and highly individualistic. They contend that

> The common theme running through these analogies is the existence of a more powerful group which states that it is the norm against which others are measured. Service users are caught in a vicious circle whereby their deviation from this supposed norm deprives them of personal power and authenticity which they would need to legitimately challenge the validity of the whole process.
>
> Just as women's experiences are sanctioned and redefined by men so are users' constantly translated and interpreted by profes- sionals (Brown and Smith, 1989, p. 109).

Providing service essentially legitimates professional authority. Empha- sizing the professional's significance encourages dependency. Chappell (1992) criticized normalization's functionalist underpinnings, its failure to seriously consider the real material constraints faced by people with learning difficulties, its idealism derived from interactionist concerns with deviance, and its emphasis on attitudes and values. Such critics believe that one of normalization's fundamental weaknesses is its failure to subject the issue of power structures and relations to any serious interrogation. Material conditions of this nature cannot be merely thought away. Emphasizing attitudinal change is an insufficient basis for the fundamental changes required to realize a more open, democratic, and just society. This requires developing a sociopolitical perspective of disability.

CONCLUSION

My mainly negative perspective has several advantages. It confirms that discussions about the experiences and well-being of disabled people must be part of a socioeconomic and historical analysis, including the division of labor and its effect on social status and opportunities. Disability is a political issue and entails examining consumer rights and raising questions about who benefits. Current ideologies and practices are neither natural nor proper; as a social creation, they can be changed. The struggle for change will require disabled people and their allies to become politicized and voice their demands. Government's position is important in developing and implementing appropriate legislation and policies. These factors encourage supporters to challenge individualized, mythical, and deficit views of disabled people; to emphasize understanding; and to change an offensive material and social world. The alternative is a form of reductionism which blames the victim and both individualizes and homogenizes the issues involved (Ryan, 1976).

Although we have a Race Relations Act and a Sex Discrimination Act in the UK, no antidiscrimination legislation protects the rights of disabled people. Several disability groups protested government's decision to scrap vital sections of the 1986 Disabled Persons' Act. Failure to implement these sections would seriously affect both advocacy and rights entitlements (Disability Now, 1991). Many disabled people are becoming politicized and demanding fundamental changes. More support is given to developing a disability movement with both practical and political aspects. But in the future the movement must decide on its continuing independence or a coalition with state forces (Oliver, 1990, p. 128).

Analyzing the schools' role in pursuing social justice and representation, Weis said that compartmentalizing issues has bedeviled attempts to change. We must 'see oppressed groups relationally, not as single instances of oppression, but also in relation to one another as well as to the dominant group' (Weis, 1991, p. 2). But he includes no reference to disability. By concentrating on class, race, and gender, it is insufficient and offensive to assume that such a topic is covered by this discourse. In the beginning of this chapter, I discussed the invisibility of this topic within sociology of education. I close with some questions: If in our work we are concerned with questions of inequality, social justice, and democracy, to what extent does the issue of disability figure in our analyses? If it does not, why not?

ACKNOWLEDGMENT

I thank members of the International Conference on 'Reproduction, Social Inequality, and Resistance: New Directions in the Theory of Education' at the University of Bielefeld, Germany, 2-4 October 1991 for their helpful comments.

5   The Repudiation of Criteriology: In Pursuit of Communities of Democracy and Hope

Siebren Miedema

ABSTRACT

It is not easy to determine major themes and achievements of education and culture in the 1980s. The social mobilization of the 1960s resulted in strong ideas of change toward democracy. The 1970s pictured different theoretical traditions in pedagogy: empirical-analytical, hermeneutical, and critical-emancipatory. Each tradition has specific ideas about content, methods, and the theory-practice relation. Which paradigm is strongest and which will ultimately win? In the early 1980s, neither of these traditions was able to cope adequately with the practical and pressing pedagogical problems such as the reform of curricula, the development of practically applicable curricula, the problems of unmotivated pupils, and the increase in the school drop-out rate.

König (1990) described four major attempts to deal with this situation. The first trend was to enlarge the number (up to 10) of paradigms; but this approach is limited since it emphasizes the internal scientific development of theory exclusively. The second was to do more research in the history of education and pedagogy, looking for certainty in the past. The third was to become practical with practitioners; the distinction between common sense and (social) scientific knowledge disappeared in the sense that scientific, institutionally embedded ideas no longer exist. A final approach, based on a certain interpretation of postmodernism, proclaims the end of pedagogy and any kind of educational theory, leaving us in a perplexing position.

THE END OF THE MODERNITY PROJECT?

One of the greatest threats to continuing the pedagogical project (related to the modernity project) comes from some developments in philosophy (Miedema, 1992). Foucault and Lyotard attack enlightenment, which Habermas defends. Foucault finds Habermas' idea of growing rationality and historical progress theoretically unacceptable. Foucault proposes a never-ending struggle between rational and irrational power. Words and signs do not refer to factual reality nor adequately represent it. They primarily refer to a network of power positions. This network constitutes the reality of spoken and written words (discourse as oration) and results from it. According to Foucault, discourses do not form a unity, converge, nor have a beginning or an end. In contrast with the enlightenment ideas, there is no unifying, permanent, neutral discourse to legitimate the diversity of discourses. Knowledge and power are related to one another circularly. There is no power relation without the fact that any field of knowing comes into being at the same time: there is no knowledge that does not presuppose and constitute power relations.

Postmodern and poststructuralist thought undermines the modern assumption of the autonomous subject. Along with source and origin, humans are always the effect, never the natural subject, of discourse. We need to speak in a twofold way about the constructed (makable) character of the subject. There is an identity between subjectivity and control or power positions. It is power alone which constitutes a subject. Subjectifying and subjection correlate. Foucault wants to develop new forms of subjectivity. He rejects the type of individuality imposed on us over the centuries (Foucault, 1984). The pressing question is: Along his line of thought, are there still possibilities for such a development beyond disciplinary and pastoral power?

Lyotard is a more radical proponent of the postmodern stance. He rejects faith in the rational subject and humanity. In postindustrial, postmodern societies, knowledge can only include disbelief in modernity's metanarratives. According to Lyotard, the heterogeneity of language games remains. There are 'narrative, but also denotative, prescriptive, descriptive and other speech elements each with their own pragmatic valencies *sui generis*. Everyone is living at the intersections of many of these valencies' (Lyotard, 1987a, p. 26). Autonomous self-determination or self-formation of the subject is impossible, he said. Humans begin by listening to the different narratives, not by speaking. The result of this process is heteronomy instead of autonomy.

MODERNITY, POSTMODERNITY, AND PEDAGOGY: THE FUTURE AND UTOPIAN THOUGHT

Reflections on pedagogy dealing with the modernity-postmodernity issue are sparse. Adalbert Rang (1988) considered the two cornerstones of the modernity project in relation to pedagogy: autonomy and rationality. Although the hypothesis that humans are autonomous was often refuted, he wanted to maintain this concept's humanizing effects. In contrast, he stressed that

> pedagogues, neither in theory nor in practice, can give up the concept of autonomy. The proposition that one could not and ought not lead children and youngsters to independency because independency and autonomy do not exist, is pedagogically speaking absurd. Those who want to defend this premise seriously would take away the whole foundation of the main idea of education (Rang, 1988, p. 16).

The second issue is related to the concept of rationality. Rang rejected a common communicative rationality. 'The lines of dissent go right through those of rationality, because reason is not based only on reason' (Rang, 1988,

p. 19). He thought it impossible to surmount difficulties caused by modern value-pluralism, by orientations in respect to normative content. 'How can one ever conclude from "is" an "ought" to be?' (Rang, 1988, p. 20). He believed normative or orienting elements could not be normative-pedagogically constructed, only historically, socially, and scientifically reconstructed.

In his preface to *Umwege* (Detours), Mollenhauer (1986) pointed to the growing doubt about the possibilities of continuing the modern pedagogical project. After the realistic, critical, and common sense (or every day) turn in pedagogy, Niess (1985) and Baacke (1985) proclaimed the next phase: the postmodern period or pedagogy as postpedagogy. In Niess' radical critique, he characterized the project of pedagogy as enlightenment as phantasmagorical. He concluded that the concept of emancipatory pedagogy is over, a *fata morgana*, an illusion of modernity (Niess, 1985, p. 13). Baacke described the disillusionment the political turn created for some educators; this led to a postmodern withdrawal. He dismissed the concept of emancipation and reduced the assumption of continuous progress to a goal of prestige-seeking scientists. Baacke adhered to the postmodern 'new wave' in pedagogy, which only had room for an 'ironical pedagogy'. 'In such a pedagogy, there is room for irritation and that is more than merely speaking on different or conflicting ideas. Liberation from the pedagogical relation may soon be possible' (Baacke, 1985, p. 212). Based on the these critics' opinions of the modernity project, the end of education and pedagogy appears unavoidable.

However, Mollenhauer stayed within the legitimation discourse of the modernity project. He sought a pedagogical concept related to the educational reality in which education gets a chance. This is the only way the modern pedagogical project and democratic ideal can survive. It is a normative choice for the 'systematic intention of ushering the younger generation along gradual stages into the given world, where in every stage humanness *sub specie aeternitatis* should not be forgotten' (Mollenhauer, 1986, pp. 174-5).

Pedagogy has always been a concrete, historically determined activity, according to Mollenhauer. It should aim at *Bildung* (education), not schooling. The latter is a form of development (*Erziehung*) that leads to a narrow, goal-oriented, methodical, and systematic interaction with children and youngsters. Then, the focus of education could change toward the potentially *Bildung* qualities of the forms of life adults model to their children. But could coercion-free presentation of one's own mature life and chosen way of living 'be accounted for in relation to and in dialogue with the issues at stake in my culture from the perspective of me and the future of my children, if I have any, or if I am responsible for any children' (Mollenhauer, 1986, p. 10)?

The *Bildungsprocess* may develop children today to aspire to a meaningful future where they will have become adults. Educators are not merely concerned with their own future, but especially, with the future of their students. Can a present postmodern 'view' of the future still accommodate pedagogical relations and actions that will serve (the good of) the children?

Beekman (1973) examined the relation between *Bildung* (maturity, future) and critique. For him, maturity meant responsibility and independence. The mature adult and the not-yet-mature child are directed to the future, to the child's later maturity. Without this potential autonomy, responsibility, and solidarity with the child, pedagogy and pedagogical reflection is impossible. Beekman thought pedagogical theory was connected with practice via an immanent and prospective critique. Through immanent critique, normative conflicts in existing situations are detected, clarified, and solved. Prospective critique helps pedagogical theorists look for new possibilities of form, new structures that eliminate the existing blockages to freedom, hindrances to opportunities for independence. Present obstacles, discovered by immanent critique, ought to be prevented in the future based on prospective critique. To realize this, one must keep the future in sight: current knowledge should be combined with utopian ideas. In Beekman's conception, utopia is

'. . . imagination, a plan for an ideal society with an ideal *Bildung*. In pedagogical theory utopia will be "the kingdom of freedom" in which the independent development of persons will be something that goes without saying. It contains the old ideals of freedom, equality and fraternity. Without these ideals every criterion is relative' (Beekman, 1973, pp. 62-3).

Continuing the modern pedagogical project requires mature adults' belief in the future. The plan for a normatively ideal future is called utopia, which plays a crucial role in pedagogical thought. It is the form of the 'not yet', the forward eye of mankind striving for greater clarity and maturity. It shows us something about people's expectations of the future. In postmodern philosophical and pedagogical views, this belief in a regulative, normative ideal was lost to a certain degree. Probably because of this loss, philosophers and pedagogues consider the concept of utopia a prime aspect of the metanarrative. Habermas' communicative theory of society considers this ideal a basic assumption that, via language and communication, will create the possibility for political awareness. Autonomy and solidarity are realizable in society.

Plans for the future can be quite varied and the choices we make are significant. In a useful (concrete, not abstract) relevant utopia, the present, past, and future must relate to one another. Utopia should have critical-constructive power. Besides evaluating the obstacles to utopia, constructive indications should be provided so today's 'not yet' could be given an active shape. 'When introducing children into an adult world, we not only have to translate that world pedagogically; we also have to believe in this world' (Dasberg, 1983, p. 125). The same is true for the pedagogical theorist as the (re)constructor of praxis. This belief Dasberg refers to has been called hope or concrete utopia. It is a regulative ideal or principle which screens reality in a critical way. An attempt is made based on available (and empirical) knowledge to realize this ideal in practice. At the same time, utopia cannot be realized in any direct, empirical way. The utopia can be adjusted on the basis of concrete pedagogical and practical-political experiences.

Sauer (1964) distinguished among a set of four utopian-pedagogical conceptions: political, rational progressive, mythical, and revolutionary. Besides these distinctions (and partly running through them) is the difference between abstract and concrete utopias (Bloch, 1963). In a concrete utopia, today and the future come together; both an analysis of the situation and of the prospective aspect are necessary. Characteristic of the abstract utopia is the absence of a critical-realistic relation with today's situation.

These positions failed, so we must create a pedagogical utopian perspective that still can be relevant to these children today. Their reality needs to be related to life in society with its cultural, social, political, economic contents and problems and philosophies. With an eye to the future, pedagogues should take an immanent critical stance in relation to today so that the individual can be related in a prospective way to both the present and future on the basis of the regulative (not absolutely interpreted) and contextualized use of autonomy and solidarity. The pedagogue should reveal the tasks and problems that need to be solved and to which the child can contribute when she/he reaches maturity. In their thoughts and actions, pedagogues must anticipate how to use the pedagogical institutions at their disposal to deal with present and future tasks and possibilities. Only when pedagogy focuses on the present, past, and future can we answer the question: What in the past has *Bildungs*-potential for today and the future, based on the regulative principles of autonomy and solidarity? 'Only that content from the past can have edifying power which could be experienced by the child or youngster as his or her past - and this naturally in a more than only biographical sense; the past has *Bildungs*-potential only when the young man or woman has entry to today and has the courage to face his or her future' (Klafki, 1958, p. 462).

At the end of the 20th century, educators and pedagogues need not feel irrelevant because the assumptions of the modernity project are disputed. It is possible to criticize a concrete-utopian, normative program; this happened throughout the history of philosophy. Criticism may result in appropriate adjustments to the hallmarks of the modernity utopia (Habermas, 1985b). It is impossible to pretend that an entire society can be created using only our educational processes. Pedagogical sciences, philosophy, politics, and praxis are directed toward independence, autonomy, and solidarity. In the first place, these three offer the possibility for 'critical negativism': to show what really is 'not yet'. Alternatively, this triumvirate becomes the regulative, the ideal for modeling the future: 'critical positivity'. The utopian aspect in pedagogy can save educators from a (probably unintended) canonization of the status quo and researchers and theorists from empiricistic, descriptive-detached, neutral conceptual-analytical, and a critical and unfruitful 'actualism'. The unknown future makes a normative pedagogical and political appeal to educators to relate their actions in theory and (research) practice to the future.

MODERNITY, POSTMODERNITY, PRAGMATISM, AND PLURALITY

Individuals, groups, and nations change in terms of biographical and social-cultural experience. This pluralization of diverging universes of discourse belongs to modern experience; shattering naive consensus is the impetus for Hegel's 'experience of reflection'. We cannot wish this experience away, only negate it. The thrust of this experience had to be worked through politically and philosophically (Habermas, 1985a, pp. 192-3; Dewey, 1940, p. 227).

Modernists (Habermas), postmodernists (Lyotard, Derrida), and neopragmatists (Rorty, Bernstein) differ about plurality. Postmodernists affirm radical plurality and heterogeneity; reject unity, totality, and universality; and do not fuse heterogeneous elements (Kunneman, 1988, p. 210). Dilthey, Weber, Jaspers, and Kolakowski anticipated their position by describing the growing pluralism of gods and demons, existential modes of being, myths, values, and metaphysical or religious world views (Habermas, 1985a). Modernists' universality claims are rejected since they imply exclusion. Lyotard (1979, 1986) rejected modernity's legitimation discourse and emancipation of the autonomous subject. Auschwitz is connected with the decline of the grand narrative of the Hegelian dialectic. The workers' revolt in Warsaw Pact countries refuted the metanarrative of communism; Western democracy was refuted in May 1968; and post-Keynesian adjustment during the crisis of 1974-9. 'In short, the modern project has gone down due to the violence brought about by its own realization. It has been submerged by the refutation of its pretensions by historical development in its reality' (Kunneman, 1988, p. 208).

Habermas (1985a, p. 193) called the pluralization of diverging universes of discourse the 'unavoidable experience of modernity'. He thinks history carries the necessary conditions for humanization. Thinking that the enlightenment project has not been superseded or could be only interrupted is very dangerous. History lets us realize a better society using rational means. The development of rationality is necessary, and sufficient for a free, just society. He tried to lay the foundations for theoretical and practical social-scientific research which could maximize problem-solving in a democratic way (Habermas, 1984, 1987). In politics, he maintains the ideal of progressive social democracy (freedom of opinion, participation in decision-making); in science, the primacy of the validity claim of truth (Habermas, 1985a, p. 194).

Habermas (1985b) claimed postmodernists played into neoconservatives' hands. He challenged modernists, saying the emancipation and progress they advocate is just a power strategy. However, Habermas probably missed the radical democratic intention behind Lyotard's criticism. Lyotard's radical normative dedication against oppression, exclusion, and injustice has no basis of legitimation in terms of nonexclusive universality because he radically eliminates the subject. But Habermas argued that it is not possible, from Lyotard's perspective, to indicate who or what is 'subjected' to violence, injustice, or oppression and why that is bad (Kunneman, 1988).

Neopragmatists Rorty and Bernstein stand between modernists and post-modernists. They take the postmodern criticism that we do not have absolute or universal criteria seriously. In following Dewey, Rorty tried to get rid of every form of criteriology (Rorty, 1987, p. 48) to develop a nonfoundational-ist, nontranscendental philosophy-as-hermeneutics position. From this per-spective, philosophy is a means to understand social practices and to contrib-ute to the ideal of social democracy by distinguishing between societies based on violence and those based on argumentation and discourse. Rorty criticizes and rejects any universalist, criteriological validity claim. He seeks to start from practical needs and problems experienced in societies and cultures.

But taking plurality seriously need not lead to an all-embracing relativism (Biesta, 1990). Neopragmatists reject every attempt to look for 'something which stands beyond history and institutions', claiming 'that a belief can still regulate action, can still be thought worth dying for, among people who are quite aware that this belief is caused by nothing deeper than contingent historical circumstance' (Rorty, 1989, p. 189). They believe we need not choose between having absolute (universal) criteria and having none at all.

Rorty and Bernstein, respectively, called their beliefs liberal utopia and phronesis. If we give up hope of finding metaphysical comfort in the *a priori* structure of any inquiry, language, or form of social life, 'we may gain a renewed sense of community. Our identification with our community - our society, our political tradition, our intellectual heritage - is heightened when we see this community as ours rather than nature's, shaped rather than found. . . . What matters is our loyalty to other human beings clinging together against the dark, not our hope of getting things right' (Rorty, 1982, p. 166).

A community needs deliberation, conversation, or communication to understand the criteria and beliefs that we currently treat as legitimized. This is not the abstract or general community of all human beings, but those 'people to whom one must justify one's beliefs . . . those who share enough of one's belief to make a fruitful conversation possible' (Rorty, 1986, p. 13).

Bernstein knows that conditions are not always fulfilled for argumenta-tive and discursive deliberation in a community. Phronesis can only render results in a community with 'a living, shared acceptance of . . . principles' (Bernstein, 1983, p. 157). Then, one has some assurance that the outcome of deliberation will not be immediately disputed. One must determine 'what material, social, and political conditions need to be concretely realized in order to encourage the flourishing of phronesis in all citizens' (Bernstein, 1983, p. 158). An unconditional prerequisite for phronesis is the existence of solidarity in a community. It can at least keep the conversation going. For Bernstein, phronesis not only requires a certain degree of solidarity in a community; but also the preeminent way to realize solidarity (Miedema and Biesta, 1990). This requires conditions which encourage discussion and expose blocking societal factors. Solidarity cannot *a priori* be presupposed.

This is the flaw in Rorty's view. He makes a sharp distinction between the public and private sides of our lives. 'Our responsibilities to others constitute only the public side of our lives, a side which competes with our private affections and our private attempts at self-creation, and which has no automatic priority over such private motives' (Rorty, 1989, p. 194). In his liberal utopia, there is a 'rigid distinction between a rich, autonomous private sphere that will enable elite "ironists" like himself to create freely the self they wish - even if that be a cruel, antidemocratic self -and a lean, egalitarian, "democratic" public life confined to the task of preventing cruelty (including that of elite ironists)' (Westbrook, 1991, p. 540). Rorty's solidarity in public life is extremely thin. We miss Bernstein's (and Dewey's) social and political communitarian vision of shared experience, a common possession, and shared power. Rorty's liberal-democratic politics 'involve little more than making sure that individuals hurt one another as little as possible and interfere minimally in the private life of each' (Westbrook, 1991, p. 541). According to his ethnocentric perspective on solidarity, we should strive for intersubjective agreement as much as possible by broadening the 'reference of us'. This implies that we need to find out whether we can weave convictions and beliefs from other cultures into our own framework of beliefs.

Bernstein wants to cultivate 'the types of dialogical communities in which phronesis, judgement, and practical discourse become concretely embodied in our everyday practices' (Bernstein, 1983, p. 223) and to deal with plurality and the irreducibility of conflict grounded in it. He is willing 'to discover some common ground to reconcile differences through debate, conversation, and dialogue' (Bernstein, 1983, p. 223). Quoting Pitkin and Shumer, he states that in democratic politics, opinions and interests are mutually revised, both individually and in common. He is looking for a 'community of communities'. However, Rorty's ethnocentric approach seems to hide under the surface of solidarity and conversation, 'colonizing' traits in relation to other cultures, traditions, and communities.

PLURALITY AND PEDAGOGY: THE CASE OF THE NETHERLANDS

As a native of the Netherlands, I was part of a specific tradition and culture. Our colonial past gives us a particular place in world history. The Dutch traveled around the world in the 16th and 17th centuries, annexed Indian land, and named it New Amsterdam (later called New York). They had colonies in Indonesia, the Caribbean islands, and Surinam.

From a political and pedagogical view, how did and do we deal with plurality in our society? The 'denominational segregation' or 'pillarization' of public life has been characteristic of our country since 1815. It fragmented almost all societal institutions and groups along denominational lines. Pillarization resulted from struggles for school emancipation. Both groups wanted their own schools and religion-based curriculum. They had serious doubts whether the mixed public schools would adequately transmit their specific religious cultures. This doubt was reinforced by social-democrats and liberals who argued against any form of pluralistic public schooling in which all religious denominations would have their place. They opted for a neutral relation or separation *qua* content of religion and state, thereby denying the cultural identity of many religious denominations. Via the education acts of 1857, 1878, 1901, and the pacification act of 1920, the school funding controversy was settled. All denominations were granted the right and funding to have their own schools. The pillarization was not restricted to education alone; all public and political life in society became organized along segregated lines: universities, political parties, trade-unions, welfare work, hospitals, and so on. This situation still exists in the Netherlands.

The vertical pillarization resulted in a 'synchronic social plurality' which blocked the way for value exchange, sharing, and mutual construction of values. During the last century, denominational segregation was the way to deal with societal plurality in the Netherlands.

Elsewhere (Miedema and Biesta, 1991), we showed that in pedagogy, implementing educational reformers' (Montessori, Parkhurst, Petersen, Freinet) ideas occurred via their instructional methods, not their social and political philosophies. These ideas were mainly treated as 'instructional psychologies' to teach any curriculum content. Untying the reformers' ideas from their political and value implications, these pedagogies were incorporated in every denominational school system without challenging the respective denominational *Weltanschauungen*. In this context, Dewey's pedagogical ideas about democracy and education were a threat to foundationalist/fundamentalist religious views (Biesta and Miedema, 1989), but even more to the pillarization that had emerged as the way to deal with societal plurality.

Until 1945, academic pedagogy was organized along pillarized lines. Langeveld (1945) was the first to try eliminating normative denominational pedagogies. Using the phenomenological approach, pedagogues could go back to the educational phenomenon itself. Langeveld maintained this phenomenon was the denominationally uncontaminated common ground for all educators. But the net result was positive: an analysis of the facts of the-lifeworld-as-it-is separately from denominational world-views. The values stayed under the denominations' authority. Along with the Dutch-Calvinistic emphasis on personal responsibility, this reinforced a way of practicing and reflecting on pedagogy in which culture, society, and politics were of secondary importance. Because of the nearly exclusive Calvinist and existentialist focus, Langeveld could only criticize society via the person as a moral, responsible individual. What began as an emancipatory process in the 19th century resulted in a complete pillarization of society that nearly blocked the possibilities for any open dialogue of cultural contents and patterns.

Our society confronts both intracultural and intercultural plurality as indicated in ethnic population proportions in Western Holland's inner city schools. For example, in the Hague inner city schools had population proportions of 90 per cent original Dutch and Dutch-speaking children and 10 per cent non-native Dutch children in the early 1970s. Now, these same schools have less than 10 per cent Dutch or Dutch-speaking children in their classes; but rather, children from Surinam, Morocco, Spain, Portugal, Turkey, and Yugoslavia. Their parents came to the Netherlands as 'guest laborers'.

There was some intercultural experience with people from the Molucces (a former Dutch colony) who always wanted to go back to their home country as soon as possible and developed a military type of organization to achieve that end in the Netherlands. This became a government problem.

In the 1970s, public policy allowed every ethnic group to keep its cultural and language heritage alive. In schools, special hours were reserved to train pupils in their own language and culture by native people who could also speak Dutch and understand western European culture and history. The ideas behind this educational policy were that 1) these children could learn Dutch much more easily when they were better trained in their own language; and 2) every culture and religion has rights. Even social democrats (who had problems with Dutch Catholics' and Calvinists' claims for religious identity and autonomy in school) promoted this idea.

But by the time the proportions changed dramatically in the schools and before the separation and distinction between 'black' and 'white' schools (Teunissen, 1989), the rights of ethnic 'minority' children to learn their original language and culture was attacked and abjured. Political conservatives lamented this expensive pluralist policy; left-wing politicians declared that complete adaptation, acculturation, or adjustment could increase these children's chances in the labor market. Adjusting to the Dutch tradition instead of their own ethnic one was promulgated as an emancipatory strategy.

ON THE WAY TO COSMOPOLITAN CITIZENSHIP

In 1981, a left-oriented principal from an inner-city elementary school (where 88 per cent of the children were non-Dutch) in The Hague told me that he opposed celebrating holidays, other than Christian and national ones, because there would be hardly any time left for regular instruction. His view is in line with and a kind of 'homogenization of society' Bernstein (1983, p. 227) wants to avoid and criticizes. It is a good example of a really insensitive and condescending practice: a colonizing attitude vis-à-vis different cultures.

I agree with Bernstein, but how do we deal with this situation from a political, cultural, and pedagogical viewpoint? This question is even more perplexing if we remember the gigantic stream of immigrants and refugees coming west from the poor areas in the east and the south after Germany's reunification, the Soviet Union's evolution into the CIS, the conflicts about nationalities and national societies in Eastern Europe, and the (economic) start of the European Community on 1 January 1993 (Habermas, 1992).

The concept of citizenship is a hot issue for politicians, academics, and commentators (Roche, 1987; Hall, 1991). Hall (1991) and Habermas (1992, p. 632) claim the sovereignty of the national state can be undermined if we support these tendencies and dismantle the welfare state, increasing international interdependence, and ongoing globalization. But the significance of the concept of citizenship is still expressed in reference to the national state.

The welfare state interpretation of 'social citizenship' (including membership, mutual rights and duties, and real participation in the community)is under pressure. Here, the state is the guarantor for citizens' political rights. These rights are a guarantee against arbitrary state power. For example, Thatcherism tried to change constituents' access to charity and philanthropy and the ability to live independently (Hall, 1991) while limiting community membership and participation. This is a concept of 'private citizenship'. Individuals are the locus of action; self-interest drives them, especially regarding the market system, without any social dimension (Roche, 1987). Hall (1991, p. 16) thinks the challenge for contemporary citizenship politics is to create a new balance between the individual and social dimensions of political rights. 'But who are members of the community?' ask the feminists, black and ethnic movements, ecologists, and vulnerable minorities (such as children). How do you deal with the plurality of needs and diverse positions and practices? Hall does not want to separate 'political (civic) rights' (the right to vote, have insight, know, get schooling and information) from 'social rights' (in relation to reproduction, the care for health and children) and 'economical rights' (having the financial means to live independently).

How can a modern society deal with political culture related to diverse and multiple cultural and social identities? According to Habermas (1996, pp. 513-4), the identity of a political community is primarily embedded in the principles of the political culture, not in a specific ethnic/cultural way of life. That is why he rejects any 'particularistic' interpretation or meaning of citizenship (in terms of a specific cultural identity), and argues in favor of a 'universalistic' (political) interpretation of citizenship. But one cannot completely separate cultural and political claims because they overlap and influence each other's territory (Hall, 1991, p. 168). In sum, Habermas (1996, p. 514) pleads for a liberal politics of immigration.

The universalistic (political) conception of 'democratic citizenship' Hall and Habermas describe can pave the way for 'cosmopolitanism' or 'world citizenship'. Habermas points to such events as the Vietnam War, the revolutionary changes in Eastern and Middle Europe, and the Gulf War that has become part of the world-wide 'public sphere' (*Öffentlichkeit*) via electronic mass media. That is why democratic (state) citizenship and cosmopolitanism need to form a continuum. Roche (1987, p. 394) also states that the study of citizenship requires making realistic but imaginative efforts to preview the future. But we also need a clear vision of what the good citizen is and is not.

CITIZENSHIP AND EDUCATION

Approaching the 'task of pedagogy' regarding democratic citizenship, we may not bypass Dewey (1927), who advocated making the 'Great Society' a 'Great Community' with a global dimension. Democracy and education (Dewey, 1916) have an internal relation. They cannot be treated separately (as politicians and social policy and welfare-state analysts often do) when 'education . . . tends to be seen as a "cultural" . . . peripheral aspect of welfare' (Roche, 1987, p. 365). The individual and society are seen as two sides of the same cultural coin. One cannot speak of education without the process of initiation in and the sharing of the culture that forms a very significant part of the pedagogical situation's environment. Education occurs in a process of 'transmission' in and by 'communication' of the habits of doing, thinking, and feeling. A society could not survive without a process of educating to give young citizens the 'reproducing and renewing' force of social life. 'The things with which man "varies" are his genuine environment' (Dewey, 1916, p. 11). Education as growth means constantly reorganizing and reconstructing experience 'which adds to the meaning of experience, and which increases the ability to direct the course of subsequent experience' (Dewey, 1916, p. 76).

Which type of community life (where change, growth, improvement, and interaction are possible) is preferable from a pedagogical and a societal viewpoint? Dewey's answer is democracy. It is more than 'a form of government; it is primarily a mode of associated living, of conjoint communicated experience' (Dewey, 1916, p. 87). He judged the degree in which a society is democratic by asking 'How numerous and varied are the interests which are consciously shared? How full and free is the interplay with other forms of association?' He also had normative ideas about distinguishing desirable and undesirable societies and what sort of education helps create democratic citizens. Dewey's ideas about the transactional relation of education, culture, politics, and democracy still are helpful. It would be a mistake to reject them out of hand (Westbrook, 1991, p. 552). Some educationalists like Tomas Englund (1986) (see Chapter 15 in this book) and Henry Giroux (1989) find Deweyan pragmatism and critical theory inspiring. They have already begun to work out for pedagogy the concept of democratic citizenship. But I think more work has to be done along this fruitful line.

6 Socialization and Economic Reproduction in Pluralistic Welfare Societies

Stefan Hradil

ABSTRACT

Much has changed in western Germany since the 1970s, including most daily living and socialization conditions. These transformations include an increase in mass prosperity, growth in education and vocational training, drastic increase in the number of highly qualified careers in the service area, and differentiation within class structures as well as exclusion of heterogeneous marginal and problem groups. This occured in spite of enlarged social security and other welfare state services; lower birth rate as well as the dwindling size of the family and household; increased economic activity of married women and mothers; decreased working hours; immigration of foreign workers, asylum applicants, and transmigrators; more labor market risks; and development of new technologies in active work and in households.

These social changes evolved almost independently of the individual's reflection and behavior and, therefore, are considered 'objective'. 'Subjective' transformations also occurred since the 1980s. Many people's mentalities and behavior patterns are different now. 'Subjective' developments (which are either directly or indirectly related to transformed 'objective' living conditions) are often summarized as 'pluralization of ways of life' (Hradil, 1987; Zapf et al., 1987). ('Way of life' is the generic term for the concepts 'form of life', 'milieu', 'subculture', 'social movement', and 'lifestyle'.)

In the 1980s, this impression of a social-cultural pluralization solidified. (Not all of the following pluralization manifestations are really new; several are comparatively old. Since they figured in the foreground of both the social scientists' and the population's attention, they were revitalized. But many mentalities, ethics, milieus, and lifestyles are new.) Some of the frequently observed manifestations are the pluralization of forms of life (more singles, nonconjugal communities, and single-parents instead of the 'ordinary family'); new (often juvenile) subcultures ('punks', 'raps', 'poppers'); 'new social movements' (women's, peace, ecological, alternative, and antinuclear power); new social milieus (city, political, technological professions, and re-strengthened regional); and differentiated lifestyles (especially in large cities).

SOCIOCULTURAL CHANGES IN A PLURALISTIC SOCIETY

The sociological analysis of these ways of life in western Germany has increased since the late 1970s. At first, such studies were carried out above all by close-to-practice disciplines (such as leisure, consumer, and political sociology), but then also by 'academic' disciplines (such as cultural sociology and social structure analysis). The results of the individual studies diverge, but when observed from afar, they agree on major points (Hradil,1992), showing a three-fold 'pluralization of ways of life'.

First, many 'new' ways of life are more independent of other living conditions and position in the class structure that many findings of the 1960s and 1970s suggested. People's ways of life are still shaped by outer factors. The most important ones are standard of education, family cycle position (for example, rearing small children), age, and disposable income. But these factors determine the way of life only to a certain extent. So, the way of life differs immensely among peers with the same standard of education, family status, age, and income (Gluchowski, 1988, p. 40). On the one hand, the reasons for partially decoupling 'subjective' lifestyles and 'objective' living conditions are an augmented degree of freedom based on increased income, improved education, higher social security, greater professional and regional mobility, fewer children, and a less strenuous everyday life. On the other hand, there is an increasing obligation to plan one's individual life due to frequent occupational crises (unemployment, rehabilitation) and private upheavals (divorce, partner's change of workplace).

Second, besides evidence of a 'causal pluralization', empirical proofs of a pluralization of ways of life in terms of their 'morphological' differentiation are accumulating. Compared with the two or three large sociocultural groups (worker consciousness, employee mentality, and so on) of former 'occupational societies', we now find more ways of life (which have little to do with the world of work). Even rough sociological attempts to acquire an overall view of social macro milieus and lifestyles lead to not only two or three, but more groupings. Empirical milieu studies by the SINUS Institute discovered eight sociocultural groupings (Hradil, 1987, p.131) which coincided with Gluchowski's (1988) findings on leisure lifestyles. The Konrad Adenauer Foundation found nine typologies of political lifestyle groupings (Gluchowski, 1987, p.28); Lüdtke found 12 (1989) and 15 (1990) lifestyle typologies; and Zapf et al. (1987) found 25 typologies for life forms or groupings.

The manifold sociocultural groupings which new western German social research invented are pluralistic insofar as they include not only traditional groups (nations, religious groups) and industrial collectives (the working class milieu), but also new formations (new social movements, new city lifestyles) stemming from spheres of labor. Apparently, these new groupings also have new characteristics. This clearly distinguishes them from conventional cultures and ways of life (for example, from the everyday Protestant culture or from the way the 'proletariat' lives):1) Many 'new' ways of life are apparently lived more consciously and purposefully and are less 'profoundly' anchored in the unconscious and habitual. 2) They do not occupy the whole 'breadth' of existence. Heterogeneous patterns can be combined (for example, in a 'workstyle' and a 'weekend lifestyle'). They are blended and inconstant, sometimes forming a 'patchwork identity' (one previously was a worker for a lifetime and in every area of life at least as far as basic values, attitudes, and behavior patterns go; one does not necessarily remain a 'Yuppie' throughout one's life nor in every situation). 3) The social limits of new ways of life cannot be clearly outlined; they intermingle. 4) They are confined to smaller groups and are probably even more transitive than industrial society or traditional ways of life.

Third, recent empirical research also showed a 'finalist' aspect of sociocultural pluralization. The 'subjective' (not so much the 'objective') ways and conditions of life determine practical life today. Increasingly often, 'inner' values, goals, and people's preferences are decisive for everyday behavior and opinions; more rarely are 'outer' rules, resources, or restrictions decisive. For example, voting, political participation, and consumer behavior today are greatly shaped by one's way of life.

Another assumption is that family socialization influences include both 'outer' living conditions and, especially, 'inner' attitudes. I believe socialization research should unravel these determining factors. Until recently, this sort of sociocultural socialization research has not progressed beyond the starting point. Empirical research which examines socialization processes depending on ways of life and possibly shaping practical behavior relevant for social mobility and the reproduction of social inequality is very rare.

THE DEFICITS OF SOCIALIZATION RESEARCH

If socialization is conceived as the 'process of emergence and development of the human personality dependent on the confrontation with social and material living conditions . . . which exist at a certain point in time in the historical development of a society' (Hurrelmann, 1986, p.14), then a lot has changed since the 1960s regarding the sociological investigation of socialization and its conditions. The stages of development can be summarized as a transition from class-specific, to social structural and multi-level, up to social ecological socialization research. This development is progressive since at least three premises which earlier impeded clarification were removed.

1. The restriction to economically based and occupationally conveyed determinants of socialization was dropped. For example, in social structural socialization research, membership in organizations and the peculiarities of the specific living area were incorporated as influential forces. The perspective of the class-specific socialization research has broadened immensely (Bertram, 1981; Grüneisen and Hoff, 1977; Steinkampf and Stief, 1978).
2. Socialization research regarding immediate determining factors has also taken intermediary authorities and mediating levels into consideration

(for example, local or family life worlds), which were recognized as factors capable of influencing the socialization processes emanating from outer conditions of existence.

3. The addition of the factors and their vertical positioning in classes and class models made room for constellation views of the social structural socialization research and for context models of social ecological socialization research (Schneewind et al., 1983; Vaskovics, 1982).

These premises, tight economism, linear determinism, and hierarchical thinking, which were rapidly removed in the 1970s and 1980s, were already simplifications and barriers to knowledge in the 1950s and 1960s.Then, there were probably more complex socialization influences than the economic, deterministic, and vertical socialization models could illustrate. In spite of that, these models were probably more suitable to the 1950s and 1960s than today because the FRG underwent immense modernization and industrialization. Thus, the spheres of economics, occupational hierarchy, materialism, and the corresponding class models were up to date. The advanced social structural, multilevels, and social ecological socialization research of the 1970s corrected old mistakes. Nevertheless, the knowledge gains remained limited. The more refined attempts at researching family socialization clearly described socialization differences in detail and explained them better than conservative class and class-structure classifications (Steinkampf and Stief 1978); but on the whole, their performance lagged behind expectations, especially considering the enormous effort involved (Steinkamp 1991).

Much socialization research from the 1970s was disappointing because it could never approach reality. It was confronted with the massive social changes in social structure and socialization conditions and with tendencies of sociocultural pluralization. Neither the advanced social structural nor the social ecological research directions considered ways of life. Even multilevel analyses treated mentalities, milieus, and lifestyles as intermediating and modifying factors of 'objective' living conditions (Oevermann et al., 1976).

RESEARCH ON SOCIALIZATION MILIEUS

If socialization research is to cope with the challenges inherent in the sociocultural pluralization of welfare societies, we need a concept which is suited to 'subjective' decisions by society's members and is capable of seriously considering people's active behavior and emerging sociocultural structures, forms of life, and groupings as autonomous determinants for socialization. The concept should respect the heterogeneous coexistence of such activities, sociocultural factors, and groupings as pluralism within an individual's existence, relevant for socialization. Also, the concept should be implemented diachronically and be capable of perceiving social and biographical changes of ways of life, as well as doing justice to the resulting processes of socialization in the life course, with its long-lasting and quickly changing shapes.

The following arguments proceed from the assumption that milieu concepts can meet these demands. To substantiate this claim, I will outline the historical development and the particular characteristics of the milieu concept. In the social sciences, a 'milieu' is generally considered an entirety of circumstances which have a determining influence on the behavior and ways of life of a certain group of people. All kinds of determining circumstances can be contemplated: natural or man-made, ecological, political or cultural, mental or physical, things or people, states of being or actions, and so on. The milieu concept has a tradition which goes beyond the establishment of sociology as an autonomous discipline. The contents of the concept, although not the term itself, emerged during the age of Enlightenment. Following the standards of natural sciences, one tried to discover the significant outer influential forces on human development. Often the essential milieu powers were seen as the climate (for example, Montesquieu, 1949, p.1328). Then as today, inheritance theories opposed the milieu concept.

With the beginning of industrialization when it was no longer possible to ignore the fact that our existence is dependent on man-made (as well as natural) circumstances, the milieu concept became a basic sociological theory (Compte, 1973, 1974; Taine, 1907; Durkheim, 1970, p.193). It implied a comprehensive determining force of the environment. But it was directed to an increasingly intricate context, consisting of natural and social components. Between the World Wars, the milieu concept turned into the 'subjective', relative, and pluralistic. That enabled the rebirth of the real pluralization of ways of life and made it appropriate for socialization research. The constituent elements of the milieu concept no longer were 'objective' (that is, independent of human thought, perception, and interpretation) environmental conditions. Max Scheler said, 'A milieu is the total of that, experienced by a single person as being effective' (quoted in Hitzler and Honer, 1984, p.61).

But in the FRG, such milieu concepts faded after World War II. The rapid establishment of the industrial society and the establishment of the sociological paradigm of the industrial society made them 'untimely'. This became very clear in Lepsius' (1966) essay outlining the political force of the 1920s 'sociomoral milieus', which receded during the period between the wars. The 'milieu' concept then directed attention to environments which belong together (above all by a particular perception such as a social-moral milieu of Catholicism) and unfold their determining power (for example, at elections) by this perception. Milieus 'objectively' can consist of very heterogenous elements (for example, the milieu of Catholicism includes all kinds of occupations, age groups, and income levels). They can be quite small (a certain suburb milieu) or biographically temporary (the milieu of a hospital doctor who spends a few hours in a certain clinic).

By contrast, the sociology of the 1950s and 1960s had very 'objective', 'centralized', and constancy-oriented ideas about important sociological environments. Ultimately, power and/or people's market position in business life was considered to be central. Occupational position and related resources (money, qualification, prestige) became behavioral determinants. Their social distribution was perceived as a consistent, vertical order. The particular status in this structure of higher and lower class membership seemed to determine thought and behavior of large groups commonly, 'objectively', and constantly. The predominant concepts of social environments up to the 1970s were 'objective', economical, deterministic (in a psychological sense), macro- and stability-oriented. These characteristics contradicted the key elements of milieu concepts. Milieu concepts seriously considered environments that are 'subjectively' seen, not small and socially or biographically changing (such as 'homeland' milieus). Consequently, the milieu concept seemed best suited to peripheral phenomena and faded into the background.

It is different now. Based on these social structure changes and the growing lack of descriptive and explanatory power of class models, the sociological milieu concept was reborn. Perhaps it was more a result of changes in the socially predominant interpretations of the social structure. The milieu concept is increasingly used to localize and explain different electoral behavior and consumer styles, especially in political (Berg-Schlosser and Schissler, 1987; Mintzel, 1988; Vester, 1992), regional (Keim, 1979), cultural (Schulze, 1990, 1992), and youth sociology (Bohnsack, 1989), as well as general social structure analysis (Hradil, 1987, 1992).

By analyzing recent milieu concepts, one notices three developments: 1)What we now call a 'milieu' shapes people not only in terms of their common perception, but also by their common active use and design of environments (for example, 'milieus' which emerge in the frame of new social movements and their networks). 2) 'Milieus' are less often conceived as the entirety of the experienced powers (as it was in Max Scheler's definition), but as one of many environmental contexts shaping the individual. 3) 'Milieu' is increasingly connected to an image of a biographical transit station. Despite it's temporary effectiveness, it is thought to produce both individual and collective (for example, political) dispositions and behavioral patterns.

We presume these conceptual developments and the current boom in milieu research not only shows it has been rediscovered (especially since the industrial society's fascination with paradigms waned), but also indicates real change. If our presumption is correct, the preceding analysis of the concept tells us something about the character of this transformation: 'Milieus' as 'objectively' founded, total, life-long, clearly defined group memberships and their inevitable influences (for example, the *déformation professionelle* of teachers) are obviously retreating. In contrast, 'milieus' in terms of an assembly of unclearly defined 'groups of like-minded people' characterized by occasionally common 'subjective' judgement, use, and change of their surroundings are increasing and becoming a central form of socialization.

The changes of the milieu concept point out that societal emphasis is shifting from the (more 'objective') 'production' and 'active work milieus' to the (more 'subjective'), 'leisure and consumer' ones. The displacement of the milieu concept also shows that some 'objectively' unchanged life circumstances today often receive a new milieu character (for example, city quarter, trade union, or professional groups) because they shape people less automatically by their 'objective' structure than by the 'subjective' meanings, uses, and activities of certain groups. The assumption is that the 'new' ('subjective'), active, temporary milieus may fulfill important functions in socialization today. Accordingly, defined concepts of milieus may be able to remove some of the shortcomings of socialization research.

Milieu concepts seem to be more suited to that than lifestyle concepts. Compared to 'lifestyle', the concept of 'milieu' applies to quite a 'close' network of interaction, a comparably 'stable' structure, and a relatively nonpersonal type of sociation. 'Milieu' is a relational category directed at contexts of environmental circumstances and what people together make of it. 'Lifestyle' is more individualistic and attributive. Lifestyle concepts aim more at the personal organization and styling of life and at the coming together of like-minded people. But in the milieu concept, outer conditions of existence are always considered (for example, a city quarter's architecture or young people's employment chances in a particular region) even if they are only perceived through the 'filter' of a certain interpretation, as a prerequisite for action, or as an object of behavior. All these attributes make it clear that shaping people is always included in the milieu concept. Thus, milieu concepts are more suited for socialization research than lifestyle concepts.

'Lifestyle' is defined as an 'unmistakable structure and form of a subjectively sensible, practiced context of the organized life of a private household, shared by a collectivity, whose members therefore, perceive and recognize each other as being socially similar' (Lüdtke 1989, p.40).

EMPIRICAL RESEARCH ON MILIEU SPECIFIC SOCIALIZATION

The suitability of the milieu concept for researching socialization processes in sociocultural plural welfare societies has been confirmed in some empirical studies. In a qualitative longitudinal study, Kurt Möller (1988) examined the socialization of youth from worker families (part of the social structure with fewer expected milieu differentiations than the service sector, for example). They were asked about milieu performances and the appearance of 'new socialization horizons' (Möller, 1988, p.116) in 'peer groups' and families to explain actual political orientations.

According to conventional class criteria, these youth would have been put into the same (working) class. Also, they were all union members, had the same occupational status, retained their parents' political attitude, and had a normal employment. This unified picture quickly dissolved when the actual everyday worlds and socialization-related milieus were examined. These were 'small spaced, historically determined, place-time limited aggregation(s) or everyday relationships which are also effective, in terms of socialization, by means of their own value system for their permanent physical members' (Möller, 1988, p.120). They were asked about the 'actually relevant determinants of socialization contexts' (Möller, 1988, p.122) on the four levels of potential orientation (behavior space, action space, self-image construction, and foreign presentation). Möller found three milieus among youth-workers:

1. A classical worker milieu: These youth belonged to different organizations such as the Social Democratic Party, Union of Public Services and Transports, worker sport associations, and public-interest groups 'against the right wing'. The *Lebensführung* (lifestyle) is rather conventional, which causes some difficulties, but they do not break out of this milieu nor enter other socialization horizons.
2. An unstable worker milieu: These youth (for example, cases involving parental divorce or erratic upbringing) do not assume their parents' values and attitudes. They often have not belonged to cliques or peer groups. Often, they seek refuge in ecstatic experiences, violent hobbies, or Rambo phantasies, for example.
3. An advancement-oriented worker milieu: These youth plan their future, usually with parental agreement and support. They realistically consider the individual achievement principle. Politics tend to be unimportant for them. Their own 'individuality' is lived out in leisure time with the help of remarkable outfits and special activities. To a certain extent, this stands opposed to the conformity of a professional life.

In summary, Möller (1988, p.134) sees a trend that 'instead of historically grown milieus with their tradition of subcultural values and interpretation systems producing homogeneity, temporarily, steadily changing "scenes" emerge which regulate membership by cognitive marks of consumption and are dependent on the laws of the capital ware market'.

In his empirical analysis, Lenz (1988) proceeds from Schütz's phenomenological social theory. In his typification of youths' 'sense placement and sense interpretation processes', he found four recurring processing and coping patterns. These 'youth types of action' prove to be dominant regarding other variables such as age, gender, social origin, and school education. They are family-oriented, hedonistic, masculine-oriented, and subject-oriented behavioral types. For experimental purposes, Lenz categorized these behavioral types into a system of social inequality. It shows that the family-

and hedonistic-oriented type appears quite independent of social origin and school education, whereby the latter tend to be equal in status to their peers. The masculine-oriented type comes from a family with a lower social status and has less school education. The subject-oriented type usually has a better school qualification and comes from a better off family.

If we look at both studies in context, one notices that each milieu in Möllers' findings corresponds to a behavior orientation Lenz illuminated. The family-oriented behavioral type emerges in the classical worker milieu. The unstable worker milieu corresponds with the masculine orientation. The advancement-oriented worker milieu is consistent with the hedonistic one. Although Möller's analysis did not find the subject-oriented type, it corresponds with Lenz's conclusion that this type hardly ever emerges among workers. The first available analyses of milieu-specific socialization show signs of convergent structures. Yet, both these pioneer studies of milieu-specific socialization brought even more concomitant factors. They confirm that socialization analyses based on milieu theories are sensible and necessary.

First, findings prove that differences in youths' orientation and personality development occur partly independent of socioeconomic, but dependent on the sociocultural, position of the parents. This trend was recognized in the mid 1980s as a structural transformation from a 'production' to a 'consumer socialization paradigm' (Heine and Mautz, 1989, p.17).

Second, differences in the parents' sociocultural orientation (as well as economic position), especially in terms of their lifestyle, often become apparent in children's behavior, but do not always lead to a similar orientation. Because other factors (for example, unstable parent/family circumstances and ensuing biographical disturbances, rising degrees of freedom for youths, and the obviously growing influence of other than family socialization instances such as school, peer groups and their families, associations, and leisure places) ensure that youths' socialization today is no longer determined solely by parental life circumstances and ways of life. In some parts of society, the family's direct socialization influence has slowly changed into an indirect one. The family is a sort of 'clearing house' where the different (sometimes contradictory) influences arising from heterogenous socialization instances of pluralistic welfare societies are clarified, assessed, weighed, molded, and, if possible, biographically 'put right again'.

Third, findings of milieu-specific socialization studies point out that socialization processes no longer form a life-long stable 'basic personality'. Rather, they convey competence in coping with one's own (often plural and changing) identity and shaping one's life course (Steinkamp, 1986, p.148).

'VERTICAL' MOBILITY AND REPRODUCTION OF SOCIAL INEQUALITY IN PLURALISTIC WELFARE SOCIETIES

If the 'sociocultural structuration of the social structure' establishes itself to such an extent in advanced industrial societies that socialization processes are greatly influenced, this has consequences for 1) the structure of social inequality and its meaning for people, 2) the mobility of people in this structure (that is, for 'vertical' mobility), and 3) the reproduction (or change) of the structure of social inequality. I will formulate some thoughts and theses based on these three consequences and will propose appropriate research categories and first empirical findings to test them.

On item 1, pluralization of the ways of life gives social inequalities (such as income levels, professional prestige, and living conditions) increasingly different meanings for people, based on their milieu membership. So in the 'traditionless-worker', the 'advancement-oriented', and the 'alternative' milieus (which play an important role in both the socialization studies previously outlined), the order of certain social-inequality dimensions is obviously very different. In the 'traditionless-worker milieu', money must be at the top because of scarcity and corresponding values; in the 'advancement-oriented milieu', education is most important; but in the 'alternative milieu', public goods and environmental conditions have to be central.

With increasing sociocultural pluralization, the 'objectivity' of the structure of social inequality loses its power. With the differentiation of (socialization) milieus, the dominance of the one-to-one-interpretation of the structure of social inequality ends where the professional hierarchy and its acquired gratifications (income, wealth, professional prestige, qualification) and corresponding materialistic-utilitarian mass culture were most important. Social inequalities prove to be related to specific cultures and to certain definitions of social inequality. The pluralization of (socialization) milieus implies a relativization of the frames of reference of social inequality. What is 'on top' and 'at the bottom' gradually becomes a question of milieu membership and the corresponding values and aims in life. With that, neither the distribution of incomes nor the structure of power changes. But their perception and practical consequences certainly do.

On item 2, the findings of milieu-specific socialization require us to reconsider the meaning of vertical mobility. Now, socialization is less founded on occupational hierarchy, but more on sociocultural heterogeneity. Socialization leaves room for multiple influences, plural identities, and active individual changes. Socialization no longer influences individual mobility only by creating unequal competence to progress, or descending a (occupational) scale, and coping with more or less complex circumstances. If different referential systems of social inequality are present, clear 'objective' mobility concepts change because the goals of life, advancement, and career interpretation become different, ambivalent, and inconstant. Mobility between milieus (where definitions of their own situation, aims, interests, and political cleavages are developed) will become as important as movement between classes. One only needs to imagine how varied and ambivalent a professional promotion (such as a move to the 'provinces') is judged. That interpretation depends on one's milieu and life phase. Conventional sociological mobility concepts, based exclusively on the professional prestige scale or qualification level, neglect the growing cultural relativity of 'vertical' mobility. Mobility concepts with fully or partly sociocultural reference frames would be better suited to the cultural definition of 'vertical' in terms of ascents and descents.

On item 3 (the reproduction of the structure of social inequality), we must draw a third consequence from the development towards milieu-specific socialization. When both the structures of social inequality and the movements within it are judged according to expanded, different, and inconstant standards, we will have to answer more complicated questions about how far the structure of social inequality is reproduced on a structural and personal level. The answer is important because, in modern societies, the legitimacy of social inequality first depends on how far its main structures (for example, income distribution) change or remain (structural reproduction of social inequality). Second, the legitimacy of social inequality particularly depends on the chances of certain social groups (women, foreigners, and professional groups) to attain or remain on (dis)advantageous levels of the structure of social inequality (personal reproduction of social inequality).

Questions about personal reproduction of social inequality can be answered if we use conventional empirical findings: Analyzing data about the life course of four cohorts, born 1919-21, 1929-31, 1939-41, and 1949-51, Mayer and Blossfeld conclude:

> In [western] Germany, the relations [among] social class origin, the achieved educational levels and professional qualifications, the position achieved at the start of a career and the career successes have become tighter rather than looser during the past decade. It turns out that the influence of the class structure is definitely not disappearing and thus must be accepted as the central, ever guiding instance for occupational choices and their beneficial results. In addition, these studies have proved that . . . the mobility processes between the social classes during working life . . . represent a process with its own quality, which is marked precisely by class limits and barriers. A comparison of our three cohorts (both men and women) shows that class limits are becoming more and more important. The class structure is becoming more rigid and is definitely not disappearing (Mayer and Blossfeld, 1990, p.307).

These and other empirical findings show an ongoing personal reproduction of social inequality. Do they contradict the conclusions drawn from the milieu-specific socialization research? Do they contradict those conclusions suggesting mobility processes that are more independent of parental homes or more inconstant, interpreted, and pursued according to different points of view, suggesting a change in the structure of social inequality? With reference to the sheer data, not necessarily. The conventional mobility and course-of-life research deals exclusively with the aspect of professional inequality, with the chain of mobility leading through the stations of family, school, and professions (and their gratifications). It deals neither with additional dimensions (such as social security, housing, environment, and integration), nor does it include the meanings of those dimensions and results of mobility for people from different social milieus with different values and goals. So, as far as our pure data can carry us, conventional mobility research and milieu-specific social structure research miss the point completely.

But in terms of its practical relevance, the findings of the 'classical' mobility research clearly contradict the discoveries of milieu-specific social structure and socialization studies. Either the professional advancement poses the central axis of ascent or descent in thoughts and behavior, in lifestyle and *Lebensführung*, in consumption and politics, or several different, competing, changing frames or reference compete for it.

Empirical mobility studies with plural milieu reference frames reveal the direction and extent of this contradiction. The object of such studies does not lie in discovering the 'subjective' satisfaction and evaluation of the 'objective' professional mobility in different milieus. In this bifurcation of 'objective' circumstances (whose 'objectivity' sociologists define) and 'subjective' judgements (which sociologists usually question individuals about) lies one of the weaknesses in current empirical social research. Milieu-specific mobility research effectively deals with unequal life conditions based on their interpretation and meaning in everyday life of different milieus. The prevalent separation of the 'objective' from the 'subjective' in current social research results more from the available empirical methods than from theoretical considerations. This dichotomy relies too much on the power of people's conscience. But in conventional social structure research, people's conscience is not awarded such a high status: From Marxist class theory up to functional stratification theory together with inherent socialization theory, man appears to unconsciously adjust to outer circumstances.

Empirical findings prove that milieu-specific mobility exists not only as sociological theses and categories, but also in reality. These results show whether the reproduced professional structure of social inequality still continues to dominate people's lives in spite of (or because of) the sociocultural pluralization of society, whether this pluralization relativizes the meaning of professional (im)mobility, or if it completely overlaps it.

The four concepts required to understand sociocultural mobility are 'social space', 'social situation', 'social milieu' and 'milieu biography'. These concepts are not new. Pierre Bourdieu (1979, 1985) uses the concept of 'social space'. 'Social situation' corresponds to the life situation concepts of Gerhard Weisser (Hradil, 1987, p.145). The development of the milieu concept was previously outlined. Vester et al. (1993) explore 'milieu biographies'. After years of synchronous research, they can now help to develop the diachronous social structure research further and to loosen it from occupational society, 'objectivistic', and purely vertical fixations.

The generalized fields of potential behavior of individual actors are called 'social spaces'. These refer to potential behavioral fields of larger social structural groupings with relatively stable behavioral conditions. Social spaces available to a group of people with a common constellation of unequal (better or worse) behavioral circumstances (resources, rules, restrictions, risks, and influences) are called 'social situations'. A group of actors who, due to a common interpretation of their material and human environment, behave accordingly, are called 'social milieus' (a group is a 'milieu' if it has unanimous values, basic attitudes, and correspondingly determined mentalities and interactions). Like social spaces, milieus are to be perceived as contexts (that is, as mutually influencing multidimensional constellations). One can best imagine social spaces and milieus as vectors running toward individual actors.

When explaining socialization differences when there are scant resources, strict norms, and manifold restrictions, consider social spaces and situations (for example, their stratification or class membership) as main explanatory variables, not milieu differentiations. With the help of 'narrow' spaces and situations, you explain certain actions; 'wide' action conditions do not. The vast opening of social spaces and situations and simultaneous differentiation (narrowing) of social milieus for most people since the 1960s makes it advisable to proceed to the milieu membership if you want to explain socialization behavior. Outer conditions of action (spaces and situations) to which members of the social milieus are exposed are going to lose explanatory power. As previously shown, the newer (more milieu-specific) socialization research arrives at its goal better than previous approaches.

'Milieu biography' renders these concepts suitable for analyzing (diachrone) socialization and mobility courses and their structural results (the reproduction or the modification, respectively, of the structure of social inequality). Four types of 'milieu biographies' can be differentiated analytically, although they are usually linked to each other: 1) 'Biographies' of milieus (the transformation of the shape of milieu cultures over time, such as the erosion of milieus of the 1968 student movement or the establishment of the milieus of emerging EDP professions). 2) Intergenerational individual 'biographies' from parental milieus (for example, an obligation and performance-oriented Protestant advancing milieu) to one's own personal milieus (perhaps a hedonistic one). 3) Intragenerational 'biographies' from one milieu to another (for example, the transition from the milieu of the 1968 student movement, at the age of 20, to that of the ministerial bureaucracy or a union at the age of 45). 4) Individual 'biographies' within a certain milieu (in particular, vertical mobility in the professional hierarchy while retaining milieu-specific mentalities and forms of relations).

The consideration and categories for pluralistic, socioculturally defined mobility processes were not taken from thin air. They exist and have considerable meaning for people. For example, this can be demonstrated by the empirical findings of Vester et al. (1993).

Figure 9.1. Milieus in western Germany

Class

Upper

Upper middle   Conservative   Technocratic   Alternative
                  Higher (9%)   (10%)   (3%)

Middle middle
                  Bourgeoisie   Promotion-oriented
                  (26%)   (24%)
                                                        Hedonistic
Lower middle   (10%)

                  Traditional
Lower   Worker (9%)   Traditionless
                                    Worker (10%)

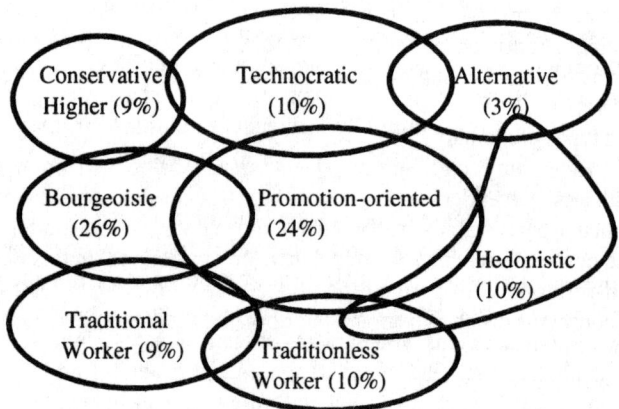

              Traditional   Materialism & Anomie   Postmaterial
              Basic   'Have'   'Consumer   New
              Orientation   Materialism Hedonism'   Orientation

---

These studies proceed from the 'opening of the social space'. Since the 1960s, individual degrees of freedom have grown via the expansion of education, new technologies in occupations and free time, new forms of life, extended state social security and infrastructures of welfare states, new possibilities for leisure and consumers, and greater everyday tolerance. The 'opening of the social space' parallels the increase of highly qualified 'new service professions' (employees and civil servants in education, research, culture, art, social work, and medicine as well as 'free professions' such as doctors, pharmacists, nonmedical practitioners, architects, and lawyers). These 'new professions' grew from 5.4 per cent (1950) to 22 per cent (1987) of the labor force of western Germany (Vester, 1992, p.152). The 'opening of the social space' resulted in changes of the 'habitus', mentalities, and milieu membership of all four types of sociocultural mobility. Figure 9.1 shows which distinct 'modern' social milieus have recently emerged in western Germany.

The growth of the 'new milieus' is based on Vester's et al. (1993) findings, not the direct consequence of the 'objective' changes of the 'social space'. Rather, the changed 'objective' life and occupational conditions posed 'challenges to learn' and cope with the new possibilities of the extended space. People reacted to this with different results (such as greater autonomy, lessening orientation, or turning toward this or that) to one or several milieus.

This is evident in the multiple 'milieu metamorphoses', 'milieu genealogical trees', and transitions from milieu to milieu. These sociocultural changes in structure and mobility movements become particularly obvious when you understand 'milieus' are not only syndromes of abstract value orientations and basic attitudes (like the 'SINUS milieus' which are confounded with socioeconomic characteristics of situations), but also concrete and practical forms of social coherence and political comprehension (Vester et al., 1993, p.181). Then, we can see how members of 'new milieus' retain some habits and types of mentalities they attained in their biographically previous milieus.

Retention is particularly evident with regard to distinction (taste, dealing with arts, perception, and evaluation of structures of social inequality). Other milieu aspects (such as self-realization demands, hedonistic leisure practices, and new male-female role models) are newly attained. In this way, the 'higher self-reflexivity' of parts of the younger generation manifests itself, making a 'conscious distance from the incorporated schemata of habits' (Vester et al., 1993, p.194) possible. Tension emerged between the originally acquired dispositions and the ideals and values of the new milieu membership. Thus, these empirical findings correspond exactly with predictions developed from changed socialization conditions and processes. The following comment exemplifies this sort of milieu mobility:

> Persons of the 'integral milieu type' are mainly advancement oriented personalities and/or come from advancement oriented families. In part, the fathers come from the same field of upper cultural-social and technical-administrative professions as the interviewed children. But some of them and the majority of grandfathers had not yet achieved such positions. Rather, they belonged to the specialized worker and craftsmen [groups]. . . . The parents thus belong to the construction generation of Western Germany who today can show off professional [achievements], housing, property, and relatively well-trained children (Vester et al., 1993, p. 214).

If one wanted to retrace how this group advanced exclusively in terms of profession, the particular way this group copes with new possibilities of the open social space would not be unique. One would not be able to tell them apart from other groups who likewise advanced professionally, but were clearly different in their aims, mentalities, and gregarious forms. One would miss highly important political, economic, and interpersonal differences. The 'integrals' have developed highly demanding aims of a self-fulfillment integrating body and soul, feelings and intellect, politics and person. They pursue these aims at work and in their partnership, where they aspire to 'relationships' and partnership-like work divisions. This also applies to consumer and free time. 'Fine taste' is celebrated here. In view of society and social inequality, a sensitive attitude is cultivated toward the ecology and Third World. These 'integrals' differ drastically from the 'humanistically active' and 'success-oriented' type, although they often share the same origin, advancement methods, and equally demanding professions in education, health care, administration, or trade (Vester et al., 1993, p. 209).

CONCLUSION

The newer milieu mobility research shows that extended absolute degrees of freedom are dealt with differently. Many milieu-specific socialization differences play a part. These milieu socialization processes and specific milieu biographies do not lead to individualization in terms of isolation. Rather, most new *Vergemeinschaftungen* (unification into social groups) are found in the growing 'new education bourgeoisie', where the most far-reaching erosion of the occupational society's collectives, most sociocultural differentiation, and most milieu mobility occur. The new milieus, lifestyles, social, and individual movements based on them can be found in the zones of particularly strongly extended possibilities.

Occupational and class-specific socialization (ascent and descent within the professional hierarchy) are not meaningless. But, just as one wave rolls over another and changes, socialization and mobility processes in the occupational and class hierarchy in 'postindustrial' service societies are increasingly shaped by social milieus and lifestyles. But also in developed, socioculturally pluralized welfare societies, it makes a difference for the members of a particular milieu which class one belongs to and comes from.

7   Inequality and Education: Changing Theoretical Conceptions

Fritz-Ulrich Kolbe, Heinz Sünker, Dieter Timmermann

ABSTRACT

Education policy is social policy. Many social science and educational theories analyze the consequences of the 'interdependence of the constitution of society and educational institutions' (Heydorn, 1980, p. 99) to investigate educational policy and the reproduction of social inequality and to distinguish among forms of educational processes which individuals experience.

Scholars discussed shared themes ('society', 'education', and 'individual') with transdisciplinary perspectives, using comparative social history and the theory of democracy (Heydorn, 1979, 1980; Collins, 1979; Timmermann and Strikker, 1986; Bowles and Gintis, 1987; Lenhart, 1987; Cole, 1988; Timmermann, 1988; Friedeburg, 1989; Sünker, 1989a and b; Richter, 1993). Anglo-Saxon contributions to these debates complement German critical educational theorists since they often identify the reproductive function of the education system for the social status quo and simultaneously illustrate difficulties in describing this function. Adorno provides a *leitmotif* for this perspective and its consequences in his 'theory of semi-education'.

> The effects of education, which have sedimented, by no means only
> in Germany, as a sort of negative objective mind, itself arose from
> the laws of social movement, or even from the very concept of
> education. It has become a socialized semi-education, an ever-pres-
> ent alienated mind (Adorno, 1972, p. 93).

The social scientific development of this idea is in Bourdieu's (1973) analysis of the relevance of the educational system for the 'structure of class relations'. This chapter includes comments on the course of the discussion in the German sociology of education debates in the 1980s, an account of the approach of the 'new sociology of education', and main theoretical points arising from a critique and reformulation of both these bodies of literature.

STATUS OF THE SOCIOLOGY OF EDUCATION

Analyses from the sociology of education are significant for arguments in critical educational thought relevant to educational theory for they include the social process of mediation. What was generally constitutive for critical educational thought was that meaningful theory formation could only arise from analyzing the 'conflictual meditation of the subjective and the objective' (Keckeisen, 1983, p. 12), of individualization and socialization in relation to educational processes and social structure, and from a method which encompassed all levels of mediation and was not subsumable under another class or category. The normative problem in the form of the postulate of emancipation which this educational theory contained was linked to three problems: 1) It was necessary to show the difference between real educational processes and emancipatory claims and to relate this to a concrete change in the relationship between the institutionalization of education and social structure as a whole. 2) A concrete critical concept of education was only possible in the context of the current social political situation (and must not displace the contradiction between education and the force of circumstance). 3) The normative standardization of pedagogic action is only possible negatively, provided through a critique of given educational processes and their institutionalization, through an indication of what is yet unresolved. Thus, educational theory remains theoretical and not directly connected to political action because the underlying critical social scientific analysis only provides findings and categories concerning the conditions and quality of institutionalized educational processes and society's requirements for this subject.

Educational sociology is central to the notions of educational theory in other ways. These encompass the critical, social-theoretically based analysis of educational processes in today's society and the historical analysis of the institutionalization of education to encourage developing basic institutional-theoretical categories. These demand a sociology of education which mediates between its object and the function of education in society.

German Educational Sociology

A starting point for examining recent German educational sociology is Friedeburg's historical analysis of 'boom and recession phases of public interest in educational politics and educational sociology' (Friedeburg, 1983, p. 157). This identifies the determination of societal politics and its processes and educational politics; however, it shows the 'conjuncture' of educational sociology in the form of corresponding analyses in the sociology of education. Besides continuing the empirical study of educational developments, macrosociological theoretical concepts and the less than favorable contextual conditions in the 1980s were not conducive for the growth of critical theory.

Discussions and assessments of theoretical strategies (ZSE, 1983; Benner, 1990) showed that then there was little further development of theoretical concepts which were critical and concerned with a materialist analysis. Discussions in educational sociology had turned more strongly toward questioning the meso- and microlevels, with the macrosociological perspective on society as a whole fading from view. By the mid 1970s, there was a strong demand that 'macrosociological and everyday cultural approaches be integrated' (Rolff, 1983, p. 205). Assessing this lack of development in theoretical concepts gives rise to the critique put forward in this period of more sophisticated models developed in reproduction theory and their acceptance in Germany (Baethge, 1984; Baethge and Teichler, 1984).

Baethge critiqued the concepts of accumulation theory, ideological structural correspondence, and reproduction of social structure. Whether in relation to the first's restricted power to explain the development of educational structures, to the concept of correspondence's lack of a 'transfer mechanism from factory to school norms', or to the third's problem of forming social norms, he established the concepts' inability 'to explain the development of educational structures and material production' (Baethge, 1984, p. 41). He pleaded for 'separation of the developmental tendencies of material production and the reproduction of subjectivity' and suggested considering the sphere of reproduction as 'substantially not subsumed to capital in relation to its regulative forms of behavior' (Baethge, 1984, p. 44). As to a theoretical system-level concept (of the relation between education and occupation systems), Baethge and Teichler preferred the distribution of status, encompassing the 'behavioral-theoretical dimension' and assuming the difference between social and system integration for the sake of historical analysis.

This critical discussion has progressed little despite attempts to take the 'new sociology of education' into account in the works of Apple and Wexler. A recent work of modernization theory (which identifies macrosociological elements) clarifies that since then, 'modernization-theoretical analyses of the educational system' (Tippelt, 1990) or a structural-functionalist method prevailed. What is desired is the further development of critical theory formation in the sense of the basic concept of social and system integration. Achieving a broader reconstruction of educational structures and the processes within them requires multilevel concepts, which argue that the development of the education sector follows an internal logic. This also reconstructs educational structures in terms of action-theoretical moments (that is, the perspective of social integration).

Recent empirical sociology of education studies included structural analyses of educational institutions and institutionalized credentialism, studies of collective learning and individual developmental processes, curriculum, and teaching studies (Beck and Kell, 1990, p. 149). Sociology of education also studies structural analyses of institutionalization. Themes included the study of different parts of the education system; 'transitions'; relations between increased educational participation and opportunities; curricula; educational planning; and vocational education. Only contributions from socialization research and microanalytical analyses of interaction stand out; 'teaching research' remains largely psychological in design and execution.

Contributions to interactionist studies of schooling or teaching emerged only recently (particularly in the works of the Dortmund Institute for Research on School Development). Approaches in terms of structural and action theory appear in more recent research on moral education and socialization.

Fend's (1990) characterization of empirical educational research is based on structural functionalism. It sees development in terms of modernization. That some contributions (like the 'school development research') also examine the internal logic of educational processes or which argue in terms of both action and structuralist theory does not change the situation that these empirical research fields paid little attention to further developing an underlying theory which does not simply mediate the various levels in a functionalist way. Representatives of the discipline conclude that there is a lack of analyses which conceptualize the whole process of the mediation of education and society as the effect of processes at other sociological levels.

The developmental tendencies of this educational research can be seen in the program of 'life course research' (Mayer, 1990; Meulemann, 1990) and in the needs identified in the studies of school development research and professional educational research. Life course research extends the sociology of education's analysis of school behavior, achievement, and equal opportunity via comprehensive longitudinal studies. In this way, individual routes through education and 'individual decisions in the life course' (Meulemann, 1990, p. 89) are considered in these categories of 'the life course'. For example, the connections between actually completed educational planning, social origins, and achievement in their contribution to educational outcomes are the focus of research. On the one hand, individual decisions and the social structure of educational institutions become recognizable 'as the outcome of the action of socially defined groups and demands of actors under given, changing contextual conditions' (Mayer, 1990). On the other hand, this considerably differentiates the question of the meaning of educational institutions relative to socially defined groups, to the demand for qualification and to status acquisition, and characterizes educational routes as functional.

As to the very differentiated 'school development research' (which studied 'institutional structures' and 'inequality in educational opportunity') and occupational research (which extends into qualification research), they emphasize needs which indicate similar research strategies. If it is claimed that the influence of the factors (especially selection) on the learning conditions of teaching should be more intensively studied in the analysis of occupational qualification, what remains unanswered is the need to examine the process of acquisition or the perspective of the learner. The conditions of the constitution of subjects or subjectivity remain unrecognized. Further development of theoretical concepts is lacking. These prerequisites of empirical research lack fundamental theoretical conceptualization. The interest in a 'new sociology' focuses on possible theoretical innovations.

NEW SOCIOLOGY OF EDUCATION

The 'new sociology of education' was developed in the social and political context of the US and Britain at the end of the 1960s, together with the New Left political movement in opposition to established educational sociology. It linked a self-understanding of its theoretical development (which played a decisive role in social critique) with the claim to a vigorous theoretical base for its subject using critical social theory.

Wexler (1987) combines three theoretical traditions: 1) Teachers and educators investigated institutionalized education's social relations of mediation as an independent study. Apple (1978) focused on reconceptualizing curriculum theory in terms of social critique. 2) American sociology and educational sociology became receptive to European sociological theory. 3) There was a tendency toward the interdisciplinary in a more differentiated sociology, which led to integration with historical and economic approaches (Wexler, 1987, p. 34; 1976). Wexler's reconstruction shows that the whole development was based on the integration of a sociology of knowledge framework, which leads to a concern with knowledge transmitted through educational institutions and interpretative and constructionist methods of analysis. Here, there is little connection with curriculum theory, which has a comprehensive concern with pedagogic processes (Young, 1971). Wexler shows that the materialist critique and the application of sociology of knowledge approaches through the political movement's social critique were decisive for the contours of the 'new sociology of education'.

Five basic premises more precisely characterize the 'new sociology of education' by contrasting its basic concepts with those of traditional, liberal sociology of education. The works of the 'new sociology of education' attempt to analyze 'social knowledge' about society in classroom teaching and the public discourse around schooling to identify its social determinants and ideological character. See the early works of Whitty and Apple (especially Young and Whitty, 1977; Apple, 1979, 1982) or Giroux (1981, 1983).

Equally opposed to liberal and structural-functionalist assumptions are two other premises concerning the school's social function. First, instead of conceptualizing the school merely as a means of individual mobility, its functions were redefined. Institutionalized education reproduces social inequality or social structures. The view of interaction in the school and its socialization function also changes. This field is investigated from the premise that one must perceive the prevailing conflicts, oppositional behavior, and resistance against school norms. The works of Wexler, Giroux, and the earlier analyses of Apple or Willis can be included here (Willis, 1977).

The key concepts are ultimately the critique of ideology and cultural reproduction. Ideology critique was a demystification program for the development of academic knowledge as well as the logical framework of the analysis of interest-bound, reality-distorting knowledge and a framework for examining the legitimating function of ideology to stabilize social relations.

Moreover, the recourse to critical social theory allowed the sociology of education to analyze education as part of cultural production. Wexler's study presents the thesis that both of the reproduction-theoretical traditions it discussed (for example, Marxist structuralism alongside the older critical theory) necessarily took the development of research away from the model of ideology critique to an analysis of institutions and levels of action.

According to Wexler, the concept of ideology was part of the former tradition (which demonstrated how ideology disintegrated the constitution of the subject in the social conditions of existence) and was more inclined to relate ideology to symbols and interaction in the context of practical actions than to analyze it as the transfer of elements of ideology. For the social-theoretical understanding of ideology, the second theory can also be identified. It aimed to analyze the reproductive moment of education and oriented the theoretical perspective toward the study of the institutions of symbolic production or the constitution of meaning and, thus, toward institutions' reproductive function.

The 'new sociology of education' finally produced educational analyses which, in the case of Bowles and Gintis (1976), interpreted the reproductive function of institutionalized education in terms of the correspondence principle or which with Apple (1979) defined the reproductive function of institutionalized education as reproducing a class-specific culture. Apple defended the thesis that the class-specific culture of the ruling social group in the school system is presented and legitimized as universal knowledge with the result that it leads to a social differentiation of constitutive knowledge.

However, central theoretical elements of the political-economic theory of schooling and the complementary conceptualization of class-specific cultural orders underwent basic changes using the concept of the distribution of ideology as 'educational knowledge'. An awareness of the relative autonomy of institutions replaced the concept of totality. 'Integration through structure' as a concept permitted the description of internal contradictions. The model of the reproduction of social domination was ultimately conceptually differentiated through the analysis of institutional conflicts.

THEORETICAL DISCUSSIONS BEYOND THE NEW SOCIOLOGY OF EDUCATION

Reexamining the Concept of Reproduction

Baethge and Wexler's critique referred to the relative autonomy of continuing processes at the level of culture in relation to the education system and the function of the state. Reproduction theory constituted the relation between the education and economic systems, although it broke apart the dialectic of structure and action in specific ways. While reproduction theory adopted a structural-functionalist perspective and action was execution of whatever seemed necessary to reproduce the unequal social structure, social democratic educational policy concentrated on education's function in reducing inequality. The concept of equality of opportunity postulated neither equality in learning conditions and processes nor equality of outcomes. But the other two concepts of equality of opportunity highlighted the contradiction between the equality of acquired education and the inequality in job positions. This contradiction did not lead to identifying the social-structural inequality of the occupational system as the real problem (as did, for example, Jencks et al., 1972; Bowles and Gintis, 1976; Carnoy and Levin, 1985). But the contradiction between the two systems was implanted into the education system as a two-fold challenge immanent to the education system: 1) between equal educational opportunity and the selection function of schooling and 2) between equality of educational opportunity and efficiency.

While social democratic educational theory and policy reflected the differential effects of unequal living conditions on the young's educational opportunity, it did not point out that the young lived in a world of unequal social positions. Reproduction theory took the opposite position: the education system should reproduce social inequality and maintain its legitimacy since the illusion of equal opportunity was constantly reproduced through meritocratic educational expansion. The weaknesses of reproduction theory were that it disregarded either the relation between ideology, culture, and state on the one hand and the economic system on the other; or that it postulated the relation between the economic structure on the one hand and ideology, culture, socialization, and curriculum on the other in a much too deterministic (economic) way. This leads ultimately to an unacceptable model of the relations between social structure and the subject, in which the actor is not only structurally dominated, but determined. Subjects (like teachers, pupils, parents) act in the reproduction model not as relatively autonomous subjects, but as marionettes without their own needs or their own will.

The experiences with educational reforms of the late 1960s suggested a closer examination of the notion of the relative autonomy of the educational system and of the processes on the level of action. A model of the connections between 'reproduction, social inequality, and action' which respects the inner logic of such structures must include a system of four loosely related structures: the social structure of the economic system, the structure of institutionalized education, the structure of the state, and the structures of the individual's life-world. Within each of these spheres, subjects act according to their roles, functions, interests, and needs as well as their position in the hierarchy. Each life-world produces its own value system, behaviors, and attitudes (toward work, politics, education) and its own cultural pattern and attitudes, which subjects bring about in accordance with their life-world. This is why there is not only the ideology of the 'ruling class', but also that of those 'subjected' to their subjugation and their various life-worlds. Their members do not limit the range of their specific cultures to the private sphere, but seek to live according to them everywhere, particularly in economic and educational institutions. In the spheres of economics, education, and state action, there is a plurality of cultures, ideologies, and interests. Part of this is attributable to the dominant 'class', others to the dominated. The economy (as much as the education system and the state) will be the arena of the conflicts between social classes. These conflicts will both take place within the given structures and bring forth new structural elements. In the framework of this model, three concepts require clarification: 1) the relative autonomy of institutionalized education, 2) subject and resistance, and 3) social structure.

The Concept of the Relative Autonomy of Institutionalized Education

The impulse for educational expansion and reform arose from the economy's increased need for educated workers. But this 'manpower approach' was not the idea which guided attempts at reform and expanded opportunities. It was more a philosophy of the 'social demand approach'. Later concepts of demands related to determining educational policy and increasing individual outcry for education reinforced this process, one stimulated by reform. Experiments in reforming the organizational structure, curriculum development, teacher education, and other elements became the fundamental object of fierce conflicts between various social groups. Reform attempts were blocked and ended in a type of educational system which neither opponents nor supporters wanted. But the growth in demand for higher education did not decline although studies show that this cannot be expected in the future.

While educational sociologists predicted a threatening legitimation crisis (either for the education system and its credentials or for the occupation system because the homogenization of the qualification profile threatened the hierarchical structure of work organization), nothing of the sort took place. Instead, the expanded participation in higher education continues. According to Lutz (1983), the entrance barriers to higher education are gradually disappearing. The selection function of education is declining while cultural pluralism and democratization of content continues to develop. Therefore, the demand for higher education has weakened the meritocratic logic behind the transition from education to employment and increasingly transfers such processes into the occupation system. This means that the occupation system runs into a legitimation crisis and has to deal with the changed supply of qualified labor. One can conclude that the educational system is only loosely linked to the other systems in its environment and that there is considerable freedom for developing different student, teacher, and parent cultures as well as for determining school content and forms of interaction.

The Concept of Subject and Resistance

Reintroducing a concept of the subject which conceptualizes it as acting independently in the sphere of production and reproduction, one recognizes the simple truth that 'class struggle' and resistance cannot be thought of without the conscious decision of individuals who realize they belong to a class and who can decide to take part in collective action. This also demands an action-based concept of the subject. Here one could draw on the concept of the subject as a productive reality-processor (Hurrelmann, 1986). This implies a concept of rational individual decision-making. The decision to adapt one's action to surrounding social relations or to oppose them is neither a chance affair nor do social conditions mechanically determine this process; it is the result of a decision, into which the formation of political goals and the effects of other factors enter. Baudelot and Establet's studies (which Giroux, 1983, and Willis, 1977, dexcribe) underline this view.

In this connection, three avenues remaining unexplored: 1) Consider the relation between resistance and education. Willis does not transfigure the phenomenon of resistance into elements of a constitution of the subject which serve as a rationale for political resistance. 2) We need to know more about intentions and goals which lead to either conformity or resistance. Particularly, we must determine if these intentions can be realized within the boundaries of life-world structures or whether they aim at structural change. 3) We must examine the connections between the intentions and outcome of action. Even action understood as resistance, which leads to political resistance, can take on destructive and constructive forms.

The Concept of Social Structure

The concept of social structure which reproduction theories use is unclear. First, the social-theoretical premises are controversial; some still use a Marxist concept of class, others the concept of social strata, both needing more definition. Second, critics claim that the applied models of vertical stratification limit their scope of validity to traditional wage labor relations.

Further queries concern the restriction of models to the vertical structure of social relations and inequality. Now, 'new' inequalities are based on other (for example, ascribed) characteristics such as ethnic identity and with respect to other social goods which mold social structures. Finally, some socialization theory arguments judge the concept of strata to be far too blunt to grasp social structures or social relations as socialization factors; new concepts such as 'lifeworld' or 'milieu' have become widespread (Hradil, 1993). The individualization thesis (Beck, 1983) goes further. It argues that while the 'old inequalities' continue to exist, they have lost their social relevance just as they have lost their significance for the subject's action-orientation. The fact that these questions have been raised leads to the conclusion that the fundamental social-theoretical premises of various concepts in reproduction theory have been critiqued and require reformulation.

The critique of the 'new sociology of education' offers new arguments. Wexler's study is a radical critique of the program. It pursues the assumptions, arguments, and internal 'dialectic' central to the program's execution. This dialectic is both immanent and operates in relation to the social function of this academic discourse. He tries to outdo the 'new sociology of education's' critique of ideology. He analyzes 'scientific discourse' as a political influence in the self-interest of those conducting it. Wexler's study shows that this 'new sociology of education' has four features.

First, 'making oneself independent' is related to the discourse of a 'reification' of the critique of ideology's pattern of argumentation, which generates an 'undialectical' concept of reproduction. The 'new sociology of education' also uses the critique of scientific knowledge. The object of critique was no longer scientific knowledge, but school knowledge or the role of the school in societal oppression. What was presumed to be part of the critique of ideology which then prevailed was that the ideological element was exclusively determined by the rationalized interests of 'the powerful' and could be exposed as such. This basic concept was maintained in the transition to the analysis of the school's reproductive function. Despite the introduction of concepts such as hegemony and cultural praxis, Wexler maintained that reproduction theory (in accordance with its object-theoretical premises) remained a theory of ideological-critique and understood symbolic forms only as ideology in relation to the process of social reproduction. The 'reproductionism' (Wexler, 1987, p. 41) this produced led to a systematically reduced emphasis on educational processes as being devoted to the reproduction of power structures.

Second, this fixation on a 'symbolic function' led the 'new sociology of education' to acquire the character of political faith and symbolic praxis. Since 'reproductionist' theory is adhered to despite thematized contradictions, using theory lapses into a statement of faith. This is clear in Willis's (1977) thesis of the subcultural resistance of working-class youth, which he regards as the constitutive moment in the social reproduction process through schooling. Giroux did not use this analytically, but to demonstrate political optimism and pedagogic commitment. In theoretical terms, it only seems that the thesis of the totality of reproduction has been abandoned because resistance is not seen as evidence of a need for revision of theoretical concepts but as an opportunity to demonstrate a political, emancipatory position.

Third, the findings of the 'new sociology of education', with the modifications (relative autonomy, structural social integration, analysis of political conflicts) it made went beyond the reproduction construct and show its theoretical deficiency. For example, the causes of social change (existing structural contradictions in the capitalist economy, relative autonomy of cultural practice, and class-specific forms of resistance) became visible.

Fourth, Wexler's application of discourse analysis shows the rhetoric of resistance's 'romantic individualism' (Wexler, 1987, p. 42) in relation to political opposition. This simultaneously forms the complement to 'reproductionism' and prevents the proponents of the 'new sociology of education' from grasping the cultural preconditions of its form of discourse. The revision of the 'new sociology of education' provides an opportunity to reconceptualize the relation between education and ideology from the perspective of social and collective action.

CONCLUSION

The relativistic character of Wexler's political-discourse analytical critique distinguishes it from one of the 'new sociology of education' posed in terms of social theory, particularly a theory of the state, such as Englund's (see Chapter 15). His critique is founded on educational theory, connecting with a sociological conceptualization of institutionalized education. Englund's thesis is that the content of institutionalized education and the knowledge it disseminates should be analyzed as part of the disputed realization of citizenship rights and as a product of political conflicts in the state's and society's public sphere. The 'new sociology of education's' ideology-critical analysis of the content of education in terms of the concept of reproduction manifests for him a reductionistic understanding because it is not free-standing and is based on implicit reductionist state- and social-theoretical foundations.

This argument is crucial because identifiable, reformulated social-theoretical foundations can be connected with a process-related normative criterion for education which concretizes emancipation, which builds on the modern social structuring of the constitution of society and participation in terms of contractual rights. If one appeals to traditional educational sociology and its structural-functionalist foundation, one can reconstruct a lost connection. The state is conceived theoretically as a modernization agent with the individual citizenship right to education as a precondition for guaranteeing the creation of the possibilities of participation in exercising civil, political, and social rights. If one adds a critical, conflict-theoretical concept of the state, then (historical) state action is grasped as a disputed 'terrain' of competing political, ideological forces. The introduction of citizenship rights was of central significance. What becomes visible is the internal logic of state action, which is anchored in the constitutive character of citizenship rights, beyond the grasp of the 'new sociology of education'. Education and its contents are part and parcel of this social conflict around state action.

This is why the 'reproduction-theoretical' analysis of school knowledge remained reductionist. In terms of educational theory, it inappropriately extended the field of subjects for which only negative rules are possible. Unjustly negated are educational processes' empirically demonstrable normative orientation, geared to process rules. Englund suggests measuring educational processes against a communitarian and citizenship rights perspective of democracy and the public sphere. For theory formation (based on a new determination of citizenship rights), this implies clarifying the ambivalent meaning of the school and examining 'educational knowledge' for its impact on it. If this image of society is transmitted, then this pedagogic concept exemplifies its socialization function.

The social-theoretically constituted category of the critical public sphere, as a medium for exercising participatory rights, opens the possibility of more closely determining the required competencies of intellectual autonomy and communication and redefines the educational system for educational-sociological analyses. Institutionalized education develops 'symbols', demonstrates an understanding of society and of what constitutes the public sphere and of what the discourses underlying collective consciousness produce.

The functional purpose of educational processes is to provide subjects with an understanding of society and of participating in the processes for the constitution of society. This functional determination represents a conceptualization of educational processes which encompasses their internal dynamics and their relation to education's subject. In terms of educational sociology and theory, this raises a conceptualization of the internal logic of educational processes on this level. The conceptualization of institutionalized education in terms of action-processes and their rules determines its new role in societal constitution and contributes to a process-oriented determination of education.

The analysis of social and educational history which Heydorn (1979) proposed is conceptualized as the unfolding of the dialectic of the institutionalization of education. It is an essential contribution to the German discussion of these issues, supporting ideology-critical perspectives which perceive the function of education to be in the interests of domination as well as their possible defeat. This connects with the hope that 'the social instrumentalization of public education becomes increasingly difficult. The reform of education is still on the agenda' (Friedeburg, 1989, p. 477; Sünker, 1992, 1993). Ultimately, we are left to repeat the insight that educational policy is social policy, through which a democratic society comes to be founded on educated (and this means active, politically engaged) citizens.

ACKNOWLEDGMENT

Robert van Krieken translated this piece from German to English.

8 Heydorn's Bildungs Theory and Content as Social Analysis

Heinz Sünker

ABSTRACT

Emancipation as a concept has no content; the problem of its realization has become the most decisive issue in educational theory. Theory is a compass. It suggests a realization which remains buried. It points to a division. The concrete and abstract remain separate, but still indicate that any cleavages can be overcome. Socrates discovered the concept of humanity, but it remained empty and the role of reason remained submerged. He was only able to discover it because it lies within us. The conditions were ripe for the concept, but not for detailing its contents. However, Socrates pointed to possibilities which are still unfolding today (see Heydorn, 1980a, p. 103).

INTRODUCTION

Heydorn (1980a) indicates the conceptual framework within which educational theory can be regarded as social theory. Based on the classical European tradition, he was oriented towards Marxist philosophy and tried to reformulate the realization of philosophy in terms of educational theory. In this sense, educational theory operates not only at the level of the concept of education, but also social theory. As Adorno said, 'The effects of education, which have sedimented, by no means only in Germany, as a sort of negative objective mind, itself arose from the laws of social movement, or even from the very concept of education. It has become a socialized semi-education, an ever-present alienated mind' (Adorno, 1972, p. 93). He went on to say that 'If, however, the mind only does what is socially approved without melting into an undifferentiated identification with society, it becomes anachronistic to persist with education after society has removed its foundations. But it has no other opportunity for survival than critical self-reflection on the semi-education for which it has become essential' (Adorno, 1972, p. 121).

Heydorn's theory of education unfolded categories developed in the history and analysis of education and society; it focused on the maieutic concept of education as 'unbound self-autonomy' (Heydorn, 1979, p. 10). Heydorn's reconstruction of the history of education concluded that human cognition and action anchored in the educational processes of species-history are distinct from the real-historical, often deficient development of society. Without denying the 'speculative moment' of education (Heydorn, 1979, p. 16), he used the concept of emancipation, which is inherent to education and includes the realization of reason in materialist transformation (Theunissen, 1970) to describe and criticize historical developments and relations.

WESTERN MARXISM

Heydorn worked within the philosophical framework of Western Marxism, which set out precisely from the adaptability of both the idealistic concept of reason and the philosophical project and the task of their materialist reformulation. He shared Lefebvre's (one of Western Marxism's proponents) intellectual roots (Hess, 1988; Sünker, 1992; Gottdiener, 1993). To illustrate, Lefebvre spoke of

> . . . philosophy, through the wide range of its interests, [which] projects the image of a 'complete human being', free, accomplished, fully realized, rational yet real. This image - implicit already in Socrates maieutic - has, for approximately twenty centuries, been refined, revised, opposed, developed and adorned with superfluities and hyperboles (Lefebvre, 1971, p. 12).

The real focus of Western Marxism's theoretical constructions is found in the study of human beings, the investigation of conditions under which subjectivity is constituted in its social contexts. I believe it is necessary to anchor Heydorn in the Hegelian Marxist tradition to avoid his work being regarded as 'speculative' and 'voluntaristic'. For instance, Korsch and Lukacs reconstructed the Marxist critique of political economy as a theory and analysis of individual and social production, where subjectivity was bound to historical development.

In the first third of the century, a major goal was to reconstruct the Marxist critique of political economy. In the 1960s, there were discussions of 'Logic and History', which began with a critique of purely philosophical interpretations of Marx's work. Developing the logical structure of the concept of capital (Reichelt, 1970) referred to the construction underlying the Marxist concept 'capital in general'. However, they were also confronted with the problem of rescuing the project of a political economy from its reduction to a critique of economy. This included debates with Althusser and others who sought to divide Marx's development into two phases: philosophical and economic. But insight into the logic of capital cannot be equated with insight into the logic of a society and its forms of interaction. This led to reflecting on the conditions of the constitution of subjectivity within the unfolding subject-object dialectic (Adorno, 1973).

Reconstructing the subject-object dialectic was linked with reformulating the concept of 'experience' (Negt and Kluge, 1972, p. 16). This attempted formulation of a critical theory of society was a reflection of the development of the second stage of Western Marxism (Anderson, 1976), 'neo-Marxism', the 'crisis of Marxism', or the 'subjective factor'.

For Markus, the realization of the meaning of subjectivity arises from the original Marxist outline of a 'theory of social revolution'. In this context, it has to demonstrate the validity of a theory which is convinced

> . . . that conscious and collective human activity *can* radically change the present conditions and the course of history; it has to dissipate all the fetishistic illusions concerning transcendent powers and immutable ends determining the fate of people and humanity. It has to be a radically immanent explanation and understanding of history, the resolute negation of the possibility of any metahistorical standpoint' (Markus, 1986, p. 117).

This can be read as a critique of the 'abstract individualism' of the Enlightenment, but also of German idealism, which focuses on a transcendental subject. Markus opposed these positions with a new understanding of intersubjectivity. Obviously, Habermas did not grasp this idea when attacking those who deal with the 'paradigm of production' (Habermas, 1985, pp. 95-103). In the context of educational theory as a critique of society, this analysis makes it necessary to pursue the relationship between reality and possibility and possible mediations between universality/species and individuality.

Dissecting the consequences of the 'interdependence of the constitution of society and educational institutions' (Heydorn, 1980a, p. 99) requires situating the history of education within that of society. The status of educational history can be approached in terms of the recent historical understandings of social history among historians. For example, as Wehler observed,

> Contemporary social history understands its object as unified, in the sense of 'society' and 'societe'; it tries to grasp as many of the underlying processes as possible which determined, and possibly still determine, the historical development of a system normally within state-political borders. In relation to the theories and categories of secularization which Max Weber developed for his universal historical studies in order - this was the original driving force - to identify as precisely as possible the peculiarity of the occidental type of society through the comparison with other cultures, three equivalent, ever-present dimensions of society can be analytically distinguished. Power, economy and culture are these three dimensions, which in principle form every society, but which also mutually penetrate and determine each other (Wehler, 1987, pp. 6-7).

Wehler's mixture of categories (interdependence in connection with Weber, totality in relation to Hegel) highlights the problems with conceptual reconstruction. With this approach, Wehler drew on the problem-formulation characteristic of the type of social analysis prevalent in the early Lukacs' Weberian Marxism and Korsch's Hegelian Marxism. The issue is applying the category of 'totality', its possibilities, and consequences of its use.

Both Lukacs and Korsch illuminated the relations of history and subjectivity, including a critique of the objectivism of the Second International. This led to emphasizing the subject-constitutive, activist content of Marxist theory. Western Marxists wanted to explain the absence of revolution in Western European countries, complementary to the 'theory-immanent' problem-formulations and debates.

The 'aspect of totality', which for Lukacs was the difference between Marxism and bourgeois science, resulted for him in the 'methodization' of the dialectic. In Marx, the dialectical method aims at understanding society as a whole (Lukacs, 1971, pp. 27-8). Lukacs answered the question of knowledge of the totality with: the Party, which embodies the Kantian transcendental principle instead of the Hegelian world spirit, having executed the realization of 'knowledge *a priori*'. For him, revolutionary development portrayed the relation between theory and social movement, which ends with pedagogy, so that the Lukacsian concept of 'totality' led to a 'Marxist holism' (Jay, 1987, pp. 301-304), which reestablished objectivism. For Korsch, the critique of the historical metaphysics of the Second International and its ontological development of the dialectic led to a productive concern with the Marxist concept of 'praxis'.

In relation to the significance of praxis as 'objective activity' which is furnished with 'revolutionary', 'practical-critical' meaning, Korsch formulated a position which escaped from the holistic consequences of the Lukacsian approach to totality. This also included a conception of the theory-praxis relationship, with which both Lefebvre and Heydorn later connected.

The second generation of Western Marxists (especially Adorno, Heydorn, and Lefebvre) were inclined toward cultural revolution and a dissolution of the concept of totality. Both of these implied the abolition of the reified structures of everyday life in favor of an emphatically understood human praxis. They developed a notion of cultural revolution as a revolution of everyday life, insisting on the possibility of developing emancipatory needs which cannot be realized within the framework of the existing social formation (Adorno, 1966, pp. 97-8; Lefebvre, 1974, p. 207; 1978, pp. 107-10; Heydorn, 1979, pp. 12-3; 1980a, p. 165; Marx, 1967, pp. 387, 426-9). In the discussion of a theory of needs, it is important to refer to Agnes Heller (1976), one of the representatives of Western Marxism who developed an analysis of 'radical needs'.

For Heydorn, the perspective of a 'totality of subject orientation' (Heydorn, 1980b, p. 297) is connected with a general social-political perspective linking abolition of alienation, 'revolution in human labor', leisure time, and needs to the development of a radical democracy (Heydorn, 1980b, p. 295) to confront the metaphysical principle of immanence and the changeability of human life and history (Heydorn, 1980c, p. 83; Sünker, 1984, pp. 4-8).

To make 'education active', to interpret it as a means of liberation (Heydorn, 1979, pp. 324, 45; 1980c, p. 117), it is necessary to analyze social relations and forms of interaction in concrete historical terms. Therefore, Heydorn distinguishes between philosophy and history. This is important when discussing the more sophisticated interprctations of his theory and analysis. A 'historical-philosophical interpretation of the relation between theory and praxis', accompanied by the 'impression of a hermetic historical dialectic' (Benner et al., 1982, pp. 87-8), misses this distinction, which focuses on the radical historicization of human history and generates findings arising from the theory of history in relation to the problem of differentiation in the concept of progress (Heydorn, 1979, pp. 53, 317).

Central here is the connection with reflections on using 'totality'. Because, according to Lefebvre, the formula of the 'dominance of the category of totality' proved dangerous, he concluded: 'We place the category of totality under that of negativity or the dialectical negation, which seems to us to be more fundamental' (Lefebvre, 1977, pp. iii, 13). For Adorno, Heydorn, and Lefebvre, the knowledge-critical approach to the category of totality and the exposing of negativity is to be read within the framework of a theory of dialectical contradiction. This approach implies a critique of the violent character of identifying thought and is connected to the principle of 'nonidentity', which is the nucleus of Adorno's thought and includes a critique of Korsch (Adorno, 1966, p. 144): 'Objectively, dialectics means to break the compulsion to achieve identity, and to break it by means of the energy stored up in that compulsion and congealed in its objectifications. In Hegel this was a partial victory over himself - being, of course, unable to admit the untruth of the compulsion to achieve identity' (Adorno, 1973, p. 157 [translation modified]).

Equally insightful was what Lefebvre showed to be the consequence of the priority of negativity over totality, which resulted in the need to demonstrate 'the relative character of structures, stabilities, invariabilities and balances' of social development (Lefebvre, 1977, pp. iii, 70). The 'experiential content of the concept of negation' (Theunissen, 1978a, p. 171) shows that negativity means 'activity, and activity in all its aspects, in which it can only completely reveal the opposite of pre-givenness' (Theunissen, 1978a, p. 73). It does this in the principle of being (embodied in the dialectical negation, which opposes totality with its claims to completeness) and in systematic limits of the totalizing movement, to be reconstructed in terms of the theory of capital and praxis philosophy. This is the core of all discussions of the 'colonization of the life world' (Habermas, 1981) or the 'colonization of space and time' (Lefebvre, 1972, 1977) which depends on its 'material substratum', which can never be completely subsumed, and seeks to encroach on it. This is the historical-systematic location of analyses of 'opposition', 'new social movements', the 'limits of social discipline' (Peukert, 1986; Arrighi et al., 1986; Offe, 1985; Hornstein, 1984): because people are never absorbed into the determination of the 'character mask' as the personification of economic relations and the form and content of the social praxis underlying changes in the status quo are produced at the same time, albeit with varying possibilities.

Precisely at this point (which links individual educational and world history), we see the significance of Western Marxism's analyses. It opened up Marx's concept of capital to its underlying historical movements, overcoming the limitations of the current critique of political economy. Thus the capitalist social formation enjoyed priority. A conception of production such as 'production of people by themselves, through their many-sided endeavors in the course of history' (Lefebvre, 1975, pp. 114-5) is common to these approaches. It opens up a perspective which can approach stages in the course of history as products of historical-social praxis, making it possible to relate questions of the potential for change in a social totality to developmental perspectives of labor's social organization and how society members interact.

The 'economy' can be regarded as a determining social development as the 'basis' and axis of society and its history without lapsing into determinism. The reference to the Marxist production paradigm emphasizes the mediation between the practical relation of humans to nature and the historically changing production of human relationships. In this sense too, we can refer to one of Markus's arguments which examines the strong explorative content of the Heydornian dialectic of educational and social history and poses a supposedly historical-philosophical bias, a 'hermetic historical dialectic'. Markus pointed out that in the seemingly paradoxical conception of the dichotomous categories of Marx's social theory (such as forces of production, social form, use-exchange value), it is possible to make a conceptual distinction within given social objectivity, representing it as the total 'product' of earlier generations, which is conceived simultaneously as human 'objectification' and social 'materialization' (Markus, 1986, p. 60).

If the constitutive conditions of individual and society are thus interrelated, for Marx, 'the dialectic of forces of production and consciousness is first exposed . . . this remains the starting point for every future theory of emancipation' (Heydorn 1979, p. 165). But it remains necessary to provide clues, absent in Marx, toward real steps in 'human history'; this corresponds with a further development of Marxism in the field of educational theory and simultaneously represents Heydorn's self-understanding.

This is also the systematic locus of educational thought based on social critique, without remaining in an abstract negativism. In the context of an analysis of determination, the critique of the social-historically (pre-)existing as the expression of human prehistory connects with the explication of human potentiality in relation to the question of the subject. The line of criticism follows the materialistically applied *topos* of the realization of reason, the identification of deficient social relationships, the perspective of a possible transcendence of this deficiency. The portrayal of social relations is simultaneously their critique. If historical development is determined as a situation of 'interdependence' (Heydorn, 1979, pp. 31, 115, 300, 335; 1980a, p. 99; 1980d, p. 262), the problem of a possible form of human development which can guarantee freedom becomes decisive (Heydorn, 1980a, p. 178). This allows for examining the development of relations between the sexes and between women's issues and educational theory (Heydorn, 1979, p. 332; 1980a, p. 107).

Education is thus the 'actualization of potential', so humans can become 'their own agents' (Heydorn, 1980a, p. 164). In defense of the project of enlightenment (Sünker, 1993, 1994a), the underlying idea is that the original approach of the idea of education, however, can be seen as a communication by human beings about their own freedom, as an attempt to bring an end to their being at the mercy of violence (Heydorn, 1979, p. 32).

What is decisive for rejecting metaphysical or life-philosophically oriented activist efforts remains reality, possibility, and utopia in Heydorn's assessment that 'human self-determination is the realization of the humanist dream and the dialectical/rational correlate of evolution' (Heydorn, 1979, p. 322). He also said that 'spontaneity requires constant referral to controlled reflection in order to take shape; but this shape draws on it for nourishment, and on its indication towards a future of liberated, redeemed, reconciled labor, of a humanity not threatened by its own history' (Heydorn, 1980b, p. 298). Possibility corresponds with a particular gestalt of spontaneity.

He captured this relationship and the essence of his theory and analysis by saying 'education is rationally mediated spontaneity' (Heydorn, 1979, p. 24). This argument allowed him to indicate both the 'playing field' of human praxis and the concrete historical conditions of the realization of this praxis (Adorno, 1966, pp. 226-7; Lefebvre, 1975, p. 337; 1977, p. III 174).

Analyzing reform pedagogy, he criticized the voluntarism emerging from belief in a presocial realm because speaking of 'nature' ends up in naturalism. The determination of human beings does not transcend a 'pure' spontaneity, but lies within the scope of 'defective life'. What Lefebvre regarded as the 'use of utopia as a method for exploring the possible' (Lefebvre, 1978, p. 115), which he also understood within the framework of a critique of the classical operations of proof (induction and deduction), with the concept 'transduction' showing the overlaps between the materialist theory of everyday life and education. Both aim to show the possibilities of realizing what in the project of the 'total person' forms an outline and awaits realization in the context of individual-social praxis (Heydorn, 1979, p. 163; Lefebvre, 1977, pp. ii, 131; Sartre, 1964, pp. 76-8).

The project of the total person provides the concept of education with a 'hinge function' to mediate between world and individual educational history. As Heydorn interpreted Marx: 'idealism and materialism are therefore aspects of an incomplete reality. The primacy of education, which constantly binds theory to practice, is easily recognizable. Education is understanding reality as it is' (Heydorn, 1979, p. 139). This project is founded on historical-theoretical explication, resting on an analysis of relations between universality/species and individuality: 'liberated individuals recognize themselves as species; they are their own totality' (Heydorn, 1979, p. 140).

What Marx regarded in his analysis of capital as the 'dumb compulsion of economic relations' can only be correctly understood when one remembers that Marx conceived the real relations in 'capital' to the extent that they corresponded to his concept. So existing capitalism does not have to correspond directly with his concept, it need not be 'self-adequate', but it is a form of existence acted upon by the movement of value, which is embedded in it (Reichelt, 1970, pp. 134-5).

The contrast to an objective reading of this analysis is the praxis-philosophically founded idea of the 'reproduction of relations of production', which decodes the production of social relations and totality, mediated through praxis (Lefebvre, 1974). Marx made this perspective clear when he placed the question of the possibility of 'the subject's self-realization, concretization, thus real freedom' (Marx, 1967, p. 505) at the front of his portrayal and critique of social relations and forms of interaction. He found the basis of this perspective in the developmental tendencies of labor (Marx, pp. 203, 231, 415, 439-40). To choose between the thesis that the dominating power of capital has priority in the dumb compulsion of economic relations (Marx, pp. 545, 908) and that of the possibility of the universal development of the individual, it is necessary to explore this opposition and examine real historical developments. But in the context of species-historical thought, the dialectic of progress illuminates perspectives which transcend a capitalization of all human relations, which cannot be represented as necessary. This comes from assessing the present as the end of an epoch during which one might believe the progress of the species could be pursued through competition between individuals (that is, through autonomous development while isolated from each other). For this reason, the species must consciously achieve its social progress through empirical individuals, who form the true subject of history (Lippe, 1974, p. 60; Berman, 1988, pp. 88-98).

The educational task of the 'totality of subjectification', the 'mass liberation, which brings to fruition the universality of the species, as the paragon of all self-determination' (Heydorn, 1980b, p. 297), can only be taken seriously as a perspective when 'the relations between education and power/domination, between external determination and self-determination, particular and universal human beings' (Heydorn, 1979, p. 28; Heller, 1984) are explored in their historical dimensions, starting from the dialectic between social materiality and human self-realization (Markus, 1986, p. 60; Heydorn, 1979, pp. 153-4, 317, 51; 1980b, p. 294; 1980a, p. 122).

EDUCATION: CONCEPT AND REALITY

The explication of the relation between concept and reality as a problem of 'equivalence' can serve as a foil for a sketch of Heydorn's work with and on the concept of education. What Theunissen said in this context about the relation between Hegel and Marx also applies to Heydorn's approach: 'Although the bearer of power is no longer "spirit", it retains the structure which Hegel attributed to spirit' (Theunissen, 1978b, p. 353).

In this sense, the *leitmotif* of the classical European tradition was introduced in *Über den Widerspruch von Bildung und Herrschaft* (Heydorn, 1979). He specified how far this mode of thought can reach, emphasizing that

> Without conceptual effort, we are left only with action, leaving us no way out. It remains in the marketplace to be exploited. To determine where we are we have to catch up with the whole of history; there is no escape from the drudgery. The contradiction between education and domination first arises as concept, gains its abstract relation to all actualizable historical interrelationships and here too indicates a dimension of consciousness with which it transcends its own history (Heydorn, 1979, p. 8).

The historical educational process can be understood in relation to the difference between historically achieved advancements in human emancipation and the real state of affairs. Consequently, we must investigate the foundations of the concept of education, the contradictions built into and developing from it, the contradiction between education and domination. Using the techniques of a critique of ideology and historical analysis, Heydorn explored the forms of educational thought and practices, drawing on the contradiction between education and domination. The contradiction he saw in the concept of education unfolds historically as the dialectic of the institutionalization of education, moving between domination and liberation. He interpreted this in relation to the historical stages in societal forms, human praxis, and development of reason as a process of human self-discovery.

To illuminate the systematic historical content of the concept of education, Heydorn surrounded it with colorful expressions, such as 'humans catching up with themselves', the 'question of human whereabouts' (Heydorn, 1979, pp. 15, 117); as 'humans thinking about themselves' (Heydorn, 1979, pp. 19, 300; 1980a, p. 179); as 'progressively liberating people to become themselves' (Heydorn, 1980b, p. 301). As a process of 'self-discovery' (1980a, p. 97), it is based on processes of 'self-help' (Heydorn, 1980b, p. 179; 1979, pp. 316, 323). 'This is its anticipatory character, which takes people beyond their self-imposed limits' (Heydorn, 1980a, p. 179).

The 'immanent tension' in the concept of education makes it the 'excavation of people and thus a challenge to reality' (Heydorn, 1980a, p. 18), so that education constitutes 'the question of the liquidation of power' (Heydorn, 1980a, p. 337). The account which emerges from this analysis of the historical process in terms of contradiction 'must reveal the contradiction, must turn education as a form of domination against itself; that era has come to an end' (Heydorn, 1980a, p. 337.) And again, 'education is not an independent revolutionary movement, it can only be so in connection with the whole movement of history' (Heydorn, 1980a, p. 100). To understand the presupposition underlying this requires knowledge of both individual and social constitutive conditions so that their necessary historical acquisition is placed at the origin of educational thought.

The emergence of education in Greek antiquity shows that two things are inherent to it: 1) a social orientation, corresponding to the bounded task of knowledge-production, aiming at improving human talents, and 2) a quality within education itself, turning these social relations around. Freedom is won from determination (Heydorn, 1979, pp. 12-3). Hegel anticipated this idea in the master-slave dialectic in *Phenomenology of Mind*. In contrast to the image of education as the 'prison of history' (Heydorn, 1979, p. 9), 'education becomes the agent of historical development, humanity finally becomes free through education, in an unintentional process' (Heydorn, 1979, p. 45).

In the Socratic maieutic, one also finds humanity approached in terms of its potential and as a reference to the connection between the form and the method of reason, which has its focus in its revelatory character in relation to society and the reason residing within human beings.

The progressive institutionalization of education in history, from the Greek Enlightenment, expressed this contradictory relation. Heydorn analyzed them on the basis of general social relationships. The polarity of emancipation and domination developed in various historical situations and epochs in differing degrees of intensity and were always related to social forms of interaction and praxis (Heydorn, 1979, pp. 36-7, 51, 73, 88, 172, 275, 316-7). A significant strength of the concept of education can be illustrated via bourgeois society, which advanced important reflections on the possibility and necessity of becoming a subject. This epoch of social interdependence and imprisonment also presented a specific solution for the relation between education and politics, the potential scope of the concept of education. Subjectivity as a generalizing principle and as the basis for a socially oriented capacity for action was an important result of the success of the principles of social change accompanying the dissolution of feudalism's frozen relations.

Heydorn's analysis of the development of neo-humanism showed the range and perspective of Humboldt's reflections, which were oriented toward equality and individuality and bore witness to the reflexive progressiveness of early bourgeois theory even though it did not yet correspond to either social conditions or individual existence. This theory rested on an opposition between social relations and the subjects who seek to transcend them. The critique of utilitarianism was based on a conception of a mediating relation among freedom, self-determination, and versatility. It showed insight into the consequences of the capitalization of society. This led Humboldt to assume a constitutive distinction between politics and pedagogy; he distinguished education from social reality because, in order to avoid existing and acting in a deluded way, the concern became 'to rescue a haven, however threatened, for humanity (Heydorn, 1979, p. 117; Heydorn, 1980d; Hohendahl, 1985). The historical failure of Humboldt's position was manifested in the fact that the demand for mass education confronted an historical process where education was turned into its opposite: socialization.

Within the 'dialectic of institutionalized education and human liberation' (Heydorn, 1979, p. 18), those who analyzed the conditions of this emancipatory process and conceptualized its promotion embodied the rise of a form of educational thought associated with Socrates, Comenius, Humboldt, Kant, Hegel, Follen, and Marx. I refer here to the work of Werner (1969; Heydorn, 1969, pp. 53-73) and Heydorn's depiction of him as a student with democratic ideas. He fought against reactionary forces in the first third part of the 19th century. Forced into exile, he lived and died in the US. With German idealism and Marxist theory, 'the history of the productive theory of education comes to a provisional conclusion' (Heydorn, 1979, p. 168).

A decline followed. Without dissolving relations of domination, the stage of development reached by the species could only move toward 'unconsciousness', which often took the form of an ideology of identity, a denial of social relations of mediation, such as the recourse to mystical ideas about 'nature'. Heydorn sketched the path of the decline from 'Caliban's entrance' to the present, without naturalizing this process. There are a few exceptions, notably Leonard Nelson and Otto Rühle.

This diagnosis of the historical development led Heydorn to the thesis of the necessary nature of the formation of consciousness, which is also essentially a historical consciousness. The generation of knowledge constitutes an attempt to struggle against the dominant relations of power because in bourgeois society, these rest on reified relations, the dominance of the abstract over the concrete (Heydorn, 1979, pp. 34, 321). It also provides the preconditions for transcending the divisions within the concept of education, which Heydorn saw in Spranger: 'For years the Privy Councillor Spranger ruled: he castrated Pestalozzi for the children of poor but respectable parents, he castrated Humboldt for the "Talmi-elite"' (Heydorn, 1979, p. 215). Under the present social historical conditions, this means: 'The new revolutionary subject, this is all that matters, is a knowing subject' (Heydorn, 1979, p. 334), so that education, as the question of the dissolution of power, is a 'revolution in consciousness' (Heydorn, 1979, p. 337). Heydorn even closed one essay with the words 'Consciousness is everything' (Heydorn, 1980b, p. 301). Heydorn critiqued the cultured middle classes and technocracy, the 'degeneration of neo-humanism into dandyism', and the 'transition from educated individuals to experts' (Heydorn, 1979, p. 171). To clarify the background to these arguments and fend off the reproach of idealist speculation, it is useful to refer to the intellectual context (the philosophy of praxis and the critique of objectivism) within which Heydorn worked and within which the possibility of the constitution of the subject is generally associated with the achievements of consciousness. Exemplary here is Adorno's negative dialectics: 'The pre-philosophical consciousness is located this side of the alternative; to a subject that acts naively and opposes itself to its environment, its own conditioning is opaque. To control this conditioning, consciousness must render it transparent' (Adorno, 1973, p. 220 [translation modified]; Bourdieu, 1987, p. 237).

This is related to the fact that the transcendence of the distinction between socialization and education, between domination and emancipation, also takes place in the empirical form of the individual via consciousness in shedding that which is individually or socially made objectivize, especially 'species-relevant objectification for itself' (Heller, 1984). Particularly the capacity, linked with the achievements of consciousness, especially the development of language (Heydorn, 1979, p. 182), to gain distance from the pre-existing provides the foundation for developing the potential for resistance against the status quo.

Because Heydorn repeatedly highlighted the connection between education and labor and analyzed the development of the social forces of production of labor, he regarded the achievements of consciousness as decisive. We should also consider the significance of educational theory as the foundation for pedagogy: 'The philosophy of education sees itself as a unity of theory and praxis; consciousness in isolation remains powerless, and praxis in isolation falls into ruin' (Heydorn, 1979, p. 152).

Isolation from consciousness or praxis can only be overcome when the potential for resistance is revealed in realization and action. This resistance stems from social historical conditions and individual education processes. Beneath is buried the 'rational structure of what technological society is concerned with', which Heydorn (1980a, p. 177; 1979, pp. 28, 312) saw representing the maturity of conditions for human emancipation, concluding 'that the elements of education which are able to overcome their disunity, rooted in class history, can become universal in a liberated species' (Heydorn, 1980b, p. 291). But liberation of consciousness through education raises the problem 'of how the deficit of consciousness, in comparison to material production, which is destroying humanity, can be transcended' (Heydorn, 1980a, p. 164; 1980b, p. 283; 1980c, p. 123; Kilian, 1971). Heydorn's account parallels the more recent discussions in industrial sociology (Kern and Schumann, 1984). Even when the growing maturity of conditions conflicts with strategies for the 'paralysis of consciousness', there remains the possibility of the alliance 'of education and revolution' (Heydorn, 1979, p. 331), the 'strategy and technique of human liberation through education, the enabling of the reason residing within it' (Heydorn, 1979, p. 311).

In this reconstruction of the history of society and education as well as educational thought, Heydorn also developed the consequences of Hegel's key definition of the mediation between the constitution of the subject and education, developing its systematic character. As he said, 'with the process of education the subject escapes its imprisonment within nature' (Heydorn, 1980e, p. 256), unburdens itself, making it possible to argue that humans are only potential subjects, 'only to be actualized as a result of education' (Koneffke, 1986, p. 72). However, Adorno's critique of this Hegelian definition as the incarnation of 'birch rod pedagogy' in which 'the abused are not educated but repressed, rebarbarized' (Adorno, 1973, pp. 336, 337) points to the underlying problem of the mediation between social and educational theory. A demonstration of the consequences for the form and content of the individual's existence includes the explication of the connection between 'self-realization and universality' (Theunissen, 1981, 1982). In the framework of an educational theory which critiques society, this includes total rejection of arguments following a logic of identity philosophy, where the particular/individual is sacrificed to the abstract generality (Adorno, 1966, p. 321; Theunissen, 1982, 1978a). For Heydorn, education becomes 'the defense of individual humans as humanity. . . . Education means the comprehensive empirical realization of humans as a species, whose potential it experiences in others' (Heydorn, 1979, p. 25).

The emphasis on 'others' is based on data on social conditions as well as insight into the maieutic character of educational processes. The requirements arising from the dialogical character of this process have consequences for the work of teachers. Here, Heydorn develops one of the paradoxes of pedagogical action which Nelson outlined as follows: 'If the goal of education is rational self-determination (that is, a situation in which people are not determined by external influences, but judge and act more on the basis of their own understanding), the questions arises, how is it possible to determine people through external influences so that they are not determined by external influences' (Nelson, 1948, p. 30). Heydorn (1979, p. 318) insisted that education involves effort and toil and established that current social institutions and emancipation 'find themselves in irreconcilable opposition' (Heydorn, 1979, p. 317).) In this regard, we may find an analysis of the relationship between processes of institutionalization and their social foundations from a social-philosophical perspective in the related work of Theunissen (1978a, p. 473) and Adorno (1966, p. 329).

CONCLUSION

Teachers who are self-aware take on an *avant garde* function: recalling the Socratic position and tradition, which refers to the significance of the personal dimension of and in educational processes, the task for teachers became, in a formulation reminiscent of Old Testament prophets: 'It articulates consciousness, helps it out of its powerlessness, it becomes the guide through the desert country' (Heydorn, 1979, p. 318; 1980c, pp. 118-9). In a complementary way, Heydorn referred to Amos Comenius, whose lecture on *lumen naturale* was a decisive model for socially critical educational thought pursuing universal human emancipation: 'Education is "educatio", leading forth' (Heydorn, 1979, p. 337). Thus, both the concept and reality of education arrive at their 'correspondence'.

ACKNOWLEDGMENT

Robert van Krieken translated this piece from German to English.

Part IV

Economics and Education

9 Educational Politics, Division of Labor, and Emancipation

Peter Leisink

ABSTRACT

Recent educational policies in the Netherlands are not easy to evaluate. They can neither be interpreted exclusively as the straightforward reproduction of social inequality, nor as policies supporting the emancipation of citizens who have a tenuous position in the labor market. We can illustrate this ambiguity using a telling example. During the 1970s, social democratic politicians and researchers committed to comprehensive education saw their ideals defeated. Christian Democrats' and Conservatives' opposition was mainly responsible for this; but, by the mid-1980s, the coalition government of Christian Democrats and Conservatives accepted certain educational reform proposals which the Scientific Council for Government Policy had elaborated along the lines of a comprehensive system. Did the government's stand mean a political conversion? Were the original goals of reducing social inequality through comprehensive education unrecognizably substituted for broadly-based training as industry required? Were these goals compatible to some extent? Answering such questions and critically examining educational policies demands an analysis of labor market developments. Any assessment of opportunities to reduce social inequality through education that ignores the relationship between education and the economic and political system will be purely idealistic. On one hand, the function of the educational system may be understood as the answer to the needs of a capitalist economy for qualified workers. On the other, education has also contributed undeniably to the emancipation and social participation of citizens in the 20th century. To evaluate how and the extent to which education performed these functions, we must consider this broader social and economic context.

This chapter reviews the two faces of educational policies in the Netherlands. This includes a brief sketch of recent labor market trends and the main educational policy lines. Then, we attempt to determine to what extent the state's educational policy offers chances for emancipation. The chapter then concludes with observations about our research needs and agenda.

LABOR MARKET TRENDS

During the first half of the 1980s, unemployment rose (peaking at 12 per cent in 1983) in the Netherlands; it has slowly decreased (to approximately 7.5 per cent) since then. Almost all OECD countries faced a similar trend, but the

Netherlands were in the category with the highest unemployment percentage (OECD, 1989 and 1991). Reduced unemployment in the Netherlands is partly due to more service sector jobs (many of them low-paid and flexible) (Elfring and Kloosterman, 1989) and partly to a change in the definition of 'labor force'. For instance, workers over the age of 57 are no longer counted as members of the labor force. In addition, official data do not adequately represent reality. For instance, only some 30 per cent of all women seeking jobs are officially registered at employment agencies (SZW, 1991a).

Unemployment reflects the parameters of social inequality by gender, ethnic origin, and educational level. Only 55 per cent of all women (versus 81 per cent of men) have a paid job. This is one of the lowest rates in the OECD countries (SZW, 1991a). Unemployment among ethnic workers is about 20 per cent (three times higher than workers of Dutch origin) since the early 1980s (Reubsaet, 1990). In large cities, such as Amsterdam and Rotterdam, 40 to 50 per cent of the Turkish and Moroccan workers are unemployed (Dercksen, van Luijk, den Hoed, 1990). To some extent, this may be explained by their relatively lower educational levels. Yet, among higher skilled immigrant workers, unemployment is not much lower. Discrimination against immigrant workers is evident through requirements that do not affect job performance (Kruyt and Fleuren, 1990; van Beek and van Praag, 1992).

The labor market position of low-skilled workers is very weak. One-third of all unemployed have only had primary education without any vocational training. In general, high unemployment rates and low educational levels are significantly correlated (OSA, 1990; SZW, 1991b). Chances of finding a job are small for low-skilled unemployed. This is caused not only by the overall shortage of jobs, but also by changes in the qualitative structure of employment. Since the late 1970s, the average qualification level for jobs has risen, partly because there are significantly fewer unskilled and low-skilled manual jobs, and partly through an overall increase in high-skilled manual and white collar jobs (Huijgen, 1989). These changes are the effect of technological innovation and economic restructuring, which turned all Western European countries into postindustrial economies (Ferner and Hyman, 1992).

Because of technological innovation, much unskilled and low-skilled manual work has disappeared and the newly created low-skilled service-sector jobs hardly match the number of workers who lost their manufacturing jobs. Also, in manufacturing and core sectors (such as the chemical and automobile industries), there is a trend to upgrade jobs (Kern and Schumann, 1984). Although new production concepts are not being introduced as quickly as Kern and Schumann (Schumann et al., 1988) originally assumed, there is a growing trend in job redesign, including job enrichment and teamwork (under headings such as lean production, Toyotaism, and Total Quality Management). Upgrading jobs is accompanied by higher skill requirements, so consequently, unskilled and low-skilled unemployed in these industries have few job prospects. Management in other industrial sectors continue to organize work using Tayloristic principles, offering low-skilled and low-paid jobs (Wood, 1989). However, forecasts for France, Germany, and the Netherlands predict that demand will decrease for unskilled workers, remain steady for skilled workers, and increase for technicians (Gordon et al., 1994).

These changes and continuities together have segmented industries and the labor market. For instance, in the financial service sector, high pay, job security, and career opportunities are prevalent; in the catering sector, low pay, no job security, and few career chances are dominant (Kloosterman and Elfring, 1991). Apart from this trend at the industrial level, there is also a tendency of segmentation at the company level. This process is well documented for the banking sector in the Netherlands, where temporary contractors (mostly female) performed data entry and other low-skilled administrative jobs before they were completely automated (Tijdens, 1989). Through this and other flexible employment (such as subcontracting), there is now a clear distinction between core and peripheral workers, much the same as Atkinson (1985) reported for Britain. Today, at least one-third of all employees in the Netherlands have some sort of flexible employment contract (Kloosterman and Elfring, 1991, p. 163). Many have a position at the periphery of the labor market. Women are overrepresented among these flexible workers, but a minority of them actually prefer it (Trommel, 1987).

To what extent this labor market segmentation has become fixed is not clear. Some (particularly the younger) temporary workers eventually get a permanent job. At the same time, it appears that core jobs (such as computer consultant and nurse) become externalized (Mok, 1994). This seems to indicate a two-way flow between core and periphery. All the same, the labor market position of unskilled and low-skilled workers is weak.

These labor market changes impact on the functions (such as qualification) of the educational system (Fend, 1974; Watts, 1984). Qualifications are the competencies or skills which enable a person to carry out a particular job.

Specific skill requirements for a job help employers select the best person. However, the qualification levels of the labor force have increased far more than the skill levels of jobs. Therefore, many workers cannot fully use their skills on the job. Many workers can actually perform a higher skilled job. One consequence of this mismatch is underutilizing skills, another is displacing low-skilled workers (Huijgen, 1989). Given the large supply of skilled workers, employers can set higher job requirements than necessary. Higher skilled applicants appear to be recruited because employers think they will sooner get used to the work and be more flexible in coping with future changes (Coenen and van de Winkel, 1988; Scholtz, 1987). However, the result is a downward displacement of workers, with low-skilled workers being banned down the social ladder or pushed into unemployment.

Employers demand other sorts of competencies in addition to higher educational qualifications. Perseverance, capacity for hard work, or loyalty are now as important as cognitive abilities (Huijgen, 1989). This has also affected the nature of education. The humanistic goals (personal development and social interaction skills) must compete with work-oriented ones for a place on the educational agenda. Watts saw similar evidence in Ireland and Britain, where 'Intrinsic educational values are subordinated to the extrinsic need to provide tickets to employment' (Watts, 1984, p. 8).

This analysis of labor market developments illustrates that competition has increased and that possessing cultural capital is an essential resource. The labor market may be regarded as an arena (van Hoof, 1987). On the one hand, there are core jobs. Highly skilled employees occupy them and are tied to the company which provides attractive employment conditions, training, and career opportunities because these workers have valuable skills. On the other, employees with medium level educational qualifications are frequently doing low-skilled jobs. Low-skilled workers fear displacement and expulsion from the labor market because they have no such guarantees. This segmentation is significantly related to educational qualifications, but it also has a gender and ethnic dimension. Women (especially those who want to re-enter the labor market after raising their children) and workers of minority or non-Dutch ethnic origin suffer disproportionate unemployment levels and must accept jobs at the periphery of the labor market. As a result of these trends, social inequality has increased in the Netherlands since the mid-1980s (SCP, 1992).

CHANGES IN EDUCATIONAL POLICY

The state has intervened in the educational system for some time. Vocational education and training has undergone fundamental changes because employers claimed it was committed to personal development, not preparation for work (Schouten, 1977). General secondary education is also changing.

During the 1980s, vocational education and training (mainly publicly funded and provided through state schools) was geared more directly to industry's needs. Mr. Wagner (a former Shell Oil Company chief executive) chaired an advisory committee which set the pace. As a result, the government recognized that industry, the educational system, and the state are jointly responsible for vocational education and training. Industry was invited to become more involved in educational policy through sectoral platforms for regular consultation between schools and representatives of employer associations. Employers were responsible for providing information about the employment structure and for supplying job profiles. By reducing central regulation or even deregulation, the state gave schools more scope to translate this information into job training profiles. Since August 1993, all curricula for secondary vocational education have been determined in this way.

Also, the structure of secondary vocational education and training was reorganized. The general move toward comprehensive education which swept through Europe during the 1960s did not alter the Dutch educational system.

Secondary education was still highly segmented and did not keep pace with industrial changes which required broad-based training. In 1986, the government reorganized secondary vocational training. The 350 upper secondary vocational training colleges were reduced to 140, turning them into multisectoral colleges. In addition to the traditional four-year course for students with a lower secondary vocational or general certificate, these colleges offer two-year courses for low achievers, without entry requirements. This sprang from concern about high drop-out rates (from 10 per cent in lower secondary to 40 per cent in upper secondary vocational education) which resulted in an estimated 40 per cent of school leavers entering the labor market without a minimum qualification level (Gordon et al., 1994, pp. 58-60).

One other structural change is still being debated. This concerns combining on-the-job and off-the-job training in all vocational education programs. Now, this apprenticeship approach exists at the lower and upper secondary levels alongside the multisectoral vocational colleges which offer full-time training with no more than some sort of practical placement.

The government hopes these changes will make vocational education more flexible. New multisectoral colleges should react more quickly and effectively to labor market changes and new job requirements resulting from technological innovation. To strengthen the labor market orientation of the vocational training colleges, the government lets them teach courses commissioned and funded by private industry. This enhances the schools' labor market orientation, uses their facilities, and generates more resources.

General secondary education is also being reformed. Proposals to form comprehensive schools, which were instituted throughout Europe during the 1960s (Watts, 1984), were unsuccessful in the Netherlands because of severe political divisions. The deadlock lasted until 1986 when the Scientific Council for Government Policy published a report (WRR, 1986) which focused on educational objectives. Comprehensive schooling was regarded as the common and general intellectual, cultural, and social development of children as a basis for further personal development. This should be conducive both to functioning socially as a member of society and making a conscious choice for further education and a career. These educational objectives were operationalized in a set of compulsory (and some optional) subjects for all students.

The Christian Democrat and Conservative government adopted these proposals partly because the segmented school system did not facilitate transfers from one track to another. The reform Parliament adopted in 1992 will establish a common curriculum for lower secondary vocational and general education. This common curriculum consists of 15 compulsory subjects (including foreign languages, mathematics, physics, information science, as well as music, visual arts, and caring), requiring 25 teaching hours per week out of a total of 32. Depending on the number and level of subject certificates, students may progress to either upper secondary vocational or upper general education. By postponing the final choice, more students may be able to proceed to upper secondary vocational education, which was too difficult for most lower secondary vocational students in the old segmented system. To keep these students in a comprehensive curriculum with many theoretical subjects, they may take practical subjects after two years, even before completing the compulsory subjects.

The optional courses are very important from the point of view of the history of education in the Netherlands. They may be used for religious training so that the constitutionally protected freedom of education is respected. All religious 'pillars' may establish schools and receive state funds, the same as the public schools. This freedom of education is the result of the 19th century 'religious wars' which resulted in a compromise which pacified the various religious pillars (Lijphart, 1968). Optional courses were also tactically important because they may be used for subjects like Greek and Latin. This prevented grammar schools from opposing the introduction of a sort of comprehensive system as they did in the 1970s.

Students progressing from the comprehensive phase to upper secondary general education will find a substantially reorganized curriculum. This reform is based on the state-commissioned report of an advisory committee, chaired by Mr. Rauwenhoff, a former member of the Board of Directors of Philips. The Interim Advisory Committee on Education and the Labor Market (1990) argued that changes in the economy (such as shorter product life spans and just-in-time production) as well as cultural and demographic changes (individualization, declining birth rates, aging population) demand that people be more flexible. In general, people should be prepared to invest in lifelong training. More specifically, several proposals encouraged a better match between education and labor. Recommendations for secondary general education curriculum included broadening subjects and compelling students to take one of four clusters rather than being free to select their own. These clusters are 'care', 'engineering', 'economy and society', and 'culture'. The government hopes that these clusters will give students a sufficiently broad base before they enter higher education.

These educational policy changes were widely discussed. The government's aims were to improve the match between education and work, reduce the drop-out rate, shorten the time spent looking for employment, make public expenditure cost-effective, and reduce inequality in educational participation which children from various social classes experienced. Against this background, it will be interesting to see to what extent educational policies may be evaluated positively as offering new chances for emancipation.

EDUCATIONAL POLICY, SOCIAL INEQUALITY AND EMANCIPATION

Since the 1970s, much research has been done on the relationship between education and social inequality. We understand more about the mechanisms behind reproducing social inequality. But simultaneously, optimism about the chances for reducing it through education has decreased. With this research in mind, we evaluated educational policies in the Netherlands and focused on two points. First, we examined the extent to which education fulfils its functions and the impact of its enhanced labor market function on social inequality. Second, we dealt with the organization and function of the educational system and the extent to which social inequality is reproduced in it.

The overall aim of government policy is to improve the educational system's labor market orientation and to match education and labor. Symbolically, both advisory committees had former captains of industry as chairpersons despite a long-standing tradition that the state is the main provider of education in the Netherlands.

The goal of catering to industry's needs for more highly qualified workers is the basis of reforms in secondary education. The comprehensive curriculum during the introductory phase (covering two years) of lower secondary education aims to raise educational qualifications for as many pupils as possible. Also the government's decision to commit itself to offering every pupil the right to obtain skilled worker qualifications reflects awareness of changes in employment's qualitative structure. To meet industry's demand for broader qualifications, the government reorganized vocational education through multisectoral colleges and curriculum reform in terms of broadly defined clusters of subjects. They also introduced contract teaching.

Even more important than these changes is the fact that the government sees the responsibility for vocational education and training as a joint effort of industry, state, and schools. Through deregulation, the state has offered industry more scope for steering training profiles and qualification standards.

Obviously, education's function to provide modern capitalism with qualified workers is dominant in state policy (Bowles and Gintis, 1976). Nevertheless, Dutch governments insist that education is geared to preparing citizens for work as well as for personal development and social participation (Ministry of Education and Science, 1991, pp. 87-8). Are these policy declarations merely rhetoric and ideology? Let's look at some considerations.

The dominant function of supplying industry with qualified workers does not override the other functions of education. In the comprehensive curriculum of lower secondary education, these are evident in such subjects as history, music, visual arts, and caring. The personal and social development function might even have a greater impact if all subjects (including 'hard' science, such as physics) would be taught with the goals of preparing people for the labor market and developing their personalities and social skills. A subject such as physics has such personal aspects and implications, but conveying that lesson demands a different approach from the traditional one based on the division of theoretical and practical subjects or the division of functional 'hard' and formative 'soft' subjects. On the other hand, the vocational education curriculum poses a real threat to education's formative function. Deregulation and government cuts combined with employers' strong influence on drawing up training profiles through the sectoral consultation platforms may seriously affect the 'soft' subjects or even eliminate them.

Also consider the importance of labor participation as a condition for (and primary means of) personal development and social participation (Coenen and Leisink, 1993). Since the late 1980s, there has been a normative reappraisal of work in this respect (WRR, 1990). Several research projects demonstrated that most unemployed want to return to employment, although work is no longer exclusively associated with paid jobs, but may also include state-sponsored 'additional' jobs (Kroft et al., 1989; van Berkel and Hindriks, 1991). During the economic crisis of the 1980s and early 1990s, severe cuts in welfare were made and modern poverty appeared (Engbersen, 1993). This situation caused a renewed interest in the concept of citizenship and the importance of labor participation as a vital part of social citizenship rights. The importance of a labor-market-oriented educational policy cannot be denied because labor participation is a key issue in the subjective appreciation of the unemployed and is regarded as a condition for, and vital element in, personal development and social participation.

To what extent does education contribute to reducing social inequality? The increasing significance of the labor market function of education implies that developments in the labor market more than ever determine the answer to this question. However, these developments do not suggest a reduction in social inequality. New production concepts only offer better quality work to a minority of highly skilled workers. Displacement and exclusion in the labor market hits hardest women, workers of minority ethnic origin, and low-skilled and unskilled workers. Personnel management appears to have a similar sort of segmentation (Williamson, 1981). For instance, companies spend increasing amounts on training their workers, but higher skilled and young employees benefit from these investments, while low-skilled and older ones tend to be excluded (Interim Advisory Committee on Education and Labor Market, 1990, pp. 25-6, 83). In sum, labor market developments do not appear to indicate a reduction in social inequality. Therefore, trying to match education and labor does not result in education's indirect contribution to reducing social inequality through labor market developments.

Since segmentation in the labor market is increasingly taking place on the basis of educational qualifications (credentialism), the relevant question is: To what extent does the educational system reproduce social inequality using the access which various social categories have as the unit of measure?

Unequal participation in education in terms of class, gender, and ethnic origin has not diminished in the Netherlands since the 1980s. Only 12 per cent of the children from working class families take upper secondary general education versus 46 per cent of children from upper class families. To a large extent, this is a result of children's performance differences at the end of primary school. This, in turn, is strongly correlated with their parents' educational levels. But this is not the only cause. Restricting the analysis to children with the same level of performance at the end of primary school, it appears that those from upper classes often opt for a higher type of education than those from the lower classes (SCP, 1990, p. 214). Turkish and Moroccan children mainly take lower secondary vocational training, which appears to be related to their parents' educational levels and their Dutch language proficiency (SCP, 1990, p. 216). Among pupils who leave secondary education without any certificate, working class children, immigrant families, and girls are overrepresented (Ministry of Education and Science, 1991).

Recognizing that a segmented educational system reproduces social inequality dates back to the 1970s (van Kemenade, 1981). Nevertheless, it was politically impossible to transcend these older institutional divisions in the Dutch educational system. Then, the choice for a particular type of education could no longer be postponed. Therefore, the introduction of a comprehensive curriculum in lower secondary education is a political breakthrough. It remains to be seen whether it will really reduce social inequality, given the institutional layout and the approach to comprehensive education.

Concentrating on the goals of comprehensive education could overcome the political deadlock at the expense of the institutional structure. But introducing comprehensive education into a formerly segmented school system seems bound for defeat if the early selection of children is based on social class. If schools are not physically integrated, working class children will continue to register at schools which formerly provided lower secondary vocational training and upper class children will attend former grammar schools. This now happens because the government has not made the actual fusion of secondary schools compulsory. The cultural dimension of reproducing social inequality (analyzed by Bourdieu and Passeron, 1977), will continue through the cultural differences between the social classes which manifest themselves in the registration at different schools.

In addition, it is hard to imagine that a school which formerly taught lower secondary vocational training will be able to teach the comprehensive curriculum at the same level as the former grammar school. This difference will have consequences for pupils' intellectual, cultural, and social development and their access to different types of upper secondary education.

Even if integrated comprehensive schools would come about voluntarily (which is happening for financial reasons), the cultural effect of social inequality must still be considered. The comprehensive curriculum's compulsory subjects are generally theoretical ones. Partly because of this, the amalgamation of different schools is not equal. In many respects, the former schools for lower secondary vocational training are inferior vis-à-vis those for secondary general education. The former have fewer pupils, fewer qualified teachers, and less social status. To understand this status difference, consider the low respect which practical knowledge commands in our societies compared to theoretical and manual work compared to mental (Meijers, 1983).

Under such circumstances, founding large colleges for comprehensive education implies that former schools for upper secondary general education (whose values and culture reflect the middle and upper classes) will play a dominant role. If this process occurs in the late 1990s, comprehensive schools will probably reproduce and enhance social inequality rather than reduce it.

Based on this unbalanced implementation of comprehensive education, cultural exclusion as a mechanism for reproducing social inequality would affect children from working class and immigrant families even more strongly than now (Willis, 1977). These pupils used to take lower secondary vocational training, often requiring an extra year to prepare for upper secondary vocational education. These pupils may not be able to master the comprehensive curriculum subjects. If the hours for optional subjects were used to learn more about the compulsory subjects, it would affect the practical subjects which are very important to motivate these pupils to complete the comprehensive curriculum. Paradoxically, holding on to the compulsory subjects of the comprehensive curriculum will demotivate these pupils and result in a greater drop-out rate (which the government wants to reduce), whereas using the optionals for practical subjects will probably result in many of these pupils not completing the compulsory subjects. If the latter choice were to be made, this would result in an early selection of pupils rather than its postponement or the reduction of social barriers which it is hoped this delay will produce.

The potential cultural effects of social inequality may be neglected due to the lack of official interest in the pedagogical aspects of comprehensive education. There is little interest in the relationship between theory and practice in teaching. For instance, in lower secondary vocational training, teachers seldom develop theoretical insights based on practical problems from everyday life. Also, individual counseling of pupils is missing. But these elements are very important to pupils who can hardly master lower secondary vocational training if they are to succeed later in comprehensive education (Valkenburg and Coenen-Hanegraaf, 1987). The same goes for pupils from immigrant families whose language problems are not fully recognized.

Educational policies are ambivalent. On the one side, the government offers extra state facilities like kindergartens, libraries, and youth health care where many working class and immigrant families live. These facilities can detect learning handicaps early and help overcome them. Similarly, the government wants to help pupils who drop out without receiving any school certificate (Ministry of Education and Science, 1991). Alternatively, the government pays little attention to the structural and pedagogical aspects of secondary school reform although these are essential for the success of marginal pupils and their opportunity to reduce their educational disadvantages. Perhaps the social balance of power permits extra state facilities at the social system's margin rather than a fundamental reform of the educational system which may cause a structural reform in those social relationships.

CONSIDERATIONS REGARDING FUTURE RESEARCH

Many 1970s theories on Dutch education and social inequality are still relevant to assess current educational policies, but three areas need more research.

First, we should analyze the relationship between changes in the educational system and the labor market. Educational research concentrates on teacher-pupil interactions in school. But education's significance in reproducing social inequality cannot be evaluated apart from labor market changes, especially since industry's investments in education are increasing. Companies invest in their human capital via training. Analyzing labor market developments is necessary since it is the context in which education fulfils its functions. For example, the government's decision to grant every citizen the right to education up to the basic level of skilled worker qualifications might be evaluated positively as a way to reduce social inequality. But this assessment is questionable because of the displacement of (relatively) skilled workers in the labor market. Thus, if the organization of work does not change, a relative increase in minimum qualification levels may not result in people getting jobs which offer further training and promotion opportunities.

Recognizing the relationship between education and labor market is also relevant for policy makers and social organizations which want to reduce social inequality. Bowles and Gintis argue that schools legitimate inequality and restrict personal development to forms compatible with subjugating youth to authority. They conclude that more economic democracy and more equality in society will enable the educational system to assist the personal development of individuals to a greater extent (Bowles and Gintis, 1976, p. 266). This analysis shows a tendency toward economic determinism. Another conclusion may be that the fight against social inequality must occur simultaneously in education and the economy, that education system reform attempts must be linked with work organization changes. We should examine the educational curriculum from this point of view and determine what qualifications education should aspire for in modern society. Watts suggests that education should not only prepare for work, but also teach 'survival skills' (to help people to overcome unemployment), 'leisure skills', 'opportunity creation skills', and 'contextual awareness' (Watts, 1984, pp. 81-2).

The second area for more research is the starting point for organizing resistance. Willis' analysis of the reproduction of social inequality ends with a consideration of his research and its implications for practical politics. He believes that schools should act at the cultural level. Teachers may help pupils discover what their own culture tells them about their position in society (Willis, 1977, p. 186). Willis agrees with Giddens' analysis of actors' 'discursive' consciousness: awareness of the unintended consequences of past actions is a condition for preventing future ones from reproducing existing social structures (Giddens, 1984). But awareness is not enough. As Sünker (following Heydorn) observed, 'Education is not an independent revolutionary agent, it can only be this in connection with the dynamics of history. Therefore, knowledge of the conditions for the constitution of the individual and society is necessary, and political education must begin with the appropriation of this knowledge in its historical context' (Sünker, 1989, p. 462). More concrete is Willis' call to link awareness and organization: political and professional organizations are needed to effect structural changes in the long run (Willis, 1977, pp. 187-8). In this respect, teachers' unions could make demands on the organization of education and the curriculum not only for working conditions, but also the opportunities education offers pupils occupying the weakest position in society. Unfortunately, few unions will accept this point of view (Valkenburg and Coenen-Hanegraaf, 1987).

Third and finally, research should pay more attention to emancipatory education opportunities which people often create for themselves in the margins of the official school system. There are several successful initiatives of this kind in the Netherlands. For instance, the women's movement and the trade unions founded a school to train women who are unskilled, unemployed, or want to re-enter the labor market for skilled jobs (Leisink and Valkenburg, 1988). Another example is trade unions teaching immigrants about the Dutch language and society during working hours (van Berkel and de Wit, 1988). Such initiatives target groups with a weak position in the labor market. These organizations offer concrete facilities and produce results now, not in the future. We can learn much from the results of such initiatives about how the entire educational system could create emancipatory opportunities.

Politicians and researchers like to debate the shibboleths of the socialist parties and trade unions. The topics of social inequality and emancipation have always been part of their agenda, although they are not the sole caretakers of these relevant issues. Perhaps some of the perspectives outlined in this chapter will be able to win the recognition and mobilization needed to improve citizens' autonomy in determining their own lives.

NOTE

For further development of the themes discussed in this chapter, see Coenen and Leisink, eds., 1993; Leisink, van Leemput, and Vilrokx, eds., 1996; Leisink, 1996 a and b; and Leisink, in press.

10 Corporatism and Identity

Philip Wexler

ABSTRACT

There is little analytical description of the social movement in education I call 'corporatist reorganization'. Emphasis on privatization and moral attacks on 'secular humanism' captured only the most salient aspects of education's social reorganization. The 'progressive', liberal platform of educational reform and 'restructuring' represents a 'partnership' of state, business, and educational professionals to change education's infrastructure and meaning.

When a new corporatist structural reorganization and redefinition of education occurs, 'workers of the school' struggle for a socially differentiated identity. Youths' everyday social existence in school is an example of decentering, lack, and absence in postmodern discourse. Socially oriented postmodernism is about macrosocial trends like 'implosion', rather than the meaning of either poststructuralism as a theory or postmodernism as a form of life where 'the subject' acts, disappears, or is 'decentered'.

Articulations of identity in a postmodern world presume that consumption is the leading social activity. Instead, we studied everyday school life in different social strata and described an institutional postmodernism with socially differentiated 'lacks'. Youth struggle with and against these absences, trying to establish distinguishable identities, 'to become somebody'.

The long-term effect of social reorganization and institutional emptying may realize postmodern predictions about reducing autonomous spheres of social life to one dimension. 'Restructuring' will likely combine 'microflexibility' of classroom production, macrointegration of social regulation, and interlocking networks of control for discipline and legitimation.

Moral conservatism is less usable for 'jet-age' education. The need for remoralization reopens questions of meaning against the current of corporatist, performance-driven 'techniflattening' and institutional emptying and desocialization. This contradiction between 'techniperformance' cultural destruction and the need for culture is the transformative site in education.

NEW CORPORATISM IN EDUCATION

The first wave of corporatism in education combined an effort to destroy the school's civic culture of republicanism (then called 'secular humanism') with rationalization leading to both the commodification and privatization of public schooling. Rationalization was a series of business/education voluntary 'partnerships'. While the arrangements were largely local, we saw them in light of Panitch's definition of corporatism as

> . . . a political structure within advanced capitalism which integrates organized socioeconomic producer groups through a system of representation and cooperative mutual interaction at the leadership level and of mobilization and social control at the mass level (Panitch, 1977, p. 66).

The old change vocabulary emphasized educational accountability, competency, and efficiency. Now, the change language and businesses' 'adopt-a-school' trend fosters improvement via national 'new' standards ('break the mold' schools). The old mold was the 'bureaucratic' factory school. The new educational reform language shows that we moved beyond corporatist school improvement to closely link education to new modes of economic production.

The 'new American school' (steming from NASDC or separate statewide and national initiatives under the aegis of educational issues, especially standardized 'outcomes', the 'educational product' and its measurement, or 'quality control') is a 'Toyota school' (Schmoker, 1992, p.23). This 'high performance' school is run by 'new collar' leaders who 'design' 'hands-on' team-organized learning of new skills for a 'restructured' workplace.

> The failure of our industrial managers to persuade more workers to design and build quality products is no different from the failure of teachers (the managers of students) to persuade more students to do quality schoolwork (Glasser, 1992, p. 32).

There is no longer an organized public institutional mediation between education and economic production. From 'the school to work transition', to the redefinition of educational knowledge, to the student, education is to be reorganized to both mirror restructured workplaces and to allow a smoother transfer of the product from student to worker. New corporatism is simultaneously the vehicle and the expression of an increasingly elite, organized, national social movement to create a post-Fordist educational apparatus to match the economic shift to 'postindustrialism' or 'capital accumulation'.

The education language is that of restructured, post-Fordist, post-industrial work. Individual schools, systems, states, and the nation need 'vision statements'. The 'crisis of productivity' and global economic competition necessitate 'the restructured workplace' (and 'restructured school'), requiring innovative (but standardized), national, computer-networked assessment of products of 'this new model of work, organization, and management'. Educators are 'vendors of schooling as a client driven, worklife derived commodity'. Education's crisis is a 'design problem'.

There are many examples of national educational reform networks based on 'restructuring'. They differ in direction and composition from moral critiques and curriculum censorship, despite the salience of the 'moral majority' line. Public financing of private education (allowing individual 'choice') stays on the agenda along with publicity for national chains of privately owned schools. But, the trend is to restructure public schools to be like restructured workplaces: 'high performance' organizations producing measurably high quality learning. This will enable high skill jobs to be competitively accomplished by 'new collar' American workers in the global marketplace.

Corporatist social forms include elite functional representation (appearing in national educational restructuring networks) and mass mobilization. Entire 'communities' are invited to join expanded coalitions. Parents work for reform. At a 'parental involvement summit', William Rioux (Executive Director of the National Committee for Citizens in Education) said,

> For me, when 23 organizations willfully and openly acknowledge the role of parents in the academic success of their children and in the success of schools overall all, that's a benchmark (Sommerfield, 1992, p.10).

Full community mobilization to restructure public schooling to the new model is a part of education's new corporatism. Reorganizing educational control via interlocking networks may increase the centralization of the 'design' function. It also needs a more 'innovative', customized, 'flexible' social organization and school culture within the controlled design network. Even standardization is justified to provide 'flexibility'. Discussing nationally standardized testing, Marc Tucker, a 'new standards project' director, said,

> Lastly, we determined that such a system must be flexible. I have already cited one example: many exams, one standard. There is another more subtle way in which flexibility is essential . . . [T]he score depends on their cumulative accomplishments over time. . . . In the first instance we expect those tasks to be centrally designed. But over time, we want them to be largely designed by classroom teachers for their own use, in their own schools, in their own classrooms. That's flexibility. That will be a world in which the teachers have internalized the standards (Wolk, 1992, p. 4).

Lauren Rescnick, the other project director, said the new standard calls for a new type of knowledge, not 'the assembly-line version'. In another resturcturing plan, the 'New Visions Schools Project,' a former New York City Schools' Chancellor described creating a flexible, less impersonal setting in experimental theme-oriented schools (Bradley, 1992, p.5).

But proponents disagree on the content of flexible, anti-assembly-line knowledge in schools. In Maine, commission reports redefined the traditional curriculum into 'core learning' with '151 goals for student learning'. The four organizing areas of knowledge are communication, 'personal and global stewardship', reasoning and problem solving, and 'the human record' (Viadero, 1992, p. 21). The most widely discussed curriculum is the Labor Department's report of the Secretary's Commission on Achieving Necessary Skills (SCANS). The report, 'Learning a Living: A Blueprint for High Performance,' calls for a 'Toyota school' approach: teamwork, collaborative learning, and changes in teacher education and professional development. The new pedagogical skills that teachers need are:

> . . . to teach in context and to develop active, collaborative learning environments; to learn new instructional management skills and use new instructional technologies that support new ways of interacting with students; and to gain experience with the principles of high performance as applied in 'restructured' workplaces (Harp, 1992, p. 10).

The commission described necessary knowledge as the productive use of resources, interpersonal skills, information systems, and technology based on fundamental thinking skills and well-developed personal qualities. They recommend that work skills be 'translated' into the academic curriculum. This involves redefining the curriculum as high-performance, workplace-relevant skills taught in 'the context of real life situations and real problems.' Arlene Penfield (president of the National School Boards Association) dissented,

> The report, for instance, goes too far in recommending that writing be reoriented from an 'academic' to a 'real world focus'. On the other hand, Albert Shanker, President of the American Federation of Teachers, observed that the report's recommendations come 'not one moment too soon' (Harp, 1992, p. 10).

New knowledge of new corporatism is the school's formal culture (the actual culture is students' social interaction) Explanations (by Harvey, 1989; Aronowitz, 1981; Wexler, 1987) of the connection between the changing organization of production (from Fordism to flexible accumulation) and postmodern culture are paralleled by the tie between the 'restructured workplace' (flexible accumulation) and the restructured, high-performance school.

In education, new knowledge is tied to the newly restructured workplace as a 'translation' of 'real life' skills to academic curriculum. This is a shift 'from an academic to a real world focus'. But all social studies or sciences, except history (the 'human record'), are absent from such a curriculum. This absence is very important because of our findings about the altered character of the informal culture of social interaction. We found a practical deconstruction of the social. Absent from the schools' class-differentiated social text are the specific elements that constitute sociality: interaction, society, and self.

The key to new knowledge and the person it positions/constructs is not only that it directly translates restructured/flexible-accumulation work needs, but also redefines meaning and subjectivity. This redefines knowing onto the one plane of high performance. Knowledge is seen as a process of translation and standardization, with innovation and flexibility occurring within the control-structured standard. This reduces the level of knowing to 'hands on task' or to horizontal (spatial or paradigmatic) knowledge. The content and rules of relation are defined by instrumental workplace skills at the furthest point and by their own, local, task relation at the nearest. The new knowledge is a 'surfacization' of knowing, removing the cultural resources and the practice of any depth, distanced, or reflexive knowledge where 'the standard' is neither skill- nor task-related, but is autonomous, different, decontextualized, and critical. What we see in the new knowledge of schooling (its formal culture) is a concrete example of 'surfacization' that postmodernism both displays and values as the new culture. It is culture without a conscience.

I call this 'technisurfacing' to differentiate it from the consumption-oriented surfacing or decentering of postmodern culture. Furthermore, this one-dimensionalizing or desocializing of knowledge/culture is not rooted in the spectacular culture of mass consumption. Instead, it displays how the redefinition of culture is mediated institutionally between production and the educational sector. Education is not simply any institutional mediation; it is one of the primary self- or subject-formative institutions. Its 'technisurfacing' and desocialization is directly relevant for identity formation.

We studied high schools after the demise of the bureaucratic, assembly-line, Fordist school. The 'design' of the 'restructured' school is being actualized; next comes a newer remoralization. This encourages cultural reconstruction as important public/private, corporatist work. The 'new culture' (which shores up institutional articulations of the new production regime) rekindles the drive toward cultural creation. Thus, an alternative may inscribe its 'vision statement' into history. This chapter's next two sections deal with middle-run desocialization and the long-run potentially transformative contradiction between culturally reconstructive regulation and a cultural alternative.

IDENTITY AND INSTITUTION

(This section is adapted from my book, *Becoming Somebody: Toward a Social Psychology of School*, 1992) The student/subject result of high performance new knowledge and a 'real world' focus is completed by interest in 'promoting healthy lifestyles'. The noncognitive, intersubjective world through which identity is formed is also 'surfacized', replacing interpersonal reflexive development with behavioral regimens for health. While these futures are 'designed', existing social institutions lose the grounds for interactively formed personal identity, without having the new technisurfaced healthy lifestyle performer 'in place' to complement postmodernism's diffused spectator in consumption as a combined substitute for identity. In our high school studies, we described youths' struggles during this transitional time.

In the school case studies, I found conditioned patterns of social withdrawal which challenge the basic constituent elements of social relations. Instead of grand theoretical challenges to the concept of society, I described specific institutional processes that reverse the constructive or 'socializing' (Touraine, 1989) establishment of society: desocialization. Something different is at stake in each case: the negation of different aspects of social relations. These practical, institutional processes of social negation represent a destruction of basic social elements, indicating a reversal of society. This is not a macro transformation of media against society, consumption rather than production, or informationalism replacing industry; it is a set of specific institutional social practices that are practical deconstructions of the social.

In each school/class, a basic constituent aspect of social relations is being destroyed. In the working class, it is interaction. The professional middle class is no longer belabored by the social whole (Horkheimer and Adorno, 1972), but by its absence. Here, society is missing at the center of school/class social relations. For the urban 'underclass' (mostly African-American and Hispanic youths), moral stigma and an inferiority complex make society's opposite (the self) tenuous if not absent. Interaction, society, and self are basic elements of social relations that are differentially expressed in each school/class, but not by their realization or fullness. Instead, the emptying and putative lack of these practices and their representations appear to stand at the center of social life.

The emptying process is unintended and overdetermined in each case. Decreased interaction is a by-product of distrust created by school administration, in harmony with its community, as it strives for order and respect. The direct effect is social selection, stratification, and polarization of student peer groups. The resultant atmosphere is one of containment and suppression. On top of this unintended by-product of the search for order and respect, additional conditions reinforce the process of emptying social interaction. Teachers took one step up from their overwhelmingly working class origins and do not want to be reminded (as professional adults) how students' bad manners and unclean appearance can threaten to throw them back socially.

Mass cultural difference reinforces class cultural difference. The social distance is opened up by fear, frustration, and displacement of the teachers' professional insecurity and threat from administrative surveillance, control, disrespect, and uncertain employment. Family differences are part of the attribution of historically and culturally newly produced deficits among students. It is easier to forgive one's own ritualistic self-distancing from the critical interaction induced by organizational and professional dynamics of failure and frustration if the interaction partner is declining beyond the bounds where reciprocity can rightfully be expected: 'they do not deserve it'.

The emptying of society is less perceptible and can occur without placing blame on the professional middle class school. Your personal self-definition and ambition is nestled in your peer associations. Students' stories of their parents' pressures and peers' ambition show a clear understanding of the social shaping of individual identities. Teachers may acknowledge that their own professionalism may cause socially divisive departmentalization. Students may complain about 'apathy' and lack of school spirit. Yet, these understandings appear as qualifications (additions to an identity built within a limited range of acceptable personal achievements) that push society out of the center of school/class. Then, they complain about its absence.

In urban schools, students fight against this emptying process because their selves are at stake. This emptying of the self occurs against the students' will, imposed forcibly and out of fear by their teachers and guards. To teachers (whose 'morale is in the pits'), injuries to student selfhood are consequences of their need to manage students to avoid overcoming students' deprivations or their own fears of students' violent uncontrollability. In-class quiet assignments avoid pedagogical encounters, while 'attacks' mounted by deans and guards usually prevent any unmanageable forms of collective self-expression. It presents problems for population management when students are overly self-expressive outside the school. This vibrant self is not harnessed and elevated, but pressed into corners and locked out by the steel doors of school time. If this fails, the therapeutic and legal ministries reach beyond the school to 'the district' and then to the city's welfare management system.

The process of self-formation or identity as compensation for a social relational lack in school life is not the whole story of how individual identities are socially produced. But, it is the part we see as high school youths struggle to become somebody. What we see is how much identity is created as a defensive compensation to a failure in modern social relations, how compensatory defensive processes are self-formative, and how hints of a postmodern succession to modern social relations are altering how society affects the self.

A more expansive view is that these school or class differences represent a divided identity labor, which when recomposed, offer a portrait of the *fin-de-siecle* self (or an institutional prologue to a postmodern transformation of self). Seen separately, there are self processes particular to each school/class: class psychology. Seen as a whole, there is an internally differentiated field upon which some historically new, postmodern sort of identity is created:

historical psychology. Each school/class represents an aspect of the self, just as each lack (interaction, society, self) is an aspect of social relations.

The emptying of social relations induces defensive self-processes to compensate for the lack. When reciprocal interaction is missing in working class schools, the result is a series of divisions to protect against a vulnerability created by an absence of caring interaction and identification with adult authority. 'Good kids and losers', disciplinary and therapeutic locales, or exaggerations of male and female are some divisions that occur when a consistent, positive identification with a listening, powerful adult is missing.

High school's organizational separation (between bureaucratic discipline and therapeutic understanding) mimics the patriarchal nuclear family's sex role divisions. But, the organizational apparatus fails to engage students. Teachers' professional insecurities and career paths, community demands for order and control, fiscal retrenchment, and a newer student/teacher difference (aided by advancing mass culture and intensified economic need) combine to dissipate trust that might produce the caring identification needed for reciprocal interaction. Division is the first line of defense, secured by exaggerating differences. But the final victor is alienated identity formation in which not a self, but an image of it emerges. The mirror replaces the subject.

For the professional middle class students, alienation or self-distancing is part of the self. It is not the apparatus, which they (unlike working class students who hope the school will care) see as powerless and irrelevant from the start, which is rejecting. Instead, through a combination of ironic humor and depression, they control limitless performance expectations (which are integral to student identity) by dampening commitment to them. Performance is both the medium and goal of self-affirmation. But, it is also a threatening enemy because it can denigrate and reject the self when not properly pacified. Its never-ending character (college beyond high school, career demands beyond college, and social conscience and economic status beyond career) instigates strategies of dampening, depression, and distance.

'The idea of the school' represents a form of society that is not a cure for excessive emphasis on individual performance. 'School spirit', like performance pressure, can unleash limitless expectations for commitment. Students can be committed to the United Nations club, math team, or band. Those are delimited obligations that can be scheduled (and contained) in commitment of self and time. The school has become 'nothing'. The character rather than the logistics of performance diminishes collective capacities for society. Socially created performance pressures have built-in defenses against limitlessness. Society (both progenitor and antithesis of individual achievement performance) is really united with that performance. Both are means of self-affirmation, but also threats to the self. They are channels of boundarylessness, uncontrollable demand, unpredictability, and self-surrender. 'Mellowing out' or getting 'psyched down' is a self-defense against performance.

Students use 'apathy' as a defense against limitless demands from performance and society. Performance can be individualized and regulated by depression; society is compartmentalized ('departmentalized' for teachers), avoided, and denied. Negation of society is part of the compensatory defense against limitless demand and the threat of an unbounded self, represented by performance. It is harder to withdraw from school performance 'pressures'; but, society can be denied. Society becomes nothing as a self-defense method. Depression is a self-defense method. Rationalized communication is a way out of social fragmentation and an absent social center. Social 'apathy', even though society seems missed, still operates to keep performance 'on track'.

Social institutions (even their lacks) shape the self. But, interactional and societal lack is different in working class, professional middle class, and urban minority 'underclass' (where self-affirmation is also lacking) schools. Self-establishment has to be repeatedly accomplished before any other shaping occurs. The compensatory process is more direct. Where the lack of self-affirmation is the basic social absence, the socially patterned defensive self-formation occurs at the basic line of self-defense: self-existence.

From the first 'hello' (that says, 'we are not who you have heard we are') to the last 'goodbye' (that reminds the world, 'we have value as human beings'), students work to create a visible, differentiated, and reputable self. By being 'good' or 'decent', the social is represented in demarginalizing self-existence. Whatever they may have to prove about their self-value at the outset of their school career is exaggerated by the school's organization around the assumption that what is lacking among the students is a decent, moral self. Morality here is not the neat concern of the upwardly mobile working class teacher, but a more basic question of the student's integrity. From the early morning meetings of the administrative staff to the close of the school day, the students are managed (at worst, as a potentially dangerous population and at best, as a deficit self to be classified, guided, or uplifted).

'Drillin' (the interaction game of verbal invidious self-distinction) and fighting (almost always self-defense against imputed moral inferiority) are preeminent social forms. The lack of an affirmed, valuable self as the determinative social organizational absence induces expressive displays as the most immediate and accessible compensation to school social relations' reinforcement of socially inherited stigma.

These defensive processes (of a self formed within institutions characterized by social practices of emptying core elements of social relations) reveal more of what postmodern society means than textualists' talk about a 'decentered' self. Our description ties self-dynamics to organized social practices in concrete everyday institutional life. Analytic recomposition of a class-divided self (formed as a compensatory defense against a class-specific institutional lack in social relations) shows an unwillingness to accept centrifugal self-dissipation as an easy herald of a new ahistorical epoch. Identity is formed in defense against social absences, not in welcoming acceptance.

A potentially emergent postmodern self would be a recomposition of what I call the class-specific 'foreshadowings' of image, communication, and network. This self also emerges out of social interactional labor to preserve self against social lacks and beyond the first line of more directly compensatory actions of self-construction. These actions are class-specific strategies of self-defense and self-construction. These primary compensations offer a guide to differences in the class self: divided, distant, and displayed.

COUNTERPOSES

Perhaps elite corporatist integrated control and techniflattening and institutional social evacuation can continue without further cultural response, indeed, without culture. Postmodernism shows that culture has not vanished. Yet, the character of postmodern culture does not offer the cultural basis for an alternative or counterpose. Rather, it extends the over-integrated, socially emptying society to culture, destroying the opportunity to culturally constitute an alternative (Mongardini, 1990).

Those who see in postmodern culture the sign of a phoenix rising from the ashes also recognize it as the cultural expression of modern society. The 'transfer of time to space' that both Olalquiaga and Harvey portray as characteristically postmodern is part of the same cultural incoherence and symbolic disruption which Mongardini asserted, with the same result (Olalquiaga, 1992, p. 22).

Mestrovic (1991, pp. 204, 207) describes the experiential aspect in more conventional sociological terms, calling postmodernism 'the institutionalization of anomie', which 'can be likened to an addiction,' where the 'postmodern self is bored, and demands an increase in the quantity of stimulation.' Castoriadis (1992, p. 22) also describes postmodernism as a 'generalized conformism' while Honneth (1991) speaks of an 'artificial pluralization of aesthetically shaped lifeworlds' that 'empty subjectivity motivationally so that the electronic media can then compensatively encroach on this emptied subjectivity with its offers of simulation.' Postmodern culture does not provide conditions to counter the integrated rationalization of control or resources for social relations to realize identity in other than hypermedia, baroque compensations. There appears to be no point of reliable resistance against which there is an opening to create 'the foundations of a new culture' (Mongardini, 1990).

Both the patriarchal presence of authority (Benjamin, 1989) and the postmodern, 'absence' of authority prevent any dialectic of differentiation and so reinforce social control integration and cultural and identity eclecticism and conformity. The reinvention of a dialectic of differentiation depends on real difference, as Vincent's (1991) 'rediscovery of the sacred amidst profane activities prevailing in everyday life'. The opening resistance to rationalizing, commodifying, social emptying 'colonization of the lifeworld' is not attained only in language, but is a socioemotional, interactional, existential process that severs the authority transferences and countertransferences which structure what is mistakenly seen as destructured, everyday institutional life.

Difference is not mere differentiation, even from a distant point, as a structuralist reading would have it. Ultimately, difference is created in light of an historic experience or memory of creation (Jonas, 1974, p. 37). Ensnarement in authority and its absence that fuels desire in rationalized life is a substitution for the desire for transformation by contact with a more different domain of difference in time through which sacred otherness sheds a transformative temporal light on instrumental mundanity. Scenarios of self-formation and struggle against ambiguous and diminished diffuse forms of authority can be replaced by what they replaced: sacred otherness occupying time that is 'inassimilable by automatic mechanisms' (Vincent, 1991).

In this view, the cultural resources required for a dereifying moment are not in the refoundationalism of religion and its texts, but in a cultural creation based in absolute (not naturalistic) differences and enables interaction, dialogue, and broad receptivity to 'otherness'. This view of culture is neither a melancholic embrace of novel experience, nor the performance anticulture of American liberalism, nor the moral conservatives' reassertion of premodern values. These are the cultural responses of a new social regime emerging in the core self-formative educational institutions. Harvey (1989, p. 302) describes how 'the emphasis upon ephemerality, collage, fragmentation, and dispersal in philosophical and social thought mimics the conditions of flexible accumulation. . . . But it is exactly at this point that we encounter the opposite reaction that can best be summed up as the search for personal and collective identity, the search for secure moorings in a shifting world'.

The collective identity solution to modern/postmodern destruction of culture and identity is not just reaction nor the moral majority's early attack on secular humanism in education or 'family values.' It includes radical 'new' movements which hope for a culturally rooted alternative to integrated control, social emptying, and conformism. However, even the new radical social movements are subject to a continuing process of societal reincorporation. Do they exemplify that 'genuine critical spirit' against postmodern conformism, which 'can only exist in and through the establishment of a distance with what there is, entailing the conquest of a point of view beyond the given, therefore in the work of creation' (Castoriadis, 1992)? Postmodern conformist culture results from a more profound problem of the 'decadence of spiritual creation'.

Creation, from the viewpoint of sacred otherness, is an existential, utopia-driven, practical desire for recognition, dialogue, and receptivity to both an unreified state and the living other, which extends to primordial moments of creation and encounter. It is the truly different, opposite counterpose to contemporary forms of idolatry; it is the starting point for articulating educational counterposes to the 'Toyota school'.

   This sort of fundamental cultural creation is an existential and practical 'calling', not a bibliographical display of postmodern exegesis. In education, it will mean teaching toward utopia, not as performance-driven techniques and external 'standards'. 'What matters is that time and again an older generation staking its entire existence on that act, comes to a younger with the desire to teach, waken and shape it; then the holy spark leaps across the gap' (Buber, 1963 and 1992). Without this commitment and the social forms of life that create and sustain it, new corporatism and institutional emptying of the social, will stand as heralds of the future of education in the new order.

ACKNOWLEDGEMENT

This is a revised version of a paper published in Australia's *Arena Journal*, No. 2, 1993/94 as 'Corporatism and Its Counterposes'.

11 Educational Reform and Politics in Israel: Change or Economic Reproduction?

Ilana Felsenthal and Chaim Adler

ABSTRACT

Although sociologists of education are well aware of the power in words and of the ideological connotations behind supposedly 'value free' narratives, our own hands are not entirely clean either. Some of the terminology sociologists of education used has acquired almost mythological dimensions. One example is the 'reproduction' concept. Everyone who prides himself or herself as a true proponent of egalitarian education is crying 'off with reproduction'. As a result, every educational system accused of being guilty of reproduction comes under fire. We are referring here to 'reproduction' as a key term in radical discourse. We do not accept Giroux's (1988, p. 113) view, attributing 'the reproductive theory of schooling' to both radical and conservative critics of education. This interpretation conceptually binds those who believe that schools should reproduce with those who claim they should not. This approach is not useful in the present context. Moreover, those conservatives who rebuke schools for not being sufficiently responsive to economic and technological developments shy away from using the rhetoric of reproduction and tend to speak in terms of efficiency and inefficiency.

In this chapter, we try to disentangle the concept of reproduction from the ideological web threatening to obscure the reality behind the rhetoric. We first dissect the concept, then apply it to educational reforms in general and to Israeli school reform in particular.

REPRODUCTION THEORY

Our first task is to break the concept of reproduction into its component parts. We claim that any reproductive theory of schooling (economic, cultural, or both) faces two conceptually separable types of questions: first, questions concerning distribution and access; second, questions concerning domination and legitimation. Although separately formulated here, the two types of questions are never fully independent of each other. Struggles for change or reform in education mostly revolve around one of these two types of issues or some combination of both.

What do educational systems distribute? What kinds of distributions should be defined as 'reproductive'? First, public educational systems distribute schooling per se. The relevant data which might enable us to answer the first question (about distribution) pertains to the number of years of free, compulsory education, size of enrollments and attendance rates, and so on (that is, information about how many stay in school for how long). In the sociological literature dealing with reproduction, such data do not attract much attention. One explanation for this dearth of interest might be that sociologists engaged in researching and writing about the reproductive theory of schooling are mostly working in countries which reached high levels of educational expansion years ago; therefore, such levels are now taken for granted. We claim that there is a group of countries in which such high levels of educational participation (especially regarding rates of attendance in secondary education) have only recently been reached. This accelerated rate of growth over a relatively short span is bound to have major effects on educational priorities and on the manner in which other distributional problems are being met.

Table 12.1 shows the accelerated growth of secondary education in Israel between 1975 and 1988. None of the other countries in this table underwent similar expansion; in 1975, most of them already had attendance rates which Israel reached only a decade later.

In terms of distribution, the rapidly rising levels of education must mean that a constantly growing percentage of the 'weaker' (educationally speaking) segments in Israel's school-age population are being drawn into the education system. Their duration of stay in this system is being significantly prolonged. In other words, the most glaring and obvious symptom of a reproductive education system (that is, the exclusion of certain disempowered groups from public schooling) is being speedily eradicated.

Let us examine this argument more closely. When one refers to the 'weak' or 'vulnerable' segments in Israeli society, which groups come to mind? The largest segment which is most likely in Israel (as elsewhere) to become a victim to reproductive trends is women. How did the accelerated growth of Israeli education affect them? Several studies indicate that women might be considered the major gainers in a process of educational expansion. To quote a survey of socioeconomic indicators in Israel as compared with OECD data which the Israeli Center for Social Policy Studies published:

> Even as general levels of education rise over time, men's education levels exceed women's in all the OECD countries participating in the study, and in Israel. It is evident, however, that a narrowing of the disparity between the sexes is part of the process. During the 1960s, Israeli men had an average of 15 per cent more schooling than women in terms of years - 8.5 versus 7.4 respectively, or a difference of 1.1 years. Today the gap has narrowed to 11.4 versus 10.9, a mere six-month advantage for men (Kop, 1988, p. 42).

This trend is clearly evident in Figure 12.1.

Table 12.1. Relative growth in school attendance (in per cent)

Country	Year	Secondary School	Postsecondary Education and University	Standard Age for Secondary School
Israel	1975	65.7	25.2	12-17
	1980	72.0	26.0	
	1986	82.0	28.0	
	1987	84.0	27.0	
	1988	83.0	27.0	
US	1975	92.0	57.0	12-17
	1980	90.0	56.0	
	1986	100.0	59.3	
Canada	1975	91.0	39.3	12-17
	1980	92.0	41.9	
	1986	103.0	54.6	
Japan	1975	92.0	24.6	12-17
	1980	93.0	41.9	
	1986	96.0	28.8	
The Netherlands	1975	88.0	25.2	12-17
	1980	92.0	30.0	
	1985	104.0	32.0	
Denmark	1975	80.0	29.4	13-18
	1980	105.0	28.6	
	1985	105.0	29.3	
France	1975	82.0	24.5	11-17
	1980	85.0	25.5	
	1986	95.0	30.2	
Great Britain	1975	83.0	18.9	11-17
	1980	84.0	20.2	
	1985	85.0	22.4	

Note: The standard age in all countries for university students is 20-24.
Source: UNESCO Statistical Yearbook, 1988, Table 3.2; Klinov (1991), Table 1,S.29.

Figure 12.1. Average school age by gender in Israel

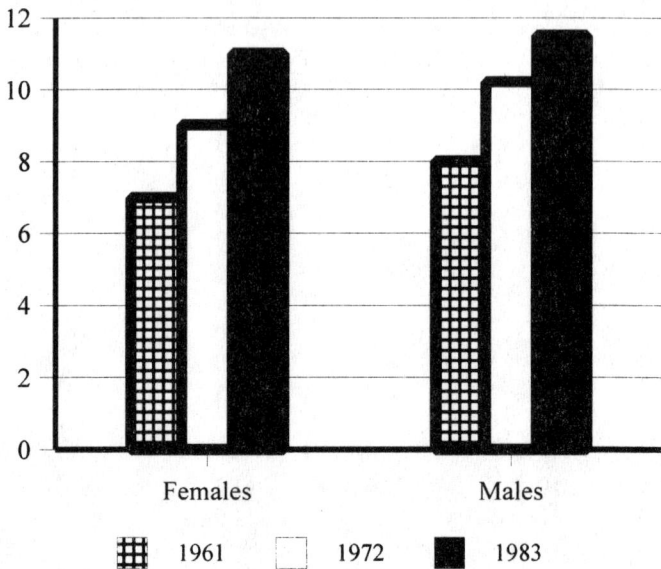

Source: Central Office for Statistics, Israel

Kfir, Ayalon, and Shapira reached similar conclusions, claiming 'girls and women raised in Israel are equal to men in the quantity of their education: more women than men complete secondary schools in the academic tracks, and more women go on to post-secondary education' (Kfir, Ayalon, and Shapira, 1990, p. 59; translated from Hebrew). We shall return to gender inequality issues in educational attainment and education, but now we discuss other 'vulnerable' groups and their shares in educational resources.

After women, the next population segment to fall prey to educational reproduction are racial, national, and ethnic minorities. Israel does not have a clearly definable racial problem, but it has a considerable national minority: its Arab citizens (1/6 of the population). Paradoxically, the other segment which has always been considered under-privileged in educational terms now constitutes the majority of the population. This major sector is frequently designated 'Oriental Jews' (those born in Asia or Africa or descendants of parents born there). Because the main wave of immigration from these countries reached Israel in the early 1950s, most of the 'Oriental' children in the educational system today are, for all intents and purposes, second generation Israelis, whose parents were either bred and born in Israel or brought there at an early age. How did these two groups (Arab citizens of Israel and 'Oriental' Jews) fare as a result of educational expansion?

Figure 12.2. School attendance of 14- to 17-year-old Arabs in Israel (in per cent)

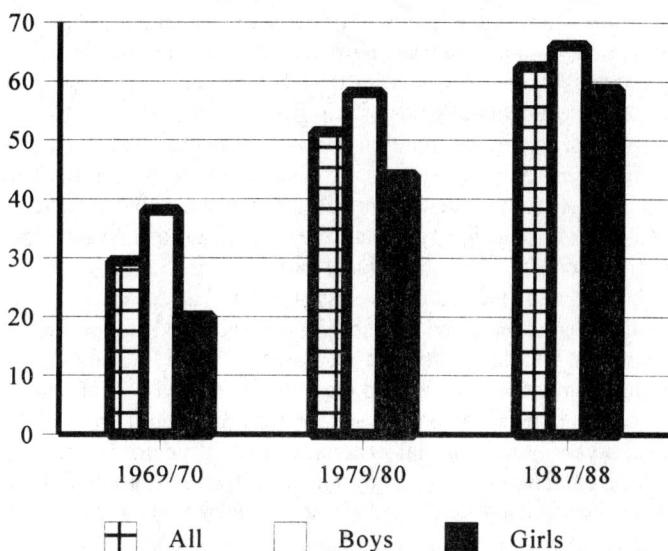

Source: Central Office for Statistics, Israel

When the State of Israel was established, the Arab minority was the least educated sector in the country, partly due to the over-representation of the better educated strata among those who left the country during the 1948 war. In 1947, 33 per cent of Arabs attended school (Mar'i, 1978); most students did not stay in the education system for more than four years. In 1970, the attendance rate of of Arab children aged 6-13 was 87.1 per cent; in 1985, it reached 94.7 per cent. The percentage of Arab students in secondary education is not as close to the national average as the numbers in primary education, but the rates of growth are nonetheless staggering (see Figure 12.2).

We have worked closely with several Arab high schools and are impressed by the vigor and motivation which principals, teachers, and students demonstrate. Their willingness to try new methods and new curricula and their somewhat naive faith in education as a key to social mobility are remarkable. Hopefully, the growing power that the fundamentalist movements have lately acquired in the Arab sector will not halt educational growth, especially for Arab women whose educational gains have not equaled those of males in this sector. But when speaking in general about the 'Arab sector', one lumps together several non-Jewish groups: Moslems, various Christian denominations, and the Druz community. Each of these groups has differing patterns of educational participation and deserves separate treatment.

How much did 'Oriental' Jews gain from the accelerated growth rates of the Israeli educational system? That they (who are more than half of the school-age population) gained is obvious in a system that enrolls close to 100 per cent of the relevant age group in primary schools and more than 85 per cent in secondary schools, this large group could not avoid being included in this 'educational boom'. If we confine ourselves to data about levels of school attendance, the educational gains of this group in general, and of women in this group in particular, are quite impressive. As a result of growing definitional difficulties (due mostly to the frequency of inter-marriage between 'Oriental' and 'Ashkenazi' Jews), our data are somewhat outdated. According to the Ministry of Education 1987 data, the percentages of 17-year-olds from Asian-African origin in the educational system were 15.8 per cent and 62.6 per cent in 1964 and 1982, respectively. During the last decade, this trend has certainly not been reversed and is especially pronounced among second and third generation Israelis, as the data presented in Table 12.2 show.

We have intentionally avoided class differences in educational attainments (a central issue in reproductive theories of schooling) for two reasons: 1) As a relatively 'young' social system, the class structure in Israel has not yet crystallized. The recent immigration from Eastern Europe is bound to create some new fluctuations in the already unstable class and status definitions so one should be careful while handling these concepts. This is not to say that Israel is a classless society, only that its system of stratification is not yet well defined. 2) Class-bound categories are nonexistent in Israeli educational statistics. Still, the extent of overlap between lower-class positions and ethnic origin turns any discussion of ethnicity into a de-facto analysis of stratification. For the first two decades after independence, this overlap was almost total; the new immigrants from Asia and Africa (who were usually less educated, more culturally traditional, with larger families) became Israel's lower class. Two decades of upward mobility (which educational expansion has partly facilitated, but mostly due to the general rise in the standard of living, combined with the influx of cheap labor from the occupied territories) changed this picture. Many 'Oriental' Jews moved into the loosely defined middle class. All over Israel one can still find some pockets of poverty, chronic unemployment, drugs, and crime. The predominant ethnic group living in such neighborhoods and communities are still Jews from 'Oriental' origins. While discussing the issue of ethnic groups, we used silence to address the problems of education and stratification. 'Oriental' Jews were constantly overrepresented in the lower economic strata.

Education systems distribute schooling. When the system expands rapidly, overtaking the rates of population growth, it distributes more schooling to more people (some of them previously excluded from formal education). The more far-reaching this process, the less reproductive the system. Education systems also distribute other and socially desirable goods: high-status knowledge, sought-after credentials, and scarce openings in prestigious educational institutions. How these 'goods' are handled and how it affects the question of reproduction are next on our agenda. Our discussion shall focus on macro-level, major policy-making strategies.

Table 12.2. Educational level of Jews (over 14 years) based on place of birth and their years in school (in per cent)

| Birthplace | Year | Total | Years in School | | | | |
			0-4	5-8	9-12	13-15	16+
Total	1975	100.0	11.9	25.5	44.9	10.7	7.0
	1985	100.0	8.1	17.3	50.2	14.2	10.2
Israel	1975	100.0	1.4	15.6	61.5	14.0	7.5
	1985	100.0	0.9	8.7	63.3	16.7	10.4
Asia or Africa	1975	100.0	28.2	33.3	31.5	4.9	2.1
	1985	100.0	23.2	27.5	38.1	7.3	3.9
Europe or US	1975	100.0	8.5	28.6	40.0	12.2	10.7
	1985	100.7*	7.0	22.6	39.3	15.9	15.9
Israel; father also born in Israel	1975	100.0	2.3	15.3	61.6	14.1	6.7
	1985	99.4*	0.8	7.9	63.5	17.1	10.1
Israel; father born in Asia or Africa	1975	100.0	1.9	25.6	65.2	6.0	1.3
	1985	100.0	1.1	12.8	72.4	10.4	3.3
Israel; father born in Europe or US	1975	100.0	0.6	6.6	58.1	21.3	13.4
	1985	100.0	0.6	3.4	50.2	24.9	20.9

* The percentages in the source text did not total 100 per cent.
Source: State of Israel, Ministry of Education (1987), Table F-4, S.55.

POLICY-MAKING STRATEGIES

Since the late 1960s, two strategies operated in Israel's education system. These strategies might seem contradictory, but they were actually complementary. The first strategy was the 1968 School Reform, Ministry of Education and Culture initiated and Israeli parliament approved. The enacted reform consisted of three facets. The first facet was concerned with the issue of educational expansion; an extra year of compulsory education was added, bringing the number up to 11. Figure 12.3 presents this achievement in a comparative cross-national perspective.

Figure 12.3. Compulsory education in Israel and selected countries (in years)

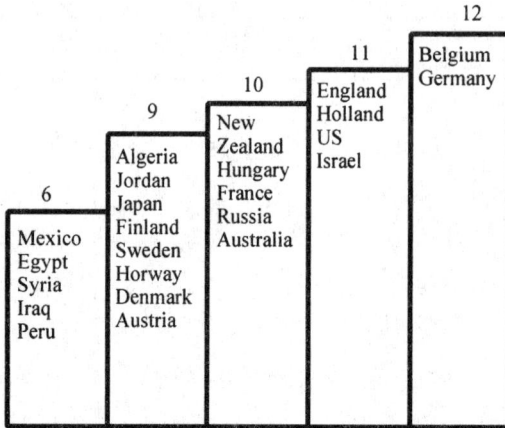

				12
			11	Belgium Germany
		10	England Holland US Israel	
	9	New Zealand Hungary France Russia Australia		
6	Algeria Jordan Japan Finland Sweden Horway Denmark Austria			
Mexico Egypt Syria Iraq Peru				

Source: UNESCO, 1988

The second facet of the proposed reform was to reorganize the school structure. Until then, the educational system in Israel had eight years of primary school and four years of secondary school. The reform implemented a three-year intermediate school (junior high school), thus creating a system of 6-3-3. This structural change had several objectives, chief among them the upgrading of teachers' educational level in the intermediate grades.

The third (and the most widely debated) facet of the 1968 reform came under the heading of 'school integration' (that is, creating socially mixed schools). The term 'socially mixed' implied bringing Jewish children of differing ethnic origins together in the same school (that is, 'Oriental' and 'Ashkenazi', the latter term implying European or American origins). Using our own distributional frame of reference (not necessarily at the expense of other goals such as solidarity and 'common culture'), school integration policy must clearly be defined as an antireproductive strategy. The worst kind of educational reproduction occurs when children of vulnerable populations are isolated in their own segregated schools. Under the prevailing conditions of scarce public resources for education, these children are apt to become the victims of the worst kind of allocation: 'poor schools for the poor'. When and where possible, school integration might be one of the best solutions to this distributional problem, the alternative being a disproportionally massive investment in segregated schools for the socially disadvantaged population.

This alternative is both unrealistic and socially unpalatable, reminiscent of the US, pre-1954, 'separate but equal' arrangement.

We do not intend to determine whether the 1968 school reform has or has not been successful. Some of its ardent opponents claim that it failed altogether; others point out some partial successes; still others hail it as a sweeping success (Katz, 1988). Empirical studies are also inconclusive, mostly indicating some statistically significant gains in scholastic achievement for average and somewhat below-average ability students. This offsets the small losses above-average ability students incurred.

Some reference to high-status knowledge and school integration seems unavoidable. Integrated schools are supposed to facilitate equal access to all types of knowledge, including high-status subjects. There are many indications that this equality of access was hindered by practices instituted in many integrated schools presumably to solve problems of instruction in mixed-ability classrooms. Some of these practices (like homogeneous classes and ability grouping in English and math, both quite prevalent in Israeli schools) actually excluded children from a disadvantaged background from high-status knowledge or gave them access to this knowledge at a very low level. Homogeneous home-room classes have been contrary to the Ministry of Education's recommended policy strategies; ability grouping in a few key subjects has been the recommended policy strategy.

At about the same time that school integration was being intensively debated, while the reform itself was implemented at a much slower pace than originally intended, another process (with some important distributional ramifications) was set into motion. This phenomenon is the creeping but constant differentiation of the Israeli high school through the steady growth in vocational education. This trend began when the administration of large portions of the vocational educational system was transferred from the Ministry of Labor to the Ministry of Education and Culture in the 1960s, when it was renamed 'Technological Education'. This presumably administrative move resulted in some extremely important changes in secondary education in Israel, first and foremost the accelerated growth of the 'technological' relative to the 'general' or academic tracks. These rates of growth are presented in Figure 12.4.

Vocational education in Israel is subdivided into three tracks (from the upper, most prestigious, co mbining technological studies in subjects like computer science and modern electronics with high-level academic subjects, down to the middle and lower tracks in which subjects such as automobile mechanics, printing, fashion design, and hairstyling are prevalent). In 1975, at the height of the process of expansion, the majority of 12th grade vocational education students (63.6 per cent) attended the middle and lower tracks (designated 'regular' and 'practical' respectively). Since then, the picture has changed significantly; in 1985, attendance in the 12th grade of the upper track reached 55.3 per cent.

Figure 12.4. Distribution of students in higher secondary schools by educational track (number of students in thousands)

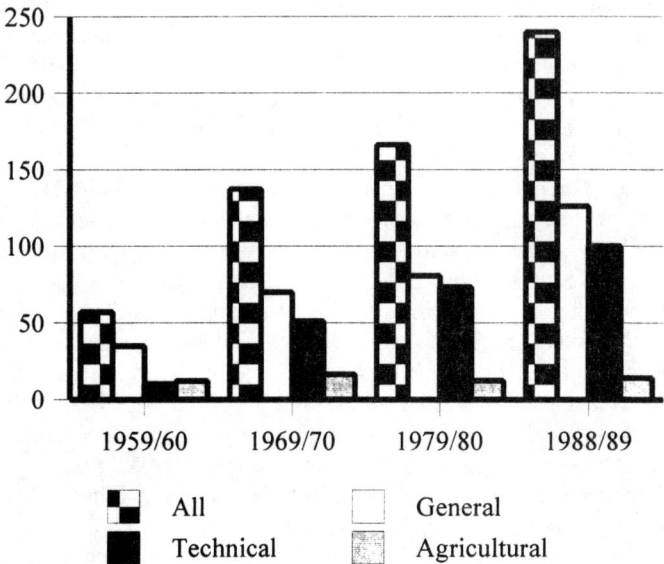

Note: Grades 10-12 in six-year secondary schools; grades 9-12 in four-year schools.
Source: Central Office for Statistics, Israel

Who are the students in vocational schools in Israel? What does attendance in this educational sector mean in terms of distribution? As a relevant Ministry of Education and Culture publication said, for the last 20 years, there was significant increase in the number of technological students. In 1987/8, some 42 per cent of upper secondary school students (grades 10-12) were studying in vocational schools. Many of the students came from 'disadvantaged sectors of the population'. Which 'disadvantaged sectors' are heavily represented in vocational education? We will concentrate on the three groups: women, Arabs, and 'Oriental' Jews.

According to 1986 data, women are much more heavily concentrated in the academic track; 57 per cent of female students in this age group chose academic schools, while 57 per cent of the male students in the same age group were studying in the various vocational tracks. Women are also over-represented in secondary education as a whole, a fact which renders these figures even more significant. In 1982, more than half of female secondary school students from 'Oriental' backgrounds were enrolled in academic schools, as opposed to a third of their male counterparts. In vocational education, the picture is less favorable to female students: they are to be found to a somewhat greater extent in the lower vocational tracks, studying such dead-end subject as hairstyling or home economics.

Vocational education was slow in reaching the Arab sector; a negligible percentage of the Arab population is enrolled in this track. This is certainly not due to any objection on the part of this group to attending such schools, but to a shortage of resources needed to develop this sort of education in Arab towns. Arab politicians and educators constantly struggle for these resources, unaware of the cul-de-sac nature of at least the lower tracks of this system. In certain respects, Arab leaders might have a point: dropout rates (the percentage of students in grades 9-11 discontinuing their education and not going on to the next grade) have been 15.3 per cent in Arab education in 1987/8 (falling from 25.3 per cent in 1970/1) while only 5.4 per cent of their Jewish counterparts were dropping out of school at the same time. This difference is partially explained if we look at the lack of the vocational alternative. Still, it seems that the Arab sector should concentrate on expanding regular academic schools, avoiding a vocational 'Trojan horse'.

While Arabs participate in vocational education to a limited extent and Jewish women to a lesser degree than men (relative to their high rates of attendance in secondary education), Jewish men of 'Oriental' origin get the lion's share of this type of schooling. This is apparently the 'disadvantaged population' referred to in the official publication. What is wrong with vocational education? It is certainly more expensive to keep a student in a vocational school than one in the academic track (Klinov-Malul, 1991). If investment is any indicator of quality, one should be better off attending the former. But, in reality, vocational education (especially in the lower tracks) tends to distribute either low-status knowledge in subjects which are not included in the matriculation exams or teach high-status knowledge at a very low level, which likewise is of limited value for these exams. The resultant statistics are presented in Figure 12.5.

Since a matriculation certificate is a prerequisite for admittance into most institutions of higher education in Israel, certainly for universities, these figures do not bode well for about half the vocational education graduates. Some might argue that a growing sector of vocational (or, according to its official designation, 'technological') education is part and parcel of the process of expansion of modern educational systems. Let us examine both this argument and the comparative data in Table 12.3.

In 1986, Israel, together with the Netherlands, boasted the highest percentages of students in vocational tracks. Yet in most countries this percentage has been going up since 1975, while in Israel it has been going down, as academic tracks were expanding. Despite this gradual decline, Israel is still far from closing the gap in this respect between itself and other developed countries.

Figure 12.5. Distribution of matriculated or student final exams by educational track 1988/89 for Jewish and Arab students (in per cent)

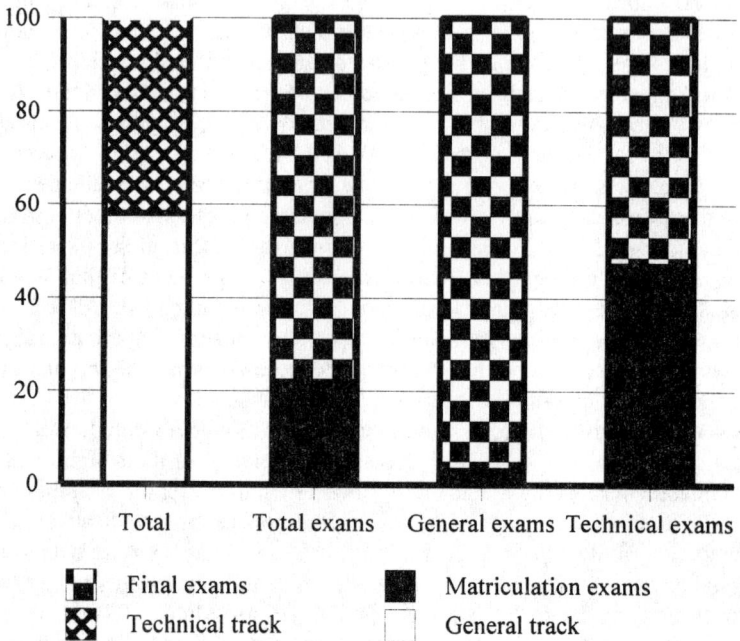

Source: Ministry for Education and Culture, Israel

We pointed out some distributional problems which the disproportional growth of vocational education created in Israel, actually suspecting it of enhancing reproductive processes with regard to certain 'vulnerable' groups. Another criticism leveled at this educational sector is based on recent cost-benefit studies showing that despite higher costs (a student in an academic track costing 80 per cent of that of a student in a vocational track), there are no significant differences in graduates' earning power (Klinov-Malul, 1991). Ruth Klinov-Malul also considered substituting formal, in-school vocational education with certain school-plus-work or on-the-job training alternatives existing in several other countries, including Germany. She rejected this possibility because of distributional considerations and the fear of aggravating ethnic gaps in educational attainment.

Table 12.3. International comparison of secondary school students in academic and vocational tracks (in per cent)

Country	Year	Academic Track	Vocational Track
Israel	1975	56.8	43.2
	1980	58.8	41.2
	1986	61.5	38.5
Canada	1975	100.0	0.0
	1980	100.0	0.0
	1986	100.0	0.0
Japan	1975	83.0	17.0
	1980	85.2	14.8
	1986	87.4	12.6
Western Germany	1975	86.2	13.8
	1980	85.8	14.2
	1985	87.8	12.2
France	1975	79.6	21.0
	1980	78.0	22.0
	1985	74.0	26.0
the Netherlands	1975	59.7	40.3
	1980	59.2	40.8
	1985	55.8	44.2
Great Britain	1975	96.0	4.0
	1980	95.2	4.8
	1986	91.7	8.3
Denmark	1975	89.6	10.4
	1980	74.7	25.3
	1985	69.1	30.9

Source: UNESCO Statistical Yearbook, 1988, Table 3.5; Klinov (1991), Table 3,S.32.

POSTSECONDARY EDUCATION

Table 12.1 showed that attendance rates in postsecondary and higher education in Israel are roughly comparable to those of the most developed countries in Europe. Clearly, Israel does not yet come close to the postsecondary attendance rates characteristic of both the US and Canada (55-60 per cent). While attendance rates in several European countries are rising, the same rates in Israel remained static since 1980. Therefore, there is no reason to complain about an 'exaggerated' growth in postsecondary education in Israel; yet, one open question is: How shall the influx of highly educated Russian immigrants affect the higher education system?

What is the fate of the three groups we discussed in the Israeli postsecondary education? Women are quite nicely represented as far as total enrollment rates are concerned. In universities, their numbers went up rapidly since 1965 (when females constituted just 36.1 per cent of the student body) to 1985 (when 47.7 per cent of the students were women). Women are also heavily represented in other postsecondary institutions (such as teacher training colleges and academic programs for hospital nurses), but their numbers in all kinds of technically oriented courses are negligible: less than 20 per cent.

Looking further, we find the majority of female university students in the humanities, but they are also enrolled in growing numbers in the behavioral sciences, in faculties of medicine and law, and in the natural sciences and mathematics. But their numbers in faculties of engineering and architecture are extremely small. In this respect, one might claim that some reproductive forces are still in evidence, but this situation is aggravated since we have less-than-proportional representation of women in postgraduate work.

Not surprisingly, representation of the Arab sector in general, and Arab women in particular, in postsecondary education (including universities) is very low. Despite the rising levels of attendance in primary and secondary education, in 1985 only 39 per cent of the relevant age group in the Arab population attended the 12th grade and 24 per cent of the same age group took the matriculation exams. No wonder that, although a sizable proportion of those possessing the matriculation certificate go on to higher education, the numbers are still very small. Arab students tend to have language difficulties in subjects requiring advanced verbal capacity in the language of instruction (Hebrew) because schools in their sector use Arabic as the main language of instruction, while Hebrew is taught as a second language. More surprising is the fact that Jews of 'Oriental' origin lagged behind in levels of schooling, especially postsecondary and higher education.

The percentage of academic degree holders among members of this group was 14.6 per cent of all academic degree holders in the Israeli population in 1984. The percentages used to be 6.6 per cent and 8.3 per cent in 1961 and 1974, respectively, so some progress was made in distributing this high-status knowledge. But is it enough? This situation was further aggravated in that since the early 1980s, there have been constant cuts in government expenditures on education. This trend might enhance the efficiency of the system, but it might also support those reproductive processes already in operation.

COVERT AND OVERT DISTRIBUTION PROCESSES

In the beginning of this chapter, we argued that reproduction is double faceted. One facet pertained to questions of distribution; the other to issues of legitimation and dominance. Now, we concentrate on the second component of the reproductive theory of education. Both covert and overt processes of distribution of whatever 'goods' (or, by the same token, 'bads') the educational system has at its disposal do not take place in a cultural and political vacuum. Distributional strategies evolve through continuous struggles inside and outside the educational arena. We try to trace these complicated processes of dominance and struggle, legitimation and delegitimation, and detail the rhetoric and practice of educational reform in Israel.

Since the 1960s, the Israeli education system has undergone several 'reforms'. The first (and most loudly debated) usually comes under the heading of 'The Reform' with a capital 'R', which we discussed in the first part of this chapter. Although this reform had several objectives (including the extension of compulsory education), the one item on its agenda that gained most of the public attention was the issue of school integration. We claim that the heated debate around school integration is not just a manifestation of conflicting educational interests between groups of parents and educators, but a symbolic representation of the ongoing struggle around some of the most basic structural and cultural issues in Israeli society. Israel's volatile stratification system is a combination of horizontal integration and vertical differentiation among Jewish ethnicities (Peres, 1985). Peres defines horizontal differences between two groups as 'the aggregate of all cultural differences . . . which are transferred by socialization'; the vertical distance meaning 'the distance between the groups' positions in the society's stratification system' (Peres, 1985, p. 39). Thus, integrating and differentiating forces are constantly working in every sphere of life in Israel, including the educational arena in which cultural integration is supposed to be forged. Unfortunately, the education system in Israel is also the breeding ground for vertical differentiation because it is connected to different social positions. It is no wonder then that school integration acquired symbolic dimensions and that such an intensive battle has been raging around it.

About the same time that the issue of school integration became the locus of educational discourse in Israel, other less-voluble changes steadily crept into the education system: the rapid growth of vocational education and a reform in the structure of the matriculation exams, enhancing the Ministry of Education's control over this major ritual of classification (Meyer and Rowan, 1978). It is interesting that both these relatively salient reforms accelerated differentiating processes. The result was tightening up the already existing 'bottle-necks', making access to high-status knowledge even more difficult and selective. The fact is that this type of reform (which serves the interests of dominant groups) has never become a focal issue for public or political struggle, while parents, teachers, and the media severely attacked the policy of integration. One could safely assume that the groups who pay for tightening controls, standardized tests, and more selective policies are those sectors which are less informed, less involved, and less empowered.

Moreover, the narrative of integration is not presented in terms of scarcity of resources and distribution problems; thus, it inadvertently creates the illusion that one can simultaneously eat the cake and have it, too. If disadvantaged students can do better when they just share the same classroom, teacher, and curriculum with their luckier peers, why should the government invest more in education? Indeed, there has been a steady decline in government expenditures on education (Klinov-Malul, 1991), while parents were gradually forced to cover a growing share of the costs of their children's education. Lately, it seems that the rhetoric of integration is slowly, but surely, being replaced. New narratives emphasizing parental choice on the one hand and school autonomy on the other have appeared. We suspect that such new narratives might (if educators, scientists, and policy makers do not negate them) tilt the delicate balance between egalitarian and nonegalitarian forces in Israel's education system toward a more reproductive trend.

12 Educational Policy as Technocratic Strategy: The Politics of Excellence

Frank Fischer and Alan Mandell

ABSTRACT

The educational crisis continues to be front-page news in the US. Daily, the media feature stories about the sad condition of America's schools. Since the mid 1970s, dozens of publications appeared. Federal and state governments, philanthropic organizations, business groups, testing organizations, and individual research teams initiated studies and reported findings. While these reports differed in substance and specific recommendations, all claimed that the crisis of education is not only real, but carries manifold consequences for American society as a whole (Altbach et al., 1985, pp. 41-2).

Even more pointedly, these educational partisans argued that the crisis in education was at the root of the troublesome decline in national productivity and central to the country's sliding competitive edge. The failure of our schools was even said to be reflected in the character of the population and the ingenuity of the American work force. The core issue was the very future of 'American prosperity, security, civility. . . . If an unfriendly foreign power had attempted to impose on America the mediocre educational performance that exists today, we might well have viewed it as an act of war. As it stands, we have allowed this to happen to ourselves' (National Commission on Excellence in Education, 1983). The threat was considered overwhelming.

These 'white papers' offered evidence of myriad symptoms of this 'mediocrity': declining test scores, failure of schools to place high academic demands on students, dangerously lax level of school discipline, absence of strict and systematically applied criteria for promotion between grades, curricula too vulnerable to the vicissitudes of student choice, and significant drops in mathematical, scientific, technological, and foreign language studies (Shapiro, 1990; Shor, 1986). There was also a lack of adequate computer training essential for participating in a technological society. It was claimed on top of these failures, the publications asserted that public support for education had declined and that confidence in the schools was at an all-time low. Taken for granted in these analyses was the assumption that the graduates of US high schools and colleges were, at best, mediocre. This 'rising tide of mediocrity' was supposedly a threat to 'our very future as a nation and as a people' (National Commission on Excellence in Education, 1983, p. 23 and *Educating Americans for the 21st Century*, Executive Summary).

EDUCATIONAL POLITICS AND POSTINDUSTRIAL PROBLEMS

Taken together, these findings and recommendations portray a society in trouble. The reports focus on key segments of the US where major social and economic conflicts had occurred. They underscore the fact that governing most institutions is an exercise in 'crisis management'. They not only point to the low quality of educational achievement *per se*, but to the failure of American schools to promote and sustain democratic values. Not surprisingly, most people (from Congressional leaders to the typical American parent) are convinced that not only do our educational institutions reflect a society in crisis, but they are also a major cause of our deteriorating social and economic conditions.

However, there are important limits to this interpretation and contradictions to unravel, which might help us understand the broader and more significant societal transformations taking place. We believe that a language of 'excellence' (which emerged in the mid 1970s) echoes in our talk of schools today. It serves as the cornerstone of a strategy to cure the malaise threatening the future of high-tech America. Underlying this historical rhetoric is an elite's attempt to instrumentalize a serious contemporary crisis for techno-industrial interests while only secondarily being concerned about improving the quality of American education. At issue here is not our educational crisis *per se* (one that is most evident in schools of the poor and in 'savage inequalities' that persist across America), but rather its interpretation and how that crisis has been manipulated to facilitate a larger elitist technocorporate, postindustrial transformation of American society (Kozol, 1991). Let us consider some of the most important working assumptions of the publications that have molded our understanding of schools and our views of contemporary society.

Nothing plays a more significant role in the portrait of the educational crisis than the failure of schools to provide students with the skills needed to succeed in high-tech America. Essential to this ideology of reform is the long-standing belief that schools must build a path to the work place. It is assumed that a basic function of modern education is to provide students with appropriate job skills and work-relevant values and attitudes. According to the Commission charges, American schools are not fulfilling this role.

The facts are more problematic. Whereas the reports typically assumed the need for high-tech training, studies of the contemporary labor market painted a radically different picture. Most job growth is occurring in areas that require the least skill, especially in the expanding service sector. Even when high-tech industries are most broadly defined, they accounted for only a small proportion of new jobs. According to the US Bureau of Labor Statistics, growth in such job categories as building custodian, cashier, secretary, kitchen helper, guard, and door-keeper are all above the percentage of total job growth in areas such as computer systems analyst, programmer, and even computer operator (Richie, Hecker, and Burgan, 1983, p. 50).

Even more fundamental is our failure to handle the uncertain relation between education and job skills. In fact, no premise is more essential to modern educational ideologies than the belief that education is basic to economic development, especially in advanced technological societies. This presupposes that schooling requirements for jobs steadily increase because of technological change and that schools provide the training demanded for more highly skilled employment. But the supporting evidence is remarkably thin. An extensive review of the literature on the link between education and jobs not only concludes that there is 'no clear contribution to economic development beyond the provision of mass literacy', but that education is often 'irrelevant' or even 'counterproductive' to on-the-job productivity (Black and Worthington, 1986, pp. 257-80; Aronowitz and Giroux, 1985; Collins, 1979; Berg, 1971). Instead, studies show that work experience itself, not formal school instruction, most effectively contributes to job competence. Schooling is not a highly efficient method of training the work force.

A second issue is the obsession with testing and test scores. While many reports emphasize the decline of national examination scores, the evidence is often misleading and sometimes inaccurate. Numerous educational experts have shown that the reality of declining scores is questionable. Moreover, even where statistical evidence of decline is valid, its causes are open to a wide range of interpretations. For example, while it is true that between 1952 and 1982, the average Scholastic Aptitude Test (SAT) verbal score fell 50 points, by 1982 (the year before most of the key national reports were made public), SAT scores had actually begun to rise, a reality which the Congressional Budget Office itself confirmed. Other indices like the NAEP (National Assessment of Educational Progress) Reading Test for 1971, 1975, and 1980 showed that 17-year-olds 'were doing about as well in their total reading ability as they were ten years earlier' (Stedman and Kaestle, 1985, pp. 204-10; Judy, 1980). There is also evidence of systematically increasing scores in law school and medical college admission tests, as well as rising scores on a significant number of the College Board's own achievement tests.

Given the complexities surrounding the problem of testing (which include possible bias in test questions, the debate over whether these tests measure aptitude or learned achievement, and the actual narrowing of the gap between minorities and whites in SAT verbal performance), the decline of scores hardly seems certain. Most test scores and their use in debates over educational crisis (including claims of success when glimmers of higher scores are perceived) have confused an already complicated situation. Instead of firmly capturing a schooled reality, the use of test scores in the debate over schools adds a layer of confusion and ideological obfuscation to an already complicated and politically charged situation.

TRADITIONAL BELIEFS AND EDUCATIONAL REFORMS

Perhaps even more important than the myth of high-tech employment and the misuse of test scores is how most reports about US schools have sought to perpetuate Americans' faith in traditional beliefs over the historical role of educational institutions in the society. In this view, schools have effectively served to further the American ideals of democracy, equality, upward mobility, and economic development. However, there are serious distortions in such a nostalgic portrait and important questions about the relation between schooling and commitment to these values that have gone unanswered. Rather than envisioning schools as the cauldrons of economic progress and social promise, a more critical analysis reveals many ways schools buttressed class-privilege, created inequalities, and undercut democratic ideals. (There are many excellent 'revisionist' histories of American education, although even among these critical analyses, there are significant methodological and theoretical differences. See Spring, 1976; Katznelson and Weir, 1985; Katz, 1971; Bowles and Gintis, 1976; Nasaw, 1979; Carnoy and Levin, 1985.)

It is the power of a 'legend' not the 'reality(ies) we have inherited' that most animates these reports and has decisively influenced public understanding of the schools (Greer, 1973, p. 33). Indeed, critical histories of American education show that schools have been regularly used to mediate economic inequalities and social dislocations which capitalist transformations have precipitated. School 'reforms' have been intimately connected with the conflicts between American democratic ethos and economic disparities. Historians identify three central junctures in which schools were called upon to rationalize and legitimate basic economic transformations. We have now entered a fourth period of American educational reform, a time that is intimately associated with the emergence of a 'postindustrial' society.

In the first reform period (from the late 1830s through the 1840s), 'common schools' were to become 'the balance wheel of the social machinery', responding to a growing urban population, the decline of the skilled craftsperson, and the demise of self-sufficient farmers (Horace Mann, cited in Curti, 1974, p. 134). The schools were promoted as 'the best antidote to the social turmoil generated by universal male suffrage, Jacksonian democracy, and a restive population of urban laborers' (Nasaw, 1979, p. 40; Bowles and Gintis, 1976, pp. 160-73). This curriculum became the basis of a new moral education molding students' character through new forms of social control.

Between 1890 and 1920, schools were again used to promote socioeconomic transformation from an entrepreneurial world to one which large-scale bureaucratic firms predominated. For these 'progressive' reformers, it was only a new professional elite of 'educational executives' (trained in the hierarchical organizational techniques of Taylor's scientific management and the canons of business efficiency) who could reshape the school in the image of a modern factory system (Tyack and Hansot, 1982; Haber, 1964; Weibe,

1967). The introduction of the 'comprehensive high school' became the institutionalized mechanism for 'Americanizing' immigrant groups often seen at the forefront of labor radicalism). The school's job was to extend the requisite training and internalize the new patterns of authority demanded for an evolving corporate managerial revolution. The need to institutionalize such new patterns of social efficiency found one of its strongest adherents in Elwood Cubberley, Dean of the School of Education at Stanford University (Bowles and Gintis, 1976, p. 199; Spring, 1972, Chapter 6).

The third period of educational reform followed World War II. It resulted in the creation of a multitiered hierarchical system that provided both a place for a new working middle class clientele and insurance that elite universities could maintain their selectivity and privileged status. While the establishment of more open-access community colleges was basically designed to train 'skilled subprofessional white collar workers', what is crucial here is the transformation on the elite front. The phrase 'skilled subprofessional white-collar workers' comes from Bowles and Gintis in their discussion of the group of 'rapidly growing occupational titles' whose training was to come from the expanding university system (Bowles and Gintis, 1976, p. 205). (See also Clark, 1960, pp. 569-77.)

The challenge was to confront an emerging 'science gap'. The 'knowledge race' required a vast outpouring of new funds for scientific research and development and the training of engineers and physical scientists. (On the emergence of 'big science', see Kargon, 1983, p. 152; Mukerji, 1989.) The profitability of research and development (R & D), the rhetoric of the Cold War, and the shift in the international division of labor that jeopardized American hegemony laid the basis for the 'federal contract university' that institutionalized the connection between the growth of higher education, US 'national security', and the expertise of a scientific elite. In fact, strengthening this relation among education, science, and technology, coupled with a growing recognition of its importance for international economic competition in the era of 'high technology', the groundwork for a new social transformation was thereby established: the appearance of 'postindustrial society' and the birth of a fourth period of American educational reform.

'Postindustrial society' remains a contested concept which is hard to define. Basic to its theoretical formulations is a recognition that, by the 1960s, the American political economy entered a new phase involving a fundamental shift from a predominantly industrial production system toward an information-based service-oriented economy. Information itself became the basic commodity; science and technology were its driving forces. Whereas the traditional industrial system had appropriated science and technology for its own purposes, they now became the productive system itself. One result was an ever-expanding commitment to research and development; another was that training scientists and technicians became a top economic priority.

POSTINDUSTRIAL TRANSFORMATION

What this postindustrial transformation means for American society is not yet clear. Discussing its implications is one of today's most critical issues. But it is clear that such a new social form demands a basic sociopolitical restructuring, raising significant issues regarding a number of fundamental values and assumptions about social inequalities, democratic participation, and political freedom. It also became clear that now dominant elites are rallying around a specific programmatic concept of technocratic postindustrial society; it involves a particular theory of postindustrialism with a specific vision of the future and a set of strategies (including an educational one) to bring it about (Bell, 1973; Beniger, 1986; Ferkiss, 1979; Lasch, 1972; Kleinberg, 1973).

Originating with such writers as Bell (1973), Brzezinski (1976), Etzioni (1968), and Reich (1983), this technocratic theory has been widely accepted. Its supporters include the leading factions of both major American political parties as well as international organizations such as the Trilateral Commission (Sklar, 1980). It calls for establishing a more scientifically managed system of governance which requires the dismantling of the traditional pluralistic system of interest-group politics. Interest groups themselves are seen as the main barriers to achieving technocratic coordination. According to the technocratic analysis, aggressive competition of self-interested groups for scarce resources created a dramatic rise in social entitlements. This caused a 'system's overload' that prevents the development of a comprehensive central plan. By deploying centralized administrative mechanisms, these technocratic strategies seek to depoliticize the interest-group process (thereby facilitating the centralization of resources for scientific and technical development) and demand a massive contraction of the social and political entitlements already held responsible for the crisis (Huntington, 1975; Dickson, 1981; Straussmann, 1978; Fischer, 1990).

Also basic to this emerging model is a new set of values and ideological undergirdings. Traditional capitalist values associated with property, wealth, and production are steadily giving way to values based on knowledge, intellect, and education. The 'professional' replaces the entrepreneur and professionalism itself becomes key to a central postindustrial ideology (Larson, 1977; Collins, 1979, pp. 131-81). Consistent with this technocratic vision, education assumes a more a prominent role. The university, the traditional house of science and enterprise, is accorded special status. Since organizing and producing research is one of the critical tasks in the new social order, the university becomes a primary 'productive agency' for the creation and dissemination of technical ideology. For example, Bell argues that 'in the postindustrial society the chief problem is the organization of science, and the primary institution [is] the university or research institution where such work is carried out' (Bell, 1973). The 'organization of science' takes numerous forms. One is the production of new knowledge; another is the training and professional certification of ever new layers of experts who will take charge of the postindustrial apparatus; a third (largely mediated through professional training) involves bringing new knowledge to bear on the problems of 'social guidance' (that is, the growth of administrative and policy sciences).

The role envisioned for educational institutions in the postindustrial (information) society has never been larger. As in the past, these institutions play a key role in an historically specific resocialization of students for work and citizenship. But in the postindustrial period, schools not only need to inculcate students with new ideologies consistent with the social, economic, and cultural demands of a technocratic society, they are now involved in creating the ideologies themselves (Peschek, 1987). For example, Huntington (1975) is certsin about the centrality of the university and its necessary alignment with the demands of 'society'. He argued, 'By now, higher education is the most important value-producing system in society. That it works poorly or at cross purposes with society should be a matter of great concern' (Huntington in Sklar, 1980, p. 41).

EXCELLENCE REIGNS SUPREME

In the context of fashioning an ideology, the language of excellence became more than hackneyed, neutral rhetoric. While there is some truth to Peterson's (1985) argument that the calls for excellence have been 'mere puff', it is certainly not coincidental that 'action for excellence', 'barriers to excellence', 'excellence competitions', 'centers for excellence', 'excellence circles', and 'excellence in teaching programs' (to name but a few) obsessively invoked a term that had powerful connotations. Beginning in the mid 1970s, excellence became an emotional shibboleth heralding a new era, a key term in the process of ideology-making and social transformation.

Rarely has a word been so widely cited. While the term itself was not new to the social reform literature, its revitalization was first announced in management literature (Gardner, 1961; Peters and Watermans, 1982; Peters and Aush, 1985; Flanders and Utterback, 1985). There, excellence was a response to problems of production, leadership, and control in the contemporary postindustrial organization. From the world of management, the term spread to every institution of society. We were soon enticed to embrace a world of excellence (from microwave ovens, to the Philadelphia Orchestra, to self-discovery and personal growth seminars). In short, excellence became the contemporary jargon of achievement and merit. Is not excellence 'what we do best'? Ronald Reagan rhetorically asked in his final State of the Union address. It even, he responded, 'makes freedom ring'.

While several of the national educational reports of the 1970s and 1980s made an effort to define this term, what is most striking in the educational literature is its amorphous nature, its ability to refer to something and nothing simultaneously. It is revealing how little substance the term excellence seems to carry and how weak is the effort to define it with any precision. However, excellence is firmly entrenched in the kind of technocratic/instrumental operationalization emblematic of the entire period. As one report declares, excellence must 'produce demonstrable improvements'; such 'improvements' should take place within 'clearly expressed' 'standards of performance', and should be achieved 'efficiently' (National Institute of Education, 1984, pp. 15-6). To write of performing 'on the boundary of individual ability' or setting 'high expectations' blurs how talk of excellence has mirrored the contours of this period, obscured the real conflicts of our times, and hidden the technocratic underpinnings that have successfully begun to permeate our schools. (For more information about the excellence movement in education, see Lazerson et al., 1985; Apple, 1987.)

The reports from the educational sphere did not alone create this moment of technocratic ideology-building nor have the many commissions and reporting bodies necessarily been staffed by people who lack concern for real problems. Instead, they have mediated the educational crisis through the conceptual lens of a postindustrial future. Wittingly or unwittingly, the reports analyzed schools from a viewpoint geared more to where they believe society is going (and where many think it should move) than to where our (many) problems really are. In this respect, the function of the commissions has been to find a way to translate ideological requirements which political and economic elites have propagated into educational policy recommendations. Their basic objective was to help shape the way we think and talk about schools and to legitimate a specific reform agenda.

For example, Michael Apple shows how the reports 'shift' the 'terrain of the debate from a concern with inequality and democratization . . . to the language of efficiency, standards, and productivity' (Apple, Summer 1987, p. 200). But it is important to notice that, even in most of the more helpful critical analyses of excellence in education, the notion and use of the term itself is never scrutinized and is often granted the same symbolic, nebulous status it gained in the reports themselves.

Even more specifically, the emphasis on excellence in education responded to three interrelated legitimacy problems the postindustrial transformation has grappled with: the need for a shared moral vision capable of overshadowing the largely instrumental thrust of technocratic postindustrialism; the extension and refinement of a set of meritocratic standards that can justify obvious social inequalities; and the introduction of a more technocratic system of authority designed to legitimate the general depolitization of decision-making.

The lack of a genuine moral vision is the Achilles heel of technocratic theory. As critical theorists eloquently argued, technocratic thought, because of its reliance on technical criteria, lacks a reflexive dimension (Stanley, 1978). It is unable to account for and consensually ground its own world-view without appealing to external normative criteria. As such, excellence announced a vision of 'the good' which attempts to compensate for technocracy's failure to supply a legitimate moral realm. The contemporary call for excellence in the postindustrial context attempted to graft a moral dimension onto an inherently valueless technocratic world view. It adds an ersatz system of shared values to an otherwise instrumental set of societal arrangements typically obsessed with 'thingness', systems, planning, and technique.

The problem of motivation is directly connected to the issue of filling a glaring moral void. In depicting a society-in-crisis and introducing excellence as a term of amelioration, commission reports, labor leaders, educators, and corporate executives purposefully relied on a word that can help remotivate individuals to play their requisite roles in the 'new' society. Many workers and students have found the goals of late corporate capitalism personally meaningless. Many opted for cynical obedience, some rejected cultural expectations for other lifestyles; perhaps the majority drudged on in apathy (Lerner, 1986; Roses, 1989; Kreisberg, 1992). Imbuing students with motivation and drive for relative achievement, especially in their later work lives, has been a central goal of educational institutions. The turn to excellence brought this educational thrust into even greater prominence.

To understand the appearance of excellence in the contemporary discussion of educational reform, it is important to see its connection to meritocracy. Historically, meritocracy has been the social form of technocracy. It is a system of hierarchy, status, and advancement based on achievement which is largely technical in nature. What provides meritocracy with its legitimacy is that it is rooted in the same source as technocracy: science and its methodology. In meritocracy, as in science, the validity of claims may be determined using objective procedures such as tests, measurements, and their pragmatic consequences. In such a framework, knowledge rather than material wealth or traditional authority becomes the basis for status and power.

But although the ideology of meritocracy has long been basic to corporate capitalism and government bureaucracies, it has recently become the subject of broad debate. Criticized for its narrow and simplistic worldview, further challenged when minority groups demanded social equality (including equal access to education), meritocratic ideology has been directly attacked. The call for excellence is also designed to reinvigorate meritocracy's claims to truth and fairness, to relegitimize its 'objective' methods and 'universal' standards. In effect, the language of excellence has been used to remold the concept of meritocracy into a higher sounding, more encompassing moral discourse and to disguise its narrower, more elitist realities.

Yet, beyond this ideological attempt to remoralize an otherwise instrumental conceptualization of meritocracy, an even more troublesome aspect of the appeal to excellence is the way it has been programmatically institutionalized in both the schools and workplace. Here, we find a set of concrete practices, extrapolated almost directly from managerial literature, designed to inculcate in both classrooms and administrators' offices, the ethos and priorities of the new social paradigm. More specifically, whereas the standard conception of achievement standards is designed to measure student ability to perform, a reformulated language of meritocracy-as-excellence adds a deeper social-psychological dynamic. The new ideological thrust seeks to instill personal meaning in an otherwise impersonal (and often personally meaningless) set of institutional goals and standards. Excellence is about personhood; it is essentially about qualities of the self.

Because excellence is most often associated with the nature of a self (rather than the workings of a system, institution, or process), its use connotes images of personhood, personal accomplishments, and individual responsibility. In effect, excellence is necessarily about how a distinctive self comes to terms with a world. But by carefully framing the ideologies of excellence within the assumptions of the meritocratic-technocratic project, these very qualities of the person are distorted by being molded to the demands of a specific crisis of legitimation and motivation that depends on the allegiance and initiative of workers, students, and citizens when their connection to the system is deemed most precarious and necessary.

To idealize excellence and bemoan 'mediocrity' in work, school, and political performance is to blame individuals for the failures of institutions and to shape a language of motivation that can persuade the individual to perform more 'productively' and act more 'responsibly'. Calls to excellence concern themselves with questions of pride and enthusiasm; they are about asking individuals to 'shine' (Peters and Watermans, 1982, p. xxiii).

Such incantations in the private realm have purposefully combined self and institution, person and performance, individual and society to create a significant misunderstanding of an individual's place in the world. Such interpretations push us to systematically blur the differences between responsibilities of the self and structural requirements of an emerging sociocultural system. In reality, as a motivational tool, the excellence strategy (and its ongoing offshoots) attempted to revive market place competition. The technique was merely to resituate it in the interpersonal world of the bureaucratic work place and school. This is blaming the victim, a process even more pernicious and effective because it comes when the security of self-definition and the sanctity of self-understanding are problematic for most people (Ryan, 1976). While this dynamic of blame plays an important role in further weakening a self, it simultaneously strengthens the ethic of meritocratic social divisions. To be judged less-than-excellent is to be relegated to a lower rung and to suffer the long-acknowledged 'hidden injuries' of class (Sennett and Cobb, 1972). The diminution and systematic 'invasion of the self' has been described sensitively in Christopher Lasch's (1978, 1984) and bell hooks (1993) works. Typically, this psychology of failure manifests itself in a further loss of self-confidence and, more often than not, passivity in the face of authority.

But what makes the present period of reform distinctive is the systematic effort to employ rigorous standards of achievement that insidiously exploit these psychological processes. In school and the workplace, criteria of excellence put success further out of reach and make failure more 'objective'. Not only does such a strategy (that, in the educational arena, included the increasing demand for national standards and curriculum and for nationwide testing) lead to greater personal pain, it also legitimates an elitism essential to the new technocratic project.

Finally, there is the system of authority itself. Basic to a technocratic/postindustrial system is the authority of science and technology. But recently, science and technology have been sharply criticized in many quarters of society. In the face of numerous crises and threats which technological 'progress' has generated (for example, governments of all political persuasions systematically plunder the environment), important voices question the fundamental legitimacy of the scientific world-view itself.

A significant literature sought to analyze the roots of the 'scientific' mindset and its pernicious effects on humanity and the ecosystem (Rifkin, 1985; McKibbens, 1989; Bordo, 1987; Berman, 1981). Again, an ideology of excellence has been called upon to relegitimize the culture of science and its system of authority. In curricular terms, many education reports that publicly introduced this fourth period of educational reform attempted to infuse excellence in the schools via rejuvenation of the liberal arts. Despite this lip service to the importance of liberal studies (to broaden historical/cultural literacy, develop critical thinking skills, return to the 'great books'), the elites' most pressing interest is with science, not the humanities.

One of the most influential efforts in the 'great books' direction can be found in Mortimer Adler (1982). Also see Kerry Walters (1990) for a valuable critique of the turn to 'critical thinking' as a central educational goal and the essays in Mark Edmundson's edited book (1993).

TECHNOLOGICAL LITERACY

One indication of these new directions was the large amounts of new money from legislative appropriations and foundation grants that poured into universities to revitalize the scientific infrastructure (laboratories, computer systems, research centers, university-industrial-parks) and to improve scientific education (both training and equipment.) Many authors described this role of the university (Kenney, 1986; Kalas, 1986; Mukerji, 1989). Another manifestation is the fact that even within the liberal arts and sciences curriculum per se, the call for excellence has been, in practice, increasingly preoccupied with 'technological literacy'.

Designed largely for students in the nonscientific disciplines, the technological literacy movement confronted a critically important problem: wide-

spread scientific and technological illiteracy in American society renders
citizens unable to participate in the ostensibly neutral domain of technology
in which political decisions are increasingly framed. That is, for democracy
to function properly, citizens must have enough scientific competence to
judge (if not actually make) technological decisions. In fact, it is argued that
only through facilitating a greater understanding of (and political involvement
in) such technically-based decisions can democracy be made viable in a high-
tech society. But, if the proclaimed purpose of technological literacy is to
facilitate democracy, how does it fit into a technocratic strategy basically
designed to depoliticize and limit citizen participation? A closer look at
'technological literacy' suggests an ironic twist.

A case can be made that an important function (the hidden latent function) of programs for technological literacy is not so much to teach competence in judging scientific and technological matters, or to provide people
with tools that empower and offer new channels of access. Its function is to
bolster the authority of science, an objective designed to counter the disrup-
tive impact of the antitechnocratic criticisms of science and technology. (Our
basic argument about the meaning and teaching of 'scientific literacy' came
from Dickson [1984]. An important connection between 'scientific' and
'computer' literacy can be found in Roszak [1986, Section III] and Bowers
[1988, especially Chapters 1 and 3].)

One clue to this goal can be found in a report on scientific education
which the National Science Foundation and the US Department of Education
(1980) issued. Concerned that schools no longer infuse students with an
appropriate attitude toward science, the report called on teachers and administrators to develop new strategies to provide a more positive climate for science, its methods, and its contents. What is significant here is not solely the
fear of a shortage of future scientists and technical workers, but the legitimacy of a culture of science and the acceptance of a world built in its image.

The primary goal of technological literacy programs may be to teach
enough of the logic and knowledge of science and technology that students
come to respect its institutions and culture, but not enough to question its
general premises or specific findings. That is, the expansion of technological
literacy (understood as the appreciation of science rather that its mastery) is
intended not to encourage skills that would enable informed citizens to critically evaluate and participate in technically based decisions, but rather to
create more willingness to accept the conclusions of scientific experts and to
exacerbate inequalities of access and understanding that have always existed.
'Scientification by a still inaccessible elite' is the vital need of an emerging
technocratic society. Michael Black and Richard Worthington describe this
new role of science in a particularly useful way:

> Instead of clarifying policy objectives, science becomes a techno-
> cratic instrument which mystifies the public by creating a language

package inaccessible to journalist and citizen alike. The result is
frustrated intervention by outsiders in the actual public policy process coupled with a real fall in democratic participatory practice
(Black and Worthington, 1986, pp. 277-278).

Given this context, this remarkable obsession with our schools cannot be
understood as simply a worry about problems teachers and students face
daily. Rather, what has become something of a societal preoccupation might
be better understood as part of a broader effort to institutionalize the vision
of political and technocratic elites who singled out a social institution easily
blamed and vulnerable to the vicissitudes of ideological manipulation.

This technocratic system and its 'new class' elites did not spontaneously
emerge in full form. A project of such scale and importance must work its
way through an entire culture, molding values, relations to authority, technologies, and status structures to its own requirements. To argue that the technocratic interpretation of postindustrialism gained significant presence through
the ideology of excellence and its various permutations in this fourth period
of educational reform is not to overlook the fact that technocratic restructuring will confront a multiplicity of obstacles to its full realization. It is, however, to acknowledge that the presence of something like an 'excellence
movement' has been extremely successful in naming the basic terrain of
discourse about socioeconomic and school failure and in creating habits of
thought we still use to rationalize an even broader attack on the legitimacy of
the entire public sphere today. There are close links between the destruction
of public lands, the attack on public funding for the arts, and the systematic
reduction of government support for public education. In terms of the latter,
in 1983-4, state taxes accounted for almost 85 per cent of the total state
operating budget for the State University of New York. In the 1995-6 budget,
that percentage dipped to 49 per cent; and that may drop to 33 per cent soon.
Similar statistics could be cited for other state university sytems. For example,
Connecticut has the highest per capita personal income in the US, but its
public share for higher education has now also been reduced to 33 per cent.

CONCLUSION

Undoubtedly, new ideologies will emerge to replace excellence after its
particular influence has been played out. Further research is needed to chart
the concrete ways in which excellence and other emergent languages have
been reshaped to fit particular interests and to examine the on-going struggles
within the schools and how rhetoric and everyday experiences work with and
against each other. Also, we must become more aware of imaginative pedagogical approaches and educational experiments that have sought equity,
quality, and hope through the birth of new sources of public language (Meier,

1995; Duckworth, 1987; McClaren, 1989; Greene, 1988; Noddings, 1992). In the final analysis, both meaningful educational reform and relevant social critique demand further investigation in this emerging postindustrial era.

ACKNOWLEDGMENTS

Earlier versions of this chapter were published in *TELOS*, No. 76, Summer 1988; and in *Bildung, Gesellschaft, soziale Ungleichheit* (Suhrkamp, 1994).

13 Pedagogy in the Age of Predatory Culture

Peter McLaren

ABSTRACT

This chapter deals with youth, schooling, taboos, apathy, postmodernism, and what pedagogy can do in this predatory age. Some of the key elements of predatory culture are pursuit of naked power, crisis mentality, stalkers and victims, social divisiveness, and dominance of capital and its concerns over democracy. Media culture pictures a mean and scary world, thanks to fear-mongering in our media presentations. Any new world order must first involve parents and educators in creating a new moral order in school and at home. A new critical pedagogy is needed to counterbalance the New Right as well as to create schools, schooling, and school systems which can respond adequately to postmodern challenges, including overcoming youth's apathy.

TABOO

We now inhabit predatory culture (Farren, 1993). Predatory culture is a field of invisibility (of stalkers and victims) precisely because it is so obvious. Its obviousness immunizes its victims against a full disclosure of its menacing capabilities. In predatory culture, identity is fashioned mainly (and often violently) around the excesses of marketing and consuming and the natural social relations of postindustrial capitalism. Life is lived through speed technology in anticipation of recurring accidents of identity and endless discursive collisions with otherness because it is virtually impossible in predatory culture to be cotemporal with what one both observes and desires. Predatory culture is the left-over detritus of bourgeois culture stripped of its arrogant pretense to civility and cultural lyricism and replaced by a stark obsession with power fed by the voraciousness of capitalism's global voyage.

It is a culture of universalism compressed into local time. Naturalized by and entrenched in primitive accumulation, it has exceeded its own wildest fantasies of acquisition and has dropped its facade of civility and compassion. It can stand naked in its unholy splendor; it can make no claims to be just and fair; it can now survive without artifice or camouflage.

Abandoning the historical criteria for making ethical judgments, predatory culture refuses to wager on the side of radical hope; instead, it cleaves false hope out of the excrement of image-value. It collapses all distinctions between the real and the imaginary and seeks to conceal its own simulating activity. Predatory culture is deceptive. We are its children.

The capitalist fear that fuels predatory culture functions at the world level by installing necessary monetary and social crises. Computers are the new entrepreneurs of history; their users are merely scraps of figurative machinery, partial subjects in the rag and bone shop of predatory culture, Manichean allegories of 'us' against 'them', 'self' against 'other'. The social, cultural, and human have been subsumed within capital. This is predatory culture.

Largely because of the way in which media shape and merchandise morality and construct certain forms of citizenship and individual and collective identities, our understanding of the meaning and importance of democracy has become impoverished in proportion to its dissolution and retreat from contemporary social life. In this time of democratic decline in the United States, ideals and images have become detached from stable and agreed-upon meanings and associations and are now beginning to assume a reality of their own. The world of the media splinters, obliterates, peripheralizes, partitions, and segments social space, time knowledge, and subjectivity to unify, encompass, entrap, totalize, and homogenize them. Missing from the educational debate is a discussion of how capitalism achieves this cultural and ideological totalization and homogenization and, through it, insinuates itself into social practices and private perceptions (Grossberg, 1988a).

Today's increasingly 'disorganized' capitalism has produced a gaudy sideshow that promotes a counterfeit democracy of flags and emblems. It harnesses the affective currency of popular culture so the average American's investment in being 'American' has reached an unparalleled high. How are the subjectivities (experiences) and identities of individuals and the production of media knowledges within popular culture mutually articulated? What is not being discussed in today's educational debate is the desperate need to create a media-literate citizenry that can disrupt, contest, and transform media apparatuses so they no longer have the power to infantilize the population and continue to beget passive, fearful, paranoid, and apolitical social subjects.

George Gerbner (1989/90) and others have pointed out that American television viewers accept a distorted picture of the real world 'more readily than reality itself'. In television reality, men outnumber women three to one; women are usually mothers or lovers, rarely work outside the home, and are natural victims of violence. It is a reality where less than ten per cent of the population hold blue collar jobs, few elderly people exist, and young blacks accept their minority status as inevitable and anticipate their own victimization. It is a world in which 18 acts of violence an hour occur in children's prime time programs. It also serves as a mass spectacle, reflecting the state's allocative power. We are facing a crisis of predatory culture forged through the unholy symbiosis of capitalism and technology (technocapitalism), a crisis that has profoundly global implications. We have been warned by the cyberpunk generation, but our eyes and ears no longer belong to us.

Educators need to realize that a new world order cannot be realistically achieved without first creating a new moral order at home (in our classrooms and living rooms) - one that refuses to challenge the received truths or accepted conventions that have provoked the current crisis of history and identity. So far, Presidents Bush and Clinton have reproduced a moral order in which young people are able to resist being motivated to enter into any logic of opposition through counterpublic spheres of cultural resistance.

It is sad that the supposed 'education president' (George Bush) invested more in the intelligence quotients of his weapons of war than in those who grow despondent in the nation's schools. While politicians self-righteously decry the retrenchment of the conservative 'hard-liners' in Russia, they fail to see the ideological affinities with their own political positions; incredibly, they see their conservative position as somehow more enlightened and the policies they support immune to the possibility that they could contribute to social ill. This has blinded them to the ways in which dominant social order continues to shut the colonized out of history, even in this so-called era of interculturalism and growth of polyethnic and polylingual communities. When debating public education, we must seriously examine how contemporary forms of schooling reproduce national images of citizenship.

The kind of curriculum focus needed in today's schools must actively contest the historical amnesia which contemporary cultural forms found in the mass media have created. Students should explore why they identify with Dirty Harry and Rambo and begin to historicize that identification in the context of the larger political and social issues facing the country.

Public opinion among the wealthy and powerful is more supportive of the public school system and current reform efforts; those disempowered because of race, socioeconomic status, or gender do not share this opinion. Conditions in this country's school systems have appreciably worsened for the populations (particularly African American and Latino youth) that will be increasing in numbers. Groups actively lobbying for minority positions on issues dealing with race, social, and welfare concerns are labeled 'ethnocentric' or 'separatist' within the conservation agenda. These accusers include Diane Ravitch, Roger Kimball, William Bennett, and Lynne V.B. Cheney. Within such an agenda (which claims to preserve the unconditional principles of civilized society), the call for diversity is sanctioned only when the converging of diverse voices collapses into a depoliticized coexistence based on capitulation to the hidden imperatives of Eurocentrism, logocentrism, and patriarchy. Educators and students who refuse to genuflect before the Western cultural tradition and see it as the apogee of cultural and political achievement are branded as perverse, ignorant, and malicious sophists who 'defiled reason' (Kimball, 1991; Ravitch, 1990). This ideological position effectively heralds the impeding demise of white culture: 'If white people have any pride in their heritage, now is the time to act because your history is under assault'! This call for white authenticity embalms the past for people of color and shrouds their histories in the thinning strands of the moral and social consciousness of a nation with social amnesia. It also shrouds domination in a white sheet of race, class, and gender purity and silences questions of racism, sexism, homophobia, and class oppression.

What Anglocentric educators who teach under the sign of 'First World' do not understand is that our schools fail many minority students precisely because of overemphasizing the status of one's cultural capital. Ironically, urban students (from places such as New York's Howard Beach, Ozone Park, and El Barrio) are likely to learn more about Eastern Europe in contexts which *soi-dissant* metropolitan intellectuals have desigend than about the Harlem Renaissance, Mexico, Africa, the Caribbean, or Aztec or Zulu culture. The sad irony is that test scores based on information filtered from the Western canon and bourgeois cultural capital and developed in the business salons of the Prozac generation are used to justify school district and state funding initiatives. The reality of schooling is that United States society is composed of differentially empowered publics. Mainstream schooling ensures that those publics which already enjoy most of the power and privilege in society will transmit their advantage to succeeding generations. This ensures intergeneration continuity: working-class students get working-class jobs; affluent students get jobs that will advance their lives and their children's.

Gangs in predatory culture are situated in what Dwight Conquergood calls a 'media demonology' that foments 'moral panics' about gangbangers who are categorized as social defectives, occupy a subterranean rogues gallery of the half-human *Untermensch*, and have been socially identified as the expendable human excrement. As Conquergood notes, public opinion of gangs (largely media motivated) deflects attention from the 'political and economic macropatterns of exclusion and displacement which shape the microtexture of everyday struggle for poor and socially marginalized people' (Conquergood, 1994, p. 54). This ignores the fact that the criminalization of gangs is directly linked to deindustrialization, disinvestment, economic polarization, residential segregation, real estate speculation, gentrification, and the abandonment, neglect ,and collapse of civic institutions such as schools in the name of retrograde fiscal responsibility. We demonize those who are physically threatening predators (like gang members) and the less dangerous, eyesore predators (such as the homeless) who serve predatory culture as little more than an affront to bourgeois sensibility and decorum.

Cultural literacy spokespersons such as Hirsch have reduced literacy to a cultural thesaurus students must memorize if they aspire to become active, engaged citizens. Yet when culture is despairingly viewed as a storehouse of dead facts, then the concept of difference (when applied to issues of race, class, gender, age, sexual preference, or disability) can be absorbed into what I call 'dead pluralism'. Dead pluralism keeps at bay the need to historicize difference, to recognize the hierarchical production of systems of difference in whose interests such hierarchies serve, and to acknowledge difference as a social construction forged within asymmetrical relations of power, conflicting interests, and a climate of dissent and opposition. The 'pluralism' that supposedly already undergirds our so-called multicultural society in the vision of Diane Ravitch and Roger Kimball is based on uncoerced consensus, interracial and intergenerational harmony, and zero-degree public unity - a perspective shrouded in the lie of democratic ubiquity. When Ravitch and Kimball call for pluralism over separatism, they are really buttressing the status quo against disempowered minorities seeking social justice.

The real danger facing education is not simply the general public's refusal to recognize its embeddedness in relations of power and privilege at the level of everyday life, but rather the fact that the public prefers to act as if few (or no) such political linkages exist. The danger is neither an apathetic nation nor a cynical one, but rather the ability of the public sphere to exist relatively uncontested. Why? I believe that it has to do with the ability of the larger public sphere to mobilize desire and secure the public's passion and the relative inability of progressive educators to analyze the social, cultural, moral, and political implications of such an ability.

In the US and Canada, work within the field of critical pedagogy is now underway during what I consider a precipitous and precarious time. We live in a moment of particular urgency and importance for the future of democracy as we bear witness to two conflicting potentialities, manifesting themselves in the worldwide struggle between democratic forms of social life and those labeled totalitarian and autocratic. A significant dimension of this crisis involves the politics of meaning and representation. We must consider the cultural logic or sensibility currently organizing aspects of everyday life, a logic which has been variously theorized under the term 'postmodern'. Since there is no shared understanding of what constitutes a 'real' postmodern political or cultural agenda, I use the term in its most general sense to refer to, among other things, the rupturing of the unitary fixity and homogenizing logic of the grand narratives of Western European thought, which Lyotard refers to as the *grands recits* of modernity (such as the dialectic of spirit, the emancipation of the worker, the accumulation of wealth, the steady march of progress leading to the classless society, and the mastery of nature). The term also covers the cultural reproduction of subjects produced from the consumer myths and images which the global dispersion of capital, the social construction of unfixed identities, and the leveling of the opposition between high art and popular art have produced. It also suggests the rejection of truth claims grounded in a transcendent reality independent of collective human existence, an abandonment of the teleology of science, the construction of lifestyles out of consumer products, and the use of cultural forms of communication and social relations that evolved from the disorganization of capitalism.

The debate surrounding postmodernity is gathering momentum in literature, social theory, cultural studies, education, and legal studies. A central thesis of postmodernism is that meaning is increasingly becoming severed from representation. '[I]n our society the sign no longer refers to a signified but always only to other signs, so that we no longer encounter anything like meaning without speech, but only move in an endless chain of signifiers' (Burger, 1989, p. 124). The unity of the sign and its ability to anchor meaning has been significantly weakened. The average person lacks a language for making sense of everyday life (Grossberg, 1988a, p. 180).

As a result of the postmodern condition, the alienation of the subject associated with modernism has been replaced by its fragmentation, which Madan Sarup (citing literary critic Fredric Jameson and economist Ernest Mandel) labels the 'refusal to engage with the present or to think historically . . . a random cannibalization of all the styles of the past . . . [an increasing incapacity] of fashioning representations of our current experiences . . . [and] the penetration and colonization of Nature and the Unconscious by contemporary forms of multinational capitalism' (Sarup, 1989, p. 145). We need not hold that poststructuralist and postmodernist theories (which recently emerged to engage and explore our location within the postmodern condition) are necessarily antagonistic to the project of emancipation.

Postmodernity involves us in the tension which modernist and postmodernist attempts to resolve the contradiction of being both the subject and object of meaning have produced. David Holt (1989, p. 174) describes two ways to order reality by asking: Does meaning generate life? Or does life generate meaning? The first question is posed within the discourse of modernity which assumes that our lives should be lived out as an explanation of a meaning prior to life, a transcendental meaning codified in a conception of metaphysical truth. The second reflects that the advent of postmodernity and the shattering of the notion of 'truth' is based on a metaphysical assumption. To live life as if it generated meaning is to live within the contingency and uncertainty of the present (in which ethics, tradition, and agency are revealed as social constructions or cultural fictions). Living within the tension created by these two questions generates others: Do we act to represent meanings or for the sake of the possible effects of our actions? Does action create identity or does it follow from identity? While various types of philosophers have always debated these questions, the postmodern condition has turned our attention to the interface between such questions. The educator must help students critically engage the politics and ideologies which inform these questions as they begin to understand themselves as both a product and producer of meaning. We claim that it is precisely by critically engaging the dialectical tension between these two questions that we must assume our role as active social agents. Living as a critical social agent means knowing how to live contingently and provisionally without the certainty of knowing the truth, while courageously taking a stand on issues of human suffering, domination, and oppression. Living with courage and conviction with the understanding that knowledge is always partial and incomplete is the 'postmodern' task of the critical educator.

Bauman lists as characteristics of postmodernity 'the widespread aversion to grand social designs, the loss of interest in absolute truths, the privatization of redemptive urges [that is, self as opposed to social transformation], the reconciliation with the retaliate - merely heuristic - value of all life techniques, the acceptance of the irredeemable plurality of the world' (Bauman, 1988-89, p. 39). He sees these characteristics as a consequence of the fact that the abolition of strangeness has risen to the level of a universal human condition.

Ineradicable plurality is now a constitutive quality of existence and represents a refusal to overcome differences for the sake of sameness. Values (uniformity and universalism) so central to modernity have become ruptured and replaced by coexistence and tolerance. Bauman writes that 'in the plural and pluralistic world of postmodernity, every form of life is permitted on principle; or, rather, no agreed principles are evident which may render any form of life impermissible'. He distinguishes between the modernist (cognitive) and postmodernist (postcognitive) questions. Modernist questions ('How can I interpret this world of which I am a part? And what am I in it?') have been replaced by postmodernist queries ('Which world is it? What is to be done in it? Which of my selves is to do it?') (Bauman, 1988-89, p. 40).

The so-called cognitive questions are not really cognitive; instead, they 'reach beyond the boundaries of epistemology'; they are fundamentally pre-epistemological. Modernist questions (such as 'What is there to be known? Who knows it? How do they know it and with what degree of certainty'?) are replaced by ones which do not locate the task for the knower but attempt to nurture the knower: 'What is a world? What kinds of worlds are there, how are they constituted, and how do they differ'? Questions demanding certainty (such as 'How is knowledge transmitted from one knower to another, and with what degree of reliability?') are positioned against 'What happens when different worlds are placed in confrontation, or when boundaries between worlds are violated'? (Bauman, 1988-89, p. 42).

Bauman's insights into the shift from a modernist quest for certainty to a postmodernist attempt to understand shifting contexts are very important. They speak to a growing tension between these two positions which possess both empowering and constraining potential for the struggle against oppression and the quest for human freedom. While we should welcome the breaking down of grand theories informed by Eurocentric and patriarchal assumptions and epistemological certainties, we are aware that questions related to oppression and liberation have a greater propensity to become lost in a new postmodernist relativism, where the question of 'How can we eliminate suffering'? collapses into 'What is suffering'? Bauman captures this tension when he writes: 'It seems in the world of universal strangeness the stranger is no longer obsessed with the absoluteness of what ought to be; nor is he disturbed by the relativity of what is' (Bauman, 1988-89, p. 42).

There are both utopian and 'dysutopian' currents to the postmodern condition and poststructuralist theorizing. But we must recognize that postmodernity has brought with it not only new forms of collective self-reflexivity but also new forms of ideological colonization. Critics as diverse as Andreas Hyssen, Todd Gitlin, and Fredric Jameson maintained that postmodernism has a specifically, though not exclusively, American strain. Cornel West (Stephanson, 1988b, p. 276) labels this 'a form of Americanization of the globe'. The rise of postmodernism has been materially tied to the rise of American capital on a global scale since the late 1950s and early 1960s era of interimperialist rivalry and multinationalization. Jameson argued that the persistence of *l'ancien regime* in Europe precluded the same kind of development there; however, in the US, a whole new system of cultural production emerged and a new, specifically American cultural apparatus or 'cultural dominant' began to serve as a form of ideological hegemony, forcing Third World countries to play 'catch up' (Stephanson, 1988a, p. 8).

Postmodernity has also been described as the era of the death of the Cartesian subject and a retreat from history. Dean MacCannell (1989, p. xiii) goes so far as to say, following Levi-Strauss, that after Hiroshima and Nagasaki and the stockpiling of weapons in accord with strategic nuclear plans, American society deemed it too risky to have history and, therefore, effectively abandoned it as its motive power of development, entering instead the 'reversible time' of so-called primitive societies which, though they are immersed in history, nevertheless try to remain impervious to it.

One strand of contemporary postmodernism grew from juxtaposing currents in American culture: emancipation and the rise of immigration in the late 19th century and assimilation into America's mythological melting pot. Here, difference is flattened out, accommodated to the values of white patriarchal capitalism. This reflects MacCannell's idea that a mere celebration of difference can become an insidious higher form of 'sucking difference out of difference, a movement to the still higher ground of the old arrogant Western Ego that wants to see it all, know it all, and take it all in, an Ego that is isolated by its belief in its own superiority' (MacCannell, 1989, pp. xiv-xv).

A critical understanding of the relationship between the self and other is one of the crucial challenges of current pedagogical practices in the postmodern age. This is especially true in light of MacCannell's observation that two dominant activities shaping world culture are the movement of institutional capital and tourists to remote regions and 'the preparation of the Third World into the First'. By this, he means the movement of refugees and displaced peoples 'from the periphery to the centers of power and affluence'. For instance, in the case of the United States, MacCannell (1989, p. xvi) has noted the profound implications which follow from cultural implosions).

The implication of this for educators is to construct a pedagogy of 'difference' which neither exoticizes nor demonizes the 'other', but rather seeks to locate difference in both its specificity and ability to provide positions for critically engaging social relations and cultural practices.

Like Grossberg (1988a), I do not conceive of postmodernity as a 'total historical rupture' that constitutes the ideological representation of late capitalism, the commodification of our decentered subjectivities, the implosion of the difference between the image and the real, or the collapse of all metanarrative, but rather as a sensibility or logic by which we appropriate (in the contemporary context) cultural practices into our own lives. That is, I wish to call attention to postmodernity as a process significantly less totalizing, as 'determining moments in culture and everyday life'. In this view, postmodernity refers to the 'growing distance, and expanding series of ruptures or gaps, between these various aspects of everyday life, between the available meanings, values and objects of desire which socially organize our existence and identity, and the possibilities for investing in or caring about them which are enabled by our moods and emotions'. There is a feeling that life no longer has any basic purpose to which we can passionately commit. He remarks that our 'mattering maps no longer correspond to any available maps of meaning'. In short, postmodernity is a crisis of meaning and feeling: 'a dissolution of what we might call the "anchoring affect" that articulates meaning and affect'. One of the dangers of postmodern culture is the establishment of what Grossberg calls a 'disciplined mobilization', meaning 'the construction of a frontier as an unbridgeable gap between the livable and the unlivable, the possible and impossible, the real and the unreal'. A disciplined mobilization refers to the temporal and spatial articulation of texts through social practices which give us both stability and mobility in everyday life. It 'defines the very possibilities of where and how we move and stop, of where and how we place and displace ourselves, or where and how we are installed into cultural texts and extended beyond them' (Grossberg, 1988a, pp. 36-40).

Such a 'typography of cultural practices' defines the sites we can occupy within culture, the investments we can make in them, and the places along which we can connect and transform them. Grossberg is especially concerned with the New Right's increasing ability to develop ideological and affective alliances among social groups. That is, looking at the postmodern frontier as a site of struggle among discourse, material practices, and representation, it can be argued that the New Right has been able to rearticulate, reconstruct, and reterritorialize the 'national popular' (the family, nationalism, consumerism, youth, pleasure, and heroes) against itself as affectively charged but ideologically empty. One example of this is the ability of New Class neoconservatives to manipulate traditional populism (Picone, 1987-88, p. 21).

YOUTH AND POSTMODERN APATHY

Even in this postmodern era, the ideological hegemony in the US, while condemnable and powerful, has its contradictory moments. Students often see the critical educator's concern for community and social justice as a threat to their general ideological commitments. For many students, critical pedagogy becomes an uncomfortable and self-contesting exercise. They are reluctant or refuse to question meanings, preferring to live them.

It is not critical pedagogy's purpose to absorb student apathy about politics and social change into traditional political categories and end up offering another 'blaming the victim' analysis of the ideological formation of today's youth. Rather, I acknowledge there are historical conditions which account for youth resistance and apathy. For instance, Grossberg notes that 'youth inserts cultural texts into its public and private lives in complex ways and we need to be aware of the complexity and contradictory nature of youth's social and political positions' (Grossberg, 1988b, p. 139). He rightly recognizes that in our postmodern era, young people exist within the space between subjectification (boredom) and commodification (terror). Our media culture has become a 'buffer zone', a 'paradoxical site' at which today's youth live out a difficult (if not impossible) relation to the future. In fact, Grossberg argues that American youth have largely been formed out of the media strategies of the 'autonomous affect' in which politics, values, and meaning have been reduced to individualized images of morality, self-sacrifice, and community. They are living the surface identities of media images in which the politics of 'feeling good' triumphs over the politics of interpretive insight.

Grossberg points to one cultural struggle in which the New Right leads: the attack on the counterculture of the 1960s and 1970s, in part through its ability to reconstruct the history of the war in Vietnam. A war which youth fought, Vietnam became 'the symbol of the moment when the identification of the postwar youth generations with America fell apart and consequently, the moment when America lost, not only its center but its faith in a center'. Yet, popular narratives in the media now attempt 'to place the war back into the familiar frameworks of traditional war narratives of personal drama'. The existence of the counterculture at that time is generally ignored in popular representations of the war. Rather, the war is interpreted as an attack on America and its sacred values, 'the moment when the postwar youth generations lost their faith, not only in America, but in the possibility of ever finding a center, an identity, in which it could invest'. The effect of ignoring the counterculture is to displace 'the ideological content from youth culture and [transform] it into purely affective relations' or 'affective nostalgia'. That students now have few grounds upon which to imagine constructing an oppositional or counterhegemonic pedagogical stance in a cultural center with no real ideological content (only feelings) makes the challenge of critical pedagogy all the more acute and pressing (Grossberg, 1988a, pp. 56-9).

Part of the problem with youth's refusal to engage in issues of class oppression and social injustice both inside and outside the classroom has to do with the fact that in the Untied States, domination and oppression are not as overt as in many Third World countries. North American civil society is less simply structured by divisions based on the conflict of labor and capital. Consequently, class relations do not appear to cause social inequality. Thus, there is a greater focus on oppressive instances of gender divisions, age differences, and ethnic conflict. In other words, we do not live within structures of terror such as those found in El Salvador or Guatemala, where workers are frequently dispatched by a *coup de grace* through the forehead. Furthermore, collective action does not seem as necessary within a climate of political and cultural pluralism, although the presence of the black underclass and the homeless is somewhat changing this spectatorial detachment towards human oppression. The point is that class, gender, and racial oppression exist, regardless of the perception by the public at large (Baum, 1987).

Grossberg admits that given the New Right's incursion into the frontier between affect and ideology, where only or mainly emotional responses are possible without benefit of ideological understanding or commitment, there is little room for Gramsci's 'optimism of the will' necessary for comprehending political struggle, understanding and confronting affective commitment outside of the system of cultural power within which such an investment is constructed, and assuming a necessary relationship between affective investment and external systems of meaning. The desire among conservatives and die-hard 'patriots' to make flag burning a crime (using either a constitutional amendment or civil blasphemy statute) as a reaction against the recent US Supreme Court ruling is an example of affective commitment in which patriotism is construed as an 'empty center' (Grossberg's term) devoid of the ideological engagement that makes it impossible to undermine any definition of what 'American' means other than absolute commitment to America itself.

In relation to what is happening on the popular front, critical pedagogy must become a strategic and empowering response to those historical conditions which have produced us as subjects and to the ways we are daily inserted into the frontier of popular culture and existing power structures. We claim that clarifying some of the practices of critical pedagogy can, as a form of intellectual labor, have transformative effects, enabling us to deconstruct and move beyond affective investments 'to a higher level of abstraction in order to transform the empirically taken-for-granted into the concretely determined' (Grossberg, 1988a, p. 68).

Dare we conspire to create a critical pedagogy that is able to provide conditions for students to reject what they experience as a given; one that includes a sharpened focus on the relationship among economies (including political, moral, sexual, capital investment, 'free' expression, and belief and identity formation) and the construction of desire and formation of human will; a pedagogy of discontent and of outrage that is able to contest the hegemony of prevailing definitions of the everyday as the 'way things are'; one that refuses the hidebound distinction between lofty expression and popular culture, between art and experience, between reason and the imagination? We need a critical pedagogy that can problematize schooling as a site for the construction of moral, cultural, and national identity and can emphasize creating the schooled citizen as a form of emplacement, as a geopolitical construction, and as a process in the formation of the geography of cultural desire. Dare we transform teaching practices in our schools into acts of dissonance and interventions, into the ritual inscription of our students, into the codes of the dominant culture; into structured refusals to naturalize existing relations of power; into the creation of subaltern counterpublics?

It only makes sense that a curriculum should have as its focus investigating the study of everyday, informal, and popular culture and how the historical patterns of power that inform such cultures are imprecated in forming individual subjectivity and identity. Pedagogy occurs not only in schools but in all cultural sites. The electronic media is perhaps the greatest site of pedagogical production that exists; you could say it is a from of perpetual pedagogy. In addition to understanding literacies applicable to print culture, students must recognize how their identities are formed and their 'mattering maps' produced through an engagement with electronic and other types of media so they will be able to engage in alternative ways of symbolizing the self and gain a significant purchase on the construction of their own identities and the direction of their desiring. In such an investigation, teachers and students become transformed into cultural workers for self and social emancipation. I call for a pedagogy of critical media literacy linked to what Paul Willis (1990) called a 'grounded aesthetics' designed to provide students with the symbolic resources for creative self- and social formation so they can more critically re-enter the vast, uncharted spaces of common culture.

I recommend that students make critical judgments about what society might mean and what is possible or desirable outside existing configurations of power and privilege. Students must be able to cross into different zones of cultural diversity and form what Trinh Minh-ha (1988) calls hybrid and hyphenated identities to rethink the relationship of self to society (or other) and to deepen the moral vision of the social order. This raises questions: How are the categories of race, class, gender, and sexual preference shaped within the margins and centers of society? How can students engage history as a way to reclaim power and identity? The critical media literacy I mentioned is structured around the notion of a politics of location and identity as border-crossing. It is grounded in the ethical imperative of examining the contradictions in US society between the meaning of freedom, the demands of social justice, and the obligations of citizenship on the one hand and the structured silence that permeates incidents of suffering in everyday life.

Critical educators must not choose the chronic dream of totality and completeness in their theoretical formulations. Rather than chart out a grand theory, they should begin to connect the cause of social transformation to a more inclusive view of the project of critical pedagogy. They should foresake the narrow vision that characterized so many previous radical educational projects which allowed themselves to work simply within the context of ideology critique, class analysis, or gender analysis. If we recast the task of critical pedagogy in a language of possibility, we can connect it more persuasively and passionately to a view of what it means to be truly empowered. In doing so, critical educators must create social spaces which break down the tightening grasp of social division and hierarchy and build on 'the embodiment of human solidarity', a task that makes it 'possible to achieve a wholehearted engagement in our societies that does not rest on illusion and bad faith' (Unger, 1987, p. 212). Critical pedagogy's task is to construct a praxis for teachers that urges active solicitude for the marginalized and dispossessed (male and female) of those whom the incursion of the logic of capital into both the rural and urban landscapes of North America have vanquished.

This praxis is lived in solidarity with all victims struggling to overcome their suffering and alienation. The irruption of the poor in our towns and cities over the last decade demands a relocation of schooling in a praxis of solidarity where the individual and personal is always situated in relation to the collective and communal (without the simple-minded cohesiveness these terms usually imply). It is a praxis that seeks to engage history by helping the powerless locate themselves in it. This means calling teachers to a cosuffering with the oppressed as they struggle both to transcend and transform the circumstances of their disempowerment (Chopp, 1985). In other words, we need to resitutate the challenge of teaching as a task of empowering the powerless from states of dependency and passivity as both an informed movement for revolutionary social and economic transformation and as means of achieving what Brain Fay calls a 'state of reflective clarity'. This is a state of liberation 'in which people know which of their wants are genuine because they know finally who they really are, and a state of collective autonomy in which they have the power to determine rationally and freely the nature and direction of their collective existence' (Fay, 1987, p. 205).

In searching for the nonidentity constitutive of a genuine experience of liberation, we seek to avoid becoming trapped within a totalizing negativity (what we refer to as an incipient antiutopianism, Left malaise, or an entrenchment of despair characteristic of those who have abandoned a language of hope and possibility). In addition, our theoretical approach is deliberately cast to avoid following a preestablished scheme, formula, or script; it is self-consciously multidisciplinary as we have chosen to collaborate with many different types of contemporary scholarship: semiotics, hermeneutics, critical theory, liberation theology, and poststructuralism. But in doing so, we maintain we are not moving away from the concrete but rather towards the complexity of the concrete (Lamb, 1982, pp. 49-50).

A pedagogy of the concrete is grounded in a politics of ethics, difference, and democracy. It is unashamedly utopian in substance and scope; it articulates a vision of and for the future, maintaining that if we have no idea of what we are working towards, we will never know if, in our struggle for human freedom, those conditions have been met. Thus, our thoughts and actions are deliberately designed to rupture the unitary fixity and cohesiveness of social life and resist attempts at asserting the homogeneity of the social and public sphere. I refer here to a pedagogy that is grounded in the importance of the 'other' and the need to develop a common ground for linking the notion of difference to a publicly shared language of struggle and social justice. Like MacCannell, I believe the positive potential within post-modernity 'depends on its capacity to recognize and accept otherness as radically other . . . the possibility of recognizing and attempting to enter into a dialogue, on an equal footing with forms of intelligence absolutely different from [our] own' (MacCannell, 1989, p. xv). However, Rosaldo (1989, p. 217) points out that radical otherness may not be as radical today as it once was.

The politics of difference that undergirds such a critical pedagogy is one in which differences rearticulate and shape identity such that students can refuse the role of cultural servant and sentinel for the status quo to reclaim, reshape, and transform their own historical destiny. The pedagogy I propose is not premised on a common culture or a transcendence of local knowledges or particularisms. It is not committed to enlightenment epistemology nor economic liberalism, but rather a new socialist imagery grounded not in specific forms of rationality but in forms of detotalized agency and the expansion of the sphere of radical democracy to new forms of social life. It is a move away from what Arnold Krupat (1991, p. 243) calls 'unself-critical humanistic universalism' and toward a 'critical cosmopolitanism' which does not ask people to discard ethnic and local attachments for more global commitments, but interrogates the universal already contained in the local and examines how the ethnic and regional is already populated by other perspectives and meanings. We live in this contested zone between local and global, dominant and subordinate meanings and social practices, seeking to rearticulate them in the interests of greater social justice and freedom. This is no small task at this time in which subjectivity is being constructed within the future anterior; where we feel nostalgia for a time that has not yet arrived; where we seek new forms of longing and of belonging; where spaces of possibility are expanding, but our belief in possibility can imagine its own extinction and, thus, a new history can be born. How we shall decide to write history is another matter, but one that we need not leave entirely to chance.

Our pedagogical homes need to become cultural spaces where students are able to form interlaced networks of intracommunal negotiation, spaces that work toward constructing intimacies and coarticulated communal patterns in classrooms and the surrounding communities, and spaces that take the project of human liberation and social justice seriously.

ACKNOWLEDGEMENTS

This chapter has drawn from two published essays (McLaren, 1992; McLaren and Hammer, 1989) and the introduction to McLaren's (1994) book, *Critical Pedagogy and Predatory Culture* (London, UK: Routledge).

Part V

Educational Reform

14 Recent Education Reform: Is It a Postmodern Phenomenon?

Geoff Whitty

ABSTRACT

This chapter discusses the 1980, '86, and '88 Education Acts and their consequences. It differentiates between Thatcherite or New Right and postmodern
impulses for change and education reform in the UK. Other facets of recent
changes in City Technical Colleges, open enrollment, local school management, grant maintained schools, and overall policies, including a national
curriculum and alternative futures, are also discussed.

INTRODUCTION

In the mid-1980s, I suggested 'corporatist' and 'market' alternatives challenged traditional social democratic policies. In the late 1980s, Thatcher's
Conservative government, increasingly under 'New Right' domination,
favored the market alternative. While state intervention, not the capitalist
market economy, was blamed for English and Welsh industrial decline and
social dislocation, interventionist policies of left-wing local education authorities (LEAs) were attacked for the poor performance of inner city schools. Just
as privatization appeared to revive the economy, the solution to urban educational problems seemed to be creating a 'market' in education.

Many provisions of the 1986 Education Acts and 1988 Education Reform
Act intended to enhance clients' rights of 'voice', 'choice' and 'exit'. Many
New Right adherents thought these rights and liberties important. But, in
addition to the philosophical case for choice, schools supposedly would be
more responsive and effective if the system were more diverse and if parents
had greater control over them. Kenneth Baker, the government minister
responsible for the 1980 Act, said 'choice and diversity are the key elements
to improve the quality of education for all London's children' (Baker, 1990).

The 1980 Education Act prefigured some of the Thatcher government's
education policies by using public money to support private education providers and encourage the public sector to behave more like the private one,
espousing competition and choice. These policies challenged the postwar
social democratic system of comprehensive secondary schools under LEA
control. By reducing the powers of LEAs, they encouraged restructuring the
whole system and eventually abolishing LEAs. Alongside the apparent devolution of power to individual schools, central government was strength-

ened, most noticeably in establishing a national curriculum, which neoconservative New Right advocates (not market-oriented neoliberals) favored.

At the end of the 1980s, Richard Johnson (1989) suggested that, as a
result of the 1980, '86, and '88 Education Reform Acts, 'the main configurations of formal schooling will be unrecognizable by the mid 1990s'. Stuart
Sexton, former Thatcher advisor and advocate of market forces on the Right,
claimed no LEAs will remain by the year 2000 if the Conservative Party takes
over. Even if Labour prevails, it will do little more than tinker with Conservative mechanisms of parental choice and LEAs will exercise the same sort of
control over schools that existed before the Education Reform Act.

RAMPANT THATCHERISM OR POSTMODERNITY?

Are some of the recent changes in education an abomination of Thatcherism
or do they indicate something deeper that requires rethinking education
policy? Although parts of the Education Reform Act seem to be a typical
New Right crusade to stimulate market forces at the expense of 'producer
interests' and the left educational establishment, that is only one way of
looking at it. Espousing choice and diversity in education encourages notions
of an open, democratic society as well as a market ideology. Thus, current
policies have a potential appeal far beyond the coteries of the New Right.

Part of their appeal is encouraging different types of schools, responsive
to needs of particular communities and interest groups. Furthermore, we are
told that diversity in types of schooling does not necessarily mean hierarchy.
Thus, one former government minister characterized the drift from comprehensive education to more specialized and differentiated types of school not
as a return to elitist approaches to educational provision, but as happening
'without any one [type] being regarded as inferior to the others'.

More sociologically, encouraging diverse provision modes may reflect
some postmodern characteristics. Current developments might be not merely
the product of the short-term ascendancy of a free-market ideology within the
Conservative Party, but part of a wider retreat from modern, bureaucratized
state education systems - the so-called 'one best system' in the US (Chubb
and Moe, 1990; Glenn, 1987) - perceived as failing to fulfill their promise.
Beside changes in how the state regulates other social activities, they might
be seen as new ways of resolving the state's core problems.

Such policies might also seem to respond to changes in the mode of
accumulation, reflecting a shift from 'Fordist' mass production to what
Stephen Ball (1990) calls the 'post-Fordist school'. New schools may be the
educational equivalent of what Stuart Hall (Hall and Jacques, 1989) labels the
rise of 'flexible specialization in place of the old assembly-line world of mass
production' in which differentiated consumption rather than mass production
is the driving force. The appearance of some of the new City Technology

Colleges and moves toward 'niche marketing' of schools might seem to support such a 'correspondence thesis'.

These moves toward different types of schools may respond to the complex patterns of political, economic, and cultural differentiation in contemporary English society which replaced the traditional class divisions of comprehensive education. Support for schools run on various principles, including those of religious minorities, might reflect a widespread collapse of a commitment to modernity. Or it may reject the totalizing narratives of the enlightenment project (either liberal or Marxist versions), replacing them with 'a set of cultural projects united (only) by a self-proclaimed commitment to heterogeneity, fragmentation and difference' (Boyne and Rattansi, 1990).

Worldwide, many politicians support diversifying provision and site-based control of schools. Thus, although school choice policies in the US were encouraged by Republicans Reagan and Bush, the growth in site-based management policies, magnet schools, and other schools of choice received broader support. A market approach to education has entered mainstream (not just narrow New Right) US social thinking (Chubb and Moe, 1990). Labour governments in Australia and New Zealand pursued similar policies while, in parts of Eastern Europe, the centrally planned Communist education systems are being replaced with experiments in educational markets. Even Japan (where the standardization of educational provision is often seen as contributing to the nation's modernization and extraordinary economic success) recently considered policies to enhance choice and diversification 'to secure such education as will be compatible with the social changes and cultural developments of our country' (Stevens, 1991, p. 148).

Many feminists and some ethnic minorities find the pluralist models of society associated with postmodernism to be attractive. In the US, Chicago school reforms mirror some of the dilemmas which such groups now face in relation to New Right policies. Those reforms sought to dismantle the vast Chicago Schools District bureaucracy which failed (even when under black politicians' control) the majority of its students. The devolution and choice policies resulted from an alliance between New Right school choice advocates, black groups seeking to control local schools, together with disillusioned white liberals and some former 1960s student radicals. In New Zealand, community empowerment advocates united with consumer choice exponents against the old bureaucratic order (Grace, 1991). At first, such alliances appear paradoxical, but they are less so in the context of postmodernity, which Lyotard (one of its leading philosophers) sees as a pluralist, pragmatic, and restless partially differentiated social orders. Social development is not seen as 'the fulfilment of some grand historical narrative' but as 'a pragmatic matter of inventing new rules whose validity will reside in their effectivity rather than in their compatibility with some legitimating discourse' (Boyne and Rattansi, 1990). In that context, 'unprincipled alliances', which once might have prevented Chicago's political configuration, are less appropriate. If major attempts at social engineering appeared to fail, less ambitious aspirations may now be in order.

In Britain, softening Labour Party policies may reflect a similar shift from class-based politics. England's emergent comprehensive education system was linked to a politics that assumed that class was the most significant dimension of social differentiation. Many black parents (who supposedly welcomed the Reform Act's opportunities to be closer to their children's schools) thought the party's traditional social democratic policies bureaucratic and alienating. While not endorsing the entire Thatcherite dream, some aspects meet their aspirations. Policies stressing heterogeneity, fragmentation, and difference signify more than a passing neoliberal fashion. They may reflect the emerging multiple social fissures and deeper change in social solidarity modes.

However, some of the groups that benefit from the devolved and pluralistic patterns of educational provision espouse more totalized philosophies than the broadly social democratic ones which formerly dominated educational politics. This argument has been used against state funding of new religious (particularly Moslem) schools in Britain. This criticism, though, can be seen as a product of arrogant enlightenment thinking, reflecting a prevailing stereotype of Eastern culture which maintains the West's sense of its own cultural superiority (Said, 1978; Halstead, 1990).

The issues and political implications of postmodernist tendencies and theories are difficult to 'read' (Giroux, 1990). Far from reflecting a real change in the nature of society, analyses that celebrate fragmentation and the atomization of decision-making at the expense of social planning and government intervention may just replace one oppressive master-narrative with that of the market. Many sociologists see espousing heterogeneity, pluralism, and local narratives as the basis of a new social order mistaking phenomenal forms for structural relations. Harvey (1989) asks if postmodernist cultural forms and more flexible modes of capital accumulation should be seen 'more as shifts in surface appearance rather than as signs of the emergence of some entirely new postcapitalist or even postindustrial society'.

RHETORIC AND REALITY

If we can read the rhetoric of choice and diversity in various ways, what can we make of current British policies? Do they encourage choice and diversity? It is too early to draw conclusions, but evidence (based on conference presentations and a research project on City Technology Colleges I worked on with colleagues in Newcastle and Birmingham) exists. I shall also comment on some key Thatcher government policies (open enrollment to state schools, local management of schools, City Technology Colleges, and Grant Maintained Schools) before looking at the 'bigger picture'. This is important since current policy studies smuggle in a pluralist orthodoxy and detract from theoretical attempts to understand the coherence (or incoherence) of education policy as a whole. First, let's look at some of the individual policies.

Open Enrollment

The Education Reform Act sought to remove 'artificial limits . . . on the ability of popular (state) schools to recruit up to their available capacity'. Abolishing the LEAs' right to set Planned Admission Limits (PALs) up to 20 per cent below a school's 'standard number' allows most schools to recruit up to the level of their 1979/80 enrollments. This increases the chances that students previously denied access to the most popular schools will be able to attend them. But, one of the ideas behind open enrollment is that it will lead to systemic benefits by forcing less popular schools to improve or close.

A full assessment of the effects of open enrollment must await its total implementation and that of Local Management of Schools, which ties funding directly to student numbers. However, in areas where open enrollment has operated for some time, it does not seem to work as envisaged. Although some schools became literally full while others fell below their old PALs and standard numbers, the latter did not necessarily become unviable. Many such schools still serve the dwindling inner city populations. The government's Audit Commission controller suggested that this policy will leave thousands of school places empty, rather than closing whole schools; he found few examples of open enrollment stimulating all schools to improve and hopeless ones to close (Bates, 1990). But popular schools, which cannot expand beyond their standard number, may become covertly selective, using artificially boosted test scores to enhance their market appeal. Open enrollment may enable some (but not all) schools to seem to improve. It may increase the gap between the best and worst schools and, in the context of national curriculum assessments, rank them on a linear scale rather than foster diversity.

The Labour Party feared that proposals such as this could result in educational apartheid and racial segregation. There are now signs of this fear being realized. While denying that segregation was part of the Bill, the government argued they did not wish to restrict parental choice of schools in any way (Blackburne 1988). In 1989, these dangers became clear when the Secretary of State rejected the Council for Racial Equality's claim that the Cleveland County Council unlawfully allowed a parent to move her child on racial grounds. Despite the complex details of the case, many people perceived that the government viewed the Education Reform Act as taking precedence over the 1976 Race Relations Act. But some might say that the social democratic dream of an integrated society is outmoded and schools for particular racial groups reflect the real diversity of postmodern societies.

Local Management of Schools (LMS)

The Education Reform Act requires LEAs to devolve the bulk of their budgets to individual schools based on age-weighted student numbers. This enhances the powers of Headteachers and Governing Bodies and constrains the LEAs' role in managing their schools. LEAs are at different stages of developing their LMS schemes. In LEAs where LMS already operates, some schools have barely changed, while others have introduced significantly new management and marketing approaches. Brian Knight (1990) suggests that LMS will produce greater differentiation between schools and that individual ones will seek to occupy different market niches. Whether these will be different but equal is questionable. Equal treatment for all schools is at the heart of the formula funding approach, but most sociologists consider treating manifestly different cases in the same way as reinforcing existing inequalities.

The effects of LMS formulae on inner city schools have caused problems. Emphasizing funding via age-weighted student numbers leads to phasing out even marginal attempts at positive discrimination that developed since the 1960s. Government's initial attempt to discourage introducing additional factors and complicated formulae to allow for social need made many LEAs reluctant to devise new forms of positive discrimination. Other elements of the government's approach to LMS will also affect inner city schools. The controversial decision to charge actual staffing costs against a budget based on average ones gives inner city schools with high turnover and many empty posts a surplus. But the effect of falling rolls in such areas had also led to merging schools and relatively high staffing costs by protecting posts and responsibility allowances after the merger. Despite some recent government concessions, such allowances will eventually be phased out.

The overall effect of the LEA formulae has been to move resources away from inner city schools or to give disproportionate benefits to suburban and rural ones. The draft formula originally produced for Avon (an LEA spanning three catchment areas) was particularly criticized. Virtually all inner city primary schools and some disadvantaged secondary schools in Bristol stood to lose significant funds (Guy and Menter, 1992). Only a concerted local campaign produced changes. However, the same general tendency exists in other authorities, especially those with heavily contrasting catchments.

Another concern about LMS relates to special education children. The House of Commons Select Committee on Education, Science and Arts (1990) argued that LMS and other Reform Act provisions may undermine progress made in mainstreaming such students. Also, many special needs formulae adopted by LEAs are too narrow to bring additional resources to cope with all the special educational needs into schools. Even after some government attempts to respond to such criticisms, needs recognized in the formulae may still not entice schools to take those students. Schools may feel that the market consequences of doing so would make them less attractive to parents whose children provide the bulk of the students whose numbers drive the funding formula (Bowe and Ball with Gold, 1992). Thus, children with special education needs could be concentrated in schools which have trouble recruiting other students. These schools may be located in the inner city and, thus, any diversity of provision would probably exacerbate social inequalities.

City Technology Colleges (CTCs)

Creating two new types of schools, completely outside the control of LEAs, could be seen as an alternative to the notion that inner city schools are under-achieving and must be escaped via the Assisted Places Scheme, offering poor families government help with private school fees (Edwards et al., 1989). CTCs, a 'new choice of school' with business sponsorship and a curricular bias toward science and technology, were to be located in or near derelict inner city areas since (as Kenneth Baker said) 'it is in our cities that the education system is at present under most pressure' (DES, 1986). Because of various setbacks, by September 1990, only seven of the projected 20 CTCs were operating and only 15 would be established. Some of them have incor-porated existing schools and are phasing in the CTC approach.

It is hard to tell what CTC education will be like and if it will develop a distinctive ethos. When they were launched, their purpose was 'to provide broadly-based secondary education with a strong technological element thereby offering a wider choice of secondary school to parents in certain cities and a surer preparation for adult and working life to their children' (DES, 1986). Their apparently modern and vocationally relevant curriculum was distinctive, offering enhanced choice to groups traditionally denied it.

Whether CTCs will provide more real opportunities for disadvantaged groups and stimulate improvements in other urban schools is unclear. Origi-nal CTC plans were concerned with the needs of inner city children. Giving CTCs exclusive catchment areas when other schools were losing theirs smacked of positive discrimination and prevented groups well-served by other schools from imitating this initiative. But both sponsors and sites were hard to find. The failure to find appropriate sites, but accepting more subur-ban areas, was partly caused by Labour councils who refused to make inner city ones available. The problem of finding sponsors was embarrassing for the government. Not only did government ministers underestimate the costs of starting such schools, but also some major industrial companies like BP and ICI publicly dissociated themselves from the scheme, preferring to contribute to existing schools. Only companies and entrepreneurs closely associated with a Thatcherite style of capitalism backed the concept amidst rumors of ministe-rial arm-twisting. However, Kenneth Baker suggests that big corporations are part of the social democratic establishment and the sorts of companies back-ing CTCs also spearhead new economic developments.

CTC students are not supposed to be selected based on academic ability. The staff of existing CTCs claim intakes meet their requirement to represent their catchment areas, though a report drawn up for the DES said that official requirements are actually unworkable (Dean, 1990). But even if CTC intakes are academically and socially broad, they are not comprehensive. Students (and parents) are selected only to the extent to which they display the desired characteristics. These characteristics, broader than the purely academic ones of the Assisted Places Scheme (APS), emphasize commitment, orientation, and motivation. The principal of Bradford CTC justified a high acceptance rate for Asian applicants since 'the strong work ethic associated with such families is exactly the sort of quality which we are looking for'. The initiative can be seen as responsive to the changing nature of British society, varying labor market needs, and tapping a different market from APS.

However, the strong competition for places in some CTCs makes it difficult to predict what form selection will take in the future and its effects on disadvantaged groups. Based on their observations at Kingshurst in the West Midlands, Walford and Miller (1991) argue that CTCs will sponsor some members of the working class from their environment, but that they will have little positive impact on that environment and some negative consequences for those who remain in it. They also believe that, as CTCs become increasingly popular, they will wish to move up the traditional hierarchy of esteem to more conventional curricular styles and thus 'deviate from (their original) role - as Kingshurst already appears to be doing'.

Grant Maintained Schools

The government claimed that Grant Maintained Schools (GMSs) would 'add a new and powerful dimension to parents' ability to select within the publicly provided sector of education' and that 'parents and local communities [would] have new opportunities to secure the development of their schools in ways appropriate to the needs of their children and in accordance with their wishes' (DES, 1987). GMSs are existing schools which parents vote to take out of LEA control and receive central government funding. (They are similar to charter schools in the US.) They hoped to make schools more responsive and reduced the power of left-wing Labour LEAs, particularly in urban areas.

Mrs. Thatcher thought most LEA maintained schools would eventually opt out, but it is unclear if this appeals to parents. Although over half the LEAs in England and Wales had schools that sought grant-maintained status by April 1991 (over a third of LEAs had at least one school whose change in status had been agreed), more than 300 that moved that way represented a small proportion of all maintained schools. The government's expectation that the first schools to opt out would be from Labour-controlled urban LEAs did not happen. Less than a third of the first 72 schools which achieved grant-maintained status were in Labour-controlled areas; Conservative-controlled shire counties have been among those most affected (Fitz et al., 1991).

Parental votes in 50 schools rejected plans to opt out and there were cases where LEAs (including left-wing urban ones) persuaded school governing bodies not to vote. On the other hand, critics allege that the government is bribing schools to go grant maintained by, for instance, granting GMSs 'over generous initial capital grant allocations' compared with schools still in the LEA- maintained sector (Halpin and Fitz, 1990). Incentives announced at the 1990 Conservative Party conference bear this out. The right to opt out, first restricted to secondary and larger primary schools, has now been extended to all primary ones. Also, ministers encouraged more schools to opt out.

Meanwhile, there is a debate about using GMS regulations to fund minority schools, especially for Muslim students (Cumper, 1990). When the Reform Bill was enacted, the 'New Right' Hillgate Group (1987) wanted the government to encourage 'new and autonomous schools . . . including church schools of all denominations, Jewish schools, Islamic schools and such other schools as parents desire'. While their argument helped pressure government to allow non-Christian voluntary aided schools (Halstead, 1986), they realized the same objective could be achieved either through state aid for independent religious schools or by existing schools opting out to develop a religious or cultural distinctiveness. Despite arguing the case on the grounds of 'natural justice', an all-party attempt in the House of Lords to allow it did not gain government support. Nevertheless, at a more general level, government ministers said that the GMS regulations should give 'schools freedom to develop individual character and compete for pupils on the basis of parents' preferences' (TES, 1991). This agrees with the notion of diversity.

But critics say grant-maintained status reintroduces academic hierarchy and creates a back door to permit academic exclusion. The government originally stated that Grant Maintained Schools would not normally be permitted to change their character or admissions policies within five years of opting out. By removing that five year rule, the government said this will enhance diversity while not necessarily encouraging GMSs to become academically selective. That remains to be seen. Grant-maintained status has been widely used to keep existing grammar schools selective. Thus, LEA maintained grammar schools facing comprehensivization can immediately apply for grant-maintained status and receive a decision before acting on any reorganization proposals. They can retain their existing selective character if they change status. Some of the earliest schools to opt out came into this category and 28 of the first 72 GMSs were selective ones.

There is little evidence that grant-maintained status produces diversity in the types of schooling available. If Walford and Miller's argument about popular CTCs seeking to emulate existing high status parts of the system is also applicable to GMSs, we can expect many of them to become increasingly academically selective in their intakes and conventional in curricular approaches. Given the many 11-18, selective, voluntary, and single-sex schools amongst the first GMS applications approved, Fitz et al. (1991) argue that the newly emerging sector may already be developing an image that appeals to parents who want 'traditional' secondary schooling for their children.

OVERALL POLICIES

What about the 'bigger picture'? Overall, the analyses of the effects of various market-oriented Thatcher government policies suggests that, far from producing genuine pluralism and interrupting traditional modes of social reproduction, they may perpetuate long-standing structural inequality. There is little evidence of a postmodernist 'break'. The Education Reform Act seems as likely to produce greater differentiation between schools on a linear scale of quality and esteem as the positive diversity some had hoped for. If so, recent reforms continue the English education history Banks (1955) described.

Walford and Miller (1991) claim that, while comprehensive schools tried to overcome historic links between diversity of provision and inequalities of class and gender, CTCs 'played a major part in re-legitimizing inequality of provision for different pupils'. They argue that the 'inevitable result' of the concept of CTCs (especially when coupled with GMSs and LMS) is 'a hierarchy of schools with the private sector at the head, the CTCs and GMSs next, and the various locally managed LEA schools following'. A senior Labour Party education spokesperson asserted that creating a hierarchy from elite private schools (through CTCs and GMSs to a residual provision of Council schools) was a deliberate Conservative Party policy.

Whether deliberate or not, there is little evidence that the Education Reform Act provides a structure that encompasses diversity and ensures equal opportunity for all students. But there is evidence that the reforms further disadvantage those unable to compete in the market and actually create a hierarchy of schools. This will predominantly affect the working class and black populations in the inner cities. While they never gained an equitable share of educational resources under social democratic policies, abandoning planning in favor of the market seems unlikely to provide a solution. Indeed, an educational underclass may emerge in Britain's inner cities.

Present policies are as likely to increase structural inequalities as challenge them, while fostering the belief that their championing of choice provides genuinely equal opportunities for all who wish to benefit from them. For members of disadvantaged groups who are not sponsored out of schools at the bottom of the status hierarchy, either because of exceptional academic ability or alternative definitions or merit, the new arrangements are another way to reproduce deeply entrenched class divisions. Visions of our moving toward a postmodern education system may be premature or reflect surface appearances. At the very most, current reforms seem to relate to a version of postmodernity that emphasizes 'distinction' and 'hierarchy' within a fragmented social order, rather than one that positively celebrates (or even tolerates) 'difference' and 'heterogeneity' (Lash, 1990).

THE NATIONAL CURRICULUM

This linearity is also evident in the national curriculum, the one element that seemed to contradict the Thatcher government's espousal of market forces. The national curriculum which the 1988 Education Reform Act established specifies study programs and attainment targets for the three 'core' subjects (English, mathematics, and science) and seven other 'foundation' ones. While some New Right neoliberals hoped the curriculum would be left to the market, the government was not persuaded to do so. Instead, the argument of neoconservative pressure groups such as the Hillgate Group prevailed. This group argues that, even if market forces ultimately become the most desirable way of determining a school's curriculum, central government's imposition of a national curriculum on all state schools is a necessary interim strategy to undermine the vested interests of a 'liberal educational establishment' which threatens educational standards and traditional values.

Hillgate Group counters pressure for a multicultural curriculum that 'has been felt throughout the Western world, and most notably in France, Germany, and the United States, as well as in Britain'. It joins defenders of 'the traditional values of Western societies, and [particularly those recognizing] that the very universalism and openness of European culture is our best justification for imparting it, even to those who come to it from other roots' (Hillgate Group, 1987). While happy that new, autonomous schools (including Islamic ones) are emerging, their commitment to market forces makes them insist that all children receive 'the knowledge and understanding that are necessary for the full enjoyment and enhancement of British Society'. 'Our' culture, including Europe's, 'must not be sacrificed for the sake of a misguided relativism, or out of a misplaced concern for those who might not yet be aware of its strengths and weaknesses' (Hillgate Group, 1987).

The Hillgate pamphlet both acknowledges difference and defuses its potential challenge to the prevailing social order. Given its influence on government policies when the Reform Act was finalized, the reading of those policies (reflecting the sort of postmodern society which celebrates heterogeneity and difference) we flirted with earlier becomes even more questionable. Within the Hillgate Group's discourse, there is a master narrative that differentiates cultures on a hierarchical basis and sees social progress largely in terms of assimilation into European culture.

Further, the national curriculum is likely to arrange schools and students on a linear scale based on the combination of LMS, competition amongst schools for students, and the publication of assessment scores. This could leave the most disadvantaged students concentrated in schools with low aggregate test scores and declining resources and morale.

ALTERNATIVE FUTURES?

The Thatcher government's approach to education is well-captured in the paradoxical concept of 'conservative modernization' (Dale, 1989) linked with other aspects of modernity, rather than something distinctively antimodern or postmodern. Despite developing new forms of accumulation and changes in the state's regulations and limited changes social and cultural differentiation patterns, the continuities are as striking as the discontinuities. Theoretically, this seems to support those who deny any radical rupture with modernity, but it is also consistent with a view that argues for a dialectic of continuity and discontinuity (Best and Kellner, 1991).

Thus, without a postmodernist 'break', Conservative policies may have been more responsive than those of other political parties to subtle social and cultural shifts. Although social class divisions still challenge our education system, traditional social democratic approaches, which favor a common school and some version of a common curriculum (Lawton, 1975; Whitty, 1985), will have to respond to the social diversity of contemporary societies. Just as current citizenship discussions on the left seek to create 'unity without denying specificity' (Mouffe, quoted in Giroux, 1990), this will be a challenge for future education policy. James Donald (1989) called for approaches based on 'participation and distributive justice rather that simple egalitarianism' or 'cultural heterogeneity rather than a shared humanity'. He argued that this questions the very idea of comprehensive education. While I am not convinced that is necessarily the case, it merits reconsidering the notion of comprehensive education and indicates the left must rethink old orthodoxies.

NOTE

This chapter is based on a paper presented to the 'Conference on Reproduction, Social Inequality and Resistance: New Directions in the Theory of Education' at the University of Bielefeld, Germany, 1-4 October 1991 and published in German as 'Ist die jüngste Bildungsreform ein postmodernes Phänomen?' (Is the Latest Education Reform a Postmodern Phenomenon?), pp. 64-88 in H. Sünker, D. Timmermann, and F. Kolbe, eds., *Bildung, Gesellschaft, soziale Ungleichheit* (Education, Society, and Social Inequality), 1994, Frankfurt am Main, FRG: Suhrkamp. Although some specific policies have been modified, the major theoretical issues remain substantially unchanged. For further discussion, see Whitty et al. (1993) and Whitty (in press).

15 Educational Discourses and Creating a Democratic Public: A Critical Pragmatic View

Tomas Englund

ABSTRACT

Pragmatism involves a conception of a critical public, free inquiry and communication, the growth of imagination, and the embodiment of purposeful habits of conduct as essential not only to the realization of inquiry but to the ultimate goals of life as well. With its claim that all knowledge is inescapably fallible, it radically opposes the fundamentalist tendencies of this age of abstraction toward final solutions (Rochberg-Halton, 1986, p. 18)

INTRODUCTION

As a social scientist, one can emphasize (as Dewey did) the moral importance of the social sciences, their role in widening and deepening our sense of community, and the possibilities open to it. Or one can emphasize (as Foucault does) how the social sciences served as instrument of 'the disciplinary society', the connection between knowledge and power, rather than that between knowledge and human solidarity (Rorty, 1983, pp. 203-4). According to Cherryholmes, one may think of these paths not as heading in different directions, but crisscrossing in irregular, unexpected ways. They are not mutually exclusive. Also, heeding Foucault's warning may be required for the success of Dewey's project (Cherryholmes, 1988, pp. 179-80).

In this chapter, I assess two research traditions within the sociology of education: the traditional and the new sociology of education. This involves assessing their theories and conceptions of state and society and their attitude to education and curriculum as a citizenship right in creating a public. Based on this assessment, I outline a 'new citizenship sociology of education and curriculum'. In the latter, the content of education is seen as contingent on and an expression of citizenship rights (in the context of liberal democracies, as continually contested, sparking-points of conflict ultimately are determined by the struggle within the society and the state apparatuses and are decisively dependent on public opinion). With a view of the content of education as a contingency related to the struggle over citizenship rights, the normative basis of interpretation and guidelines which the new sociology of education did not take over from traditional sociology of education is reconstituted in the sociology of education. This can be used as a criterion for evaluating the character of educational contents in creating a public.

TRADITIONAL SOCIOLOGY OF EDUCATION

The traditional sociology of education (which American, British, and Swedish educational sociologists adopted in the 1950s and 1960s) was deeply rooted in a structural functionalist scientific model of a technological society and an unproblematic view of the state as an evolutionary force. The educational system's expansion and increasing differentiation were seen as inevitable outcomes of technologically determined changes in occupational structure, requiring even more intricate skills. Concurrently, the drive for educational efficiency was congruent with the traditional socialist critique of unequal educational opportunity between classes. A fundamental aspect of British and Swedish research traditions was an effort toward educational equality in terms of equal opportunities. A commitment to a version of Fabian socialism/social democracy and social engineering via education also influenced these traditions. Like the policy makers with whom they became associated, the sociologists were concerned with increasing access to schooling rather than examining the nature of the education they sought to distribute more widely. There was a confident assumption that we took for granted that education was a 'good' in itself and that it was in the interests of both individuals and the national economy that they should receive more of it (Whitty, 1985, p. 9).

EDUCATION AS AN INDIVIDUAL CITIZENSHIP RIGHT

One theoretical foundation for these traditions was 'T. H. Marshall's analysis of the rise of the welfare state as a principle of citizenship exercising increasing countervailing power against the force of class stratification, [which] strongly supported the possibility of realizing a welfare society in which equality and liberty would be optimally balanced' (Karabel and Halsey, 1977, p. 10). This perspective of access to education as an individual citizenship right has historically legitimated a social democratic educational policy. Marshall posited the gradual emergence of three different types of citizenship rights: civil, political, and social (Marshall, 1964, p. 71- 2).

Marshall viewed the right to education as a social right. But, he defined social rights in relatively vague terms and left much room for interpretation regarding the concrete meaning of 'to the full' and 'the life of a civilized being'. Marshall did, though, set out the more detailed meaning of education as a social right and its relationship to citizenship and the other rights:

> The education of children has a direct bearing on citizenship, and, when the state guarantees that all children shall be educated, it has the requirements and the nature of citizenship definitely in mind. It is trying to stimulate the growth of citizens in the making. The right to education is a genuine social right of citizenship, because

the aim of education during childhood is to shape the future adult. Fundamentally it should be regarded, not as a right of the child to go to school, but as the right of the adult citizen to have been educated. And there is here no conflict with civil rights as interpreted in an age of individualism. For civil rights are designed for use by reasonable and intelligent persons, who have learned to read and write. Education is a necessary prerequisite of civil freedom (Marshall, 1964, p. 81-2).

Here, Marshall stressed education as a prerequisite for the adult citizen to exercise his/her rights. But, Marshall is also unproblematically idealistic and instrumental in his view of the state guaranteeing these rights.

THE STATE AS AN EVOLUTIONARY FORCE

In his critical assessment of Marshall's theory, Giddens (1982) (who highly valued Marshall's analysis) presents a perspective that develops this further. He argued that Marshall wrote as though the development of citizenship rights evolved as a natural process, helped along where necessary by the beneficent hand of the state, but failed to emphasize that citizenship rights have been substantially achieved only via struggle (Giddens, 1982, p. 171).

What Giddens criticized is Marshall's unproblematical view of the state as an evolutionary force. Giddens (1982, pp. 126, 174) also sought to define how the struggle for citizenship rights relates to the state. He put greater emphasis than Marshall on the constant struggle for citizenship rights and on how the real substance of these rights can constantly change. Furthermore, in contrast with a Marxist tradition that tended to undervalue various 'bourgeois rights', Giddens highlighted the importance of the struggle (primarily by labor movements of different countries) over the formal status of these rights, with a view to their realization. The tangible implications of the different forms of citizenship are not self-evident; they only assume meaning and are realized in a specific historical, social context. Their concrete interpretation will be decisively dependent on how well-rooted they are in public opinion, what significance they have to different groups within society, and what actual scope different groups in society have to realize their citizenship rights.

EDUCATIONAL POLICY IMPLICATIONS OF THE TRADITIONAL SOCIOLOGY OF EDUCATION

This educational policy regards education as a source of social mobility but is rather uncritical of educational content, which it believes is a simplification of scientific progress and adjustment of the curriculum to scientifically investigated demands of the technological society's needs. This educational policy and curriculum perspective is called a scientific-rational conception (Englund, 1986). Popkewitz's hypothesis is that syllabus writing based on the 'discipline-centered' principle ignores the social nature of knowledge and the differing approaches existing in the various disciplines and that the reconstructed scientific logic does not reflect the conflicts in the real-life scientific community. Instead, syllabuses and teaching materials present a uniform systems view of the social context, describing society as a closed system whose parts work together in stable harmony (Popkewitz, 1976, 1977a, b).

In curriculum history research (Goodson, 1985, 1987; Popkewitz 1987), it has been shown how school subjects are legitimated and mythologized; their association with scientific disciplines produces this result. In Sweden, the syllabus analyses of the late 1950s used a range of empirical studies to establish overall course content requirements. The 'demand analyses' which the Upper Secondary School Committee conducted in the 1960s can be seen as examples of the so-called scientific-rational conception of education (Englund, 1986). Traditional sociology of education is part of a vulgar pragmatism which values functional efficiency and is premised on unreflective acceptance of explicit and implicit standards and conventions.

This policy perspective is also uncritical in the sense that it does not see/ does not want to see (as Marshall observed in a lecture as early as 1949) the reproduction of class-based relationships and class structures 'through education in its relationship with occupational structure . . . [and that] citizenship operates as an instrument of social stratification' (Marshall, 1964, p. 110). Marshall says there is no reason to deplore this, but we should be aware of its consequences. The status acquired by education is carried into the world bearing the stamp of legitimacy because an institution designed to give the citizen his/her just rights conferred this honor (Marshall, 1964, p. 110).

I shall not comment on Marshall's assessment, but his well-informed remark as an expert on the development of citizenship rights leads to the question of how the educational system is to be a legitimate force in the maintenance of and a qualification for exercising citizenship rights, not only as individual rights, but also in a collective perspective, in creating a critical public. In the further extension of these questions, both a critical perspective of the new sociology of education (in spite of its, in many respects, more sophisticated analysis compared with traditional sociology) and a 'new citizenship sociology of education and curriculum' can be developed.

THE NEW SOCIOLOGY OF EDUCATION - OUTLINE OF A CRITIQUE

In contrast with the concern of the traditional sociology of education and social mobility, the effectiveness of education, the question of 'power and ideology in education' (for example, see Karabel and Halsey, 1977) is a question the so-called 'new sociology of education' has raised. But the movement this term represents is far from uniform. In its initial stage of development (Young, 1971) as well as later, different emphases can be determined (Whitty, 1985). A point of departure stemming from the new sociology of education which is important in the present context is the view of knowledge (particularly school knowledge) which the movement follows up and develops. School knowledge is historically and socially determined. It is a manifestation of certain power relations and is one element in the reproduction of a specific society. The attitude of the new sociology of education to school knowledge is to ask not primarily about effective transmission, but about how the knowledge concerned has been constituted, what forces support it, and what conditions it helps reproduce.

EDUCATION REPRODUCING THE EXISTING SOCIAL ORDER

During the 1970s, the dominant metaphor for the place of education in society within this tradition and others related to the new sociology of education is that of a Marxist and Durkheimian nature. This means that the education system is regarded exclusively as an institution for reproducing the existing social order. In the various neo-Marxist traditions, the main emphases are on laying bare how socialization legitimizes certain fundamental social conditions (chiefly in Marxist socialization research), how the demands of capital accumulation predetermine the structure and content of the education system (mainly in German educational economics), how the structure of the school system corresponds to the demands of economic development and the workplace (mainly in American neo-Marxist research), or how ideology reproduces existing conditions (chiefly French research). Many of the works within these basic approaches became classics (Althusser, 1971; Bourdieu and Passeron, 1977; Bowles and Gintis, 1976) and attracted many followers. The functionalist-oriented correspondence principle (Bowles and Gintis, 1976) the accumulation demands of 'capital logic', and the reproduction metaphor (Althusser, 1971; Bourdieu and Passeron, 1971) for a long time overshadowed any interest in the meaning of structural change and in content as change factor.

A notable exception, partly based on traditions, is the 'reconceptualization' (critical curriculum theory) movement in the US in the late 1970s and early 1980s (Apple, 1979). As in the phenomenological approach of the new sociology of education (for example, Esland, 1971), American reconceptualists/critical curriculum theorists mainly see the individual (particularly the teacher) as the key change agent. Change is a matter of transforming the consciousness of classroom actors (Giroux, 1981 and 1983). But, a problem with both these traditions is their view of change as primarily a matter of raising individual consciousness in the classroom, separated from an analysis of the state and its role as an ultimate boundary-setting power relation in education.

TOWARDS A RELATIONAL THEORY OF THE STATE

Within the new sociology of education, a societal perspective on education as reproduction and a theory of the state progressively developed from its originally interactive sociology-of-knowledge beginnings. But for a long time, the state was analyzed within a biased perspective and neither research based on 'capital logic', nor correspondence theory-based research, nor reproduction research of the kind which Althusser (1971) and other reproductionists (except for Poulantzas) inspired, problematized the manifestations of social tension in the struggle for state power.

Not until quite late in the theoretical development of the new sociology of education do tendencies toward more sophisticated perspectives evolve (Dale, 1982). Yet, they are not applied and seldom go further than self-critical observations (such as the notion that hegemony is not free floating). Tied to the state in the first place, hegemony is not an already accomplished social fact but a process whereby dominant groups and classes 'manage to win active consensus of those over whom they rule' (Apple, 1981, p. 38, referring to Mouffe, 1979, p. 10). Apple later asked himself if 'the State only serves the interests of capital or is it more complex than that? Is the State instead an arena of class conflict and a site where hegemony must be worked for, not a foregone conclusion where it is simply imposed?' (Apple, 1982, p. 14).

It is only with the incorporation of the 'late' Poulantzas' (1979, 1980) state analysis, which Carnoy (1984) primarily mediated, that a perspective evolves according to which, rather than being directly determined by the needs of capital, the curriculum (like other aspects of society) was increasingly conceptualized as contested terrain and, hence, a site of struggle between competing political and ideological forces. However, there was considerable controversy about the extent to which these should be achieved as essentially class forces (Carnoy and Levin,1985; Whitty, 1987, p. 110). In an evaluation of the new sociology of education and critical curriculum theory, Wexler comments that internal critiques of reproduction (especially among educational new sociologists [Apple, 1981; Giroux, 1981]) modify but preserve the basic logic of analysis. Adding terms like 'contested reproduction' or 'structural autonomy' does not displace an organic view of society as a natural integrated social order (Wexler; 1987, p. 79; Englund, 1986). Referring to the later, Giroux stressed his treatment of public philosophy and the crisis in education (Giroux, 1984) and citizenship, public philosophy and the struggle for democracy (Giroux, 1987, 1988). During the 1980s, Apple also developed many themes that transcended his earlier 'basic logic of analysis', such as the tension between person and property rights. Carnoy and Levin write, with reference to Poulantzas (1980) that

> . . . the State apparatuses are the materialization and condensation of class relations. . . . Power struggles originate outside the State, but insofar as they are political struggles, they have to include the State. . . . Education can thus be understood in the context of social conflict, as part of a social conflict that changes as a result of previous struggle (Carnoy and Levin, 1985, pp. 46, 48).

This perspective has not enjoyed success within the new sociology of education/critical curriculum theory research; the authors Whitty apostrophized (Carnoy and Levin, 1985) hardly use their perspective to analyze curriculum questions and they instead develop the problematic of the traditional sociology of education in a conflict perspective. Carnoy and Levin present a view of education as subject to tension between two conflicting dynamics attempting to influence the control, purpose, and operation of the schools. On the one hand, schools traditionally reproduced the unequal, hierarchial relations of the nuclear family and capitalist workplace; on the other, they represented the expansion of economic opportunity for subordinate groups and the extension of human rights (Carnoy and Levin, 1985, pp. 14, 24).

Their main interest is access to education; they do not apply their perspective to curriculum questions. In my previous study 'Curriculum as a Political Problem', where the curriculum question is emphasized, the starting point is similar to that of Carnoy and Levin. I also view the institutional compulsory education system in a capitalist democracy as being situated in a field of force, pulling it between social integration and change. This tension becomes visible if one examines the role of the education system in relation to those groups in society whose education prepares them for, and who when they leave school mainly occupy, subordinate and manual positions in the social division of labor. 'Education for social integration' refers to the adjustment of the working class and other subordinate groups to an existing economic and political system. 'Education for change' relates to a strengthening of the position of these groups in society. The progressive potential of education can be seen by giving such groups the resources needed to assume greater power or share more fully in decision making in society and/or to enable them to use their education to influence their social environment, thus facilitating a collective development of freedom. The tension between the socially integrative (conservative) and change-oriented (progressive) aspects of education I assume to center on the 'citizenship education' which schools provide (Englund, 1986, pp. 16, 18). In both these analyses (Carnoy and Levin, 1985; Englund, 1986), the state is seen (according to a state theory built on Poulantzas [1979, 1980] late works) as the crucial and ultimate power relation, where the conditions for education are settled.

It is through the conservative restoration, the reconstitution of the state, and the nationalized curriculum movement (especially in the US and UK in the 1980s and 1990s) that the freedom of action within the state apparatus and its dependence on a public philosophy, which Poulantzas (1980) primarily and theoretically developed, has become obvious. My hypothesis is that the imperfection of state theory (the maintenance of an interpretation of educational phenomena in terms of their reproducing the status quo [that is, education reproduces the social classes and conditions of capitalism] with the state seen as the instrument used to guarantee class domination) together with one-sided (in the UK, mostly locally governed) progressivism (Hamilton, 1988) and with regard to curriculum issues (the long-decided belief during the postwar period of social democratic consensus that such issues should be treated as matters of professional judgment [Whitty, Barton, and Pollard 1987, p. 171] created specific conditions in two areas: 1) for 'the character of the disaster' (for example, that politicians of the right rather than the left reestablished the curriculum as a significant site of struggle) and 2) for 'the undermining of the progressive constituency' (Dale, 1988, p. 46) (for example, undervaluing potential political/parliamentary constituencies) in the political education movement.

The new sociology of education has been too busy viewing the state as subordinate to the demands of capitalism and, within that frame, has been associated with forces trying to create local progressive constituencies. On the other hand, the state apparatus has not been viewed as a condensation of class forces and a potential expression of democracy. One book in the US

> . . . recognizes - unlike the neo-liberal wing of the Democratic Party - that without an effective public sector, corporate-dominated private markets will skew the US political economy in fundamentally undemocratic and socially destructive ways . . . [and in which the] immodest aim is to contribute to the development of a new public philosophy in the United States - one that comprises communitarian values, a state capable of effective action in the public interest, a participatory political culture, and a democratic, accountable process of public choice (Levine, 1988, pp. 2, 10).

THE FORGOTTEN CITIZENSHIP PERSPECTIVE

Related to this imperfect theory of the state was the fact that the new sociology of education totally neglected the citizenship (right) perspective of the traditional sociology of education. The new sociology of education had rightly criticized the traditional sociology of education because its educational view was restricted to the question of access to education. Instead, the new sociology of education focused on the content of education, but did not relate it to any sort of moral or normative criteria. Locking the new sociology of education to the reproduction and social control metaphors, and later to resistance and pervasive progressivist ambitions, meant that the question of the proper content never appeared on the agenda. This question could have been posed if the citizenship perspective of the traditional sociology of education had been extended educational content. This might also have meant that the new sociology of education would have taken the initiative on the curriculum front and been able to respond to conservative demands for a curriculum related to citizenship rights.

For a long time, the normative base was not developed in new sociology of educationists/critical curriculum theory. We only had Apple's (1979) declaration that all of this centers around a theory of social justice. My own inclination is to argue for something left of a Rawlsian stance. For a society to be just, it must (as a matter of both principle and action) contribute most to the advantage of the least advantaged (Apple, 1979, pp. 11-2).

The commonly accepted basis for the more or less Marxist-inspired new sociology of education/critical curriculum theory seemed to be a mixture of a rather broad standard of social justice and an elementary conception of freedom. While these claims appear to accord with a general interpretation of the Marxist tradition, they are not developed in any substantial manner and are far from secure (Liston, 1988, p. 125).

As Apple also says in the introduction to Liston (1988), this critical literature has a common set of political beliefs about the importance of so-called 'person rights'. In the struggle between property and person rights that lies in the heart of our economy, the individuals within this critical tradition support the extension of person rights and democratic principles to all social institutions (Apple, 1988, p. 2; Bowles and Gintis, 1986; Carnoy and Levin, 1985). Most striking in these traditions is the emphasis on an individualistic (human rights) perspective of freedom from or against the state as an expression of emancipation, not a collective, communitarian citizenship perspective of democracy and civic life related to the role of education.

A NEW CITIZENSHIP, SOCIOLOGY OF EDUCATION, AND CURRICULUM - SOME STARTING POINTS

Consequently, the fundamental point of reference to which I believe a new citizenship, sociology of education, and curriculum would be coupled is a theory on citizenship rights in which education and educational content/curriculum are seen in relation to the development of citizenship rights. In certain respects, Marshall's theory concerning theories about state and society needs to be revaluated, emphasizing citizenship rights as contingent on conflicts between social forces in society and the state as the essence of a basic political/economic power struggle.

It is also important to know how schools relate to this problematic and especially how it affects educational content (for example, what image of society, forming entirely different bases for thinking about society, different educational conceptions) so that education has a fundamental political social-ization role. Education is a fundamental (social) citizenship right in itself, but only as an instrument for raising awareness and maintaining all our citizen-ship rights can the role of education be analyzed.

Williams (1961) distinguishes three different images of society as bases for thinking about it. One starting point is the monarchy and the social order built up around this institution. This image of society is one of an organism 'in which each person in the society has "his part to play"' (Williams, 1961, p. 102). The second image Williams distinguishes is that of society as a market: 'a free market involves radical dissent from any rigid, prescriptive establishment: in this sense it continually overlaps with the kind of demo-cratic spirit which accompanied it' (Williams, 1961, p. 105). The starting point here is production and trade. These activities are central to society; all the other institutions and organizations of society have to be molded to the demands of economic activity. The basis for the third image of society is 'the rights of man'; perhaps the basic difficulty has been that 'the interpretation of rights has been ordinarily selective' and that 'the idea is in part conven-tional, in part abstract: it has sought to unite the necessarily limiting idea of the liberty of the subject, and the necessarily universal idea of the brother-hood of man' (Williams, 1961, p. 107).

Comparisons can be made with Wood's (1984, 1988) protectionist and participatory models of democracy and schooling and Battistoni's (1985) different (liberal and participatory-republican) conceptions of democratic citizenship related to schooling. As Beyer (1988) noticed: first, democracy is intimately tied to a set of values regarding such issues as the nature of social justice, equality, freedom, and the like. To be engaged in democratic action is to guide one's actions in ways consistent with such values, principles, and commitments (begging the question of what these principles and commit-ments should be); second, this view of democracy has an affinity with some recent literature concerning a reconstructed civic education. Several critical analyses of the concept of civic education have appeared, suggesting a new role for a public philosophy. These writers 'look upon political philosophy as a form of civic educational agency, exploring its value as a moral and cogni-tive message system, judging it by its capacity to inspire just action in daily life' (Finkelstein, 1985, p. 15; Beyer, 1988, p. 222).

Private or public school organization is central here. Publicly financed and controlled education for everybody, public education as a citizenship right (Englund, 1989), creates totally different prerequisites for educational content/curriculum than a system where 'an individualistic perspective [in which] parents are seen as having a "prior right" to choose their children's schools' is dominant (Edwards, Fitz, and Whitty, 1985, p. 39). As Reese

(1988) stresses, democracy is a sham without a system of public schools that introduces everyone to a world of ideas, values, and knowledge and takes all children beyond their own narrow and private worlds. Public schools must stand above and in tension with private concerns. The tension between private and public visions will always exist (Reese, 1988, p. 440).

CHANGING PUBLIC IDEALS - METADISCOURSES OF EDUCATION

The (public) educational systems in most Western democracies have a historically based symbolic function to shape our sense of community and create a public (Boli, Ramirez, and Meyer, 1985). However, shaping a sense of community produces different discourses/practices, with different meanings. Previously (Englund, 1986), I identified three educational conceptions (patriarchal, scientific-rational, and democratic) which can be seen as mass- or metadiscourses for public identity formation. I analyze (compulsory) public education systems as systems for identity formation on a mass scale.

Historically, public education in Western countries has been characterized as patriarchal. In the patriarchal curriculum conception, adherence to the principles of democracy is primarily formal and the idea of equality plays a very minor role. The patriarchal conception's ideas about the social role of the ruling groups are often associated with a view of society as an organism in which different strata are expected to occupy predetermined, totally distinct, and explicitly hierarchically ordered positions. The 'national interest', as ruling social groups so interpret it, leaves little room for maneuver for conflicting ideologies within the nation. Perennialism is historically a crucial part of the patriarchal conception, but it is not related to the compulsory education system. Perennialism more 'automatically' influences it via a traditional perennialist ideal in higher education, speaking to the problems of educating the nation's elite. One can also see how strong the perennialist educational philosophical tradition is during the 20th century since it is based in university level humanities subjects (Englund, 1986; Bloom, 1987). Bloom fails to understand that the development of a public involves a critical dialogue in which respect for the interpretations of others is a part of rational inquiry processes (Feinberg, 1989, p. 136). With progressivism in the UK, I refer to a rather specific educational practice (Cunningham, 1988; Dale, 1988). However, in an American context, it is more difficult to use that term (Englund, 1986, pp. 234). The term educational 'progressivist' is not to be confused with the term 'progressive' (education for change) which is linked to specific social developments. Progressivism does not necessarily mean progressive social development (Englund, 1986).

The scientific-rational conception entails a functional view of democracy. In such a system, it is 'rational' to allow certain groups to receive more in-depth education, while other groups are not considered to need it. It does, however, allow more scope than the patriarchal concept for different ideologies within the framework of a democratic superideology. There is an emphasis on equal opportunity, with the aim of putting the individual gifts of all social groups to good use. The conception implies an image of society with a heavy emphasis on the market. The key activities of society are market-related and the other social institutions (such as legislative assemblies, central government, and the education system) are shaped to market demands while evolving specific technologies to meet these demands. This is an ends-means rationality with science as a value-free instrument of social engineering. In educational philosophical terms, there is a balance in this conception between progressive psychological and essentialist disciplinary claims.

There have been many (American) examples of essentialist visions (Hirsch, 1988; Ravitch and Finn, 1988), supporting commitment to educational excellence, but also recognizing that education has a moral mission (the creation of a public in a democratic society). The progressive proposals have been fewer. The role of public education in the progressive tradition is (also) to create a public voice in an otherwise inarticulate, uninformed mass. However, progressivism still holds out the possibility that science, both as a method and a community of inquiry, would serve as the modern world's replacement for foundationalism (Feinberg, 1989).

Thus, the idea that drives the patriarchal and the scientific-rational conceptions is the view that there is a preestablished standard to determine membership in the public. Education's function is to see that everyone has the opportunity to learn to act in accordance with a specific ideal. The three mass- or metadiscourses (or conceptions) are described in condensed form in Table 15.1. (For an additional 'literacy' dimension, see McLaren, 1988).

What is the specific difference between the scientific rational and the democratic conception? I will try to develop that theme, especially analyzing the three terms the public, text, and teacher.

TOWARD A DEMOCRATIC CONCEPTION? CREATING A CRITICAL PUBLIC: A NEOPRAGMATIC SKETCH

The idea of a critical public (which education can create) suggests, as Dewey (1927) pointed out, a sense of shared experience and a commitment to communicating the meaning of that experience with and to others. Reese also declares that 'democracy is a sham without a system of public schools that introduces everyone to a world of ideas, values, and knowledge that takes all children beyond their own narrow and private worlds' (Reese, 1988, p. 440). Dewey (1927) also criticizes the idea of natural inalienable rights that are given prior to politics, claiming instead that inalienable rights are constituted in and through the social process. Dewey's concept of the public is rooted in a perspective based on the recognition and regulation of indirect consequences of human communicative acts.

Table 15.1. Three mass- or metadiscourses

Conceptions	Patriarchal	Scientific-rational	Democratic
Democracy:	Formal	Functional	Participatory
Equality:	Practical inequality	Equality of opportunity	Equality of results
Image of society:	Organistic	A market	Focusing on rights of man
Mode of rationality:	Value-based	Scientific-technological	Communicative, pluralistic
View of science:	Idealistic	Positivistic-empiricist	Relativistic, neopragmatic
Individual/society:	Social dominance	Individualism	Communitarian
Purpose of public education:	Preparation for national citizenship	Vocational preparation	Preparation of a critical public
School organization:	Segregated school system, mass-elite	'Rational' differentiation, individuals' choice	Laterdifferentiation, higher level of general education for all
Educational philosophies:	Reform pedagogy perennialism	Mass progressivism/ elite essentialism	Reconstructionism
Higher-status subjects:	Religious instruction, history	Mathematics, science	Social studies
Politics and social order:	Constitutional, mass subordination of conflict to national interests	Apolitical, subject-subject-based, related to technological development	'Political education', related to conflicts
Literacy:	Functional (mass), cultural (elite)	Functional	Critical

Note: See Chapter 3 in this volume for Apple's discussion of the roles of the public, text, and teacher.

In Englund (1986), the analysis there ends with a reference to the debate in the US concerning citizenship education. With Giarelli (1983), a reference is made to the necessary distinction between state and society or, more specifically, between the teacher's role as a state official/transmitter of the state's ideology and his/her role as a servant/educator of the public. If we principally see these two roles as interconnected and the state aspect as primary, we neglect the role of teachers as a resource for the public/society (that is, for every citizen) we want to create. What Giarelli emphasizes is that the job of teachers, rather than being to transmit a state ideology from above, is to create conditions for public discussion and to develop 'reasonable citizens discharging their civic purpose, the formation of new publics' (Giarelli, 1983, p. 35). For a program (radically grounded argumentation) to achieve this aim, see Giroux (1988); for a liberally based line of argument in the same direction, see Gutmann (1987).

> ... 'political education' - the cultivation of virtues, knowledge, and skills necessary for political participation - has moral primacy over other purposes of public education in a democratic society. Political education prepares citizens to participate in consciously reproducing their society (Gutmann, 1987, p. 287).

Giarelli takes his general starting points from Dewey (1927). These points can be developed into a specific conceptual frame of reference, a perspective of the role of institutionalized socialization. Figure 15.1 illustrates Habermas' (1984/1988) analysis of the interplay of four basic sectors.

Figure 15.1. Habermas' analysis of the interplay among four sectors

	Public	Private
System	Public administrative system, state power	Market, money
Life world	Society, public sphere, communication	Private sphere, intimacy

According to Habermas, democratic citizenship consists of the capacity to form independent opinions and the opportunity for intellectual autonomy. These are formed in the 'life world' through primary socialization in the family and later in the educational system and other forms of institutionalized socialization (which are situated between state and society), through opinion formation and participation in the public sphere.

Shaping the prerequisites for people to attain a communicative competence may be considered crucial in the fulfilment of citizenship rights in two mutually dependent ways. The content of institutionalized socialization can be analyzed both as a criterion for the inherent significance of conditions governing the exercise of citizenship rights (education as a means of enabling every citizen to exercise his/her own rights) and as necessary in shaping a 'community' and establishing the common good. Here, it is consistent to speak of the political community as natural because it is a necessary condition for the essential manifestation of a dignified human life.

THE TEACHER AND THE TEXT

What is the role of the text in creating the public? What is the relationship between text and curriculum? Referring to educational policy documents as historical-social products and national curricula (when extant) as political compromises (Englund, 1986), the educational text/textbook generally can be seen as an authoritative interpretation/curriculum of what students can learn (McCutcheon, 1982, p. 19;. Cherryholmes, 1988, p. 133).

What kind of texts are we referring to when we say texts create a public? The textbook is one dominating medium. The textbook, with its specific political economy (Apple, 1986), has a certain genre and style. Genre refers to things regularly done and style to a regular way of doing things (Scholes, 1985). The genre of textbooks can be thought of as collections of statements that make authoritative knowledge claims. They make statements about subject matter, social values and arrangements, what counts as knowledge, and what information is more or less important. They define, using inclusion or exclusion, what is important and unimportant to study and present the meaning of words as fixed. Students and others are told little to the contrary in the overwhelming majority of textbooks in any subject at any level, except in some areas in literature and philosophy (Cherryholmes, 1988, p. 51).

Within the present prevailing educational conception, the scientific-rational, textbooks are predicated on two rules with respect to meaning. First, they tend to approach meaning structurally; meanings are presented using definitions, referents, and linkages. Second, they advance meaning, if up-to-date, that represents the current state of 'authoritative knowledge' (Cherryholmes, 1988, p. 55). Cherryholmes also emphasized that 'neither teachers nor students are likely to ask how meanings came to be what they are if textbooks do not self-consciously draw attention to the social construction and context dependence of meanings' (Cherryholmes, 1988, p 55).

The text/textbook is one crucial link in the structural process of meta-discourses, which express specific values and interests related to specific rules, the latter in turn reflecting ideological relationships. Texts and textbooks are parts of these structural processes (Giddens, 1979) which can be conceptualized in terms of governing the continuity or transformation of structures. The power to alter textbooks is, ultimately the power to change the world; without it, we remain unwitting captives of past texts and discourses.

If the text is seen as a vehicle for eternal truth (religious or scientifically 'proven'), the teacher's function is to guide the student toward the correct interpretation of the text, so that the truth might stand revealed. But if the text is understood as partial or its truth value varies in relation to historical changes, this sort of interpretation will not suffice. If wisdom, creative reflective intelligence (Dewey 1916/1966), or some less grandiose notion such as heightened awareness is to be the end of our endeavors, we shall have to see it not as something transmitted from the text to the student but as something developed in the student who questions the text.

One way of distinguishing the different discourses/practices in the scientific-rational and the democratic conceptions is to differentiate between ways of becoming part of the public. The traditional way (patriarchalistic and scientific-rational) means learning the proper response to the text as an item stimulus. The democratic approach is to enter the text as a part of the conversation about the significance of a flow of historical events and about the meanings attached to them. Giarelli (1983) discussed this basic difference when he made the necessary distinction between state and society or, more specifically, between the teacher's role as a state official/transmitter of the state's ideology and his or her role as a servant/educator of the public.

Teachers continually choose whether to reinforce knowledge claims presented as authoritative and structured or to expose their partiality. The choices are pragmatic. If they reinforce dominant structures, they enact an uncritical and vulgar pragmatism. If they question structural and positivist meanings and standards, they enact a critical pragmatism. We build our communities, educational or otherwise, and social life with choices such as these (whether vulgar or critical); our identification with our community (our society, political tradition, intellectual heritage) is heightened when we see it as ours rather than nature's, shaped rather than found (Rorty, 1983, p. 166).

We operate publicly in reference to a system of multiple meanings and as 'multiplicity of meanings is the element in which all thought must move in order to be strict thought' (Heidegger, 1968) it becomes all the more important to try to foster and nurture those forms of communal life in which dialogue, conversation, phronesis, practical discourse, and judgment are concretely embodied in our everyday practice (Bernstein, 1983, p. 229; Bernstein, 1987).

The last decade, simultaneous with the conservative restoration of learning and the movement of authoritarian populism, witnessed a revival of interest in pragmatism. The heritage of Dewey, which Bernstein (1983, 1987), Rorty (1979, 1983), and Habermas (1984/1988) revitalized called attention to the need for nonfoundationalism (for example, the impossibility of a philosophical justification of standard school knowledge) and communication.

These scholars also highlighted (a sense of) community, democracy, and solidarity as crucial issues. Bernstein (1983) elaborated on the concept of community with reference to the Aristotelian concept of 'phronesis'. According to Bernstein, an indispensable prerequisite for phronesis is the existence of a certain degree of solidarity in a community. This kind of solidarity can keep the conversation going even when, in the community of inquirers, the outcome of a free and unforced argument is 'tolerant disagreement' (Rorty, 1987, p. 48).

Rorty (1987) tried to get rid of every form of 'criteriology', criticizing and rejecting any universalist, criteriological claim that sees philosophy as a means of understanding social practices. At the same time, he contributed to the ideal of social democracy as he distinguished between societies based on violence and on argumentation and discourse. Summarizing some aspects of the neopragmatic tradition, I view it (in spite of Rorty's anticriteriological stance) as working within a criteriology that is not universalist, but nonetheless a reference point for making judgements.

But is it possible and worth striving for creating a critical public in an age of authoritarian populism? The possible choice between different interpretations of what education as a citizenship right actually means shows the contingent and political character of education. Are we going to retain the national curriculum as the one remaining symbol and potential instrument of a common education system which people can struggle collectively over? Or will we let all provision emerge from the individual exercise of choice (or nonchoice) in the marketplace?

16 Summary/Conclusions: The Future as Seen from the Present

Russell F. Farnen

ABSTRACT

This chapter has four parts. The first reviews some American and English critical theorists' ideas about the politics, sociology, and economics of education in the mid-1990s. The second part describes the impact mass media has on educational issues and reforms, while part three lists highlights and major themes from the previous chapters. Part four presents core areas of agreement and ideational consensus among the contributors to this volume as well as a few areas of disagreement among representative critical theorists.

INTRODUCTION

A common theme running through this book is a shared sense of democratic intellectual outrage with New Right social, political, economic, and educational philosophy, reasoning, and curriculum proposals. Taken together, the contributors to this volume look at the conservative restoration as neither conservative nor restoring anything worth the effort. That is, the New Right clearly supports the economic reproduction process. This is a system in which educated individuals are so much economic raw material or technological fodder for new-age industry. This rightist movement has also duped some liberal allies into a partnership based on enlightenment and 19th century liberal individualistic ideas of autonomy, localism, choice, merit, and excellence. However, its true purpose is not only to seize control of governments and public schools, but also to ensure that a new medieval religious conformity is imposed on students. Its primary goal is to make them 'educated' only in business/industrial terms while being anti-union, docile, and obedient workers in an Orwellian '19- or 2084' world. This odd alliance of religious fanatics, industrial/electronic/service authoritarians, and individualistic liberals against social liberals, democrats, and social justice adherents is a drama being played out on a stage where the distracted public is mesmerized by tabloid news, sports, entertainment, violence, sex, and media mindlessness. This chapter summarizes some of the book's critical comments on this contemporary saga (for example, mass media and education, technology and excellence, and authoritarian populism).

The theme of this chapter (the future as seen from the present) allows us to review topics such as reconceptualism in the 1990s; resisting/overcoming hegemony (how do you do it? and is postmodernism compatible with critical theory?); the disabled as a new ally in gender, race, and class solidarity; realities of postindustrial life and education; potential horrors of the Toyota School and its feudal, undemocratic structuralism; promises of democratic schooling and productive education for democracy; Western European and US trends in Western European in critical theory; prospects for educational reform in a 'predatory' age; economic, political, and social reform and schools; and cross-national opportunities to create democratic schools, communities, and movements of hope and vision in the 21st century.

EDUCATIONAL POLITICS IN THE US AND UK: CRITICAL THEORY, RADICAL EDUCATION, AND RECONCEPTUALISM

This section focuses on some current trends in critical theory. It summarizes, compares, and contrasts some recent work of Anyon, Apple, Levin, Giroux, and McLaren (Giroux and McLaren, 1994) and reviews parallel trends in England, using the work of Edwards and Whitty.

Jean Anyon and the Case Against Postmodernism

Anyon's work on ideology and history textbooks, social class and curriculum options, inner city school reform, and gender and class is well-known to educators, critical theorists, and civic education specialists. Anyon (1994, pp. 115-33) wrote that since neo-Marxist thought has been largely abandoned because it became dead-ended, critical scholars (the 'Left') have turned their attention to student-teacher empowerment and change, using postmodern and poststructuralist theories. They are searching for a more equitable and progressive educational, social, political, and economic system.

Anyon finds commendable Henry Giroux's emphasizing the contingent, specific, and historical and allowing students and marginalized 'others' to speak. However, theory belies practice. No students, no marginalized, no African Americans, no 'others' do much speaking in his works. Instead, bell hooks' views are used to harshly evaluate 'radical critical theorists'.

According to hooks, the use of the 'other' is a mask and is oppressive. It annihilates and erases; usurps 'others' speech; interposes better trained interlocutors, pain merchants, reporters, story tellers, recreators, authorities, colonizers, and speaking subjects using 'others' merely as a focus of attention. Additionally, the abstractions found in Giroux's work make it inaccessible to those whose emancipation is claimed. This discourse is not only nonempirical, but creates a metalanguage by drawing on the theoretical constructs of others to discuss the ideology of 'transcendental subjects' and 'border pedagogy'. Observable reality, which deals with school climate and the hidden curriculum, must be related to practical theoretical constructs. Obscurantist concepts become barriers to communication about changing schools and teachers. As a result, 'abstract theorizing agency is displaced into discourse'. Language is separated from events; it becomes independent from lived existence; ideology is empowered instead of people/actors and personal agency. This unproductive process means that 'ideological production concepts become fetishized' and 'ideology functions as a kind of "currency" - a medium of exchange among ideologists'. Political language can be useful for political resistance or for promoting direct political action and legitimate political struggle. In this way, postmodernism/structuralism serves the producers' interests, not that of popular emancipation (Anyon, 1994, p. 129).

Anyon says that more useful social theory should combine theory and action and judiciously employ concepts and empirical facts. It is not merely ad hoc or local since it must connect social structures, daily life, and the complexities of a middle-range theory of local connections to societal constraints. Such theory would also include space for personal agency, social problems, and reasoned indeterminacy, yet also focus on political action, practice, and ending oppression. Anyon is convinced that the underlying basis of school reform theory in the US is inadequate and must itself be deconstructed and reconstructed if schools are to be upgraded.

Henry Giroux, Committed Postmodernist and Civic Educator

Giroux's interest in curriculum reform, multiculturalism, language, leadership, 'critical citizenship' education, and the 'reconstruction of democratic public life' is unflagging. For example, Giroux (May/June 1991, pp. 305-8) pitted the current 'ethics of adaptation' against 'an ethics responsive to the imperatives of a critical democracy'. He interrogates the current curriculum and present school organization by asking: Whose history is being taught? Whose experience is embodied in the school setting? Who speaks for whom and under what conditions/for which and whose purposes? What kind of citizens are we producing? What kind of society do we want to create?

He claims that it is neither moral nor ethical for schools to preach good work habits, patriotism, or testing skills as substitutes for effective democratic education. Instead, democratic education requires students to learn to 'imagine otherwise' and 'to make choices, think critically, and believe they can make a difference'. Critical educators must sanction and interrogate students' prior knowledge, appreciate democratic political culture, and practice 'cooperation, sharing, and social justice' in schools. This means studying history, oppression, racism, sexism, equality, and justice. Such practices allow 'dialogue, trust, and solidarity' to develop in the discussion of ethnic and ideological differences. Students must be 'border crossers', reconstructionists, and risk-takers. They must learn to cross 'over into cultural zones that provide a critical resource for rethinking how the relations between dominant and sub-ordinate groups are organized'. Such border crossers examine their relation to structured dominance and learn what is required to promote social justice and democracy by appreciating differences and diversity. The school curriculum must be concerned with the problems of everyday life, school-community relations, school democracy, and both critical and moral citizenship.

In 1992, Giroux discussed current attacks on critical theorists as being utopian, opaque writers, using unclear and ambiguous prose, coining new terms, and fostering incomprehensibility while using inaccessible concepts. Giroux finds this charge reductionist, trivializing, and culturally monistic, antideconstructionist, and elitist. Complexity and difference are important since effective educators are border crossers in language, theory, and the politics of difference. They are engaged in creating a new society instead of being continually marginalized. They can accept such linguistic risks. Furthermore, he cries foul regarding a charge Apple made in 1988 that the Left should avoid mystification and unrealistic claims that cannot be clarified of verified. The more arcane this work, Apple said, the more likely it is to be marginalized, its concepts to remain vague, and to unduly suffer from its unclear writing, which itself is undemocratic in character and essence.

Giroux said that such criticisms mask old positive empiricist claims, oversimplify schooling to a matter of reproduction versus resistance, and falsely split theory and practice, while ignoring one's own linguistic partiality (that is, answers the question: Who speaks, under which conditions, and for whom?) and the contextual question (Who reads what under which conditions?). It fails to realize that linguistic diversity is important to democracy. New projects need a new language so educators will develop multiple literacies based on differences rather than totalizing theories. Languages can also be critical and subversive so they need not all be 'plainspeak', he says. Language itself should be used to repeatedly rewrite everyday experiences. Giroux ends his defense of linguistic variety by summarizing his views on democracy, democratic culture, and citizenship. He uses terms such as self-management, transfer of horizontal power, resource access, informed decision making, control over life, and emancipation in a community setting in which public service is valued (Giroux, 1992, pp. 219-27).

Giroux and McLaren (1992) analyze the excesses of language and its relation to questions of identity, inequality, struggle, and the current context in which there is 'a populist authoritarian ideology that ties it to a tidy relation among national identity, culture, and literacy'. Language today divides dominant from subordinate groups, whites from blacks, and schools from meeting democratic imperatives. Language needs to be seen as how it subjectively relates to 'history, power, and authority'. Critical theory is seen as deficient since it has not moved beyond 'critique and domination' in its language. Language as it relates to 'subjectivity and praxis' is also discussed, along with the use of language in describing a social reality which influences educational and social change. Language seems 'to socially construct and moderate reality' and 'interacts with experience to shape subjectivity'. They discuss the question of critical theories' use of language as being 'too abstruse and impractical'. A new classroom critical pedagogy must empower learners to appreciate differences, shape self and community, and produce social justice.

Henry Levin, School Reformer and Economist

Levin tries to accelerate disadvantaged children's learning through his cost-effective accelerated schools model. One basic idea of this approach substitutes a 'gifted and talented' strategy for a 'remedial' model for teaching at-risk students. He began his work in the early 1980s when he visited schools and conducted demographic research. He saw administrators and teachers engaged mostly in disciplining students, while the latter were bored as they routinely completed worksheets. Teachers used negative words to define average pupils and positive words to define gifted and talented students. Whereas average students were said to need remedial work since they were either not well prepared or acted out, talented kids were believed to need hands-on programs, an enriched curriculum, and more advanced work. His conclusion was that defining students determines how you educate them.

Thus, Levin looked for remedial students' talents and strengths. Students responded to his enrichment plans and linking the schools to their experiences, culture, and community. He redefined the problem to build on the strengths of talented teachers and staff, not just those of students. The same was true for parents, whose hidden resources he also sought and found. Schools were reformed so that all members could make better and more informed decisions after an internal transformation of the school's culture. Providing enrichment mathematics programs throughout a school was one element in such a transformation; it seemed to work. A cultural transformation also means that staff are more engaged and enthusiastic and the educational setting becomes friendly and open to parents. Volunteers work there and other family members join in after-hours events. These schools are noisy places, but children communicate there, build their vocabularies, are curious, and want to own things they produce in school. Test scores, while improving, are just a byproduct (not the goal) of schooling. School budgets have not been inflated in these schools, which usually take five to six years to reform.

Levin (1994) examines heightened educational needs for turn-of-the-century workers and the projected impact of test scores on productivity. He concludes that any concern about education should be directed to improving human capabilities, not just satisfying some narrow, misunderstood 'economic imperative'. His research finds that skill upgrading for new occupations will be an unlikely result of any new changes in computer technology. This is so for a variety of reasons, including the fact that workers are easily replaced for this work. The increased educational needs of technical and professional workers are also examined. Such future needs are not likely to be very different from the present. There is also an unlikely need for more college-educated workers whose wages are already declining and who are already in oversupply. So there is no skills gap, no rosy future for college graduates, and no new technology or work organization which will mobilize any such changes. In sum, no worker shortages are forecast.

Michael Apple: Gender, Text Analysis, and a Multidisciplinary Approach

In 1992, Apple warned that the influx of computers into schools must be guided so the new technology benefits all citizens. The computer revolution is costly to schools and may interfere with their humanistic and political education goals. The computer invasion may outpace teachers, may discriminate against poor/minority students, and may be for naught since no one can predict the future job market (Apple, February 1992, pp. 47-52). He wrote about screening science films and employing new mathematics standards and how these contribute to conservative educational causes. He also discussed the financial crisis of education; school-based inequality and the use of mathematics to maintain such inequality; grounding a curriculum in problem solving and student experience; and the complexities of teachers' lives. His views on textbooks as official knowledge serving the ruling elite and their purposes appeared in his 'official knowledge' book in 1993. Texts may be fought for or against on the basis of a moral regulation, a teaching aid, or a means for democratization. Although seeming progressive, textbooks are still hegemonic. Teachers must work with students to deconstruct the text and its multiple meanings. Textbooks (as instruments and cultural artifacts) remain political/economic commodities and so have to be studied through political economy and cultural studies. Such an analysis can explain the mystery of state textbook adoption practices and their influence on publishers, along with the interstate politics of how textbook content is selected, used, and for what purposes (Apple, October 1992 and 1993; Apple and Christian-Smith, 1991).

The UK Situation: Misery Likes Company

Some of the educational issues which predominate on the policy agenda in the US and Canada are also before the public in the UK. For example, in November 1992, the *Journal of Moral Education* focused on 'citizenship and diversity'. The articles dealt with identity, the just community, back to basics, peace, pluralism, decency, diversity, and civic education within the UK's new national curriculum. In the 1990s, writers (such as Geoff Whitty, Tony Edwards, and Joseph Tamney) are concerned about quality control, reform, and teacher education; parental choice in the UK and the US; teacher education, conservative government, and religious education; and differential rates of funding for city technology colleges and those in nonurban locations. Teacher education standards, partnerships to define standards, core competencies, quality control, public accreditation/accountability, and local/national needs are being discussed. The question of parental choice is scrutinized not from reasserting 'old-style collectivist principles', but rather in line with striking a balance between collective goods and private rights, the pessimism of those wanting change versus 'free market' optimists, and the likely prospect that such a political initiative will allow escape for the privileged, no reform for what remains behind, and further benefits to those who already prosper from their 'free market' advantages (Edwards and Whitty, 1992, pp. 101-17).

Recent Trends in US/UK Critical Theory

In *Between Capitalism and Democracy*, Svi Shapiro writes about 'educational reform and liberal democracy' and 'from critical theory to the politics of educational change'. The basic elements of such a plan would include empowerment, social justice, unified social and educational crises, and incorporation of 'new themes, moral concerns, and social vision into the general discourse on education' (Shapiro, 1989, pp. 1, 23, and 79).

Shapiro's comments are useful guides which (when joined with Anyon's observations) allow us to use some internally generated criteria to assess the worth, durability, and utility of the foregoing analysis. Few critical theorists (with the notable exception of Apple) are willing to tell us who is doing something beneficial and worth emulating. Furthermore, the level of postmodern/poststructural abstraction for the dynamic discourse used in critical arguments is either an asset or a liability. This depends on the shared perspective and academic consanguinity of the reader and writer. Shapiro decries the overliberalization of individualism. Since this is the key feature of the American myth, it deserves challenge; but in all likelihood, it will resist change until more pragmatic alternatives appear.

American critical theorists surveyed here may be unified in their analysis of (and opposition to) conservatism in the US, but they have done little to arrange for a return of the radical and revolutionary leftist language which the right has expropriated. American conservatives turned the meaning of revolution, radical, reactionary, and anarchy upside down. For example, they want to turn the clock back, but say they are not reactionary; are revolutionary, but want to conserve the mythical past; and are radical, but never get to the root of matters since they are victims of their own superficial ideology of God, country, work, television, sports, and (home-based) motherhood.

Some critical theorists (for example, Anyon and Levin) are very practical in their approach to real educational reform. They have tried and discarded certain of their own group-prescribed remedies. Instead, they employ older or revised versions of useful theories which have encouraged new thought to redefine practical educational problems. We have seen some of this in action as well. Keep in mind who writes about which disciplinary fields: Giroux is a specialist on civics and citizenship; Apple on gender, texts, science, and mathematics; Anyon and Levin on practical educational reform; and Levin on challenging the New Right's economic predictions (on which they base their educational reform plans) for the 21st century.

US political culture is in a transitional phase to which the Republican Party seems to have momentarily adjusted. As for the Democrats, their degree of change, adaptation, or chances for turning public attitudes around all are problematic. Given such public attitudes, there is little likelihood that a Left liberal or radical educational plan will be adopted anywhere, except for cities in the most dire straits. (Even then, privatization is likely to be the preferred alternative, as in Hartford, CT; Boston, MA; Baltimore, MD; and Minneapolis, MN where it has been tried and, in almost every case, rejected.) Most writers on politics and/of education will likely continue to be structural/functionalists since their convictions are most known and in favor around the country. But, it is possible to use relevant findings from the research on politics and education which could prove useful for critical educators who want to institute a local school or systemwide experiment, reform, or project. Generally, unless the school system is politically contextualized, there is little chance that any reform will work, even with Levin's broadly applicable accelerated schools program. Since all educational reconceptualists do not agree on the worth of poststructural and postmodern analytical frames, language, and perspective, it is a sign of strength for neo-Marxists to accept the relevant and reject the useless parts of the latest philosophical fads.

As we look at the hardening conservative political trends in the UK, Canada, and the US, we see the 'curse' of reactionary illiberal politics extends throughout the English-speaking union, with certain notable exceptions (such as New Zealand). While these national and international trends are important, we must remember that, as former Speaker of the US House of Representatives 'Tip' O'Neill said, 'All politics are local politics'. The US right has recognized the strength of this dictum in that they run local candidates for state legislatures, city councils, school boards, and even dog catchers as stepping stones to monopolize political control from the bottom up.

Even more basic is the contested site of the classroom. Democratic public education is (by nature) essentially political. While some teachers may claim neutrality on partisan party choices, it is preferable to explore the worth of various policy options in classrooms. Here, teachers can fairly make their reasoned choices known to the class. Using the 'on the one hand' and 'on the other' politics of nonchoice is the politics of frustrated decision making.

Professors, teachers, students, parents, and community members must accept the charge of democratic politics to be involved and informed on public choices. In this endeavor, critical theorists must provide a viable social theory or cognitive schema to rationalize schooling and its subject matter, textbooks, organization, and curriculum. This means examining political topics dealing with power relationships and the authoritative allocation of values within a democratic political system in which daily conflict is inevitable. Thus, reconceptualists are responsible for making the effort, if not for determining the outcomes of this process. Just as there are cycles of critical elections every generation or so, there are also swings in the ebb and flow of authoritarianism and liberal/conservative political values. When the earth must spin around on its axis for a while before the humanistic/progressive cycle returns, the critical educator's job is to keep these options not only open but alive, relevant, and available for the right (or left) educational or political moment.

MASS MEDIA'S INFLUENCE ON EDUCATION

The mass media are quick to cover school controversies, issues, and problems when the topics are crime, violence, drugs, strikes, or political divisiveness. However, they do not regularly and responsibly cover students as learners, teachers as workers, curricular changes, extracurricular activities, or educational finance and governance. Consequently, many of the public's views on schooling stem from media's failure to provide useful context and their distortion of educational realities (Dennis and La May, 1993, pp. ix-xii, 1-3).

The public's views on schools and schooling focus on 'mediacentric' issues such as vouchers, choice, reform, restructuring, privatization, excellence, Channel One or ITV, national curriculum/standards/testing, racial/ethnic segregation, and other highly visible questions. These are issues which intrigue newspaper editors, TV broadcasters, and news managers whose sole purpose is to turn a profit, regardless of whether entertainment or education provide the impetus to 'sell' subscribers, readers, or viewers.

The real stuff of education deals only incidentally with such questions. It involves issues such as teachers' salaries/benefits (approximately 75 per cent of school budgets), career advancement, promotion, tenure and merit policies, school administration, and management. It is important to ask who pays for education, what corporations want/deserve from schools, who benefits from what kinds of educational information, and what stake special interests have in school politics, economics, and social reform. As with their evaluation of politicians, the public often rates their own local schools much higher than 'other' systems, even those a short distance away. This is partly a product of the overall favorable coverage local schools receive in the local media as well as personal experiences with local schools and their personnel.

If public opinion is uninformed about a radical democratic educational reform agenda and alternatives to conservative pleas to nationalize curricula, no one has informed the mass public about textbooks, tests, and TV influences which already have both corporate and national cultural guidelines as part of their very essence. If the public knows little of deindustrialization, postmodernism, disability, emancipation, corporatism, and democratic educational options at home and abroad, this is partly a result of democratic reconceptualists' failure to make their case in the media. Also, it is a result of mass communication's (both public and private) failure to include left-of-liberal spokespersons in these conversations while simultaneously excluding the poor, women, handicapped, ethnic minorities, and others who are not older, white, upper class, male hegemons. (More often, this happens at the state and local levels in the US where racism's concrete effects are so perniciously obvious.) Also ignored are questions about the (dis)utility of school reform (reaction) or the democratization (elitization) of educational politics. Such agenda items would allow critical educators to contribute to public discussions, providing a missing piece of the communications puzzle now lacking in most Western European and American educational dialogue and debate.

SOME MAJOR THEMES AND SPECIFIC CONCLUSIONS

When selecting some of our major themes and conclusions, we try to avoid repeating those mentioned in the introductory chapter and in the contributions themselves. However, the following short list of summary ideas and conclusions may help to bring several of these generalizations together in one place.

Conclusions About Politics and/of Education

1. Instead of keeping politics out of education, it is clear that schooling is a contested political site in which ideational, party, and ideological views are debated heatedly with questions of who 'owns' public schools, whose tax dollars are to be spent, and whose values will be paramount in the educational institution.
2. The politics of schooling makes it clear that vocational versus humanistic or liberal arts curricula as organizational frameworks reflect different value orientations such as education for consumerism, work, self-development, or lifelong learning. This divisive question about the primary emphasis of schooling pits parents against educators and politicians against business persons. We know that education for work has significant costs associated with this self-serving goal. For example, while many business representatives joined some politicians in berating public schools and promoting educational reform, the basic questions of who

(parents, professionals, employers, or public officials) shall fund and control the educational enterprise are still contested issues.

3. When a country introduces an examination system and national goals, we again see a clash of values because these goals, the questions posed, and the grading and reporting system have no one clear choice which is self-evidently superior to other alternatives. We must also ask how these goals will be implemented and how the test results will be used for and against children, teachers, and schools.

4. The American and European New Right clearly wants to capture public schooling so education can service their interests while supporting popular and conventional moral, spiritual, family, and religious values in line with conservative views of a new era of antimodern postindustrialism. The New Right has the benefit of strong political sponsorship, for example, from major parties in England, the US, and Germany. Thus, advocates of big defense spending benefit from a combination of receiving additional government dollars which are simultaneously linked to governmental deregulation and devolution. They are willing to pay the meager price associated with the reassertion of traditional values in the face of the 'reflexive modernization' of our 'risk society', which is rapidly changing before we have clear answers to the new questions we face every day (Beck, 1992; Giddens, 1994). These issues center around work, family, and gender as well as ecology, war, democracy, shared abundance, and other serious questions. This includes the value of 'utopian realism' where the educational system plays a significant role in achieving happiness, self-actualization, and security which can counter the reactionary forces of fundamentalism, insecurity, fragmentation, and totalitarianism (Giddens, 1994, pp. 100-1, 169, and 246-53).

5. This book challenges New Right adherents partly because they are self-serving, mean-spirited, and fundamentalistic antimodern political curmudgeons. They are out of step with the increasing globalization of communications and the postindustrial, postpostmodern age which requires developing a new spirit and the positive elements of a new ecology, public welfare, civic virtue, and democracy. They are irrelevant to developing a new democratic politics going beyond classic individualistic liberalism and false claims to 19th century conservative (Tory) values to the growth of a dialogic democracy based on civic associations, solidarity, deliberation, cosmopolitanism, and substantive reforms of the welfare state and the market economy both in theory and practice.

6. Different proposals from the autonomous and functionalist groups in critical educational theory reflect education's role as a social discriminator or equalizer which teaches obedience or independence. They also reflect some basic ambiguities and vagaries in Western educational practice and theory. Similarly, the disparate emphasis on competition and excellence versus compensatory education, equity, and affirmative action

is another example of different themes which critical theorists emphasize even while they may agree on certain elemental views about education and reproduction, correspondence, and agency.

7. It is important to have clearly defined ideas about what terms such as nation, state, government, or regime mean as well as how the economic system relates to each (for example: Is a democratic political system or civil society possible without a market economy?). The pervasive hidden curriculum (which is based on class lines) plus the countering forces of emancipation, resistance, or agency all assume an economic dimension.

8. One frequently asserted suggestion is that teachers should assume a more activist role in curriculum revision, educational finance, workplace democracy, gender equality, and other key initiatives. Such reforms, along with democratizing schools, teaching decision-making skills, decentralizing and debureaucratizing the system, encouraging professional teamwork, and using counterhegemonic actions can together synergistically ensure systemwide educational renewal.

9. Ethnographic as well as qualitative and quantitative methods are valuable in classroom research. Different contributors also expressed their views about key terms (such as social reproduction, correspondence theory, human capital, enlightenment, praxis, and oppression) in different educational, social, political, and economic settings. Other concepts clarified include the force of cultural reproduction of historical conditions, ideologies, and individual dispositions which impede students' counterhegemonic tendencies and emancipatory impulses (subject to the influence of externally imposed hegemonic restraints) along with border crossings to achieve racial diversity amidst social unity.

10. The general worth of cultural reproduction theory must be evaluated in terms of its optimistic or pessimistic possibilities or usual outcomes and whether it produces hegemonic or democratic school and social conditions in different national settings.

11. There has been a lack of uniformity or unanimity in critical theory during the last two decades despite overall agreement on the baneful effects of using schools to serve production and business interests rather than encouraging individual development and social justice. Several critiques of neo-Marxist positions have analyzed these same questions.

12. Interrelationships between political science trends and critical theory's contributions to political science and civic education were discussed in several chapters. Decision and policy making, state theory, everyday politics, cultural studies, political socialization research, and political education are areas where political science as a discipline and critical pedagogical reconceptualism are mutually useful and informative.

13. Since education is involved with the politics of culture, those in power decide what knowledge is privileged; how it is organized, taught, and evaluated; and who will be credentialed to promote social differentiation

and discrimination between the 'haves' and 'have nots' in different classes. These are key areas of agreement among various types of critical theorists emphasizing different aspects of social inequality, for example.

14. Since the US now virtually has a national textbook and curriculum system, goals, and testing, there is no use in emulating the UK and Japan to raise standards or ensure accountability. As most educational reconceptualists would agree, if that is done, the country's elite are sure to benefit, but the poor and disadvantaged most likely will not.

15. Despite claims to the contrary, the authoritarian populism of the New Right advocates the values of choice, civilization, and family in the cause of consumerism and free-enterprise capitalistic business. The so-called revolutionary conservative restoration in the US and UK is based on privatization, centralization, vocationalization, and differentiation. Thus, it produces a dual system of education with market (private) and minimum (public) schools. Neoconservatives and their neoliberal allies unite on fundamentalism and classic market competition to benefit the consumer while speaking of choice and privatization to establish a 'socialized' or 'nationalized' curriculum, standards, and tests. But, they either fail to realize or will not admit that these initiatives will result in discrimination, division, resistance, and exclusion of 'others' (such as the poor, women, gays, and minorities) from the 'common' culture, especially as this myth exists in the UK, Germany, the US, and the Netherlands.

16. The New Right ignores the 'pornography of poverty' (which is the West's real educational challenge), favors elitist solutions for the privileged classes, and leads outward from democracy to support a longstanding 'structured inequality' and 'educational apartheid'. Yet, the spreading battle over a national curriculum could forge new teacher, parent, and oppressed group alliances. But the price we shall pay for the newest educational products of the grand market narrative is too great since we are now surrounded by so many of its obvious flaws (such as poverty, racism, ecocide, and a permanent state of war since 1939).

Conclusions About the Sociology of Education and Education and Society

1. The disabled have been largely ignored in the sociology of education and in critical theory and educational reconceptualism. Researching marginality and disability provides insights into the general society and produces social goods in and of itself. Categorization, definitions, legitimation, professionalization, normality, and ideology are key topics involved in this process. Disability can be considered a form of oppression. Thus, equal political opportunity to participate fully in social decision making is a major liberation and empowerment goal. The idea of normalization

is as inadequate as much current national legislation to protect the disabled. When we do not include the disabled, when we discuss inequality, social justice, and democracy, who else is being left out, marginalized, or excluded as 'others' (that is, those outside 'normal' society)?

2. The postmodern project attacks the enlightenment, autonomy, science, rationality, and today's metanarratives. Pedagogy, education, and schooling must come to terms with the postmodernist challenge through concepts such as mobility, imagination, and concrete or abstract utopias (political, rational, progressive, mythical, and/or revolutionary). There are two types of utopian visions: where present and future come together in a critical way with today's reality (concrete) or they do not do so (abstract). This use of the utopian framework has actual *Bildungs*-potential, does not sanctify the present, and directs our future research. Educational modernists, postmodernists, neopragmatists, and pluralists also have varying views on the utility of utopianism and topics such as criteriology.

3. While a mature cosmopolitan citizenship may be part of the ideal type that describes effective democratic citizens, we may all benefit from reexamining Dewey's original formulations of these ideas from the 1930s and 1940s since they are still pedagogically useful and are a basis for neopragmatist writers in this field.

4. Both objective (technological) and subjective (milieus) conditions of German life have changed dramatically in the last 25 years. These sociological changes occurred in an increasingly pluralistic society, but sociological research has failed to stay abreast. This is partly because of the deficit of useful milieu research guidelines for socialization studies (for example, youth who fit the classical, unstable, and advancement- or family-oriented, hedonistic, masculine, or subject-oriented worker types). These orientations were based on socialization contexts or social inequality considerations. Social space, situation, milieu, and milieu biography are other useful concepts needed to understand sociocultural mobility.

5. German milieu research indicates that the continuation of class and milieu type breaks down to conservative, technocratic, and alternative (upper middle) bourgeois, and traditional/traditionless workers exhibiting materialistic, hedonistic, or postmaterial orientations. As one moves up or down in the society, the influence of one's past origins and present class membership are equally important, if not equally influential.

6. Since educational policy is social policy, the sociology of education plays a mediating role between social analysis and the study of education. A new sociology of education emerged in the US and UK in the late 1960s. It developed our basic approaches to and understanding of correspondence, social domination, and reproductive theory as part of the cultural studies and critical theory movements.

7. The concept of reproduction and relations between the educational and economic systems should be reexamined. The determinism and lack of

agency (which the reproduction model postulates) ignore the interplay of the economy, education, state, and individual. There is much autonomy in educational institutions; dominated subjects can resist; and social structures can and do change. We must study the resistance process plus how it is practiced in different settings and the relative importance of ethnicity, race, and gender contrasted with important class influences.

8. Heydorn's contributions to critical educational theory (such as the concepts of emancipation, education as social theory, and education for autonomy) were developed in the framework of Western Marxism. Education is seen as liberation, self-actualization, transduction, and praxis.

Conclusions About the Economics of Education

1. Any consideration of educational policy making must not only be concerned about competing views of emancipation, comprehensive schooling, social inequality, correspondence, and reproduction, but also with the dynamics of an operative national political and economic system, including division of labor and labor market trends.

2. The Netherlands increased social inequality for women and minority workers since the 1980s. Simultaneously, secondary general and vocational education and comprehensive schools were reformed in the early 1990s with the imposition of a common curriculum along with provision for certain optional courses (such as classical languages). The comprehensive curriculum in lower secondary education allows a delay in one's choice of a future educational track; this could lessen present segmentation while reducing social inequality if schools are physically integrated, curricula equalized, school quality enhanced, and equality of status improved. Children from working classes and immigrant families will be differentially affected by these reforms. Thus, attention to dropout rates, counseling, dynamic monitoring of outcomes/results, and other modifications may be necessary to salvage the reform agenda.

3. Linking educational reform to labor market changes is the first step for research in this area. Education should not only be vocational, it should teach people to prepare for work, find jobs, survive in the economy, enjoy leisure, improve life opportunities, and promote personal awareness and responsiveness. It can inspire group resistance and involvement via practical politics, professional organizations, and teachers' unions; it can provide emancipatory opportunities for women returning to work or recent immigrants seeking language training and self-improvement.

4. The Toyota School's advocacy of teams, performance, quality, and management goals is the latest successor to the old bureaucratic, corporatist, industry-based models. The post-Fordist school serves postindustrialism and postmodernism. Restructuring, productivity, customer satisfac-

tion, flexibility, commodification, standards, and consumerism are new watchwords. Forgotten today is how society and self interact socially; studying history is all that is left of the old social studies movement.

5. The processes of emptying schools, desocialization, and inattention to identity formation are products of postmodern anomie and conformism in a culture of change, uncertainty, identity crisis, and division. This culture pits fundamentalist 'family values' against 'secular humanism'.

6. The concept of economic reproduction (using the educational system to breed a new work force) involves questions of resource distribution, social legitimation, and hegemony/dominance/struggle. In Israel, women, recent immigrants, and the Arab minority share the least in the decreasing educational abundance. If and when these groups are more fully integrated into Israel's educational and social/economic system, their disempowerment may radically change the Israeli reproduction system.

7. Israel's 1968 educational reforms added a year of compulsory education, instituted a 6-3-3 structural change, and integrated schools. The result is debatable. Israel's vocational education history is also perplexing. The Israeli guideline of horizontal integration and vertical differentiation is furthered by the educational system where cultural integration is promoted while vertical social differentiation is not. Israel's new but conservative metanarratives of parental choice and school autonomy now underway may foster even more economic reproductive tendencies.

8. The language of rhetorical excellence has dominated American educational discourse since the 1970s. Despite the fact that our schools are labeled high tech failures, the existing jobs are low tech enough so that even high school graduates may seem overeducated. Appropriately, job experience rather than schooling determines success in the work world. The emphasis on testing is also part of this cult of excellence; test results are distorted in the mass media to prove that schools are failing; but these results are at least debatable and probably wrong.

9. Instead of US schools being responsible for democracy, mobility, and economic progress, they buttress privilege, inequality, and the present economic order. US schools performed these roles in the Progressive, post-1945, and present postindustrial era of information, science, technology, communications, education, and professionalism. Excellence, the key term here, is totally devoid of meaning. Other overused terms (such as improvements, performance standards, and efficiency) which mass media hype popularized share this fate. These education goals do not chart where schools have been as much as they develop policies for where they should go. A new moral vision, meritocracy, new social inequalities, technocratic authority and control, legitimacy, and depoliticization are opposites of mediocrity, bureaucracy, failure, and lack of progress. Technological literacy, not humanism, is postindustrialism's

goal. Democracy, public support, equity, quality, and hope are not part of the postindustrialist language of science and excellence.

10. The US and European debate about the definition of democratic citizenship and citizenship education in the postindustrial and postmodern era centers around concepts such as race, gender, ethnicity, Euro/Anglocentrisim, age, disability, homophobia, and class oppression. The empowered use schooling, examinations, and job rewards to ensure their continuing dominance. Mass media demonizes gang members and ignores the homeless who are seen as affronts to middle class sensibilities. The cultural police guard the sanctity of the English language, its history, and its 'dead pluralism' which forces consensus, harmony, and unity down our throats. Meanwhile, people leave the public shpere and are uninterested in these issues because of a lack of passion, motivation, knowledge, progressive education, and a pedagogy of 'difference'.

11. Critical educational theory in North America and Europe must deal with poststructuralism, postindustrialism, postmodernism, and the assault on our grand narratives about progress, historicism, classlessness, teleology, emancipation, wealth, nature, language, scientism, consumerism, free market democracy, truth, pluralism, and the production of meaning.

12. Today's youth do not willingly accept postmodernism or critical education. Both views challenge contemporary ideology and media images of the truth which gloss over social justice, oppression, community fragmentation, the underclass, social conflict, and psuedopatriotism. Critical pedagogy attempts to problematize economics, everyday life, identity, schooling, popular culture, and the mass media. Critical education must help students empower themselves, reject prevailing conventions and grand theories, accept the possibility of solidarity, and join other contemporary reformers and concrete realists with a utopian vision.

Conclusions About Educational Reform

1. We examined recent UK educational reforms to see how well they promoted choice and diversity. Topics included open enrollment (which neither closed underenrolled schools nor improved all schools, but rather widened the gap between the best and worst ones, especially in the case of increased racial segregation); local school management (formula funding did not uniformly improve either school self-management or equality of treatment but ended affirmative action plans, moved scarce resources from inner city schools to suburban and rural ones, and concentrated disabled students in urban schools with depleted overall enrollments); City Technical Colleges (eventually scaled back since local sites and business sponsors are hard to find and their impact on the working class, other than a small group of Asian students, hard to measure); and

Grant Maintained Schools (in practice, a direct grant, pro-choice, non-LEA controlled scheme to nurture religious and academically selective schools without promoting true diversity and nontraditional education).

2. Current UK educational trends are also market, choice, and New Right or Thatcherite based. The LEA's powers were drastically reduced and their existence threatened. This postmodern movement is antibureaucratic, post-Fordist, and fragmented; it is pluralistic and pragmatic, seeking to define an emerging postcapitalist or postindustrial society. Their experience with open enrollment, local school management, City Technical Colleges, Grant Maintained Schools, and educational capitalism has not produced pluralism nor reduced social reproduction, correspondence, resistance, or hegemony. Instead, traditional structural inequality persists among the underclass in inner cities. This new postmodernity reflects hierarchy, distinction, and fragmentation, not toleration, difference, and heterogeneity. The new national curriculum is also designed to counter liberalism as well as to promote fundamentalism, monoculturalism, Westernism, and 'conservative modernization', a typical political paradox of espousing both continuity and change.

3. Seeing critical education as an informed choice which can include pragmatism and democratic theory allows one to both challenge the fundamentalism of this new age of dead traditionalism and pedagogical nonsense and link much of last century's predominant educational theory to the educational demands we shall likely face in the next. Instead, a more resonable choice is between the traditional and new sociologies of education. The latter views education as a citizenship right to create a public as well as to produce a democratic state, economy, and society.

4. The present and proposed democratic discourse (contrasted with traditional/patriarchal and scientific-rational views) is the project of the pragmatic participatory society, producing equal results, human rights, communicative and relativistic reasoning in the communitarian public sphere, in which critical citizens use probabalistic rationality and critical literacy to resolve conflicts (which political education and social studies in a reconstructed school would have helped them develop).

5. Education can be seen as a person's basic citizenship right which results from both past struggles and future contestation. Essentially, citizenship definitions are class, occupational, and stratification by source concepts.

6. The contribution of the so-called new sociology of education is not concerned as much with schools as ideological production lines, but also with the production of knowledge (for example, see the Whitty and Apple chapters), its sources, supports, and results. This is the critical curriculum theory approach. It views teachers as key change agents who help students transform themselves as well as change the state, politics, and the economy. A thorough discussion of the state and its ideological products and apparatuses can be a fruitful aspect of contemporary critical

theory. The New Right has not only monopolized these public discussions, but has also dominated the related curriculum debates and disorganized its democratic opposition. Instead, the goal of a public-spirited political philosophy (which takes its democratic state as a given and a powerful tool to be used) is to develop nonconservative community values, state action, political participation, and public choice/accountability based on advantaging the least-advantaged through social justice and furtherance of citizen's basic human rights.

7. In the context of the democratic/participatory metadiscourse, the role of political/citizenship education is critical. It helps develop public morality and train and encourage citizens to create new publics (combining a radical and liberal view). Teachers, text revisions, and new curricula can change educational discourses. Thus, students are taught to critically examine the text, engage in dialogue, and practice critical pragmatism. They can mobilize against the undemocratic forces of an authoritarian popular criteriology. Students must learn both to tolerate or embrace disagreement as well as to promote community solidarity when possible and practical. (For a discussion of many of these themes from a US perspective, including a theory of the state, correspondence theory, agency, Deweyism, and postmodernism, see Brosio, 1994. For a cross-national view, including France, Ecuador, Taiwan, Mexico, Bolivia, Nepal, US Chicanos, and American Indians, see Levinson et al., 1996.)

COMMON ASSUMPTIONS, THEMES, AND PRODUCTS

The ideas presented in this book benefitted from their advocates being mutually informed about one another's views. In this regard, the volume contains a series of conversations about common interests. Some of the major themes and findings which result from these studies include these conclusions:

1. Critical theory/reconceptualism is one of the few academic and educational areas which is willing to contest New Right philosophical, economic, and educational views head on.
2. A socially valuable stance of radical pedagogy is its inclusiveness (that is, of race, gender, disability, age, sexual preference, ethnicity, and so on) in general public dialogue. Such topics are not used to exclude, but rather treated as constructive elements to be included in the societal celebration of our shared uniqueness, otherness, and unity in diversity.
3. The radical critique serves as a balance for the arrogance of business representatives. They neither want to pay taxes nor submit to government regulation, but they want schools to serve their self-serving purposes. As self-appointed and publicly accepted educational 'experts', business

representatives want to reform schools that do not pass muster or mirror the reproduction/correspondence image.

4.   Two other common themes in this book are the utility of studying concepts such as state, citizenship, and civic education on the one hand and the possibility of providing continuity with the last 50 years through a combination of critical pedagogy, a new progressive education, and pragmatic educational theory. For example, the exercise of repudiating criteriology is a claim for the seriousness with which (neo)pragmatism should be considered as an educational philosophy.

5.   The contributors to this volume share an understanding of the paramount value of human rights, community solidarity, political participation, and democratic societies of hope and promise, and optimistically endorse the necessary economic and educational reforms to manage an emerging postindustrial society with its still indefinite postmodern claims.

6.   Throughout this book, we repeatedly question past social, economic, political, and educational reform attempts (with their seemingly harmless emphasis on excellence) or claims for purposive education for work or vocation (which often has a hidden agenda). Since these often have serious effects for the unwary, we challenged claims in our studies, found many of them lacking substance, and that each served one special interest or another, not the well-being of the polity as a whole.

7.   While not all of the contributors have either the same understanding of (or appreciation for) postmodernism, all have been willing to discuss this philosophical phenomenon in terms of its economic, political, social, and (especially) educational significance. Above all, the postmodern force/condition may be symptomatic of even more massive changes as we move from economic postindustrialism to a new form of philosophical postmodernism, whose outlines are only dim and vaguely visible on a distant, fuzzy horizon.

8.   The contributors approached the topics of critical educational theory, radical educational reform, and pedagogical reconceptualism from their own perspectives and disciplinary interests. While there was no attempt to mold these views into a common pattern, there is a general agreement on the nature of our basic educational problems as well as a positive philosophy and realistic means to resolve some of the outstanding questions we face today and tomorrow. Hopefully, others will find these conclusions useful for their own education, society, and public policy.

9.   The major ideas presented in this book are, on balance, more optimistic than pessimistic, more faithful to democracy and its educational systems, and more committed to the achievement of greater shared prosperity and well-being of people in their local, national, and global settings. Indeed, all of the contributors (individually and as a group) have commited themselves to furthering these humanistic goals.

References

REFERENCES FOR CHAPTER 2

Almond, G. (Fall 1988). 'Separate Tables: Schools and Sects in Political Science', pp. 828-42 in *PS: Political Science and Politics,* Vol. 21, No. 4.

Altbach, P., R. Berdahl, and P. Gumport, eds. (1994). *Higher Education in American Society,* 3rd edition. Amherst, NY: Prometheus Books.

Althusser, L. (1971). *Lenin and Philosophy and Other Essays.* New York, NY: Monthly Review Press.

Anderson, L., et al. (April 1990). *The Civics Report Card.* Princeton, NJ: Educational Testing Service.

Anyon, J. (1979). 'Ideology and United States History Textbooks', pp. 21-39 in R. Dale, et al., eds. (1981) *Education and the State,* Vol. 1. Lewes, Sussex, UK: Falmer Press.

Anyon, J. (1980). 'Social Class and the Hidden Curriculum of Work', pp. 317-41 in H. Giroux, A. Penna, and W. Pinar, eds. (1981), *Curriculum and Instruction.* Berkeley, CA: McCutchan.

Anyon, J. (1983). 'Intersections of Gender and Class: Accommodation and Resistance by Working Class and Affluent Females to Contradictory Sex Role Ideologies', pp. 19-37 in S. Walker and L. Barton, eds., *Gender, Class, & Education.* Lewes, Sussex, UK: Falmer Press.

Apple, M. (Spring 1979). 'What Correspondence Theories of the Hidden Curriculum Miss', pp. 101-12 in *The Review of Education,* Vol. 5, No. 2.

Apple, M. (Spring 1980). 'Analyzing Determinations: Understanding and Evaluating the Production of Social Outcomes in Schools', pp. 55-76 in *Curriculum Inquiry,* Vol. 10.

Apple, M. (1982a). *Education and Power.* Boston, MA: Routledge and Kegan Paul.

Apple, M., ed. (1982b). *Cultural and Economic Reproduction in Education. Essays on Class, Ideology, and the State.* London, UK: Routledge and Kegan Paul.

Apple, M. (1983). 'Work, Class, and Teaching', pp. 53-67 in S. Walker and L. Barton, eds., *Gender, Class, & Education.* Lewes, Sussex, UK: Falmer Press.

Apple, M. (1988). *Teachers and Texts.* New York, NY: Routledge, Chapman and Hall.

Apple, M. and N. King (1983). 'What Do Schools Teach?' pp. 82-99 in H. Giroux and D. Purpel, eds., *The Hidden Curriculum and Moral Education: Deception or Discovery.* Berkeley, CA: McCutchan.

Apple, M. and L. Weiss, eds. (1983). *Ideology and Practice in Schooling.* Philadelphia, PA: Temple University Press.

Arnot, M. and G. Whitty (1982). 'From Reproduction to Transformation: Recent Radical Perspectives on the Curriculum for the USA' pp. 93-103 in *British Journal of Sociology,* Vol. 3, No. 1.

Aronowitz, S. and H. Giroux (1985). *Education Under Siege.* South Hadley, MA: Bergin and Garvey.

Aronowitz, S. and H. Giroux (1991). *Post-modern Education.* Minneapolis, MN: University of Minnesota Press.

Bell, C., ed. (1973). *Growth and Change.* Encino, CA: Dickenson.

Bernstein, R. (1978). *The Restructuring of Social and Political Theory.* Philadelphia, PA: The University of Pennsylvania Press.

Bourdieu, P. (1973). 'Cultural Reproduction and Social Reproduction', pp. 487-511 in J. Karabel and A. Halsey, eds. (1977), *Power and Ideology in Education*. New York, NY: Oxford University Press.

Bourdieu, P. (1977). *Outline of Theory and Practice*. Cambridge, UK: Cambridge University Press.

Bourdieu, P. (1984). *Distinction: A Social Critique of the Judgement of Taste*. Cambridge, MA: Harvard University Press.

Bourdieu, P. and J. Passeron (1977). *Reproduction in Society, Education, and Culture*. London, UK and Beverly Hills, CA: Sage.

Bourdieu, P. and J. Passeron (1979). *The Inheritors. French Students and Their Relation to Culture*. Chicago, IL: University of Chicago Press.

Bowles, S. and H. Gintis (1976). *Schooling in Capitalist America*. New York, NY: Basic Books.

Bowles, S. and H. Gintis (1986). *Democracy and Capitalism*. New York, NY: Basic Books.

Bowles, S. and H. Gintis (1988). 'Contradiction and Reproduction in Educational Theory', pp. 16-32 in M. Cole, ed., *Bowles and Gintis Revisited: Correspondence & Contradiction in Educational Theory* Lewes, Sussex, UK: Falmer Press.

Brademas, J. (1987). *The Politics of Education: Conflict and Consensus on Capitol Hill*. London, UK and Norman, OK: University of Oklahoma Press.

Carnoy, M. (1984). *The State and Political Theory*. Princeton, NJ: Princeton University Press.

Carnoy, M. (1985). 'The Political Economy of Education', pp. 157-73 in *International Social Science Journal*, Vol. 37, No. 2.

Carnoy, M. and H. Levin (1985). *Schooling and Work in the Democratic State*. Stanford, CA: Stanford University Press.

Carnoy, M. and H. Levin (1986). 'Educational Reform and Class Conflict', pp. 35-46 in *Journal of Education*, Vol. 168, No.1.

Carnoy, M. and H. Levin (Winter 1986). 'But Can It Whistle?', pp. 528-41 in *Educational Studies*, Vol. 17, No. 4.

Carnoy, M. and J. Werthein (1977). 'Socialist Ideology and the Transformation of Cuban Education', pp. 573-84 in J. Karabel and A. Halsey, eds., *Power and Ideology in Education*. New York, NY: Oxford University Press.

Cole, M., ed. (1988a). *Bowles and Gintis Revisited: Correspondence & Contradiction in Educational Theory*. Lewes, Sussex, UK: Falmer Press.

Cole, M. (1988b). 'From Reductionist Marxism and Revolutionary Socialism to Post-Liberal Democracy and Ambiguity . . .', pp. 452-62 in *British Journal of Sociology*, Vol. 39, No. 3.

Cole, M. (1989). '"Race" and Class or "Race" Class, Gender, and Community', pp. 118-29 in *British Journal of Sociology*, Vol. 40, No. 1.

Dryzek, J. (May 1986). 'The Progress of Political Science', pp. 301-20 in *The Journal of Politics*, Vol. 48, No. 2.

Dryzek, J. and S. Leonard (December 1988). 'History and Discipline in Political Science', pp. 1245-60 in *American Political Science Review*, Vol. 82, No. 4.

Englund, T. (1986). *Curriculum As A Political Problem*. Stockholm, Sweden: Almqvist & Wiksell.

Farnen, R. (1990). *Integrating Political Science, Education, and Public Policy*. Frankfurt am Main, FRG: Verlag Peter Lang.

Farnen, R. (1993a). 'Cognitive Political Maps: The Implications of Internal Schemata (Structures) versus External Factors (Content and Context) for Cross-National Political Research', pp. 212-81 in G. Csepeli, L. Keri, and I. Stumpf, eds., *State and Citizen*. Budapest, Hungary: Institute of Political Science, Hungarian Academy of Sciences.

Farnen, R. (1993b). 'Reconceptualizing Politics, Education, and Socialization: Cross-National Perspectives on Cognitive Studies, Problem Solving, and Decision making', pp. 375-459 in R. Farnen, ed., *Reconceptualizing Politics, Socialization, and Education: International Perspectives for the 21st Century.* Oldenburg, FRG: University of Oldenburg BIS.

Farnen, R. (1994a). 'Politics, Education, and Reconceptualism: Current Trends in Critical Theory, Political Science, and Socialization in the United States' (published in German as 'Politik, Bildung und Paradigmenwechsel: Jüngste Trends in der Kritischen Pädogogik, in den politischen Wissenschaften, in den politischen Socialisation un in der politischen Bildung in den Vereinigten Staten', pp. 338-84 in H. Sünker, D. Timmermann, and F. Kolbe, eds., *Bildung, Gesellschaft, soziale ungleichheit* (Education, Society, and Social Inequality). Frankfurt am Main, FRG: Suhrkamp Verlag.

Farnen, R. (1994b). 'Nationality, Ethnicity, Political Socialization and Public Policy: Some Cross-National Perspectives', pp. 23-101 in R. Farnen, ed., *Nationalism, Ethnicity, and Identity: Cross-National and Comparative Perspectives.* New Brunswick, NJ and London, UK: Transaction Publishers.

Farnen, R. (1994c). 'Political Decision making, Problem Solving, and Decision making: American and Cross-National Perspectives', pp. 129-53 in S. Miedema et al., eds., *The Politics of Human Science.* Brussels, Belgium: VUB Press.

Farnen, R. (1996a). 'Politische Sozialisation, Erziehung und kritische Theorie: Politik und Erziehung in den Vereinigten Staten' (Political Socialization, Education, and Critical Theory: Politics and Education in the United States), pp. 135-69 in W. Helsper, H. Krüger, and H. Wenzel, eds., *Schule und Gesellschaft im Umbruch: Theoretische und internationale Perspektiven* (School and Society in Upheaval: Theoretical and International Perspectives), Vol. 1. Weinheim, FRG: Deutscher Studienverlag.

Farnen, R. (1996b). 'Nationalism, Democracy, and Authority in North America and Europe since 1989: Lessons for Political Socialization and Civic Education', pp. 39-105 in Farnen et al. *Democracy, Socialization, and Conflicting Loyalties in East and West: Cross-National and Comparative Perspectives.* New York, NY: St. Martin's Press and London, UK: Macmillan.

Finkelstein, B. (November 1984). 'Thinking Publicly about Civic Learning: An Agenda for Education Reform in the '80s', pp. 23-4 in A. Jones, ed. (1985), *Civic Learning for Teachers: Capstone for Educational Reform.* Ann Arbor, MI: Prakken.

Fischer, F. (1990). *Technocracy and the Politics of Expertise.* Newbury Park, CA: Sage.

Fischer, F. and J. Forester, eds. (1987). *Confronting Values in Policy Analysis.* Newbury Park, CA: Sage.

Giarelli, J. (1983). 'The Public, The State, and Civic Education', pp. 33-6 in A. Bagley, ed., *Civic Learning in Teacher Education.* Minneapolis/St. Paul, MN: College of Education, University of Minnesota

Gintis, H. and S. Bowles (1981). 'Contradiction and Reproduction in Educational Theory', pp. 45-59 in R. Dale et al., eds., *Education and the State,* Vol. 1. Lewes, Sussex, UK: Falmer Press

Giroux, H. (1981a). *Ideology, Culture, and the Process of Schooling.* Philadelphia, PA: Temple University Press.

Giroux, H. (1981b). 'Toward a New Sociology of Curriculum', pp. 98-108 in H. Giroux, A. Penna, and W. Pinar, eds., *Curriculum and Instruction.* Berkeley, CA: McCutchan.

Giroux, H. (1984). 'Public Philosophy and the Crisis in Education', pp. 186-94 in *Harvard Educational Review,* Vol. 54, No. 2.

Giroux, H., ed. (1991). *Post-modernism, Feminism, and Cultural Politics.* Albany, NY: State University of New York Press.

Giroux, H. and A. Penna (1981). 'Social Education in the Classroom: The Dynamics of the Hidden Curriculum', pp. 209-30 in H. Giroux, A. Penna, and W. Pinar, eds., *Curriculum and Instruction.* Berkeley, CA: McCutchan.

Giroux, H. and D. Purpel, eds. (1983). *The Hidden Curriculum and Moral Education: Deception or Discovery.* Berkeley, CA: McCutchan.

Hagendoorn, L. (November 1991). 'Authoritarianism, Education, and Democracy'. Paper presented at the International Conference on 'How To Be A Democrat In A Post-Communist Hungary', Center for Political Science, Hungarian Academy of Sciences, Balatonföldvár, Hungary.

Hanna, J. (1982). 'Public School Policy and the Children's World: Implications of Ethnographic Research for Desegregated Schooling', pp. 316-55 in G. Spindler, ed., *Doing the Ethnography of Schooling.* New York, NY: Holt Reinhart and Winston.

Huebner, D. (1981). 'Toward a Political Economy of Curriculum and Human Development', pp. 124-38 in H. Giroux, A. Penna, and W. Pinar, eds., *Curriculum and Instruction.* Berkeley, CA: McCutchan.

Illich, I. (1970). *Deschooling Society.* New York, NY: Harper and Row.

Jennings, M. (June 1980). 'Comment on Richard Merelman's "Democratic Politics and the Culture of American Education"', pp. 333-7 in *American Political Science Review,* Vol. 74, No. 2.

Jennings, M. (March 1981). 'Comment on the Merelman-Jennings Exchange', pp. 155-6 in *American Political Science Review,* Vol. 75, No. 1.

Kelly, E. (1995). *Education, Democracy, and Public Knowledge.* Boulder, CO: Westview Press.

Klein, E. (25 August 1991). 'We're Talking About a Revolution', pp. 4-7 in *Parade Magazine.*

Liston, D. (May 1988). 'Faith and Evidence: Examining Marxist Explanations of Schools', pp. 323-50 in *American Journal of Education,* Vol. 96, No. 3.

Macpherson, C. (1977). 'Do We Need a Theory of the State?', pp. 61-75 in R. Dale, et al., eds. (1981), *Education and the State,* Vol. 1. Lewes, Sussex, UK: Falmer Press.

Masemann, V. (February 1982). 'Critical Ethnography in the Study of Comparative Education', pp. 1-15 in *Comparative Education Review,* Vol. 26, No. 1.

Meloen, J. (1992). 'A Critical Analysis of Forty Years of Authoritarianism Research', pp. 128-65 in R. Farnen, ed., *Nationalism, Ethnicity and Identity: Cross-National and Comparative Perspectives.* New Brunswick, NJ and London, UK: Transaction Publishers.

Merelman, R. (June 1980). 'Democratic Politics and the Culture of American Education', pp. 319-32 in *American Political Science Review,* Vol. 74, No. 2.

Merelman, R. (March 1981). 'Reply', pp. 156-8 in *American Political Science Review,* Vol. 75, No. 1.

Monroe, K., et al. (March 1990). 'The Nature of Contemporary Political Science: A Roundtable Discussion', pp. 34-43 in *PS: Political Science and Politics,* Vol. 23, No. 1.

Offe, C. and V. Ronge (1975). 'Theses on the Theory of the State', pp. 77-85 in R. Dale, et al., eds. (1981), *Education and the State,* Vol. 1. Lewes, Sussex, UK: Falmer Press.

Peterson, S. (1990). *Political Behavior. Patterns in Everyday Life.* Newbury Park, CA: Sage.

Popkewitz, T. (May 1985). 'Intellectuals, Sciences, and Pedagogies: Critical Traditions and Instrumental Cultures', pp. 429-36 in *American Journal of Education,* Vol. 93, No. 3.

Shirley, D. (1986). 'A Critical Review and Appropriation of Pierre Bourdieu's Analysis of Social and Cultural Reproduction', pp. 96-112 in *Journal of Education,* Vol. 168, No. 2.

Smith, M., J. O'Day, and D. Cohen (Winter 1990). 'National Curriculum American Style', pp. 10-17 and 40-7 in *American Educator.*

Spring, J. (1993). *Conflict of Interests: The Politics of American Education,* 2nd. Edition. New York, NY: Longmans.

Tirozzi, G. (19 May 1991). 'Bush's Education Plan is Too Limited to Have a Real Impact', p. E3 in *The Hartford Courant.*

Tobin, J. (1989). 'Visual Anthropology and Multivocal Ethnography: A Dialogical Approach to Japanese Preschool Class Size', pp. 173-87 in *Dialectical Anthropology,* Vol. 13.

Tyack, D. (1995). *Tinkering Toward Utopia: A Century of Public School Reform.* Cambridge, MA: Harvard University Press.

Wilcox, K. (1982a). 'Differential Socialization in the Classroom: Implications for Equal Opportunity', pp. 268-309 in G. Spindler, ed., *Doing the Ethnography of Schooling.* New York, NY: Holt Reinhart and Winston.

Wilcox, K. (1982b). 'Ethnography as a Methodology and Its Application to the Study of Schooling: A Review', pp. 456-88 in G. Spindler, ed., *Doing the Ethnography of Schooling.* New York, NY: Holt Reinhart and Winston.

Willis, P. (1981). 'Cultural Production Is Different from Cultural Reproduction is Different from Social Reproduction is Different from Reproduction', pp. 48-67 in *Interchange on Educational Policy,* Vol. 12, Nos. 2-3.

Willis, P., et al. (1988). *The Youth Review: Social Conditions of Young People in Wolverhampton.* Aldershot, Hants, UK: Avebury, Gower.

Wood, G. (Spring 1982). 'Beyond Radical Educational Cynicism', pp. 55-71 in *Educational Theory,* Vol. 32, No. 2.

REFERENCES FOR CHAPTER 3

Apple, M. (1985). *Education and Power.* New York, NY: Routledge, ARK Edition.

Apple, M. (1988). *Teachers and Texts: A Political Economy of Class and Gender Relations in Education.* New York, NY: Routledge.

Apple, M. (Spring 1988). 'Social Crisis and Curriculum Accords', pp. 191-201 in *Educational Theory,* Vol. 38.

Apple, M. (1989). 'American Realities: Poverty, Economy and Education', pp. 205-23 in L. Weis, E. Farrar, and H. Petrie, eds., *Dropouts from School.* Albany, NY: State University of New York Press.

Apple, M. (1990). *Ideology and Curriculum,* second edition. New York, NY: Routledge.

Apple, M. (1993). *Official Knowledge: Democratic Education in a Conservative Age.* New York, NY: Routledge.

Apple, M. and L. Christian-Smith, eds. (1990). *The Politics of the Textbook.* New York, NY: Routledge.

Apple, M. and S. Jungck (Summer 1990). 'You Don't Have to be a Teacher to Teach this Unit', pp. 227-51 in *American Educational Research Journal,* Vol. 27.

Bastian, A., N. Fruchter, M. Gittell, C. Green, and K. Haskins, eds. (1986). *Choosing Equality.* Philadelphia, PA: Temple University Press.

Bernstein, B. (1977). *Class, Codes and Control*, Volume 3. New York, NY: Routledge.

Bernstein, B. (1990). *The Structuring of Pedagogic Discourse:Class Codes and Control*, Volume 4. New York, NY: Routledge.

Best, S. and D. Kellner (1991). *Postmodern Theory: Critical Interrogations*. London, UK: Macmillan.

Bourdieu, P. (1984). *Distinction*. Cambridge, MA: Harvard University Press.

Burtless, G., ed. (1990). *A Future of Lousy Jobs?* Washington, DC: The Brooking Institution.

Dale, R. (1989). 'The Thatcherite Project in Education', pp. 156-7 in *Critical Social Policy*, Vol. 9, No. 3.

Darling-Hammond, L. (March/April 1992). 'Bush's Testing Plan Undercuts School Reforms', p. 18 in *Rethinking Schools*, Vol. 6.

Education Group II, eds. (1991). *Education Limited*. London, UK: Unwin Hyman.

Edwards, T., S. Gewirtz, and G. Whitty (1992). 'Whose Choice of Schools?', pp. 151-6 in M. Arnot and L. Barton, eds., *Voicing Concerns: Sociological Perspectives on Contemporary Educational Reforms*. London, UK: Triangle Books.

Ellsworth, E. (August 1989). 'Why Doesn't This Feel Empowering', pp. 297-324 in *Harvard Educational Review*, Vol. 59.

Gould, S. (1981). *The Mismeasure of Man*. New York, NY: W. W. Norton.

Green, A. (1991). 'The Peculiarities of English Education', p. 27-30 in Education Group II, eds., *Education Limited*. London, UK: Unwin Hyman.

Haraway, D. (1989). *Primate Visions*. New York, NY: Routledge.

Harding, S. (1991). *Whose Science, Whose Knowledge?* Ithaca, NY: Cornell University Press.

Harding, S. And J. Barr, eds. (1987). *Sex and Scientific Inquiry*. Chicago, IL: University of Chicago Press.

Hirsch, Jr., E. (1986). *Cultural Literacy*. New York, NY: Houghton-Mifflin.

Honderich, T. (1990). *Conservatism*. Boulder, CO: Westview Press.

Hunter, A. (1988). *Children in the Service of Conservatism*. Madison, WI: University of Wisconsin - Madison Law School, Institute for Legal Studies.

Johnson, R. (1991). 'A New Road to Serfdom?', pp. 11-82 and 'Ten Theses on a Monday Morning', pp. 319-20 in Education Group II, eds., *Education Limited*. London, UK: Unwin Hyman.

Karp, S. (March/April 1992). 'Massachusetts "Choice" Plan Undercuts Poor Districts', p. 4 in *Rethinking Schools*, Vol. 6.

Kozol, J. (1991). *Savage Inequalities*. New York, NY: Crown.

Liston, D. (1988). *Capitalist Schools*. New York, NY: Routledge.

Lowe, R. (March/April 1992). 'The Illusion of "Choice"', pp. 21-3 in *Rethinking Schools*, Vol. 6.

Melzer, W. (1995). 'The Syndrome of Right-Wing Extremism Among School Children: An East-West Comparison', pp. 93-116 in G. Neubauer and K. Hurrelmann, eds., *Individualization in Childhood and Adolescence*. Berlin, FRG and New York, NY: Walter de Gruyter.

Rose, S. (1988). *Keeping Them Out of the Hands of Satan*. New York, NY: Routledge.

Sarason, S. (1995). *Parental Involvement and the Political Principle: Why the Existing Governance Structure of Schools Should be Abolished*. San Francisco, CA: Jossey-Bass.

Smith, M., J. O'Day, and D. Cohen (Winter 1990). 'National Curriculum, American Style: What Might It Look Like?', pp. 10-7, 40-7 in *American Educator*, Vol. 14.

Tuana, N., ed. (1989). *Feminism and Science*. Bloomington, IN: Indiana University Press.

Whitty, G. (1997). 'Recent Education Reform: Is It a Postmodern Phenomenon?' Chapter 14 in this book.

Whitty, G. (1992). 'Education, Economy and National Culure', p. 290-94 in R. Bolock and K. Thompson, eds., *Social and Forms of Modernity*. Cambridge, MA: Polity Press.

Williams, R. (1989). *Resources of Hope*. New York, NY: Verso.

REFERENCES FOR CHAPTER 4

Abberley, P. (1987). 'The Concept Oppression and The Social Theory of Disability', pp. 5-19 in *Disability, Handicap and Society*, Vol. 2, No. 1.

Alaszewski, A. and B. Ong, eds. (1990). *Normalisation in Practice: Residential Care for Children with a Profound Mental Handicap*. London, UK: Routledge.

Arnot, M. (1991). 'Democracy, Equality and Social Justice: A Decade of Struggle over Education', pp. 447-66 in *British Journal of Sociology of Education*. Vol. 13, No. 4, Special Issue on Democracy.

Ayer, S. and A. Alaszewski (1984). *Community Care and the Mentally Handicapped: Services for Mothers & their Mentally Handicapped Children*. London, UK: Croom Helm.

Ball, S. (1990). *Politics and Policy Making in Education and Explorations in Policy Sociology*. London, UK: Routledge & Kegan Paul.

Banks, O. (1955). *Parity and Prestige in Enqlish Secondary Education*. London, UK: Routledge & Kegan Paul.

Barton, L., ed. (1986). *The Politics of Special Educational Needs*. Lewes, Sussex, UK: Falmer Press.

Barton, L., ed. (1989). *Inteqration: Myth or Reality?* Lewes, Sussex, UK: Falmer Press.

Barton, L. and R. Meighan, eds. (1978). *Sociological Interpretations of Schooling and Classrooms: A Reappraisal*. Driffield, UK: Nafferton Books.

Barton, L. and M. Smith (1989). 'Equality, Rights and Primary Education', pp. 76-89 in C. Roaf and H. Bines, eds., *Needs, Riqhts and Opportunities*. Lewes, Sussex, UK: Falmer Press.

Barton, L. and S. Tomlinson (eds.) (1981). *Special Education: Policy, Practices and Social Issues*. London, UK: Harper & Row.

Barton, L. and S. Tomlinson, eds. (1984). *Special Education and Social Interests*. Beckenham, UK: Croom Helm.

Barton, L. and S. Walker (1978). 'Sociology of Education at the Crossroads', pp. 269-84 in *Educational Review*, Vol. 30, No. 3.

Bishop, M. (1987). 'Disabling the Able?', p. 98 in *British Journal of Special Education*, Vol. 14, No.3.

Borsay, A. (1986). 'Personal Trouble or Public Issue? Towards a Model of Policy for People with Physical and Mental Disabilities', pp. 179-86 in *Disability, Handicap and Society*, Vol. 1, No. 2.

Branson, J. and D. Miller (1989). 'Beyond Integration Policy - The Deconstruction of Disability', pp. 144-67 in L. Barton, ed., *Integration: Myth or Reality?* Lewes, Sussex, UK: Falmer Press.

Brisenden, S. (1986). 'Independent Living and the Medical Model of Disability', pp. 173-8 in *Disability, Handicap and Society*, Vol. 1, No. 2..

Brown, H. and H. Smith (1989). 'Whose "Ordinary Life" Is It Anyway?', 105-19 in *Disability, Handicap and Society*, Vol. 4, No. 2.

Carrier, J. (1990). 'Special Education and the Explanation of Pupil Performance', pp. 211-26 in *Disability, Handicap and Society*, Vol. 5, No. 3,.

Carrington, B. (1986). 'Social Mobility, Ethnicity and Sport', pp. 3-18 in *British Journal of Sociology of Education*, Vol. 7, No. 1.

Chappell, A. (1992). 'Towards a Sociological Critique of the Normalisation Principle', pp. 35-52 in *Disability, Handicap and Society*, Vol. 7, No. 4.

David, M. (1986). 'Teaching Family Matters', pp. 35-58 in *British Journal of Sociology of Education*, Vol. 7, No. 1.

Davies, L. (1984). *Pupil Power: Deviance and Gender in School*. Lewes, Sussex, UK: Falmer Press.

Demaine, J. (1989). 'Race, Categorisation and Educational Achievement', pp. 195-214 in *British Journal of Sociology of Education*, Vol. 10, No. 2.

Disability Now (1991). 'National Protest Over Loss of Advocacy Rights', pp. 1 and 3 in *Disability Now*, June.

Douglas, J. (1964). *The Home and the School*. London, UK: Panther.

Findlay, B. (1991). 'Disability, Empowerment and Equal Opportunities' (unpublished paper).

Floud, J., A. Halsey, and F. Martin (1956). *Social Class and Educational Opportunity*. London, UK: Heinemann.

Ford, J., D. Mongon, and M. Whelan (1982). *Special Education and Social Control: Invisible Disasters*. London, UK: Routledge & Kegan Paul.

Foucault, M. (1977). *The Archaeology of Knowledge*. London, UK: Tavistock.

Fulcher, G. (1989). *Disabling Policies? A Comparative Approach to Education Policy and Disability*. Lewes, Sussex, UK: Falmer Press.

Gillborn, D. (1988). 'Ethnicity and Educational Opportunity: Case Studies of West Indian Male - White Teacher Relationships', pp. 371-86 in *British Journal of Sociology of Education*, Vol. 9, No. 4.

Glass, D. (1954). *Social Mobility in Britain*. London, UK: Routledge & Kegan Paul.

Glendinning, C. (1991). 'Losing Ground: Social Policy and Disabled People in Great Britain, 1980 - 90', pp. 3-20 in *Disability, Handicap and Society*, Vol. 6. No. 1.

Hahn, H. (1985). 'Towards a Politics of Disability', pp. 87-105 in *Social Science Journal*, Vol. 22, Part 4.

Hahn, H. (1986). 'Public Support for Rehabilitation in Programs: The Analysis of US Disability Policy', pp. 121-38 in *Disability, Handicap and Society*, Vol. 1, No. 2.

Hall, S. (1988). *The Road to Renewal*. London, UK: Verso.

Hudson, B. (1988). 'Do People with a Mental Handicap Have Rights?', pp. 227-38 in *Disability, Handicap and Society*, Vol. 3, No.

Hurrelmann, K. And J. Maggs (1995). 'Health Impairments in Adolescence: The Biophsychosocial "Costs" of Modern Life-Style', pp. 53-70 in G. Neubauer and K. Hurrelmann, eds., *Individualization in Childhood and Adolescence*. Berlin, FRG and New York, NY: Walter de Gruyter.

Jackson, B. (1964). *Streaming: An Education System in Miniature*. London, UK: Routledge & Kegan Paul.

Jackson, B. and D. Marsden (1962). *Education and the Working Class*. Harmondsworth, UK: Penguin.

Karabel, J. and A. Halsey, eds. (1977). *Power and Ideology in Education*. Oxford, UK: Oxford University Press.

Lauder, H. (1988). 'Traditions of Socialism and Educational Policy', pp. 20-49 in H. Lauder and P. Brown, eds., *Education in Search of a Future*. Lewes, Sussex, UK: Falmer Press.

Leach, B. (1989). 'Disabled People and the Implementation of Local Authorities' Equal Opportunities Policies', pp. 65-77 in *Public Administration*, Vol. 67, No. 1.

Mason, M. (1990). 'Disability Equality in the Classroom - A Human Rights Issue', pp. 363-6 in *Gender and Education*, Vol. 2, No. 3.

Mills, C. (1970). *The Sociological Imagination*. Harmondsworth, UK: Penguin.

Morris, J., ed. (1989). *Able Lives: Women's Experience of Paralysis*. London, UK: The Women's Press.

Oliver, M. (1988). 'The Political Context of Educational Decision Making: The Case of Special Needs', pp. 13-31 in L. Barton, ed., *The Politics of Special Educational Needs*. Lewes, Sussex, UK: Falmer Press.

Oliver, M. (1989). 'Disability and Dependency: A Creation of Industrial Societies', pp. 6-22 in L. Barton, ed., *Disability and Dependency*. Lewes, Sussex, UK: Falmer Press.

Oliver, M. (1990). *The Politics of Disablement*. London, UK: Macmillan.

Oliver, M. (1991). 'Speaking Out: Disabled People and State Welfare', pp.156-62 in G. Dalley, ed., *Disability and Social Policy*. London, UK: Policy Studies Institute.

Oliver, M. and F. Hasler (1987). 'Disability and Self Help: A Case Study of the Spinal Injuries Association', pp. 113-25 in Disability, Handicap and Society, Vol. 2, No. 2.

Reid, I. (1978). *Sociological Perspectives on School and Education*. London, UK: Open Books.

Robinson, P. (1981). *Perspectives on the Sociology of Education*. London, UK: Routledge & Kegan Paul.

Ryan, W. (1976). *Blaming the Victim*. New York, NY: Vintage Books (revised edition).

Saporiti, A. (1995). 'Childhood and Poverty: From the Children's Point of View', pp. 237-48 in L. Chisholm et al., eds., *Growing Up in Europe: Contemporary Horizons in Childhood and Youth Studies*. Berlin, FRG and New York, NY: Walter de Gruyter.

Tomlinson, S. (1982). *A Sociology of Special Education*. London, UK: Routledge & Kegan Paul.

Tomlinson, S. (1985). 'The Experience of Special Education', pp. 157-65 in *Oxford Review of Education*, Vol. 11, No. 2.

Tomlinson, S. (1988). 'Why Johnny Can't Read: Critical Theory and Special Education', pp. 45-58 in *European Journal of Special Needs Education*, Vol. 3, No. 1.

Weiner, G. (1986). 'Feminist Education and Equal Opportunities: Unity or Discord?', pp. 265-74 in *British Journal of Sociology of Education*, Vol. 7, No. 3.

Weis, L. (1991). 'Issues of Disproportionality and Social Justice in Tomorrow's Schools', pp. 1-13 in *Education Action*, Vol. 1, No. 2.

Williams, R. (1983). *Towards 2000*. London, UK: Chatto & Windus.

Williams, J. (1986). 'Education and Race: The Racialisation of Class Inequalities?', pp. 135-54 in *British Journal of Sociology of Education*, Vol. 7, No. 2.

Wolfensberger, W. and S. Thomas (1983). *Program Analysis of Service Systems' Implementation of Normalisation Goals: Normalisation and Ratings Manual*. Toronto, Canada: National Institute on Mental Retardation (second edition).

REFERENCES FOR CHAPTER 5

Baacke, D. (1985). 'Bewegungen beweglich machen: Oder Plädoyer für mehr Ironie' (To Make movements Movable: Or in Favor of More Irony), pp. 190-213 in D. Baacke et al., *Am Ende Post-Modern? Next Wave in der Pädagogik* (Postmodern in the End? Next Wave in Pedagogy. Weinheim/München, FRG: Juventa.

Beekman, A. (1973). *Dienstbaar inzicht* (Ministering in Sight). Groningen, the Netherlands: Tjeenk Willink.

Bernstein, R. (1983). *Beyond Objectivism and Relativism: Science, Hermeneutics, and Praxis*. Oxford, UK: Basil Blackwell.

Biesta, G. (1990). 'Pluraliteit, pragmatisme en pedagogiek' (Plurality, Pragmatism, and Pedagogy), pp. 7-30 in *Comenius*, Vol. 10, No. 1.

Biesta, G. and S. Miedema (1989). 'Assessing Dewey's Influence Abroad'. Paper presented at the AERA Conference/John Dewey Society, San Francisco, CA on 28 March 1989.

Bloch, E. (1963). 'Über die Bedeutung der Utopie' (On the Meaning of Utopia), pp. 124-32 in E. Bloch *Tübinger Einleitung in die Philosophie I* (Tübinger Introduction to Philosophy I). Frankfurt am Main, FRG: Suhrkamp.

Cavalli, A. (1995). 'The Value Orientations of Young Europeans', pp. 35-42 in L. Chisholm et al., eds., *Growing Up in Europe: Contemporary Horizons in Childhood and Youth Studies*. Berlin, FRG and New York, NY: Walter de Gruyter.

Dasberg, L. (1983). 'Pedagogy in the Year 2000', pp. 117-26 in *Phenomenology & Pedagogy*, Vol. 1, No. 2.

Dewey, J. (1916). *Democracy and Education*. New York, NY: Free Press.

Dewey, J. (1927). *The Public and Its Problems*. New York, NY: Holt Company.

Dewey, J. (1940). 'Creative Democracy - The Task Before Us', pp. 220-8 in S. Ratner, ed., *The Philosopher of the Common Man*. New York, NY: G.P. Putnam's Sons.

Englund, T. (1986). *Curriculum as a Political Problem. Changing Educational Conceptions, with Special Reference to Citizenship Education*. Uppsala/Lund, Sweden: Studentlitteratur Chartwell-Bratt.

Foucault, M. (1984). 'What is Enlightenment?', pp. 32-50 in P. Rabinow, ed., *The Foucault Reader*. New York, NY: Pantheon Books.

Giroux, H. (1989). *Schooling for Democracy. Critical Pedagogy in the Modern Age*. London, UK: Routledge.

Habermas, J. (1984). *The Theory of Communicative Action*, Volume I. London, UK: Heinemann.

Habermas, J. (1987). *The Theory of Communicative Action*, Volume II. Cambridge, MA: Polity Press.

Habermas, J. (1985a). 'Questions and Counterquestions', pp. 192-216 in R. Bernstein, ed., *Habermas and Modernity*. Oxford, UK: Basil Blackwell.

Habermas, J. (1985b). *Die Neue Unübersichtlichkeit: Kleine politische Schritten V* (The New Complexity: Brief Political Writings V). Frankfurt am Main, FRG: Suhrkamp.

Habermas, J. (1992). *Faktizität und Geltung. Beiträge zur Diskurstheorie des Rechts und des demokratischen Rechts-staats* (Between Facts and Norms: Contributions to a Discourse Theory of Law and Democracy. Frankfurt am Main, FRG: Suhrkamp.

Habermas, J. (1996). *Between Facts and Norms: Contributions to a Discourse Theory of Law and Democracy*. Cambridge, MA: MIT Press.

Hall, S. (1991). *Het minimale zelf en andere opstellen* (The Minimal Self and Other Essays). Amsterdam, the Netherlands: Sua.

Hurn, C. (1993). *The Limits and Possibilities of Schooling: An Introduction to the Sociology of Education*, 3rd edition. Boston, MA: Allyn and Bacon.

Klafki, W. (1958). 'Die Erziehung im Spannungsfeld von Vergangenheit, Gegenwart und Zukunft' (Pedagogy in the Area of Tension Between Past, Present, and Future), pp.448-62 in *Die Sammlung*, Vol. 13.

König, E. (1990). 'Bilanz der Theorieentwicklung in der Erziehungswissenschaft' (An Evaluation of Theory Development in Pedagogy), pp. 919-36 in *Zeitschrift für Pädagogik*, Vol. 36, No. 6.

Kunneman, H. (1988). 'De betekenis en de beperkingen van het postmodernisme als politieke filosofie' (The Meaning and Limitations of Postmodernism as Political Philosophy), pp. 201-13 in *Socialisme en Democratie*, Vol. 50, No. 7/8.

Levine, D. and R. Havinghurst (1992). *Society and Education*, 8th edition. Boston, MA: Allyn and Bacon.

Lyotard, J. (1979). *La condition postmoderne* (The Postmodern Condition). Paris, France: Minuit.

Lyotard, J. (1986). *Le Postmoderne expliqué aux enfants* (Postmodernism Explained to Children). Paris, France: Galilée.

Miedema, S. (1992). 'The End of Pedagogy? A Plea for Concrete Utopian Acting and Thinking', pp. 28-37 in *Phenomenology and Pedagogy*, Vol. 10.

Miedema, S. (1994). 'The Relevance for Pedagogy of Habermas' "Theory of Communicative Action"', pp. 195-206 in *Interchange*, Vol. 25, No 2.

Miedema, S. (1996). 'De-pillarization, pedagogization and particularization' (Historical and Recent Trends in the Relation of State and School in the Netherlands), in J. Fernandes et al., eds., *Escola e Democracia: Cidadania e Desenvolvimenta* (School and Democracy: Citizenship and Alienation). Faro, Portugal: Escola Superior de Educaçao.

Miedema, S. and G. Biesta (1990). 'Outlines of a Democratic and Community Based Critical-Pragmatic Methodology: On the Way to Relevant Pedagogical Inquiry', pp. 76-87 in R. Evans, A. Winning, and M. van Manen, eds., *Reflections on pedagogy and Method*. Volume I. Edmonton, Canada: University of Alberta.

Miedema, S. and G. Biesta (1991). 'The European Situation in Education and Pedagogical Science from a Critical Perspective: Needs, Tasks, and Responsibilities'. Paper presented to the Department of Educational Leadership, Miami University, Oxford, Ohio, 15 April 1991.

Mollenhauer, K. (1986). *Umwege: Über Bildung, Kunst und Interaktion* (Detours: On Education, Art, and Interaction). Weinheim and München, FRG: Juventa.

Mulkey, L. (1993). *Sociology of Education: Theoretical and Empirical Investigations*. Fort Worth, TX: Harcourt Brace Jovanovich.

Niess, M. (1985). 'Das postmoderne Begehren nach Unvernunft. Oder: Das Vergnügen, einen Jaguar zu fahren' (The Postmodern Lust for Idiocy: Or the Joy of Driving a Jaguar), pp. 12-22 in D. Baacke et al., *Am Ende Post-modern? Next Wave in der Pädagogik* (At the End of the Postmodern? Next Wave in Pedagogy). Weinheim and München, FRG: Juventa.

Rang, A. (1988). *Pedagogiek en moderniteit* (Pedagogy and Modernity). Nijmegen, the Netherlands: Sun.

Roche, M. (1987). 'Citizenship, Social Theory, and Social Change', pp. 363-99 in *Theory and Society*, Vol. 16.

Rorty, R. (1982). *Consequences of Pragmatism*. Brighton, UK: Harvester Press.

Rorty, R. (1986). 'Solidarity or Objectivity?', pp. 3-19 in J. Rajchman and C. West, eds., *Post-analytisc Philosophy*. New York, NY: Columbia University Press.

Rorty, R. (1987). 'Science as Solidarity', pp. 38-52 in J. Nelson, et al., eds., *The Rhetoric of the Human Sciences: Language and Argument in Public Affairs*. Madison, WI: University of Wisconsin Press.

Rorty, R. (1989) *Contingency, Irony, and Solidarity*. Cambridge, UK: Cambridge University Press.

Sauer, K. (1964). *Der utopische Zug in der Pädagogik* (The Utopian Feature in Pedagogy). Weinheim, FRG: Belz.

Steiner, I. (1995). 'Growing Up in Twelve Cities: The Families in Which Pupils Live', pp. 73-84 in L. Chisholm et al., eds., *Growing Up in Europe: Contemporary Horizons in Childhood and Youth Studies*. Berlin, FRG and New York, NY: Walter de Gruyter.

Teunissen, J. (1989). '"Witte" en "zwarte" scholen in de grote steden' (White and Black Schools in the Big Cities), pp. 62-84 in W. Pols, S. Miedema, and B. Levering, eds., *Opvoeding zoals het is* (Education As It Is). Amersfoort and Leuven, the Netherlands: Acco.

Westbrook, R. (1991). *John Dewey and American Democracy*. Ithaca, NY and London, UK: Cornell University Press.

REFERENCES FOR CHAPTER 6

Beck, U. (1992). *Risk Society: Towards a New Modernity*. London, UK: Sage.

Berg-Schlosser, D. and J. Schissler, eds. (1987). *Politische Kultur in Deutschland. Bilanz und Perspektiven der Forschung*(Political Culture in Germany: End Result and Prospects for Research). Special issue of the journal *PVS*, No. 18.

Bertram, H. (1981). *Sozialstruktur und Sozialisation. Zur mikroanalytischen Analyse von Chancengleichheit* (Social Structure and Socialization: On Microanalytical Analysis of Equal Opportunities). Darmstadt and Neuwied, FRG: Luchterhand.

Bohnsack, R. (1989). *Generation, Milieu und Geschlecht* (Generation, Milieu, and Gender). Opladen, FRG: Leske & Budrich.

Bourdieu, P. (1979). *Entwurf einer Theorie der Praxis* (Draft of a Theory of Practice). Frankfurt am Main, FRG: Suhrkamp.

Bourdieu, P. (1985). *Sozialer Raum und 'Klassen'* (Social Space and 'Classes'). Frankfurt am Main, FRG: Suhrkamp.

Durkheim, E. (1970, first 1895). *Regeln der soziologischen Methode* (Rules of the Sociological Method). Neuwied, FRG: Luchterhand.

Gluchowski, P. (1987). 'Lebensstile und Wandel der Wählerschaft in der Bundesrepublik Deutschland' (Lifestyles and Change of the Electorate in the Federal Republic of Germany), pp. 18-32 in *Aus Politik und Zeitgeschehen* (Poltics and Current Events) (supplement to the weekly magazine *Das Parlament*), B 12, 21.3.1987.

Gluchowski, P. (1988). *Freizeit und Lebensstile* (Leisure and Lifestyles). Erkrath, FRG: DGFF.

Grüneisen, V. and E. Hoff (1977). *Familienerziehung und Lebenssituation* (Family Education and Situation in Life). Weinheim, FRG and Basel, Switzerland: Beltz.

Heine, H. and R. Mautz (1989). *Industriearbeiter contra Umweltschutz?* (Industrial Worker Versus Conservation). Frankfurt am Main, FRG: Campus.

Hitzler, R. and A. Honer (1984). 'Lebenswelt - Milieu - Situation. Terminologische Vorschläge zur theoretischen Verständigung' (Life World - Milieu - Situation: Terminological Suggestions for Theoretical Notification), pp. 56-74 in *Kölner Zeitschrift für Soziologie un Sozialpsychologie 36*.

Hradil, S. (1987). *Sozialstrukturanalyse in einer fortgeschrittenen Gesellschaft. Von Klassen und Schichten zu Lagen und Milieus* (Analysis of the Social Structure in an Advanced Society: Concerning Classes and Strata in Layers and Milieus). Opladen, FRG: Leske & Budrich.

Hradil, S. (1992). 'Alte Begriffe und neue Strukturen. Die Milieu-, Subkultur- und Lebensstilforschung der 80er Jahre' (Old Concepts and New Structures: Research of Milieu, Subculture, and Lifestyle in the 1980s), pp. 15-56 in S. Hradil, ed., *Zwischen Bewußtsein und Sein. Die Vermittlung 'objektiver' Lebensbedingungen und 'subjektiver' Lebensweisen* (Between Consciousness and Existence: The Mediation of 'Objective' Living Conditions and 'Subjective' Ways of Living). Opladen, FRG: Leske & Budrich.

Hurrelmann, K. (1986). *Einführung in die Sozialisationstheorie. Über den Zusammenhang von Sozialstruktur und Persönlichkeit* (Introduction to the Theory of Socialization: Concerning the Connection Between Social Structure and Personality). Weinheim, FRG: Beltz.

Keim, D. (1979). *Milieus in der Stadt. Ein Konzept zur Analyse älterer Wohnquartiere* (Milieus in the City: A Program to Analyze Older Living Quarters). Stuttgart and Berlin, FRG: Kohlhammer.

Lagrée, J. (1995). 'Young People and Employment in the European Community: Convergence or Divergence?', pp. 61-72 in L. Chisholm et al., eds., *Growing Up in Europe: Contemporary Horizons in Childhood and Youth Studies*. Berlin, FRG and New York, NY: Walter de Gruyter.

Lenz, K. (1988). *Die vielen Gesichter der Jugend* (Many Faces of Youth). Frankfurt am Main, FRG: Campus.

Lepsius, M. (1966). 'Parteiensystem und Sozialstruktur: zum Problem der Demokratisierung der deutschen Gesellschaft' (Systems of Parties and Social Structure: Concerning the Problem of Democratization of the German Society), pp. 371-93 in W. Abel, K. Borchardt, H. Kellebenz, and W. Zorn, eds., *Wirtschaft, Geschichte und Wirtschaftsgeschichte* (Economy, History, and History of Economy), special issue to celebrate Friedrich Lütge's 65th birthday. Stuttgart, FRG: Fischer.

Lüdtke, H. (1989). *Expressive Ungleichheit. Zur Soziologie der Lebensstile* (Revealing Inequality: Concerning the Sociology of Lifestyles). Opladen, FRG: Leske & Budrich.

Lüdtke, H. (1990). 'Lebensstile als Dimension handlungsproduzierter Ungleichheit. Eine Anwendung des Rational-choice Ansatzes' (Lifestyles as a Dimension of Action-Produced Inequality: An Application of the Rational Choice Theory), pp. 433-54 in P. Berger and S. Hradil, eds., *Lebenslagen, Lebensläufe, Lebensstile* (Life Situations, Life Courses, Lifestyles), special issue of the magazine *Soziale Welt*, Vol. 7.

Mayer, K. and H. Blossfeld (1990). 'Die gesellschaftliche Konstruktion sozialer Ungleichheit im Lebensverlauf' (The Social Construction of Social Differences in Life Course), pp. 297-318 in P. Berger and S. Hradil, eds., *Lebenslagen, Lebensläufe, Lebensstile* (Situations in Life, Life Courses, Lifestyles), special issue of the magazine *Soziale Welt*, Vol. 7.

Mintzel, A. (1988). 'Sozialwissenschaftliche Analysen lokaler und regionaler politischer Kulturen: Westdeutsche Ansätze und Ergebnisse' (Social Science Analysis of Local and Regional Political Cultures: Western German Approaches and Results). Working paper, Passau, FRG.

Möller, K. (1988). 'Milieu-Einbindung und Milieu-Erosion als individuelle Sozialisationsprobleme' (Integration Into and Erosion of Milieu as Individual Problems of Socialization), pp. 115-44 in *Zeitschrift für erziehungswissenschaftliche Forschung* (Journal for Pedagogical Research), Vol. 34, No. 2.

Montesquieu, C. (1949). *Oeuvres complètes* (Complete Works). Paris, France: Nagel.

Morrow, R. (1995). *Social Theory and Education: A Critique of Theories of Social and Cultural Reproduction*. Albany, NY: State University of New York Press.

Müller, H. (1992). 'Sozialstruktur und Lebensstile. Zur Neuorientierung der Sozialstrukturforschung' (Social Structure and Lifestyles: Concerning the Reorientation of Research on Social Structure), pp. 57-55 in S. Hradil, ed., *Zwischen Bewußtsein und Sein* (Between Consciousness and Existence). Opladen, FRG: Leske & Budrich

Oevermann, U. (1976). 'Die sozialstrukturelle Einbettung von Sozialisationprozessen: Empirische Ergebnisse zur Ausdifferenzierung des globalen Zusammenhangs von Schichtzugehörigkeit und gemessener Intelligenz sowie Schulerfolg' (Social-Structural Embedding of Processes of Socialization: Empirical Results About the Modification of the General Connection of Strata-Affiliation and Measured Intelligence as well as Success in School), pp. 167-99 in *Zeitschrift für Soziologie und Sozialpsychologie*, Vol. 5.

Preuss-Lausitz, U. (1995). 'Contradictions of Modern Childhood Within and Outside School', pp. 221-8 in L. Chisholm et al., eds., *Growing Up in Europe: Contemporary Horizons in Childhood and Youth Studies*. Berlin, FRG and New York, NY: Walter de Gruyter.

Rerrich, M. and G. Voß (1992). 'Vexiebild soziale Ungleichheit. Die Bedeutung alltäglicher Lebensführung für die Sozialstrukturanalyse' (Picture Puzzle of Social Inequality: The Meaning of Everyday Life Conduct for the Analysis of the Social Structure), pp. 251-66 in S. Hradil, ed., *Zwischen Bewußtsein und Sein* (Between Consciousness and Existence). Opladen, FRG: Leske & Budrich.

Schneewind, K. (1983). *Eltern und Kinder* (Parents and Children). Stuttgart, FRG: Kohlhammer.

Schulze, G. (1990). 'Die Transformation sozialer Milieus in der Bundesrepulbik Deutschland' (Transformation of Social Milieus in the Federal Republic of Germany), pp. 409-32 in P. Berger and S. Hradil, eds., *Lebenslagen, Lebensläufe, Lebensstile* (Situations in Life, Life Courses, Lifestyles), special issue of the magazine *Soziale Welt*, Vol. 7.

Schulze, G. (1992). *Die Erlebnisgesellschaft, Kultursoziologie der Gegenwart* (Society of Events: Cultural Sociology of the Present). Frankfurt am Main, FRG and New York, NY: Campus.

Steinkamp, G. (1986). 'Jugendbezogene Lebenslagenforschung als interdisziplinäre Mehrebenenanalyse' (Research on Adolescence as Interdisciplinary Multilevel Analysis), pp. 133-54 in W. Heitmeyer, ed., *Interdisziplinäre Jugendforschung* (Interdisciplinary Research of Adolescence). Weinheim, FRG: Juventa.

Steinkamp, G. (1991). 'Sozialstruktur und Sozialisation' (Social Structure and Socialization), pp. 251-78 in K. Hurrelmann and D. Ulich, eds., *Neues Handbuch der Sozialisationsforchung* (New Handbook of Socialization Research), 4th edition. Weinheim, FRG and Basel, Switzerland: Beltz.

Steinkamp, G. and W. Stief (1978). *Lebensbedingungen und Sozialisation* (Living Conditions and Socialization). Opladen, FRG: Westdeutscher Verlag.

Taine, H. (1907). *Philosophie der Kunst* (Philosophy of Art). Jena, FRG: Diederichs.

Vaskovics, L. (1982). *Umweltbedingungen familialer Sozialisation. Beiträge zur sozialökologischen Sozialisationsforchung* (Environmental Conditions of Family Socialization: Contributions on Social-Ecological Research of Socialization). Stuttgart, FRG: Enke.

Vester, M. (1992). 'Die Modernisierung der Sozialstruktur und der Wandel von Mentalitäten' (The Modernization of the Social Structure and the Change of Mentalities), pp. 223-50 in S. Hradil, ed., *Zwischen Bewußtsein und Sein* (Between Consciousness and Existence). Opladen, FRG: Leske & Budrich.

Vester, M. et al. (1993). *Soziale Milieus im gesellschaftlichen Strukturwandel: Zwischen Integration und Ausgrenzung* (Social Milieus in the Changing Structure of Society: Between Integration and Marginality). Köln, FRG: Bund-Verlag.

Williams, J. (1994). *Classroom in Conflict: Teaching Controversial Subjects in a Diverse Society*. Albany, NY: State University of New York Press.

Zapf, W. et al. (1987). *Individualisierung und Sicherheit* (Individualization and Security). München, FRG: Beck.

Zinnecker, J. (1995). 'The Cultural Modernisation of Childhood', pp. 85-94 in L. Chisholm et al., eds., *Growing Up in Europe: Contemporary Horizons in Childhood and Youth Studies*. Berlin, FRG and New York, NY: Walter de Gruyter.

REFERENCES FOR CHAPTER 7

Adorno, T. (1972). 'Theorie der Halbbildung' (Theory of Partial Education), pp. 93-121 in T. Adorno, *Soziologische Schriften 1* (Sociological Writings 1), Frankfurt am Main, FRG.: Suhrkamp.

Apple, M. (1978). 'The New Sociology of Education: Analyzing Cultural and Economic Reproduction', pp. 495-6 in *Harvard Educational Review*, Vol. 48, No. 1.

Apple, M. (1979). *Ideology and Curriculum.* Boston, MA and London, UK: Routledge and Kegan Paul.

Apple, M. (1982). *Cultural and Economic Reproduction in Education.* Boston, MA and London, UK: Routledge and Kegan Paul.

Baethge, M. (1984). 'Materielle Produktion, gesellschaftliche Arbeitsteilung und Institutionalisierung von Bildung' (Material Production, Division of Labor, and Institutionalization of Education), pp. 21-53 in *Enzyklopädie Erziehungswissenschaft Band 5* (Encyclopedia of Educational Knowledge Vol. 5). Stuttgart, FRG: Klett.

Baethge, M. and U. Teichler (1984). 'Bildungssystem und Beschäftigungssystem', Educational System and Occupational System, pp. 206-24 in *Enzyklopädie Erziehungswissenschaft Band. 5* (Encyclopedia of Educational Knowledge Vol. 5), Stuttgart, FRG: Klett.

Beck, K. and A. Kell (1990). 'Symposion 4: Bilanz der Bildungsforschung' (Symposium 4: Balance of Educational Research), pp. 149-68 in D. Benner, ed., *Bilanz für die Zukunft: Aufgaben, Konzepte und Forschung in der Erziehungswissenschaft* (Balance for the Future: Exercises, Concepts, and Research in Educational Knowledge). Weinheim, FRG and Basel, Switzerland: Beltz.

Beck, U. (1983). 'Jenseits von Klasse und Stand? Soziale Ungleichheit, gesellschaftliche Individualisierungsprozesse und die Entstehung neuer sozialer Formen und Identitäten' (Beyond Class and Position? Social Inequality, Business Individualization Processes, and the Formation of New Social Forms and Indentities), pp. 35-74 in R. Kreckel, ed., *Soziale Ungleichheiten, Soziale Welt, Sonderband 2* (Social Inequalities, Social World, Edition 2), Göttingen, FRG: Schwartz.

Bowles, S. and H. Gintis (1976). *Schooling in Capitalistic America.* New York, NY: Basic Books.

Bourdieu, P. (1973). 'Kulturelle Reproduktion und soziale Reproduktion' (Cultural and Social Reproduction), pp. 88-137 in P. Bourdieu and J. Passeron, *Grundlagen einer Theorie der symbolischen Gewalt* (Basis of a Theory of Symbolic Power). Frankfurt am Main, FRG: Suhrkamp.

Carnoy, M. and H. Levin (1985). *Schooling and Work in the Democratic State.* Stanford, CA: Stanford University Press.

Cole, M., ed. (1988). *Rethinking Bowles and Gintis.* Philadelphia, PA: Falmer Press.

Collin, R. (1979). *The Credential Society: A Historical Sociology of Education an Stratification.* New York. NY: Academic Press.

Fend, H. (1990). 'Bilanz der empirischen Bildungsforschung' (Balance of Empirical Educational Research), pp. 687f in *Zeitschrift für Pädagogik*, Vol. 36.

Friedeburg, L. von (1983). 'Zur Einführung: Konjunkturphasen öffentlichen Interesses an Bildungspolitik und Bildungssoziologie'(Introduction: Trends of Official Interest in Educational Politics and Sociology), pp. 157-64 in *Zeitschrift für Sozialisationsforschung und Erziehungssoziologie* (Magazine for Socialization Research and Educational Sociology), Vol. 3.

Friedeburg, L.von (1989). *Bildungsreform in Deutschland. Geschichte und gesellschaftlicher Widerspruch* (Educational Reform in Germany: History and Social Conflict). Frankfurt am. Main, FRG: Suhrkamp.

Giroux, H. (1981). *Ideology, Culture and the Process of Schooling*. Philadelphia, PA: Temple University Press.

Giroux, H. (1983). *Theory and Resistance in Education: A Pedagogy for the Opposition*. London, UK: Heinemann.

Helsper, W. (1992). 'Rezension zu: Tippelt, R. 1990: Bildung und sozialer Wandel' (Review of R. Tippelt's 1990: Education and Social Change), pp. 329-32 in *Zeitschrift für Pädagogik*, Vol. 38, No. 2.

Heydorn, H. (1979). *Über den Widerspruch von Bildung und Herrschaft* (Concerning the Conflict Between Education and Power). Frankfurt am Main, FRG: Syndikat.

Heydorn, H. (1980). 'Zu einer Neufassung des Bildungsbegriffs' (Toward a New Draft of the Concept of Education), pp. 95-184 in H. Heydorn, *Ungleichheit für alle* (Inequality for All). Frankfurt am Main, FRG: Suhrkamp.

Hurrelmann, K. (1986). 'Das Modell des produktiv realitätsverarbeitenden Subjekts in der Sozialisationsforschung' (The Model of the Productive Reality Process of Subjects in Socialization Research), pp. 71-123 in K. Hurrelmann, ed., *Lebenslage, Lebensalter, Lebenszeit* (Life Situations, Age, Lifetime). Weinheim, FRG and Basel, Switzerland: Beltz.

Jencks, C. et al. (1972). *Chancengleichheit* (Equal Prospects). Reinbek, FRG: Rowohlt.

Keckeisen, W. (1983). 'Kritische Erziehungswissenschaft' (Critical Educational Science), pp. 117-38 in *Enzyklopädie Erziehungswissenschaft Bd. 1* (Encyclopedia of Educational Science Vol. 5). Stuttgart, FRG: Klett.

Lenhart, V. (1987). *Die Evolution erzieherischen Handelns* (The Evolution of Educational Action). Frankfurt am Main, FRG: Lang.

Lutz, B. (1983). 'Bildung und soziale Ungleichheit. Eine historisch-soziologische Skizze' (Education and Social Inequality: An Historical-Sociological Outline), pp. 221-45 in R. Kreckel, ed., *Soziale Ungleichheiten, Soziale Welt, Sonderband 2* (Social Inequalities, Social World, Edition 2). Göttingen, FRG: Schwartz.

Mayer, K. (1990). 'Lebensverläufe und sozialer Wandel. Anmerkungen zu einem Forschungsprogramm' (Life Processes and Social Change: Observations for a Research Program), pp. 7-21 in K. Mayer, ed., *Sonderheft der Kölner Zeitschrift für Soziologie und Sozialpsychologie 1990* (Special Edition of the Cologne Magazine for Sociology and Social Psychology 1990).

Meulemann, H. (1990). 'Schullaufbahnen, Ausbildungskarrieren, und die Folgen im Lebensverlauf. Der Beitrag der Lebenslaufforschung zur Bildungssoziologie' (School Courses, Career Development, and their Lifelong Consequences: The Contribution of Curriculum Vitae Research for Educational Sociology), pp. 89-117 in K. Mayer, ed., *Sonderheft der Kölner Zeitschrift für Soziologie und Sozialpsychologie 1990* (Special Edition of the Cologne Magazine for Sociology and Social Psychology 1990).

Richter, E. (1993). 'Interkulturelle Bildung als Aufgabe der Schule' (Intercultural Education as a Duty of the Schools), pp. 249-74 in W. Schubarth and W. Melzer, eds., *Schule, Gewalt und Rechtsextremismus* (School, Violence, and the Extreme Right). Opladen, FRG: Leske & Budrich.

Rolff, H. (1983). 'Bildungspolitik und bildungssoziologische Forschung im Bereich Schule - kulturelle Modernisierung im Klassenkonflikt' (Educational Politics and Sociology of Education Research in the Sphere of School and Cultural Modernization in the Class Conflict), pp. 201-12 in *Zeitschrift für Sozialisationsforschung und Erziehungssoziologie* (Magazine for Socialization Research and Educational Sociology), Vol. 3.

Saporiti, A. (1995). 'Childhood and Poverty: From the Children's Point of View', pp. 237-48 in L. Chisholm et al., eds., *Growing Up in Europe: Contemporary Hori-*

zons in Childhood and Youth Studies. Berlin, FRG and New York, NY: Walter de Gruyter.

Sünker, H. (1989a). *Bildung, Alltag und Subjektivität* (Education, Everyday Life, and Subjectivity). Weinheim, FRG: Deutscher Studienverlag.

Sünker, H. (1989b). 'Heinz-Joachim Heydorn: "Bildungstheorie als Gesellschafts-kritik"' (Heinz-Joachim Heydorn: Educational Theory as Social Criticism), pp 447-70 in O. Hansmann and W. Marotzki, eds., *Diskurs Bildungstheorie II* (Discourse on Educational Theory II). Weinheim, FRG: Deutscher Studienverlag.

Sünker, H. (1992). 'Bildungstheorie als pädagogisch-politisches Paradigma' (Educational Theory as Pedagogical-Political Paradigms), pp. 59-74 in W. Marotzki and H. Sünker, eds., *Kritische Erziehungswissenschaft - Moderne - Postmoderne 1* (Critical Educational Science - Modern - Postmodern 1). Weinheim, FRG: Deutscher Studienverlag.

Sünker, H. (1993). 'Politische Kultur und institutionalisierte Bildung in Deutschland' (Political Culture and Institutionalized Education in Germany), pp. 173-85 in W. Schubarth and W. Melzer, eds., *Schule, Gewalt und Rechtsextremismus* (School, Power, and the Extreme Right). Opladen, FRG: Leske & Budrich.

Sünker, H. (1994). 'Pedagogy and Politics', pp. 113-28 in S. Miedema et al., eds., *The Politics of Human Science*. Brussels, Belgium: VUB Dreh.

Sünker, H. (1995). 'The Politics of Childhood, Children's Rights and the UN Convention', pp. 269-74 in L. Chisholm et al., eds., *Growing Up in Europe: Contemporary Horizons in Childhood and Youth Studies*. Berlin, FRG and New York, NY: Walter de Gruyter.

Timmermann, D. (1988). 'Die Abstimmung von Bildungs- und Beschäftigungs-system. Ein Systematisierungsversuch' (The Division of the Educational and Business Systems: A Systematic Experiment), pp. 25-82 in H. Bodenhöfer, ed., *Bildung, Beruf und Arbeitsmarkt* (Education, Profession, and the Labor Market). Berlin, FRG: Duncker und Humblot.

Timmermann, D. (1995). 'Human Capital Theory and the Individualization Theorem', pp. 223-46 in G. Neubauer and K. Hurrelmann, eds., *Individualization in Childhood and Adolescence*. Berlin, FRG and New York, NY: Walter de Gruyter.

Timmermann, D. and F. Strikker (1986). 'Bildung, Ausbildung und was dann? Feine Signale und harte Fakten. Überlegungen zur Abstimmung von Bildungs- und Beschäaftigungssystem' (Education, Improvement, and What Then? Subtle Signals and Hard Facts), pp. 110-81 in *Mehrwert*, Vol. 27.

Tippelt, R. (1990). *Bildung und sozialer Wandel* (Education and Social Change). Weinheim, FRG: Deutscher Studienverlag.

Wexler, P. (1976). *The Sociology of Education: Beyond Equality*. Indianapolis, IN: Bobbs-Merrill.

Wexler, P. (1987). *Social Analysis of Education: After the New Sociology*. London, UK and New York, NY: Routledge.

Willis, P. (1977). *Learning to Labor: How Working Class Kids get Working Class Jobs*. Lexington, MA: D.C. Heath.

Young, M. (1971). *Knowledge and Control: New Directions for the Sociology of Education*. London, UK: Collier-Macmillan.

Young, M. and G. Whitty, eds. (1977). *Society, State and Schooling*. Lewes, Sussex, UK: Falmer Press.

ZSE (Zeitschrift für Sozialisationsforschung und Erziehungssoziologie) (Magazine for Socialization Research and Educational Sociology) Vol. 3 (1983). Heft 2 (Book 2).

REFERENCES FOR CHAPTER 8

Adorno, T. (1966). *Negative Dialektik* (Negative Dialectic). Frankfurt am Main, FRG: Suhrkamp.

Adorno, T. (1972). 'Theorie der Halbbildung' (Theory of Partial Education), pp. 31-122 in T. Adorno, *Soziologische Schriften 1* (Sociological Writings 1). Frankfurt am Main, FRG: Suhrkamp.

Adorno, T. (1973). *Negative Dialectics*. London, UK: Routledge & Kegan.

Anderson, P. (1976). *Considerations on Western Marxism*. London, UK: New Left Books.

Arrighi, G., T. Hopkins, and I. Wallerstein (1986). 'Dilemmas of Antisystemic Movements', pp. 185-206 in *Social Research*, No. 53.

Benner, D., F. Brüggen, and K. Göstemeyer (1982). 'Heydorn's Bildungstheorie' (Heydorn's Theory of Education), pp. 73-92 in *Zeitschrift für Pädagogik*, No. 28.

Berman, M. (1988). *All That Is Solid Melts Into Air: The Experience of Modernity*. New York, NY: Penguin.

Bourdieu, P. (1987). *Sozialer Sinn: Kritik der theoretischen Vernunft* (Social Sense: Critique of Theoretical Rationality). Frankfurt am Main, FRG: Suhrkamp.

Connell, R. (1983). *Which Way is Up? Essays on Sex, Class and Culture*. Sydney, Australia: George Allen & Unwin.

Connell, R., D. Ashenden, S. Kessler, and G. Dowsett, eds. (1982). *Making the Difference: Schools, Families and Social Division*. Sydney, Australia: George Allen & Unwin.

Gottdiener, M. (1993). 'A Marx for Our Time: Henri Lefebvre and the Production of Space', pp. 129-34 in *Sociological Theory*, No. 11.

Habermas, J. (1981). *Theorie des kommunikativen Handelns* (The Theory of Communication Action). Frankfurt am Main, FRG: Suhrkamp.

Habermas, J. (1985). *Der philosophische Diskurs der Moderne: Zwölf Vorlesungen* (The Philosphical Discourse of Modernism: Twelve Lectures). Frankfurt am Main, FRG: Suhrkamp.

Hegel, G. (1955). *Grundlinien der Philosphie des Rechts* (Philosophical Baseline for Law). Hamburg, FRG: Meiner.

Heller, A. (1976). *The Theory of Need in Marx*. London, UK: Vallison & Busby.

Heller, A. (1984). *Everyday Life*. London, UK: Routledge & Kegan.

Hess, R. (1988). *Henri Lefebvre et l'aventure du siècle* (Henri Lefebvre and the Adventure of the Century). Paris, France: Métailié.

Heydorn, H. (1979). *Über den Widerspruch von Bildung und Herrschaft* (About the Contradition Between Education and Power). Frankfurt am Main, FRG: Syndikat.

Heydorn, H. (1980a). 'Zu einer Neufassung des Bildungsbegriffs' (A New Version of the Term 'Education'), pp. 95-184 in H. Heydorn, *Ungleichheit für alle* (Inequality for Everyone). Frankfurt am Main, FRG: Syndikat.

Heydorn, H. (1980b). 'Überleben durch Bildung: Umriß einer Aussicht' (Surviving with Education: The Outline of A View), pp. 282-310 in H. Heydorn, *Ungleichheit für alle* (Inequality for Everyone). Frankfurt am Main, FRG: Syndikat.

Heydorn, H. (1980c). 'Zum Bildungsproblem in der gegenwärtigen Situation' (The Problem of Education in Contemporary Society), pp. 75-135 in H. Heydorn, *Zur bürgerlichen Bildung* (On Civic Education). Frankfurt am Main, FRG: Syndikat.

Heydorn, H. (1980d). 'Abstand und Nähe. Wilhelm von Humboldt' (Distance and Closeness: Wilhelm von Humboldt), pp. 247-266 in H. Heydorn, *Zur bürgerlichen Bildung* (On Civic Education). Frankfurt am Main, FRG: Syndikat.

Heydorn, H. (1980e). 'Bildungstheorie Hegels' (Hegel's Theory of Education), pp. 231-68 in H. Heydorn, *Ungleichheit für alle* (Inequality for Everyone). Frankfurt am Main, FRG: Syndikat.

Hohendahl, P. (1985). 'Reform als Utopie: Die preußische Bildungspolitik 1809-17' (Reform as Utopia: The Prussian Politics of Education 1809-17), pp. 250-72 in W. Voßkamp, ed., *Utopieforschung. 3. Bd.* (Utopia Research, volume 3). Frankfurt am Main, FRG: Suhrkamp.

Hornstein, W. (1984). 'Neue soziale Bewegungen und Pädagogik' (New Social Movements and Pedagogy), pp. 147-67 in *Zeitschrift für Pädagogik*, No. 30.

Jay, M. (1987). 'Lukacs, Bloch und der Kampf um eine marxistische Totalitätskonzeption' (Lukacs, Bloch, and the Struggle for a Marxist Conception of Totalitarianism), pp. 298-306 in: M. Löwy et al., eds., *Verdinglichung und Utopie* (Objectification and Utopia). Frankfurt am Main, FRG: Suhrkamp.

Kern, H. and M. Schumann (1984). *Das Ende der Arbeitsteilung? Rationalisierung in der industriellen Produktion* (The End of the Division of Labor? Rationality in Industrial Production). München, FRG: Beck.

Kilian, H. (1971). *Das enteignete Bewußtsein: Zur dialektischen Sozialpsychologie* (The Stolen Consciousness: Dialectic Social Psychology). Neuwied, FRG: Luchterhand.

Koneffke, G. (1986). 'Revidierte Allgemeinbildung: Anmerkungen zu einer Diskussion des Bildungsbegriffs' (Revised General Education: Notes of a Discussion of the Term 'Education'), pp. 67-75 in *Widersprüche*, Vol. 21, No. 6.

Lefebvre, H. (1971). *Everyday Life in the Modern World*. London, UK: Allen Lane.

Lefebvre, H. (1972). *Die Revolution der Städte* (The Revolution of the Cities). München, FRG: List.

Lefebvre, H. (1974). *Die Zukunft des Kapitalismus: Die Reproduktion der Produktionsverhältnisse* (The Future of Capitalism: The Reproduction of the Relation of Production). München, FRG: List.

Lefebvre, H. (1975). *Metaphilosophie: Prolegomena* (Metaphilosophy). Frankfurt am Main, FRG: Suhrkamp.

Lefebvre, H. (1977). *Kritik des Alltagslebens: Mit einem Vorwort zur deutschen Ausgabe* (Critique of Everyday Life: With a Foreword to the German Edition), D. Prokop, ed. Kronberg, FRG: Athenäum.

Lefebvre, H. (1978). *Einführung in die Modernität: 12 Präludien* (Introduction to Modernity: 12 Preludes). Frankfurt am Main, FRG: Suhrkamp.

Lippe, R. zur (1974). *Naturbeherrschung am Menschen I. Körpererfahrung als Entfaltung von Sinnen und Beziehungen in der Aera des italienischen Kaufmannskapitals* (Domination of Nature Over Humans: Physical Experience as Development from Feelings and Relations in the Era of the Italian Merchant Capitalists). Frankfurt am Main, FRG: Suhrkamp.

Lukacs, G. (1971). *History and Class Consciousness: Studies in Marxist Dialectics*. London, UK: Merlin Press.

Markus, G. (1986). 'On the Paradigm of Production: Marxian Materialism and the Problem of the Constitution of the Social World', pp. 41-125 in G. Markus *Language and Production: A Critique of the Paradigm*. Dordrecht, the Netherlands: Reidel.

Marx, K. (1967). *Grundrisse der Kritik der politischen Ökonomie* (Outlines of a Critique of Political Economy). Frankfurt am Main, FRG: EVA.

Negt, O. and A. Kluge (1972). *Öffentlichkeit und Erfahrung: Zur Organisationsanalyse von bürgerlicher und proletarischer Öffentlichkeit* (Public and Experience: Organizational Analysis of a Civic and Proletarian Public). Frankfurt am Main, FRG: Suhrkamp.

Nelson, L. (1948). 'Die sokratische Methode' (Socratic Methods), pp. 15-48 in L. Nelson, *Drei Schriften zur kritischen Philosophie* (Three Essays on Critical Philosophy). Wolfenbüttel, FRG: Wolfenbüttler Verlagsanstalt.

Offe, C. (1985). 'New Social Movements: Challenging the Boundaries of Institutional Politics', pp. 817-68 in *Social Research*, No. 52.

Peukert, D. (1986). *Grenzen der Sozialdisziplinierung: Aufstieg und Krise der Deutschen Jugendfürsorge 1878-1932* (Frontiers of Social Discipline: Rise and Fall of German Youth's Welfare 1878-1932). Köln, FRG: Bund.

Reichelt, H. (1970). *Zur logischen Struktur des Kapitalbegriffs bei Karl Marx* (The Logical Structure of the Concept of Capital by Karl Marx). Frankfurt am Main, FRG: EVA.

Sartre, J. (1964). *Marxismus und Existentialismus* (Marxism and Existentialism). Reinbek, FRG: Rowohlt.

Schmied-Kowarzik, W. (1983). *Die Dialektik der gesellschaftlichen Praxis: Zur Genesis und Kernstruktur der Marxschen Theorie* (The Dialectic of Social Practice: The Genesis and Main Structure of Marxist Theory). Freiburg, FRG: Alber.

Sünker, H. (1984). *Bildungstheorie und Erziehungspraxis* (Educational Theory and Practical Experience). Bielefeld, FRG: Kleine Verlag.

Sünker, H. (1992). 'Everyday Life', pp. 326-34 in G. Széll, ed., *Concise Encyclopedia of Participation and Co-Management*. Berlin, FRG and New York, NY: De Gruyter.

Sünker, H. (1993). 'Education and Enlightenment or Educational Theory Contra Postmodernism', pp. 39-57 in *Education*, No. 48.

Sünker, H. (1994a). 'Are Intellectuals the Keepers of Political Culture? Some Reflections on Politics, Morality, and Reason', pp. 193-204 in R. Farnen, ed., *Nationalism, Ethnicity and Identity*. New Brunswick, NJ and London, UK: Transaction Books.

Sünker, H. (1994b). 'Alienation, Reproduction and the Social Organization of Work', pp.101-10 in W. Ehlert, R. Russell, and G. Széll, eds., *Return of Work, Production and Administration to Capitalism*. Frankfurt am Main, FRG and New York, NY: Peter Lang.

Theunissen, M. (1970). *Die Verwirklichung der Vernunft: Zur Theorie-Praxis-Diskussion im Anschluß an Hegel. Philosophische Rundschau. Beiheft 6* (The Realization of Rationality: Theory-Practice-Discussion in Connection with Hegel. Philosophical Review. Supplement 6).

Theunissen, M. (1978a). *Sein und Schein: Die kritische Funktion der Hegelschen Logik* (Being and Seeming: The Critical Function of Hegelian Logic). Frankfurt am Main, FRG: Suhrkamp.

Theunissen, M. (1978b). *Begriff und Realität: Hegel's Aufhebung des metaphysischen Wahrheitsbegriffs* (Term and Reality: Hegel's Uplifting of the Metaphysical Concept of Truth), pp. 324-59 in: R. Horstmann, ed., *Seminar: Dialektik in der Philosophie Hegel's* (Seminar: Dialectic in Hegel's Philosophy). Frankfurt am Main, FRG.: Suhrkamp.

Theunissen, M. (1981). *Selbstverwirklichung und Allgmeinheit: Zur Kritik des gegenwärtigen Bewußtseins* (Self-realization and the General Public: Critique of Current Knowledge). Berlin, FRG: De Gruyter.

Theunissen, M. (1982). 'Die verdrängte Intersubjektivität in Hegel's Philosophie des Rechts' (The Supplanted Intersubjectivity in Hegel's Philosophy of Law), pp. 317-81 in D. Henrich and R. Horstmann, ed., *Hegel's Philosophie des Rechts: Die Theorie der Rechtsformen und ihre Logik* (Hegel's Philosophy of the Law: The Theory of Forming Laws and Their Logic). Stuttgart, FRG: Klett-Cotta.

Wehler, H. (1987). *Deutsche Gesellschaftsgeschichte. Erster Band. Vom Feudalismus des Alten Rechts bis zur Defensiven Modernisierung der Reformära 1700-1815* (German Social History. First Volume. From Feudalism of the Old Laws to the Defensive Modernization of the Reformation 1700-1815). München, FRG: Beck.

Werner, H. (1969). *Geschichte des politischen Gedichts in Deutschland von 1815 bis 1848* (History of Political Poetry in Germany from 1815 to 1848). Berlin, FRG: Akademie Verlag.

REFERENCES FOR CHAPTER 9

Abrams, D. (1993). *Conflict, Competition, or Cooperation: Dilemmas of State Education Policymaking.* Albany, NY: State University of New York Press.

Atkinson, J. (1985). 'Flexibility: Planning for an Uncertain Future', pp. 25-30 in *Manpower Policy and Practice,* Vol. 1, Summer.

Bourdieu, P. and J. Passeron (1977). *Reproduction: In Education, Society and Culture.* London, UK: Sage.

Bowles, S. and H. Gintis (1976). *Schooling in Capitalist America.* New York, NY: Basic Books.

Coenen, H. and P. Leisink, eds. (1993). *Work and Citizenship in the New Europe.* Aldershot, UK: Edward Elgar.

Coenen, H. and R. van de Winkel (1988). *Onderwijs en arbeidsmarkt gecoördineerd? Knelpunten in de grafische sector in de provincie Utrecht.* (Are Education and the Labor Market Coordinated?: Bottlenecks in the Graphics Industry in the Province of Utrecht). Utrecht, the Netherlands: Jan van Arkel.

Dercksen, W., E. van Luijk, and P. den Hoed (1990). *Werkloosheidsbestrijding in Amsterdam, Rotterdam, Den Haag en Utrecht* (Tackling Unemployment in Amsterdam, Rotterdam, the Hague, and Utrecht). Den Haag, the Netherlands: Wetenschappelijke Raad voor het Regeringsbeleid.

Elfring, T. and R. Kloosterman (1989). *De Nederlandse 'Job Machine': De snelle expansie van laagbetaald werk in de dienstensector, 1979-1986* (The Dutch 'Job Machine': The Rapid Expansion of Low Paid Jobs in the Service Sector, 1979-86). Amsterdam, the Netherlands: University of Amsterdam.

Engbersen, G. (1993). 'Modern Poverty and Second-Class Citizenship', pp. 35-47 in H. Coenen and P. Leisink, eds., *Work and Citizenship in the New Europe.* Aldershot, UK: Edward Elgar.

Fend, H. (1974). *Gesellschaftliche Bedingungen schulischer Sozialisation* (Social Conditions of Socialization at School). Weinheim, FRG: Beltz.

Ferner, A. and R. Hyman, eds. (1992). *Industrial Relations in the New Europe.* Oxford, UK: Blackwell.

Giddens, A. (1984). *The Constitution of Society.* Cambridge/Oxford, UK: Polity Press.

Gordon, J., J. Jallade, and D. Parkes (1994). *Structures of Vocational Education and Training and the Match between Education and Work: An International Comparison.* Den Haag, the Netherlands: OSA (Organisatie voor Strategisch Arbeidsmarktonderzoek).

Huijgen, F. (1989). *De kwalitatieve structuur van de werkgelegenheid in Nederland* (The Qualitative Structure of Employment in the Netherlands). Den Haag, the Netherlands: OSA (Organisatie voor Strategisch Arbeidsmarktonderzoek).

Interim Advisory Committee on Education and the Labor Market (1990). *Onderwijs - Arbeidsmarkt: Naar een werkzaam traject* (Education and the Labor Market: Toward Effective Coordination). Alphen aan den Rijn, the Netherlands: Samson H. D. Tjeenk Willink.

Kern, H. and M. Schumann (1984). *Das Ende der Arbeitsteilung?* (The End of the Division of Labor?). München, FRG: Verlag C. H. Beck.

Kloosterman, R. and T. Elfring (1991). *Werken in Nederland* (Work in the Netherlands). Schoonhoven, the Netherlands: Academic Service.

Kroft, H., G. Engbersen, K. Schuyt, and F. van Waarden (1989). *Een tijd zonder een Job* (A Time Without a Job). Leiden, the Netherlands and Antwerpen, Belgium: Stenfert Kroese.

Kruyt, A. and W. Fleuren (1990). 'Juridische aspecten' (Legal Aspects), pp. 31-50 in H. Entzinger and P. Stijnen, eds., *Etnische minderheden in Nederland* (Ethnic Minorities in the Netherlands). Meppel/Heerlen, the Netherlands: Boom/Open Universiteit.

Leisink, P. (1994). 'National Development and Social Rights of the Citizen: The Prospect of Europe', pp. 110-22 in *Bulgarian Sociological Review*, Vol. 18, No. 4-5.

Leisink, P. (1996a). 'Dutch and Flemish Industrial Relations: Theory and Practice', pp. 69-92 in *European Journal of Industrial Relations*, Vol. 2, No. 1.

Leisink, P. (1996b). 'Trade Unions and worker Participation in the Netherlands', pp. 95-103 in G. Kester and H. Pinaud, eds., *Trade unions and Democratic participation in Europe*. Aldershot, UK: Avebury.

Leisink, P. (in press). 'Citizenship and Work in Europe' in M. Roche and R. van Berkel, eds., *European Citizenship and social Exclusion*. Aldershot, UK: Avebury.

Leisink, P. and B. Valkenburg (1988). *Die Gewerkschaften und marginale Gruppen auf dem Arbeitsmarkt* (Trade Unions and Marginal Groups in the Labor Market). Bremen, FRG: Universität Bremen.

Leisink, P., J. van Leemput, and J. Vilrokx, eds. (1996). *The Challenges to Trade Unions in Europe*. Aldershot, UK: Edward Elgar.

Lijphart, A. (1968). *The Politics of Accommodation: Pluralism and Democracy in the Netherlands*. Berkeley, CA: University of California Press.

Meijers, F. (1983). *Van ambachtschool tot LTS* (From the Technical School to Lower Technical Vocational Training). Nijmegen, the Netherlands: SUN.

Ministry of Education and Science (1991). *Profiel van de 2e fase voortgezet onderwijs* (The Profile of the Second Phase of Secondary Education). Den Haag, the Netherlands: Ministerie van Onderwijs en Wetenschappen.

Mok, A. (1994). *Arbeid, bedrijf en maatschappij* (Work, Firm, and Society). Leiden, the Netherlands and Antwerpen, Belgium: Stenfert Kroese.

OECD (1989). *Employment Outlook 1989*. Paris, France: OECD.

OECD (1991). *Economic Outlook 1991*. Paris, France: OECD.

OSA (1990). *OSA-Rapport 1990 Arbeidsmarktperspectieven* (The Organization for Strategic Labor Market Research 1990 Report on the Labor Market Outlook). Den Haag, the Netherlands: Organisatie voor Strategisch Arbeidsmarktonderzoek.

Reubsaet, T. (1990). 'Arbeidsmarkt en arbeidsbstel' (Labor Market and Work-based Society), pp. 51-73 in H. Entzinger and P. Stijnen, eds., *Etnische minderheden in Nederland* (Ethnic Minorities in the Netherlands). Meppel/Heerlen, the Netherlands: Boom/Open Universiteit.

Scholtz, H. (1987). 'Nieuwe technologieën; de kloof tussen vooropleiding en beroepspraktijk' (New Technologies and the Gap Between Education and Occupational Practice), pp. 38-45 in *Tijdschrift voor Arbeidsvraagstukken*, Vol. 3, No. 1.

Schouten, W., ed. (1977). *Ach meneer, ze kunnen tegenwoordig geen hamer meer vasthouden* (Sir, They Can't Even Hold a Hammer Nowadays). Scheveningen, the Netherlands: SMO.

Schumann, M., V. Baethge, U. Neumann, and R. Springer (1988). *Trend Report on Industrial Rationalization*. Amsterdam, the Netherlands: SISWO.

SCP (1990). *Sociaal en Cultureel Rapport 1990* (Social and Cultural Report 1990). Rijswijk, the Netherlands: Sociaal en Cultureel Planbureau.

SCP (1992). *Sociaal en Cultureel Rapport 1992* (Social and Cultural Report 1992). Rijswijk, the Netherlands: Sociaal en Cultureel Planbureau

Sünker, H. (1989). 'Heinz-Joachim Heydorn: Bildungstheorie als Gesellschaftskritik' (Heinz-Joachim Heydorn: Educational Theory as Social Criticism), pp. 447-70 in O. Hansmann and W. Marotzki, eds., *Diskurs Bildungstheorie II: Problemgeschichtliche Orientierungen* (Discourse on Educational Theory II: Historical Problems of Orientation). Weinheim, FRG: Deutscher Studienverlag.

SZW (Ministry of Social Affairs and Employment) (1991a). *Rapportage Arbeidsmarkt 1991* (Report on the Labor Market 1991). Delft, the Netherlands: Ministerie van Sociale Zaken en Werkgelegenheid.

SZW (1991b). *Notitie werkgelegenheids- en arbeidsmarktbeleid* (Report on Employment and Labor market Policies). Den Haag, the Netherlands: Ministerie van Sociale Zaken en Werkgelegenheid.

Tijdens, K. (1989). *Automatisering en vrouwenarbeid. Een studie over beroepssegregatie op de arbeidsmarkt, in de administratieve beroepen en het bankwezen* (Automation and Women's Jobs: A Study of Occupational Segregation in the Labor Market, in the Clerical Jobs, and the Banking Sector). Utrecht, the Netherlands: Jan van Arkel.

Trommel, W. (1987). *Flexibele arbeid: een werknemerstypologie* (Flexible Employment: A Typology of Workers). 's Gravenhage, the Netherlands: Wetenschappelijke Raad voor het Regeringsbeleid.

Valkenburg, B. and M. Coenen-Hanegraaf (1987). *Basisvorming voor alle leerlingen?* (Comprehensive Education for All Pupils?). Utrecht, the Netherlands: Jan van Arkel.

van Beek, K. and B. van Praag (1992). *Kiezen uit sollicitanten: concurrentie tussen werkzoekenden zonder baan* (Selecting from Job Applicants: Competition Between Job Seekers Without a Job). 's Gravenhage, the Netherlands: Wetenschappelijke Raad voor het Regeringsbeleid.

van Berkel, R. and T. de Wit (1988). 'Niet bij taal alleen.....' (Not by Language Alone . . .), pp. 13-21 in *Landelijke Werkgroep Nederlands op de Werkvloer*. Beekbergen, the Netherlands: Landelijke Werkgroep Nederlands op de Werkvloer.

van Berkel, R. and T. Hindriks (1991). *Uitkeringsgerechtigden en vakbeweging* (Welfare Claimants and Trade Unions). Utrecht, the Netherlands: Jan van Arkel.

van Hoof, J. (1987). *De arbeidsmarkt als arena* (The Labor Market as an Arena). Amsterdam, the Netherlands: SUA.

van Kemenade, J., ed. (1981). *Onderwijs: bestel en beleid* (Education: Institutional System and Policy). Groningen, the Netherlands: Wolters-Noordhoff.

Watts, A. (1984). *Education, Unemployment and the Future of Work*. Milton Keynes, UK: Open University Press.

Williamson, O. (1981). 'The Economics of Organization: the Transaction Cost Approach', pp. 548-77 in *American Journal of Sociology*, Vol. 87, No. 3.

Willis, P. (1977). *Learning to Labor*. Aldershot, UK: Gower.

Wood, S., ed. (1989). *The Transformation of Work?* London, UK: Unwin Hyman.

WRR (Scientific Council for Government Policy) (1986). *Basisvorming in het onderwijs* (Comprehensive Schooling in Secondary Education). Den Haag, the Netherlands: Wetenschappelijke Raad voor het Regeringsbeleid.

WRR (Scientific Council for Government Policy) (1990). *Een werkend perspectief* (A Working Perspective). Den Haag, the Netherlands: Wetenschappelijke Raad voor het Regeringsbeleid.

REFERENCES FOR CHAPTER 10

Aronowitz, S. (1981). *The Crisis in Historical Materialism: Class, Politics, and Culture in Marxist Theory*. New York, NY: Praeger, AJF Bergin.

Benjamin, J. (1989). *The Bonds Of Love*. New York, NY: Random House.

Bradley, A. (1 April 1992). 'N.Y.C. To Create Small, Theme-Oriented High Schools', p. 5 in *Education Week*, Vol. XI, No. 28.

Buber, M. (1963). *Israel and the World: Essays in a Time of Crisis*, New York, NY: Schocken.

Buber, M. (1992). *On Intersubjectivity and Cultural Creativity*. Chicago, IL: University of Chicago Press.

Castoriadis, C. (1992). *Philosophy. Politics. Autonomy*. New York, NY: Oxford University Press.

Glasser, W. (13 May 1992). 'Quality, Trust, and Redefining Education', p. 32 in *Education Week*, Vol. XI, No. 34.

Harp, L. (15 April 1992). 'Panel Blueprint Seeks To Relate School To Work', p. 1 in *Education Week*, Vol. XI, No. 30.

Harvey, D. (1989). *The Condition of Postmodernity: An Inquiry into the Origins of Cultural Change*. Oxford, UK and New York, NY: Blackwell.

Honneth, A. (1991) 'Pluralization and Recognition: On the Self-Misunderstanding of Postmodern Social Theorists', *Thesis Eleven*. Boston, MA: Massachusetts Institute of Technology.

Horkheimer, M. and T. Adorno (1972). *Dialectic Of Enlightenment*. New York, NY: Herder and Herder.

Jonas, H. (1974). *Philosophical Essays*. Englewood Cliffs, NJ: Prentice-Hall.

Mestrovic, S. (1991). *The Coming Fin De Siecle: An Application of Durkheim's Sociology to Modernity and Postmodernism*. London, UK: Routledge.

Mongardini, C. (1990). 'The Decadence of Modernity: The Delusions of Progress and the Search for Historical Consciousness', p. 53 in J. Alexander and P. Sztompka, eds., *Rethinking Progress*. Boston, MA: Unwin Hyman.

Olalquiaga, C. (1992). *Megalopolis: Contemporary Cultural Sensibilities*. Minneapolis, MN: University Of Minnesota Press.

Panitch, O. (1977). 'The Development Of Corporatism in Liberal Democracies', pp. 61-90 in *Comparative Political Studies*, Vol. 10, No. 1.

Schmoker, M. (13 May 1992), 'What Schools Can Learn from Toyota America', p. 23 in *Education Week*, Vol. XI, No. 34.

Sommerfield, M. (15 April 1992), 'National Commitment to Parent Role in Schools Sought', p. 1 in *Education Week*, Vol. XI, No. 30.

Touraine, A. (1988). *Return of the Actor: Social Theory in Postindustrial Society*. Minneapolis, MN: University of Minnesota Press.

Viadero, D. (15 April 1992). 'Maine's "Common Core" Offers a Lesson in Standards', p. 21 in *Education Week*, Vol. XI, No. 30.

Vincent, J. (1991). *Abstract Labour: A Critique*. New York, NY: St. Martin's Press.

Wexler, P. (1987). *Social Analysis of Education: After The New Sociology*. New York, NY; London, UK: Routledge, Chapman and Hall.

Wexler, P. et al. (1992). *Becoming Somebody: Toward a Social Psychology of School*. Washington, DC; London, UK: Falmer Press.

Wolk, R., ed. (17 June 1992). 'A New "Social Compact" for Mastery in Education', p. 4 in *Education Week*, Vol. XI, No 39.

REFERENCES FOR CHAPTER 11

Giroux, Henry A. (1988). *Schooling and the Struggle for Public Life*. Minneapolis, MN: University of Minnesota Press.

Kfir, D., H. Ayalon, and R. Shapira. (1990). *Women's and Girls' Education in Israel - Trends, Achivements and their Social Significance*. Research Report No. 2.90. Tel Aviv, Israel: Tel Aviv University, The Unit for Sociology of Education and the Community. (In Hebrew.)

Klinov-Malul, R. (1991). *The Allocation of Public Resources for Education: Priorities*. Jerusalem, Israel: Center for Social Policy Studies. (In Hebrew.)

Kop, Y. (1988). *Socio-Economic Indicators*. Jerusalem, Israel: Center for Social Policy Studies.

Mar'i, S. (1978). *Arab Education in Israel*. Syracuse, NY: Syracuse University Press.

Meyer, J. and B. Rowan (1978). 'The Structure of Educational Organizations', pp. 78-109 in J. Meyer et al., eds., Environments and Organizations. San Francisco, CA: Jossey Bass.

Peres, Y. (1985). 'Horizontal Integration and Vertical Differentiation Among Jewish Ethnicities in Israel', pp. 39-58 in A. Weingrod, ed., *Studies in Israeli Ethnicity*. London, UK: Gordon and Breach.

___ (1987). *The Educational System Reflected in Numbers - 1987*. Jerusalem, Israel: State of Israel, Ministry of Education. (In Hebrew.)

REFERENCES FOR CHAPTER 12

Adler, M. (1982). *The Paideia Proposal: An Educational Manifesto*. New York, NY: Macmillan.

Apple, M. (1987). *Teacher and Texts: A Political Economy of Class and Gender Relations in Education*. New York, NY: Routledge and Kegan Paul.

Apple, M. (Summer 1987). 'Producing Inequality: The Ideology and Economy in the National Reports on Education', pp. 195-200 in *Educational Studies*, Vol. 18, No. 2.

Aronowitz, S. and H. Giroux (1985). *Education Under Seige: The Conservative, Liberal and Radical Debate Over Schooling*. South Hadley, MA: Bergin and Garvey.

Bell, D. (1973). *The Coming of Postindustrial Society*. New York, NY: Basic Books.

Beniger, J. (1986). *The Control Revolution: Technological and Economic Origins of the Information Society*. Cambridge, MA: Harvard University Press.

Berg, I. (1971). *Education and Jobs: The Great Training Robbery*. Boston, MA: Beacon Press.

Berman, M. (1981). *The Reenchantment of the World*. Ithaca, NY: Cornell University Press.

Berube, M., ed. (1995). *Higher Education Under Fire: Politics, Economics, and Crisis of the Humanities*. London, UK: Routledge.

Black, M. and R. Worthington (1986). 'The Center for Industrial Innovation at RPI: Critical Reflections on New York's Economic Recovery', pp. 257-280 in M. Schoolman and A. Magad, eds., *Reindustrializing New York State*. Albany, NY: State University of New York Press.

Bordo, S. (1987). *The Flight to Objectivity: Essays on Cartesianism and Culture*. New York, NY: State University of New York Press.

Bowers, C. (1988). *The Cultural Dimensions of Educational Computing*. New York, NY: Teacher's College Press.

Bowles, S. and H. Gintis (1976). *Schooling in Capitalist America*. New York, NY: Basic Books.

Brzezinski, Z. (1976). *Between Two Ages: America's Role in the Technocratic Era*. New York, NY: Viking.

Carnoy, M. and H. Levin (1985). *Schooling and Work in the Democratic State*. Stanford, CA: Stanford University Press.

Clark, B. (May 1960). 'The "Cooling Out" Function in Higher Education', pp. 569-77 in *The American Journal of Sociology*, Vol. 65, No. 6.

Collins, R. (1979). *The Credential Society: An Historical Sociology of Education and Stratification*. New York, NY: Academic Press.

Curtis, M. (1974). *The Social Ideas of American Educators*. Totowa, NJ: Littlefield, Adams.

Dickson, D. (January 1981). 'Limiting Democracy: Technocrats and the Liberal State', pp. 61-79 in *Democracy*, Vol. 1, No. 1.

Dickson, D. (1984). *The New Politics of Science*. New York, NY: Pantheon.

Duckworth, E. (1987). *The Having of Wonderful Ideas and Other Essays*. New York, NY: Teacher's College Press.

Edmundson, M., ed. (1993). *Wild Orchids and Trotsky*. New York, NY: Penguin Books.

Educating Americans for the 21st Century: A Plan of Action for Improving Mathematics, Science and Technology Education for all American Elementary and Secondary Students so that Their Achievement is the Best in the World by 1995. (1984). 'Executive Summary'. Washington, DC: The National Science Board Commission on Precollege Education in Mathematics, Science, and Technology.

Etzioni, A. (1968). *The Active Society*. New York, NY: The Free Press.

Ferkiss, V. (Fall 1979). 'Daniel Bell's Concept of Postindustrial Society: Theory, Myth, and Ideology', pp. 61-102 in *The Political Science Reviewer*, Vol. 9.

Fischer, F. (1990). *Technocracy and the Politics of Expertise*. Newbury Park, CA: Sage.

Flanders, L. and D. Utterback (May/June 1985). 'The Management Excellence Inventory: A Tool for Management Development', pp. 403-410 in *Public Administration Review*, Vol. 45, No. 3.

Gardner, J. (1961). *Excellence: Can We Be Equal and Excellent Too?* New York, NY: Harper and Row.

Greene, M. (1988). *The Dialectic of Freedom*. New York, NY: Teacher's College Press.

Greer, C. (1973). *The Great School Legend: A Revisionist Interpretation of American Public Education*. New York, NY: Viking.

Haber, S. (1964). *Efficiency and Uplift: Scientific Management in the Progressive Era, 1890-1920*. Chicago, IL: The University of Chicago Press.

Heggade, O. (1992). *Economics of Education*. Eliot, ME: Apt Books.

hooks, b. (1993). *Sisters of the Yam*. Boston, MA: South End Press.

Huntington, S. (Fall 1975). 'The Democratic Distemper', pp. 36-37 in *The Public Interest*.

Judy, S. (1980). *The ABC's of Literacy: A Guide for Parents and Educators*. New York, NY: Oxford University Press.

Kalas, J. (1986). 'Reindustrialization in New York: The Role of the State University', pp. 257-280 in M. Schoolman and A. Magad, eds., *Reindustrializing New York State*. Albany, NY: State University of New York Press.

Katz, M. (1971). *Class, Bureaucracy, and Schools*. New York, NY: Praeger.

Katznelson, I. and M. Weir (1985). *Schooling for All*. New York, NY: Basic Books.

Kargon, R. (1983). 'The Future of American Science: An Historical Perspective', p. 152 in M. Kann, ed., *The Future of American Democracy*. Philadelphia, PA: Temple University Press.

Kenney, M. (1986). *Bio-Technology: The University Industrial Connection*. New Haven, CT: Yale University Press.

Kleinberg, B. (1973). *American Society in the Postindustrial Age: Technology, Power and the End of Ideology*. Columbus, OH: Charles E. Merrill.

Kozol, J. (1991) *Savage Inequalities*. New York, NY: Crown.

Kreisberg, S. (1992). *Transforming Power: Domination, Empowerment and Education*. Albany, NY: State University of New York Press.

Lagrée, J. (1995). 'Young People and Employment in the European Community: Convergence or Divergence?', pp. 61-72 in L. Chisholm et al., eds., *Growing Up in Europe: Contemporary Horizons in Childhood and Youth Studies*. Berlin, FRG and New York, NY: Walter de Gruyter.

Lasch, C. (1972). 'Toward a Theory of Postindustrial Society,' pp. 36-50 in M. Hancock and G. Sjoberg, eds., *Politics in the Post-Welfare State*. New York, NY: Columbia University Press.

Lasch, C. (1978). *The Culture of Narcissism: American Life in an Age of Diminishing Expectations*. New York, NY: W.W. Norton and Company.

Lasch, C. (1984). *The Minimal Self: Psychic Survival in Troubled Times*, New York, NY: W.W. Norton and Company.

Lazerson, M. et al. (1985). *An Education of Value: The Purposes and Practices of Schools*. Cambridge, UK: Cambridge University Press.

Lerner, M. (1986). *Surplus Powerlessness*. Oakland, CA: The Institute for Labor & Mental Health.

McKibbens, B. (1989). *The End of Nature*. New York, NY: Random House.

Meier, D. (1995). *The Power of Their Ideas*. Boston, MA: Beacon Press.

Mukerji, C. (1989). *A Fragile Power: Scientists and the State*. Princeton, NJ: Princeton University Press.

Nasaw, D. (1979). *Schooled to Order: A Social History of Public Schooling in the United States*. New York, NY: Oxford University Press.

National Commission on Excellence in Education (1983). *A Nation at Risk: The Imperative for Educational Reform*. Washington, DC: US Government Printing Office.

National Institute of Education (October 1984). *Involvement in Learning: Realizing the Potential of American Higher Education*. Washington, DC: National Institute of Education, US Department of Education.

National Science Foundation and the US Department of Education (1980). *Science and Engineering for the '80s and Beyond*. Washington, DC: US Government Printing Office.

Noddings, N. (1992). *The Challenge to Care in Schools: An Alternative Approach to Education*. New York, NY: Teacher's College Press.

Peschek, J. (1987). *Policy Planning Organizations: Elite Agendas and America's Rightward Turn*. (Philadelphia, PA: Temple University Press.

Peters, T. and N. Aush (1985). *A Passion for Excellence: The Leadership Difference*. New York, NY: Warner Books.

Peters, T. and R. Watermans (1982). *In Search of Excellence*. New York, NY: Warner Books

Peterson, P. (1985). 'Did the Education Commissions Say Anything?', pp. 57-74 in P. Altbach, G. Kelly, and L. Weiss, eds., *Excellence in Education*. Buffalo, NY: Prometheus Books.

Reich, R. (1983). *The New American Frontier*. New York, NY: Times Books

Richie, R., D. Hecker, and J. Burgan (November 1983). 'High-technology Today and Tomorrow: A Small Slice of the Employment Pie', p. 50 in *Monthly Labor Review*.

Rifkin, J. (1985). *Declaration of a Heretic*. Boston, MA: Routledge and Kegan

Roses, M. (1989). *Lives on the Boundary*. New York, NY: Penguin Books.

Roszak, T. (1986). *The Cult of Information*. New York, NY: Pantheon.

Ryan, W. (1976). *Blaming the Victim*. New York, NY: Vintage Books.

Schoppmeyer, W., ed. (1992). *The Economics of Education: An Introduction*. Granville, OH: Trudy Knox.

Sennett, R. and J. Cobb (1972). *The Hidden Injuries of Class*. New York, NY: Vintage Books.

Shamos, M. (1995). *The Myth of Scientific Literacy*. New Brunswick, NJ: Rutgers University Press.

Shapiro, S. (Winter 1984). 'Crisis of Legitimation: Schools, Society, and the Declining Faith in Education', pp. 26-39 in *Interchange*, Vol. 15, No. 4.

Shapiro, S. (1990). *Between Capitalism and Democracy: Educational Policy and the Crisis of the Welfare State*. New York, NY: Bergin and Garvey.

Shor, I. (1986). *Culture Wars: School and Society in the Conservative Restoration, 1969-1984*. Boston, MA: Routledge & Kegan Paul.

Sklar, H., ed. (1980). *Trilateralism: The Trilateral Commission and Elite Planning for World Management*. Boston, MA: South End Press.

Spring, J. (1972). *Education and the Rise of the Corporate State*. Boston, MA: Beacon.

Spring, J. (1976). *The Sorting Machine: National Education Policy Since 1945*. New York, NY: McKay.

Stanley, M. (1978). *The Technocratic Conscience*. Chicago, IL: The University of Chicago Press.

Stedman, L. and K. Kaestle (November 1985). 'The Test Score Decline is Over: Now What?', pp. 204-10 in *Phi Delta Kappan*.

Straussmann, J. (1978). *The Limits of Technocratic Politics*. New Brunswick, NJ: Transaction Books.

Tyack, D. and E. Hansot (1982). *Managers of Virtue: Public School Leadership in America: 1920-1980*. New York, NY: Basic Books.

Walters, K. (July/August 1990). 'Critical Thinking, Rationality, and the Vulcanization of Students', pp. 448-67 in *Journal of Higher Education*, Vol. 61, No. 4.

Weibe, R. (1967). *The Search for Order: 1877-1920*. New York, NY: Hill and Wang.

REFERENCES FOR CHAPTER 13

Baum, G. (1987). *Compassion and Solidarity: The Church for Others*. Montreal, Canada and New York, NY: CBC Enterprises.

Bauman, Z. (1988/89). 'Strangers: The Social Construction of Universality and Particularity', pp. 7-42 in *Telos*, Vol. 78.

Burger, P. (1984). *Theory of the Avant-gard*. Minneapolis, MN: University of Minnesota Press.

Burger, P. (1989). 'The Disappearance of Meaning: a Postmodern Reading of Michel Tournier, Botho Strauss, and Peter Handke', pp. 124-39 in *Polygraph*, Vol. 2, No. 3.

Chopp, R. (1985). *The Praxis of Suffering*. Maryknoll, NY: Orbis.

Conquergood, D. (1994). 'Homeboys and Hoods: Gang Communication and Cultural Space', pp. 23-55 in L. Frey (ed.) *Group Communication in Context*. Hillsdale, NJ: Laurence Erlbaum Associates.

Farren, M. (December 3, 1993). 'Theater of the Disturbed', pp. 8-11 in *Los Angeles Reader*, Vol. 16, No. 8.

Fay, B. (1987). *Critical Social Science.* Ithaca, NY: Cornell University Press.

Gerbner, G. (1989/90). 'TV vs. Reality', p. 12 in *Adbusters*, Vol. l.

Grossberg, L. (1988a). *It's A Sin.* Sydney, Australia: Power Publications.

Grossberg, L. (1988b). 'Rockin' with Reagan, or the Mainstreaming of Modernity', pp. 123-49 in *Cultural Critique*, Vol. 10.

Holt, D. (1989). 'Complex, Ontology and Our Stake in the Theatre', pp. 166-75 in J. Shotter and K. Gergen (eds.) *Texts of Identity.* London, UK: Sage.

Kimball, R. (1991). 'Tenured Radicals', pp. 4-13 in *The New Criterion,* Vol. 9.

Krupat, A. (1991). *Ethnocriticism.* Berkeley, CA: University of California Press.

MacCannell, D. (1989). *The Tourist.* New York, NY: Basic Books.

McLaren, P. (1992). 'Education as a Political Issue: What's Missing in the Public Conversation about Education'?, pp. 249-62 in J. Kincheloe and S. Steinberg, eds., *Thirteen Questions: Reframing Education's Conversation.* Frankfurt am Main, FRG: Peter Lang.

McLaren, P. (1994). *Critical Pedagogy and Predatory Culture.* London, UK and New York, NY: Routledge.

McLaren, P. And R. Hammer (1989). 'Critical Pedagogy and the Postmodern Challenge: Toward a Critical Postmodernist Pedagogy of Liberation', pp. 29-62 in *Educational Foundations*, Vol. 3, No. 3.

Minh-ha, T. (1988). 'Not You/Like You: Post Colonial Women and the Interlocking Questions of Identity and Difference', pp. 71-7 in *Inscriptions*, Vol. 3, No. 4.

Ravitch, D. (1990). 'Multiculturalism', pp. 337-54 in *The American Scholar*, Vol. 59.

Rosaldo, R. (1989). *Culture and Truth: The Remaking of Social Analysis.* Boston, MA: Beacon Press.

Sarup, M. (1989). *An Introduction to Post-Structuralism and Postmodernism.* Athens, GA: University of Georgia Press.

Stephanson, A. (1988a). 'Regarding Postmodernism: A Conversation with Fredric Jameson', pp. 3-30 in A. Ross, ed., *Universal Abandon?* Minneapolis, MN: University of Minnesota Press.

Stephanson, A. (1988b). 'Interview with Cornel West', pp. 269-86 in A. Ross, ed., *Universal Abandon?* Minneapolis, MN: University of Minnesota Press.

Unger, R. (1987). *Social Theory: Its Situation and Its Task.* New York, NY: Cambridge University Press.

Willis, P. (1990). *Common Culture.* Boulder, CO: Westview Press.

REFERENCES FOR CHAPTER 14

Baker, K. (30 March 1990). 'A Bright New Term for London's Children' p. 7 in *Evening Standard.*

Ball, S. (1990). *Politics and Policymaking in Education.* London, UK: Routledge.

Banks, O. (1955). *Parity and Prestige in English Secondary Education.* London, UK: Routledge.

Bates, S. (13 December 1990). 'Unfilled Primary Schools Places Cost £140m', p. 5 in *The Guardian.*

Best, S. and D. Kellner (1991). *Postmodern Theory: Critical Interrogations.* Basingstoke, UK: Macmillan.

Blackburne, L. (13 May 1988). 'Peers Back Policy on Open Enrolment', *The Times Educational Supplement.*

Bowe, R. and S. Ball with A. Gold (1992). *Reforming Education and Changing Schools: Case Studies in Policy Sociology.* London, UK and New York, NY: Routledge.

Boyne, R. and A. Rattansi (eds.) (1990). *Postmodernism and Society.* London, UK: Macmillan.

Chubb, M. and T. Moe (1990). *Politics, Markets, and America's Schools.* Washington, DC: Brookings Institution.

Cumper, P. (1990). 'Muslim Schools: The Implications of the Education Reform Act 1988', pp. 379-89 in *New Community,* Vol. 16, No. 3.

Dale, R. (1989). 'The Thatcherite Project in Education', pp. 156-7 in *Critical Social Policy,* Vol 9, No 3.

Dean, C. (21 September 1990). 'CTC Selectors Face an "Impossible Task"', p. 1 in *The Times Educational Supplement.*

DES (1986). *City Technology Colleges: A New Choice of School.* London, UK: DES.

DES (1987). *Grant Maintained Schools: Consultation Paper.* London, UK: DES.

Donald, J. (1989). 'Interesting Times', pp. 39-55 in *Critical Social Policy,* Vol 9, No 3.

Edwards, T., J. Fitz, and G. Whitty (1989). *The State and Private Education.* London, UK and New York, NY: Falmer Press.

Fitz, J., D. Halpin, and S. Power (Spring 1991). 'Grant Maintained Schools: A Third Force in Education?', pp. 36-8 in *Forum,* Vol. 33, No. 2.

Giroux, H., ed, (1990). *Postmodernism, Feminism, and Cultural Politics.* New York, NY: State University of New York Press.

Glenn, C. (1987). *The Myth of the Common School.* Amhurst, MA: University of Massachusetts Press.

Grace, G. (1991). 'Welfare Labourism and the New Right: The Struggle in New Zealand's Education Policy', pp. 37-48 in *International Studies in Sociology of Education,* 1.

Guy, W. and I. Menter (1992). 'Local Management of Schools: Who Benefits?', pp. 151-68 in D. Gill, B. Mayor, and M. Blair, eds., *Racism and Education: Structures and Strategies.* London, UK: Sage.

Hall, S. and M. Jacques, eds. (1989). *New Times.* London, UK: Lawrence and Wishart.

Halpin, D. and J. Fitz (1990). 'Local Education Authorities and the Grant Maintained Schools Policy'. Paper presented to the Annual Conference of the British Educational Research Association.

Halstead, J. (1986). *The Case for Muslim Voluntary-Aided Schools.* Cambridge, UK: The Islamic Academie.

Harvey, D. (1989). *The Condition of Postmodernity.* Oxford, UK: Basil Blackwell.

Hillgate Group (1987). *The Reform of British Education.* London, UK: Claridge Press.

House of Commons Select Committee on Education, Science and Arts (1990). *Staffing for Pupils with Special Educational Needs.* London, UK: HMSO.

Johnson, R. (1989). 'Thatcherism and English Education: Breaking the Mould or Conforming the Pattern?', pp. 91-121 in *History of Education,* Vol. 18, No.2.

Knight, B. (1990). 'Research on Local Management of Schools'. Paper presented to the Annual Conference of the British Educational Research Association.

Lash, S. (1990). *Sociology of Postmodernism.* London, UK: Routledge.

Lawton, D. (1975). *Class, Culture, and the Curriculum.* London, UK: Routledge.

Said, E. (1978). *Orientalism.* London, UK: Routledge.

Stevens, M. (1991). *Japan and Education.* London, UK: Macmillan.

TES (8 March 1991). 'Clarke Senses a Bloom Time Ahead', p. 3 in *The Times Educational Supplement.*

Tomlinson, T. And A. Tuijnman, eds. (1994). *Education Research and Reform: An International Perspective*. Paris, France: Organization for Economic Cooperation and Development, Center for Educational Research and Innovation; Washington, DC: Office of Educational Research and Improvement, US Department of Education.

Walford, G. and H. Miller (1991). *City Technology College*. Buckingham, UK: Open University Press.

Whitty, G. (1985). *Sociology and School Knowledge: Curriculum Theory, Research and Politics*. London, UK: Methuen.

Whitty, G. (in press). 'Citizens or Consumers? Continuity and Change in Contemporary Education Policy' in D. Carlson and M. Apple, eds., *Critical Educational Theory in Unsettling Times*. Minneapolis, MN: University of Minnesota Press.

Whitty, G. And I. Menter (1989). 'Lessons of Thatcherism: Education policy in England and Wales, 1979-88', pp. 42-64 in *Journal of Law and Society*, Vol. 16, No. 1.

Whitty, G., T. Edwards, and S. Gewirtz (1993). *Specialisation and Choice in Urban Education*. London, UK: Routledge.

REFERENCES FOR CHAPTER 15

Althusser, L. (1971) 'Ideology and Ideological State Apparatuses. Notes Towards an Investigation', pp. 127-86 in L. Althusser, *Lenin and Philosophy and Other Essays*. New York, NY: Monthly Review Press.

Apple, M. (1979). *Ideology and Curriculum*. London, UK: Routledge.

Apple, M. (1981). 'Reproduction, Contestation and Curriculum: An Essay in Self-Criticism', pp. 5-22 in *Interchange*, Vol. 12, No. 3.

Apple, M. (1982). 'Reproduction and Contradiction: An Introduction', pp. 1-31 in M. Apple, ed., *Cultural and Economic Reproduction in Education: Essays on Class, Ideology and the State*. London, UK: Routledge & Kegan Paul.

Apple, M. (1986). *Teachers and Texts*. London, UK: Routledge.

Apple, M. (1988). 'Series Editor's Introduction', pp. 1-10 in D. Liston, *Capitalist Schools: Explanation and Ethics in Radical Studies of Schooling*. London, UK: Routledge.

Battistoni, R. (1985). *Public Schooling and the Education of Democratic Citizens*. Oxford, MS: University Press of Missisippi.

Bernstein, R. (1983). *Beyond Objectivism and Relativism: Science, Hermeneutics and Praxis*. Philadelphia, PA: University of Pennsylvania Press.

Bernstein, R. (1987). 'The Varieties of Pluralism', pp. 509-25 in *American Journal of Education*, Vol. 95, No. 4.

Beyer, L. (1988). 'Schooling for the Culture of Democracy', pp. 219-38 in L. Beyer and M. Apple, eds., *The Curriculum: Problems, Politics and Possibilities*. Albany, NY: SUNY Press.

Boli, J., F. Ramirez, and J. Meyer (1985). 'Explaining the Origins and Expansion of Mass Education', pp. 145-70 in *Comparative Education Review*, Vol. 29, No. 2.

Bloom, A. (1987). *The Closing of the American Mind*. New York, NY: Simon & Schuster.

Bowles, S. and H. Gintis (1976). *Schooling in Capitalist America*. New York, NY: Basic Books.

Bowles, S. and H. Gintis (1986). *Democracy and Capitalism: Property, Community, and the Contradictions of Modern Social Thought*. New York, NY: Basic Books.

Carnoy, M. (1984). *The State and Political Theory*. Princeton, NJ: Princeton University Press.

Carnoy, M. and H. Levin (1985). *Schooling and Work in the Democratic State.* Stanford, CA: Stanford University Press.

Cherryholmes, C. (1988). *Power and Criticism.* New York, NY and London, UK: Teachers College Press.

Cunningham, P. (1988). *Curriculum Change in the Primary School Since 1945: Dissemination of the Progressive Ideal.* Lewes, UK: Falmer.

Dale, R. (1982). 'Education and the Capitalist State: Contributions and Contradictions', pp. 127-61 in M. Apple, ed., *Cultural and Economic Reproduction in Education: Essays on Class, Ideology and the State.* London, UK: Routledge & Kegan Paul.

Dale, R. (1988). 'Implications for Progressivism of Recent Changes in the Control and Direction of Education Policy', pp. 39-62 in A. Green and S. Ball, eds., *Progress and Inequality in Comprehensive Education.* London, UK: Routledge.

Dewey, J. (1916/1966). *Democracy and Education.* New York, NY: MacMillan. Glencoe, IL: Free Press.

Dewey, J. (1927/1985). *The Public and Its Problems.* Athens, OH: Ohio University Press.

Edwards, T., J. Fitz, and G. Whitty (1985). 'Private Schools and Public Funding: a Comparison of Recent Policies in England and Australia', pp. 29-45 in *Comparative Education*, Vol. 21, No. 1.

Englund, T. (1986). *Curriculum as a Political Problem: Changing Educational Conceptions, with Special Reference to Citizenship Education.* Uppsala, Sweden: Studentlitteratur/Uppsala Studies in Education 25.

Feinberg, W. (1989). 'Foundationalism and Recent Critiques of Education', pp. 133-8 in *Educational Theory*, Vol. 39, No. 2.

Finkelstein, B. (1985). 'Thinking Publicly about Civic Learning: An Agenda for Education Reform in the '80s', pp. 23-4 in A. Jones, ed., *Civic Learning for Teachers: Capstone for Educational Reform.* Ann Arbor, MI: Prakken.

Giarelli, J. (1983). 'The Public, the State and the Civic Education', pp. 33-6 in A. Bagley, ed., *Civic Learning in Teacher Education: College of Education.* Minneapolis, MN: University of Minnesota, Society of Professors of Education (SPE) Monograph Series.

Giddens, A. (1979). *Central Problems in Social Theory.* Berkeley, CA: University of California Press.

Giddens, A. (1982). *Profiles and Critiques in Social Theory.* New York, NY and London, UK: Macmillan.

Giroux, H. (1981). *Ideology, Culture and the Process of Schooling.* Philadelphia, PA: Temple University Press.

Giroux, H. (1983). *Theory and Resistance in Education: A Pedagogy for the Opposition.* South Hadley, MA: Bergin & Garvey.

Giroux, H. (1984). 'Public Philosophy and the Crisis in Educatiuon', pp. 186-94 in *Harvard Educational Review*, Vol. 54, No. 2.

Giroux, H. (1987). 'Citizenship, Public Philosophy and the Struggle for Democracy', pp. 103-20 in *Educational Theory*, Vol. 37, No. 2.

Giroux, H. (1988). *Schooling and the Struggle for Public Life.* Minneapolis, MN: University of Minnesota Press.

Goodson, I., ed. (1985). *Social Histories of the Secondary Curriculum.* London, UK: Falmer Press.

Goodson, I. (1987). *School Subjects and Curriculum Change.* London, UK: Falmer Press.

Gutmann, A. (1987). *Democratic Education.* Princeton, NJ: Princeton University Press.

Habermas, J. (1984/1988). *The Theory of Communicative Action* (2 Volumes). Cambridge, MA: Polity Press.

Hamilton, D. (1988). 'Some Observations on Progressivism and Curriculum Practice', pp. 23-38 in A. Green and S. Ball, eds., *Progress and Inequality in Comprehensive Education*. London, UK: Routledge.

Heidegger, M. (1968). *What Is Called Thinking*. New York, NY: Harper & Row.

Hirsch, E. (1988). *Cultural Literacy: What Every American Needs to Know*. New York, NY: Vintage Books.

Karabel, J. and A. Halsey (1977). 'Introduction. Educational Research: A Review and an Interpretation', pp. 1-85 in J. Karabel and A. Halsey, eds., *Power and Ideology in Education*. Oxford, UK: Oxford University Press.

Levine, M. et al. (1988). *The State and Democracy*. London, UK: Routledge.

Liston, D. (1988). *Capitalist Schools: Explanation and Ethics in Radical Studies of Schooling*. London, UK: Routledge.

Marshall, T. (1964). *Class, Citizenship and Social Development*. Garden City, NY: Doubleday.

McCutcheon, G. (Winter 1982). 'What in the World is Curriculum Theory?', pp. 18-22 in *Theory into Practice*, Vol. 21.

McLaren, P. (1988). 'Culture or Canon: Critical Pedagogy and the Politics of Literacy', pp. 213-34 in *Harvard Educational Review*, Vol. 58, No. 2.

Mouffe, C. (1979). 'Introduction: Gramsci Today', pp. 1-18 in C. Mouffe, ed., *Gramsci and Marxist Theory*. London, UK: Routledge and Kegan Paul.

Popkewitz, T. (March 1976). 'Myths of Social Science in Curriculum', pp. 317-28 in *Educational Forum*, Vol. 60.

Popkewitz, T. (1977a). 'The Latent Values of the Discipline-centered Curriculum', pp. 41-60 in *Theory and Research in Social Education*, Vol. 5, No. 1.

Popkewitz, T. (1977b). 'Craft and Community as Metaphors for Social Inquiry Curriculum', pp. 310-21 in *Educational Theory*, Vol. 27, Fall.

Popkewitz, T., ed. (1987). *The Formation of School Subjects: The Struggle for Creating the American Institution*. London, UK: Falmer Press.

Poulantzas, N. (1979). *Classes in Contemporary Capitalism*. London, UK: Verso Editions, Routledge, Chapman and Hall.

Poulantzas, N. (1980). *State, Power, Socialism*. London, UK: Verso Editions, Routledge, Chapman and Hall.

Reese, W. (1988). 'Public Schools and the Common Good', pp. 431-40 in *Educational Theory*, Vol. 38, No. 4.

Rochberg-Halton, E. (1986). *Meaning and Modernity: Social Theory in the Pragmatic Attitude*. Chicago, IL: University of Chicago Press.

Rorty, R. (1979). *Philosophy and the Mirror of Nature*. Princeton, NJ: Princeton University Press.

Rorty, R. (1983). *The Consequences of Pragmatism*. Minneapolis, MN: University of Minnesota Press.

Rorty, R. (1987). 'Science as Solidarity', pp. 38-52 in J. Nelson et al., eds., *The Rhetoric of the Human Sciences: Language and Argument in Scholarship and Public Affair*. Madison, WI: The University of Wisconsin Press.

Scholes, R. (1985). *Textual Power: Literary Theory and the Teaching of English*. New Haven, CT: Yale University Press.

Stanley, W. (1992). *Curriculum for Utopia: Social Reconstruction and Critical Pedagogy in the Postmodern Era*. Albany, NY: State University of New York Press.

Wexler, P. (1987). *Social Analysis of Education: After the New Sociology*. London, UK: Routledge.

Whitty, G. (1985). *Sociology and School Knowledge*. London, UK: Methuen.

Whitty, G. (1987). 'Curriculum Research and Curricular Politics', pp. 109-17 in *British Journal of Sociology of Education*, Vol. 8, No. 2.

Whitty, G., L. Barton, and A. Pollard (1987). 'Ideology and Control in Teacher Education: A Review of Recent Experience in England', pp. 161-83 in T. Popke-witz, ed., *Critical Studies in Teacher Education: Its Folklore, Theory and Practice*. London, UK: Falmer Press.

Williams, R. (1961). *The Long Revolution*. London, UK: Chatto & Windus.

Wood, G. (1984). 'Schooling in a Democracy: Transformation or Reproduction?', pp. 219-39 in *Educational Theory*, Vol. 34, No. 3.

Wood, G. (1988). 'Democracy and Curriculum', pp. 166-87 in L. Beyer and M. Apple, eds., *The Curriculum: Problems, Politics and Possibilities*. Albany, NY: SUNY Press.

Young, M., ed. (1971). *Knowledge and Control. New Directions for the Sociology of Education*. New York, NY and London, UK: Collier Macmillan.

Zinnecker, J. (1995). 'The Cultural Modernisation of Childhood', pp. 85-94 in L. Chisholm et al., eds., *Growing Up in Europe: Contemporary Horizons in Child-hood and Youth Studies*. Berlin, FRG and New York, NY: Walter de Gruyter.

REFERENCES FOR CHAPTER 16

Anyon, J. (Summer 1994). 'The Retreat of Marxism and Socialist Feminism: Post-modern and Poststructural Theories in Education', pp. 115-33 in *Curriculum Inquiry*, Vol. 24, No. 2.

Apple, M. (February 1992). 'Computers in School: Salvation or Social Disaster?', pp. 47-52 in *The Education Digest*, Vol. 57.

Apple, M. (October 1992). 'The Text and Cultural Politics', pp. 4-19 in *Educational Researcher*, Vol. 21.

Apple, M. (1993). *Official Knowledge: Democratic Education in a Conservative Age*. New York, NY: Routledge.

Apple, M. and L. Christian-Smith, eds. (1991). *The Politics of the Textbook*. New York, NY: Routledge.

Beck, U. (1992). *Risk Society: Towards a New Modernity*. London, UK: Sage Publica-tions.

Bernstein, B. (1973). *Class, Codes, and Control*, Vols. 1 and 2. London, UK: Rout-ledge and Kegan Paul.

Brosio, R. (1994). *A Radical Democratic Critique of Capitalist Education*. New York, NY: Peter Lang.

Dennis, E. And C. La May, eds. (1993). *American Schools and the Mass Media*. New Brunswick, NJ and London, UK: Transaction Publishers.

Edwards, T. And G. Whitty (May 1992). 'Parental Choice and Educational Reform in Britain and the United States', pp. 101-17 in *British Journal of Educational Studies*, Vol. 40, No. 2.

Farnen, R. (1996). 'Politische Sozialisation, Erziehung und kritische Theorie - Politik und Erziehung in den Vereinigten Staaten' (Political Socialization, Education, and Critical Theory - Politics and Education in the United States), pp. 135-69 in W. Helsper, H. Krüger, and H. Wenzel *Schule und Gesellschaft im Umbruch* (School and Society in Turmoil). Weinheim, FRG: Deutscher Studienverlag.

Giddens, A. (1994). *Beyond Left and Right: The Future of Radical Politics*. Stanford, CA: Stanford University Press.

Giroux, H. (May/June 1991). 'Beyond the Ethics of Flag Waving: Schooling and Citizenship for a Critical Democracy', pp. 305-8 in *The Clearing House*, Vol. 64.

Giroux, H. (Summer 1992). 'Language, Difference, and Curriculum Theory: Behond the Politics of Clarity', pp. 219-27 in *Theory Into Practice*, Vol. 31, No. 3.

Giroux, H. and P. McLaren (1992). 'Writing from the Margins: Geographics of Identity, Pedagogy, and Power', pp. 7-30 in *Journal of Education*, vol. 174, No. 1.

Giroux, H. and P. McLaren, eds. (1994). *Between Borders*. New York, NY: Routledge.

Karabel, J. and A. Halsey (1977). 'Educational Research: A Review and an Interpretation', pp. 1-85 in J. Karabel and A. Halsey, eds. *Power and Ideology in Education*. New York, NY: Oxford University Press.

Levin, H. (Spring 1994). 'Educational Workplace Needs', pp. 132-8 in *Theory Into Practice*, Vol. 33, No. 2.

Levinson, B., D. Foley, and D. Holland (1996). *The Cultural Production of the Educated Person*. Albany, NY: SUNY Press.

Shapiro, S. (1989). *Between Capitalism and Democracy*. Westport, CT: Bergin and Garvey and Greenwood Press.

Index of Names

Abberley, P., 66-7, 255
Abel, W., 261
Abrams, D., 269
Adler, C., vi, 153, 179, 273
Adler, M., vi, 153, 179, 273
Adorno, T., 39, 101, 113-4, 116-7, 119, 124-5, 146, 263, 266, 272
Alaszewski, A., 70, 255
Alexander, J., 272
Almond, G., 34, 249
Altbach, P., 169, 249, 275
Althusser, L., 23, 28, 114, 215-6, 249, 279
Anderson, L., 15, 249
Anderson, P., 115, 266
Anyon, J., 20-1, 39, 41, 230-1, 236, 249, 282
Apple, M., v, ix, 4-5, 18, 20-3, 26, 28, 30, 41, 45-59, 103, 105-6, 176, 215-6, 219, 225, 230, 232, 234-6, 246, 249, 253, 263, 273, 279-80, 282
Arnot, M., 20, 63, 69, 249, 254-5
Aronowitz, S., 17, 23-6, 144, 171, 249, 272-3
Arrighi, G., 118, 266
Ashenden, D., 266
Atkinson, J., 131, 269
Aush, N., 175, 275
Ayalon, H., 156, 273
Ayer, S., 70, 255
Baacke, D., 75, 257, 259
Baethge, M., 103, 106, 263
Baethge, V., 270
Bagley, A., 251, 280
Baker, K., 199, 205, 277
Ball, S., 65, 200, 205, 255, 277-8, 280-1
Banks, O., 63, 208, 255, 277
Barr, J., 47, 254
Barton, L., v, ix, 5, 63-72, 218, 249, 254-5, 257, 282
Bastian, A., 50, 253
Bates, S., 203, 277
Battistoni, R., 279
Baum, G., 193, 276
Bauman, Z., 188, 189, 276
Beck, K., 103, 263
Beck, U., 109, 239, 260, 263, 282
Beek, K. van, 130, 271

Beekman, A., 76, 257
Bell, C., 9, 41, 249
Bell, D., 174, 178, 273
Beniger, J., 174, 273
Benjamin, J., 150, 272
Benner, D., 102, 117, 263, 266
Berdahl, R., 249
Berg, I., 90, 171, 260, 273
Berger, P., 261, 262
Berkel, R. van, x, 136, 140, 270-1
Berman, M., 120, 179, 266, 273
Bernstein, R., 45, 55-6, 78-80, 82-3, 226-7, 249, 254, 257-8, 279, 282
Bertram, H., 87, 260
Berube, M., 273
Best, S., 53, 210, 254, 277
Beyer, L., 220, 279, 282
Biesta, G., 79-81, 258-9
Bines, H., 255
Bishop, M., 68, 255
Black, M., x, 171, 180-1, 273
Blackburne, L., 203, 277
Blair, M., 278
Bloch, E., 77, 258, 267
Bloom, A., 221, 278-9
Blossfeld, H., 95, 261
Bodenhöfer, H., 265
Bohnsack, R., 90, 260
Boli, J., 221, 279
Bolock, R., 255
Borchardt, K., 261
Bordo, S., 179, 273
Bourdieu, P., 18, 45-6, 96, 124, 137, 215, 250, 254, 260, 263, 266, 269
Bowe, R., 205, 278
Bowers, C., 180, 273
Bowles, S., 4, 18, 20, 23, 25-31, 101, 106-7, 135, 139, 172-3, 215, 219, 250-1, 263, 269, 274, 279
Boyne, R., 201, 278
Brademas, J., 250
Bradley, A., 143, 272
Branson, J., 70, 255
Brisenden, S., 66-7, 255
Brosio, R., 247, 282
Brown, H., 70, 255
Brown, P., 256
Brüggen, F., 266
Brzezinski, Z., 174, 274
Buber, M., 152, 272

285

Burgan, J., 171, 276
Burger, P., 188, 276
Carlson, D., 279
Carnoy, M., 17-9, 27-30, 36, 38, 107, 172, 216-7, 219, 250, 263, 274, 279-80
Carrier, J., 64, 255
Carrington, B., 256
Castoriadis, C., 150-1, 272
Cavalli, A., 258
Chappell, A., 70, 256
Cherryholmes, C., 211, 225, 280
Chisholm, L., xii, 257-9, 261-2, 264-5, 275, 282
Chopp, R., 195, 276
Christian-Smith, L., 47, 54, 58, 234, 253, 282
Chubb, M., 200-1, 278
Clark, B., 173, 274
Cobb, J., 178, 276
Coenen, H., x, 131, 136, 140, 269
Coenen-Hanegraaf, M., 138, 140, 271
Cohen, D., 15, 48, 253-4
Cole, M., 29-30, 101, 250, 263
Collin, R., 263
Collins, R., 101, 171, 174, 274
Connell, R., 266
Conquergood, D., 186, 276
Csepeli, G., 250
Cumper, P., 207, 278
Cunningham, P., 221, 280
Curtis, M., 274
Dale, R., 50, 59, 210, 216, 218, 221, 249, 251-2, 254, 278, 280
Dalley, G., 257
Darling-Hammond, L., 254
Dasberg, L., 76, 258
David, M., 63, 188, 256
Davies, L., 63, 256
Dean, C., 173, 190, 206, 278
Demaine, J., 63, 256
Dennis, E., 237, 282
Dercksen, W., 130, 269
Dewey, J., 18, 26, 28, 41, 57, 59, 78-9, 84, 211, 222, 224, 226, 242, 247, 258, 260, 280
Dickson, D., 174, 180, 274
Donald, J., 210, 278
Douglas, J., 63, 256
Dowsett, G., 266
Dryzek, J., 35, 250
Duckworth, E., 182, 274
Durkheim, E., 89, 260

Edmundson, M., 274
Edwards, T., xii, 50, 56-7, 205, 220, 230, 235, 254, 278-80, 282
Ehlert, W., 268
Elfring, T., 130-1, 269
Ellsworth, E., 53, 254
Engbersen, G., 136, 269-70
Englund, T., vi, ix, 11-2, 15, 32, 84, 112, 211-27, 250, 258, 280
Entzinger, H., 270
Etzioni, A., 9, 174, 274
Evans, R., 259
Farnen, R., iii-vi, viii-ix, 3-12, 15-43, 229-48, 250-2, 268, 282
Farrar, E., 253
Farren. M., 183, 277
Feinberg, W., 221-2, 280
Felsenthal, I., vi, x, 9, 153
Fend, H., 124, 131, 263, 269
Ferkiss, V., 174, 274
Fernandes, J., 259
Ferner, A., 130, 269
Findlay, B., 67-9, 256
Finkelstein, B., 36, 220, 251, 280
Fischer, F., vi, x, 9, 19, 32, 36, 169-82, 251, 261, 274
Fitz, J., 207-8, 220, 278, 280
Flanders, L., 175, 274
Fleuren, W., 130, 270
Floud, J., 63, 256
Foley, D., 283
Ford, J., 64, 256
Forester, J., 36, 251
Foucault, M., 53, 65, 73-4, 211, 256, 258
Frey, L., 276
Friedeburg, L. von, 101-2, 112, 263
Fruchter, N., 253
Fulcher, G., 64-5, 256
Gardner, J., 175, 274
Gerbner, G., 184, 277
Gergen, K., 277
Gewirtz, S., xii, 56-7, 254, 279
Giarelli, J., 26, 32, 224, 226, 251, 280
Giddens, A., 139, 213, 225, 239, 269, 280, 282
Gill, D., 278
Gillborn, D., 63, 256
Gintis, H., 4, 18, 20, 23, 25-31, 101, 106-7, 135, 139, 172-3, 215, 219, 250-1, 263, 269, 274, 279
Giroux, H., 4, 17-8, 20-6, 28, 32, 40-2, 84, 105, 109-10, 171, 202, 210,

215-6, 224, 230-2, 236, 249, 251-2, 258, 264, 273, 278, 280, 282-3
Gittell, M., 253
Glass, D., 63, 256
Glasser, W., 142, 272
Glendinning, C., 67-8, 256
Glenn, C., 200, 278
Gluchowski, P., 86, 260
Gold, A., 205, 278
Goodson, I., 214, 280
Gordon, J., 131, 133, 269, 273
Göstemeyer, K., 266
Gottdiener, M., 114, 266
Gould, S., 47, 254
Grace, G., 193, 201, 278
Green, A., 50, 52, 57, 254, 280-1
Green, C., 253
Greene, M., 182, 274
Greer, C., 172, 274
Grossberg, L., 184, 188, 190-3, 277
Grüneisen, V., 87, 260
Gumport, P., 249
Gutmann, A., 224, 280
Guy, W., 204, 278
Haber, S., 172, 274
Habermas, J., 6, 73, 77-9, 83, 115, 117, 224, 226, 258, 266, 281
Hagendoorn, L., 39, 252
Hahn, H., 65-6, 256
Hall, S., 69, 83, 200, 256, 258, 278
Halpin, D., 207, 278
Halsey, A., 63, 212, 215, 250, 256, 281, 283
Halstead, J., 202, 207, 278
Hamilton, D., 218, 281
Hammer, R., 196, 270, 277
Hancock, M., 275
Hanna, J., 33, 252
Hansmann, O., 265, 271
Hansot, E., 172, 276
Haraway, D., 47, 254
Harding. S., 47, 254
Harp, L., 144, 272
Harvey, D., 144, 150-1, 202, 272, 278
Haskins, K., 253
Havinghurst, R., 259
Hecker, D., 171, 276
Hegel, G., 19, 115, 117, 121-3, 266, 268
Heggade, O., 274
Heidegger, M., 226, 281
Heine, H., 93, 260
Heitmeyer, W., 262

Heller, A., 116, 120, 124, 266
Helsper, W., 251, 264, 282
Henrich, D., 268
Hess, R., 114, 266
Heydorn, H., 101, 112-26, 139, 264-6, 271
Hindriks, T., 136, 271
Hirsch, E., 54, 186, 222, 254, 281
Hitzler, R., 89, 260
Hoed, P. den, 130, 269
Hoff, E., 87, 260
Hohendahl, P., 123, 267
Holland, D., 283
Holt, D., 28, 188, 277
Honderich, T., 49, 51-2, 254
Honer, A., 89, 260
Honneth, A., 150, 272
Hoof, J. van, 132, 271
hooks, b., 178, 230, 274
Hopkins, T., 266
Horkheimer, M., 146, 272
Hornstein, W., 118, 267
Horstmann, R., 268
Hradil, S., v, x, 6, 85-100, 109, 260-2
Hudson, B., 68, 256
Huebner, D., 42, 252
Huijgen, F., 130, 131, 269
Hunter, A., 50, 254
Huntington, S., 174-5, 274
Hurn, C., 258
Hurrelmann, K., 87, 109, 254, 256, 260, 262, 264-5
Hyman, R., 130, 254, 269, 271-2
Illich, I., 252
Jackson, B., 63, 256
Jacques, M., 200, 278
Jallade, J., 269
Jay, M., 116, 267
Jencks, C., 107, 264
Jennings, M., 40-1, 252
Johnson, R., 50-1, 53-4, 200, 254, 278
Jonas, H., 151, 272
Jones, A., 251, 280
Judy, S., 171, 274
Jungck, S., 56, 253
Kaestle, K., 171, 276
Kalas, J., 179, 274
Kann, M., 275
Karabel, J., 63, 212, 215, 250, 256, 281, 283
Kargon, R., 173, 275
Karp, S., 57, 254
Katz, M., 161, 172, 274

Katznelson, I., 172, 274
Keckeisen, W., 102, 264
Keim, D., 90, 261
Kell, A., 103, 263
Kellebenz, H., 261
Kellner, D., 53, 210, 254, 277
Kelly, E., 252
Kelly, G., 275
Kemenade, J. van, 137, 271
Kenney, M., 179, 275
Keri, L., 250
Kern, H., 124, 130, 267, 269
Kessler, S., 266
Kester, G., 270
Kfir, D., 156, 273
Kilian, H., 124, 267
Kimball, R., 185, 187, 277
Kincheloe, J., 277
King, N., 23, 41, 249
Klafki, W., 77, 258
Klein. E., 43, 252
Kleinberg, B., 174, 275
Kloosterman, R., 130-1, 269
Kluge, A., 114, 267
Knight, B., 204, 278
Kolbe, F., v, xi-ii, 6, 101-12, 210, 251
Koneffke, G., 125, 267
König, E., 73, 258
Kop, Y., 154, 273
Kozol, J., 28, 55, 59, 170, 254, 275
Kreckel, R., 263, 264
Kreisberg, S., 177, 275
Kroft, H., 136, 270
Krüger, H., 251, 282
Krupat, A., 196, 277
Kruyt, A., 130, 270
Kunneman, H., 78-9, 258
La May, C., 237, 282
Lasch, C., 174, 275
Lash, S., 209, 278
Lauder, H., 69, 256
Lawton, D., 210, 278
Lazerson, M., 176, 275
Leach, B., 69, 256
Leemput, J. van, x, 140, 270
Lefebvre, H., 114, 116-20, 266-7
Leisink, P., vi, x, 7, 129-40, 269-70
Lenhart, V., xi, 101, 264
Lenz, K., 92-93, 261
Leonard, S., 35, 123, 250
Lepsius, M., 261
Lerner, M., 177, 275
Levering, B., 260

Levin, H., 17-9, 27-30, 107, 172, 216-7, 219, 230, 233, 236, 250, 263, 274, 280, 283
Levine, D., 259
Levine, M., 218, 281
Levinson, B., 247, 283
Lijphart, A., 134, 270
Lippe, R. zur, 120, 267
Liston, D., 29-31, 53, 219, 252, 254, 279, 281
Lowe, R., 57, 254
Löwy, M., 267
Lüdtke, H., 86, 91, 261
Luijk, E. van, 130, 269
Lukacs, G., 114, 116, 267
Lutz, B., 108, 264
Lyotard, J., 73-4, 78, 187, 201, 259
MacCannell, D., 190, 196, 277
Macpherson, C., 19, 36, 252
Magad, A., 273, 274
Maggs, J., 256
Mandell, A., vi, xi, 9, 169-82
Manen, M. van, 259
Markus, G., 115, 118, 120, 267
Marotzki, W., xii, 265, 271
Marsden, D., 63, 256
Marshall, T., 212-4, 281
Martin, F., 27, 256
Marx, K., 116, 118-21, 123, 266-8
Mar'i, S., 157, 273
Masemann, V., 33, 252
Mason, M., 65, 69, 256
Mautz, R., 93, 260
Mayer, K., 95, 104, 261, 264
Mayor, B., 278
McCutcheon, G., 225, 281
McKibbens, B., 179, 275
McLaren, P., vi, xi, 4, 10, 183-96, 222, 230, 232, 277, 281, 283
Meier, D., 181, 275
Meighan, R., 63, 255
Meijers, F., 137, 270
Meloen, J., 39, 252
Melzer, W., 254, 264-5
Menter, I., 204, 278-9
Merelman, R., 37, 40-1, 252
Mestrovic, S., 150, 272
Meulemann, H., 104, 264
Meyer, J., 167, 221, 273, 279
Miedema, S., v, xi, 6, 73-84, 251, 258-9, 265
Miller, D., 70, 255
Miller, H., 206, 208, 279

Mills, C., xi, 64, 68, 256
Minh-ha, T., 194, 277
Mintzel, A., 90, 261
Moe, T., 200-1, 278
Mok, A., 131, 270
Mollenhauer, K., 75, 259
Möller, K., 91-2, 261
Mongardini, C., 150, 272
Mongon, D., 256
Monroe, K., 34, 252
Montesquieu, C., 89, 261
Morris, J., 68, 257
Morrow, R., 261
Mouffe, C., 210, 216, 281
Mukerji, C., 173, 179, 275
Mulkey, L., 259
Müller, H., 261
Nasaw, D., 172, 275
Negt, O., 114, 267
Nelson, J., 259, 281
Nelson, L., 123, 125, 267
Neubauer, G., xii, 254, 256, 265
Neumann, U., 270
Niess, M., 75, 259
Noddings, N., 182, 275
Oevermann, U., 88, 261
Offe, C., 19, 28, 36, 118, 252, 268
Olalquiaga, C., 150, 272
Oliver, M., 67-8, 71, 257
Ong, B., 70, 255
O'Day, J., 48, 253-4
Panitch, O., 142, 272
Parkes, D., 269
Passeron, J., 23, 137, 215, 250, 263, 269
Penna, A., 41, 249, 251-2
Peres, Y., 167, 273
Peschek, J., 175, 275
Peters, T., 175, 178, 275
Peterson, P., 275
Peterson, S., 37, 252
Petrie, H., 253
Peukert, D., 118, 268
Pinar, W., 249, 251-2
Pinaud, H., 270
Pollard, A., 218, 282
Pols, S., 259
Popkewitz, T., 21, 214, 253, 281-2
Poulantzas, N., 216-8, 281
Power, S., 278
Praag, B. van, 130, 271
Preuss-Lausitz, U., 262
Prokop, D., 267

Purpel, D., 40-2, 249, 252
Rabinow, P., 258
Rajchman, J., 259
Ramirez, F., 221, 279
Rang, A., 74, 75, 259
Ratner, S., 258
Rattansi, A., 201, 278
Ravitch, D., 185, 187, 222, 277
Reese, W., 220-2, 281
Reich, R., 9, 174, 275
Reichelt, H., 114, 120, 268
Reid, I., 63, 257
Rerrich, M., 262
Reubsaet, T., 130, 270
Richie, R., 171, 276
Richter, E., 101, 264
Rifkin, J., 179, 276
Roaf, C., 255
Robinson, P., 63, 257
Rochberg-Halton, E., 211, 281
Roche, M., x, 83-4, 259, 270
Rolff, H., 103, 264
Ronge, V., 19, 28, 36, 252
Rorty, R., 78-80, 211, 226-7, 259, 281
Rosaldo, R., 196, 277
Rose, S., 54, 254
Roses, M., 177, 276
Ross, A., 277
Roszak, T., 180, 276
Rowan, B., 167, 273
Russell, R., 268
Ryan, W., 71, 178, 257, 276
Said, E., 202, 278
Saporiti, A., 257, 264
Sarason, S., 254
Sartre, J., 119, 268
Sarup, M., 188, 277
Sauer, K., 77, 259
Schissler, J., 90, 260
Schmoker, M., 142, 272
Schneewind, K., 88, 262
Scholes, R., 225, 281
Scholtz, H., 131, 270
Schoolman, M., 273, 274
Schoppmeyer, W., 276
Schouten, W., 132, 270
Schubarth, W., xi, 264, 265
Schulze, G., 90, 262
Schumann, M., 124, 130, 267, 269-70
Schuyt, K., 270
Sennett, R., 178, 276
Shamos, M., 276
Shapira, R., 156, 273

Shapiro, S., 169, 235, 276, 283
Shirley, D., 23, 253
Shor, I., 169, 276
Shotter, J., 277
Sjoberg, G., 275
Sklar, H., 174, 175, 276
Smith. H., 70, 255
Smith, M., 15, 48, 64, 253-5
Smith, R., xii
Sommerfield, M., 143, 272
Spindler, G., 252-3
Spring, J., 172-3, 253, 276
Springer, R., 270
Stanley, M., 176, 276
Stanley, W., 281
Stedman, L., 171, 276
Steinberg, S., 277
Steiner, I., 259
Steinkamp, G., 88, 93, 262
Stephanson, A., 190, 277
Stevens, M., 201, 278
Stief, W., 87-8, 262
Stijnen, P., 270
Straussmann, J., 174, 276
Strikker, F., xii, 101, 265
Stumpf, I., 250
Sünker, H., iii-v, vii, viii, xii, 6-7, 101-26, 139-40, 210, 251, 265, 268, 271
Széll, G., 268
Sztompka, R., 272
Taine, H., 89, 262
Teichler, U., 103, 263
Teunissen, J., 82, 259
Thomas, S., 70, 257
Thompson, K., 255
Tijdens, K., 131, 271
Timmermann, D., v, vii, xii, 101-12, 210, 251, 265
Tippelt, R., 103, 264-5
Tirozzi. G., 16, 253
Tobin, J., 33, 253
Tomlinson, T., 64, 255, 257, 279
Touraine, A., 146, 272
Trommel, W., 131, 271
Tuana, N., 47, 254
Tuijnman, A., 279
Tyack, D., 172, 253, 276
Ulich, D., 262
Unger, R., 195, 277
Utterback, D., 175, 274
Valkenburg, B., 138, 140, 270-1
Vaskovics, L., 88, 262

Vester, M., 90, 97-100, 262
Viadero, D., 144, 272
Vilrokx, J., x, 140, 270
Vincent, J., 151, 272
Voß, G., 262
Voßkamp, W., 267
Waarden, F. van, 270
Walford, G., 206-8, 279
Walker, S., 63, 249, 255
Wallerstein, I., 266
Walters, K., 179, 276
Watermans, R., 175, 178, 275
Watts, A., 131-3, 139, 271
Wehler, H., 115-6, 268
Weibe, R., 172, 276
Weiner, G., 63, 257
Weingrod, A., 273
Weir, M., 172, 274
Weis, L., 71, 253, 257
Weiss, L., 24, 249, 275
Wenzel, H., 251, 282
Werner, H., 123, 269
Werthein, J., 38, 250
West, C., 190, 259, 277
Westbrook, R., 80, 84, 260
Wexler, P., vi, xii, 8, 103, 105-6, 110-1, 141-52, 216, 265, 272, 281
Whelan, M., 256
Whitty, G., vi, xii, 4, 10-1, 20, 47, 52, 54, 56-7, 59, 105, 199- 210, 212, 215-7, 220, 230, 234-5, 246, 249, 254-5, 265, 278-82
Wilcox, K., 33-4, 253
Williams, J., 63, 257, 262
Williams, R., 58, 63, 220, 255, 257, 282
Williamson, O., 136, 271
Willis, P., 4, 20, 25, 28, 39-40, 105, 109, 138-40, 194, 253, 265, 271, 277
Winkel, R. van de, 131, 269
Winning, A., 259
Wit, T. de, 140, 271
Wolfensberger, W., 257
Wolk, R., 143, 272
Wood, G., 21, 25-6, 253, 282
Wood, S., 131, 271
Worthington, R., 171, 180-1, 273
Young, M., 105, 215, 265, 282
Zapf, W., 85-6, 262
Zinnecker, J., 262, 282
Zorn, W., 261

Index of Subjects

affirmative action, 3, 4, 239, 245
agency (educational, human, personal, social), 21-2, 30, 188, 196, 220, 231, 240, 243, 247
apathy, 177, 183, 191, 192
Australia, 11, 201
authoritarianism, ix, xi, 4, 8, 23, 25, 27, 33-4, 36, 39, 52, 54, 65, 70, 81, 139, 148, 150-1, 173, 176-81, 237, 244
autonomy, 6-7, 9-10, 18, 21, 28, 45, 55-6, 67, 74, 76-7, 82, 99, 106-8, 110-2, 140, 168, 195, 224, 229, 242-4
Bildungs theory, vii, xi, xii, 6, 75, 76, 113-26, 182, 210
Canada, 3, 16, 25, 155, 165, 187, 234, 236
capitalism, 23, 28, 30-1, 66, 120, 135, 142, 177, 183-4, 187, 190, 205, 218, 235, 246
citizenship, x, 6, 11-2, 17, 32, 35, 41-2, 82-4, 111-2, 136, 175, 184-5, 194, 210-4, 216, 218-20, 223-5, 227, 232, 236, 242, 245-8
  democratic, 17, 84, 220, 224
City Technology Colleges (CTCs), 11, 205-8
civics, new, 20
class (caste), 3-11, 17-8, 20-1, 23-4, 27-31, 33-4, 36, 38-9, 41, 43, 46-7, 53, 55, 57, 59, 63-4, 68, 71, 85-8, 90, 92, 95-8, 100-2, 106, 109-11, 124, 136-8, 145-50, 158, 172-3, 178, 186, 191-4, 201-2, 206, 208, 210, 212, 214, 216-8, 230, 236, 238, 240, 242-3, 245-6
corporatism, vi, 3, 141-52, 238
correspondence, theory of, 20, 22-3, 37, 216, 240, 247
cosmopolitanism, 84, 239
criteriology, v, 73-84, 227, 242, 247-8
critical functionalists, 28
critical theory, v, 3-4, 7, 10, 15-43, 84, 102-3, 106, 114, 176, 195, 229-30, 232, 235-7, 239-43, 245, 247-8
culture
  common, 4-5, 10, 52, 54, 58, 194, 196

  national, 54
  political, 15, 30, 37, 83, 218, 231, 236
  predatory, vi, xi, 3, 10, 183-96
curriculum, ix, 6, 8, 10, 18, 27, 31-3, 37, 42-3, 81, 103, 105, 107-8, 133, 143-4, 168, 172, 179, 185, 194, 205, 210-1, 213-21, 229-34, 247
  comprehensive, 134-5, 137-40, 243
  hidden, 20-3, 40-1, 231, 240-1
  national, v, 4-5, 11, 15-6, 45-59, 199-200, 203, 209, 225, 227, 234, 237, 241, 246
decision making, x, 10, 16, 18, 34, 37-9, 42, 217, 232, 236, 241
deconstruction, 7, 145
democracy, v, ix, 3-4, 6, 9-10, 12, 16, 21, 24-7, 29, 32, 37, 39, 40, 42, 51, 56-7, 72-84, 101, 112, 116, 139, 172-80, 183-4, 187, 195-6, 212, 216-21, 223, 227, 230, 232, 235, 239-42, 244-5, 248
disability, v, ix, 3, 5-6, 19, 63-72, 186, 230, 238, 241-42, 245, 247
discrimination, 3, 8, 38, 63-4, 68, 71, 130, 204-5, 241
distribution process, covert and overt, 167
diversity, ix, 4, 11, 24, 54, 73, 185, 194, 199-200, 202-3, 205, 207-8, 210, 232, 234, 240, 245-7
Eastern Europe, 10-1, 83, 158, 186, 201
education
  and the economy, 3, 139
  as individual citizenship right, 212
  Bildungs theory, v, 113
  citizenship, 17, 35, 42, 224, 245, 247
  civic, ix, 4, 15, 32, 35-6, 40-1, 220, 230, 234, 240, 248
  economics of, i, iii, xii, 3, 12, 243
  Erziehung, 75, 251
  institutionalized, 105-8, 111-2, 123
  policy concerns of, vi, vii, ix, 6-7, 9-10, 23, 35, 39, 43, 49, 82, 101, 107-8, 112, 129, 132, 134, 136, 169-82, 212-4, 225, 242, 243

political, 35, 41-2, 140, 218, 224, 234, 240, 246
political economy of, 17, 27, 29
politics and, vi, 39, 102, 129, 170, 202, 230, 238
politics of, 32, 35, 37
postsecondary, 165, 166
progressive, 245, 248
reform, vi, 9-10, 16, 27, 36, 48, 129, 141-3, 153, 167, 172-3, 177, 179, 181-2, 197-210, 223, 230, 236, 238, 243, 245, 248
sociology of, xii, 3, 5-7, 11, 63, 71, 101-3, 105-6, 211-9, 241-2, 246
special, 5, 64, 204-5
technical, 4
theories of, xi, xii, 15, 22, 29, 34-5, 73, 101-2, 107, 111, 113, 115, 118-9, 124-5, 239, 243, 245-6, 248
vocational, xii, 9, 24, 103, 132-5, 138, 161-4, 167, 243-4
El Salvador, 193
elitism, 3, 8, 36, 179
emancipation, vi, 3, 7, 23, 26-7, 75, 78, 81, 102, 111, 113, 121-2, 124-6, 129-40, 187-8, 190, 194, 219, 230-2, 238, 240, 243, 245
enlightenment, xi, 22, 25, 89, 115, 122, 196, 229
project, 11, 73, 75, 78, 119, 201-2, 240, 242
equal opportunity, 5, 19, 27, 32-3, 63, 69-70, 104, 107, 208, 212, 222
equality, 3, 4, 11, 18-9, 25-8, 30-3, 68, 76, 107, 122, 139, 161, 172, 177, 212, 220-1, 223, 231, 240, 243, 245
equity, 3, 11, 18, 36, 181, 239, 245
ethnicity, ix, 3, 6, 53, 158, 243, 245, 247
ethnography, 33, 34, 39
excellence, vi, 9-10, 19, 31, 169-82, 222, 229, 237, 239, 244-5, 248
Finland, 16
France, x, 16, 22, 131, 155, 165, 209, 247
gender, 3-4, 8, 21, 23-4, 27, 29-31, 37-8, 43, 45, 47, 50, 55, 63-4, 69, 71, 92, 130, 132, 136, 156, 185-6, 193-4, 208, 230, 234, 236, 239-40, 243, 245, 247

Germany (FRG), iii, vii-xii, 3, 6-7, 22, 42, 72, 85-6, 88-9, 95, 98-9, 101-3, 112-3, 115, 123, 126, 131, 164-5, 210, 215, 239, 241-2
Grant Maintained Schools (GMS), 11, 206-8
Guatemala, 193
guest laborers, 6
hegemony, 3-4, 21-2, 24, 26-7, 30, 39, 54, 110, 173, 190-1, 193, 216, 229, 244, 246
hermeneutics, 6, 79, 195
heterogeneity, 11, 54, 74, 78, 94, 201-2, 209-10, 246
homophobia, 186, 245
human capital, 139, 240
humanism, 7, 11, 49, 122-3, 151, 244
identity (personal, group, national, and cosmopolitan), vi, ix, xii, 7-9, 52, 68-9, 74, 81-3, 93, 109, 117, 123, 125, 141-52, 183, 185, 188, 191-4, 196, 221, 232, 234, 244-5
immigrants, 6, 83, 140, 158, 166, 243, 244
inequality, v, vii, x, xii, 3, 11, 18, 22, 26, 28, 30, 40, 63, 69, 156, 176, 208, 223, 232-4, 244, 246
and education, 101-12
social, vii, x, xii, 5-9, 72, 87, 92, 94-7, 99-101, 105, 107, 129-30, 132, 134-40, 192, 210, 241-3
integration, 9, 25, 66, 96, 103, 105, 110, 150, 160-1, 167-8, 217, 244
Israel, vi, ix, x, 3, 9, 153-68, 244
Japan, 11, 16, 47, 56, 155, 165, 201, 241
labor, division of, vi, 23, 31, 71, 129-40, 173, 217, 243
labor market, xii, 7, 82, 85, 129-36, 139-40, 170, 206, 243
segmentation of, 131
lifestyle, varieties of, 86, 91-3, 96, 146
literacy, cultural, 179, 186
local education authorities (LEAs), 11, 199-200, 204-8, 246
local management of schools (LMS), 204, 208-9
marginalization, 5, 10, 65, 67, 70
marketization, 51, 55, 58
Marxism, 4, 25-6, 29, 114-6, 118, 243
neo-Marxism, 15, 34-5, 40-1, 215, 230, 240

mass media, ix, 29, 84, 185, 229, 237, 244-5
meritocracy, 3, 9, 177-8, 244
metadiscourse, 34, 247
   patriarchalistic, 226
   scientific-rational, 12, 32, 214, 221-3, 225-6, 246
milieu, types of, 6, 86, 89-100, 242
minority, 7, 11, 18-9, 34, 38, 58, 131-2, 136, 149, 156-7, 177, 184-6, 207, 234, 243-4
modernism, 6, 8, 11, 22, 73-5, 77-8, 187-9, 201, 210, 252, 255, 258-60, 266-7, 272, 281-2
modernity project, 73-5, 77
Morocco, 82
motivation, 6, 31, 70, 157, 177-8, 206, 245
multiculturalism, xi, 4, 11, 34, 40, 43, 49, 54, 187, 209, 231
nationalism, ix, 3, 39, 191
neoconservatism, 5, 32, 36, 42, 48-50, 209
neoliberalism, 5, 48, 50-1, 57, 202, 241
neopragmatism, 242
Netherlands, x, xi, 3, 6-8, 17, 80-2, 129-37, 139-40, 155, 163, 165, 241, 243
New Left, 15, 35, 40, 105
New Right, 4, 10-2, 49, 53-4, 183, 191-2, 199-201, 209, 229, 239, 241, 246-7
   conservative restoration, 3, 4, 10-2, 46, 49, 50, 53-4, 59, 183, 191-2, 199-201, 209, 218, 226, 229, 239, 241, 246-7
New Zealand, 11, 201, 236
normalization, 70, 241
oppression, v, 3, 5-7, 22, 30, 43, 63-84, 110, 186, 188-9, 192-3, 231, 240-1, 245
pedagogy, vi, x, xi, 6, 10, 12, 21, 24-5, 35, 42-3, 46, 48, 53-4, 56, 73-7, 80-1, 84, 116, 119, 123-4, 183-96, 223, 233, 242, 245, 247-8
phronesis, 79-80, 226-7
pillarization, 6, 81-2
pluralism, 3, 6, 11, 25, 34-5, 41, 43, 56, 75, 78-83, 108, 186-7, 189, 193, 202, 208, 234, 245-6
   sociocultural, 87, 88, 94, 96
policy making, vii, 3, 24, 34, 36, 39, 240, 243

political science, iii, vii, ix, x, 15, 34-8, 40-2, 240
politics
   and education, vii, ix, 32, 37, 236, 251
   and/of education, v, 4, 13-60, 236, 238
   conservative, v, 45-60, 49
   educational, 129-40
   everyday, 15, 24, 37, 240
Portugal, 82, 259
postindustrialism, 3-4, 6, 8-11, 22, 36, 38, 74, 130, 142, 170, 174-7, 179, 181-3, 202, 230, 239, 243-6, 248
postmodernism, vi, xi, xii, 3-4, 6, 8, 10, 24-5, 73-6, 78-9, 141, 144-5, 147, 149-52, 183, 187-92, 196, 199-210, 229-31, 235-6, 238, 242-8
poststructuralism, 8, 74, 141, 188-9, 195, 230, 235-6, 245
pragmatism, xi, 3, 6, 11, 78, 84, 211-28, 247-8
praxis, vii, 7, 10, 22, 25, 31, 33, 41, 76-7, 110, 116-22, 124, 195, 240, 243
privatization, 3, 4, 8, 46, 50-2, 55-6, 58, 141, 199, 236-7, 241
public
   democratic, vi, 11, 25, 211-28, 231, 236
   policy, x, 3, 34, 36, 38, 82, 181, 248
race, 3-4, 21, 23-4, 29, 31, 38, 43, 50, 53, 55, 57, 63-4, 68, 71, 185-6, 194, 203, 230, 243, 245, 247
rationality, 6, 12, 21, 23-4, 32, 73-4, 78, 196, 222-3, 242, 246
reconceptualism, v, 15, 20, 42-3, 229-30, 240-1, 247-8
reproduction
   cultural, 21, 26, 37, 105, 187, 240
   economic, v-7, 28, 85-100, 153-68, 229, 244
   theory of and education, v, vi, 3, 5-7, 9, 12, 18-22, 25-30, 37, 39, 41, 43, 63, 83, 85-101, 103, 105-7, 109-111, 129, 139, 153-68, 187, 208, 210, 214-6, 219, 229, 232, 240, 242-4, 246, 248
resistance, vii, 7, 20-6, 37, 39, 41-2, 56, 72, 105, 108-11, 124, 139, 150, 185, 192, 210, 219, 231-2, 240-1, 243, 246

risk society, 260, 282
social
   analysis, v, 3, 113-26, 242
   inequality, 94, 174, 176, 205, 244
   justice, 10, 12, 18, 42, 68, 71-2,
      187, 191, 194, 196, 219-20, 229,
      232-3, 235, 240, 242, 245, 247
   mobility, 6, 49, 55, 63, 86-7,
      94-100, 105, 157-8, 172, 191,
      213-4, 242, 244
   reoganization, 141
   reproduction, 5, 22, 30, 63, 110,
      208, 240, 246
   structure, ix, x, 7, 15, 86, 88, 90-1,
      96-7, 102-4, 107-9
socialization, v, ix, x, 3, 6, 15, 33-6,
     38-42, 85-100, 102-5, 107, 109,
     112, 123-4, 215, 220, 224-5, 240,
     242
   political, ix, 35, 38-42, 220, 240
sociology, of education, ix, 102, 105,
     111-2
Spain, 82
state
   as evolutionary force, 212, 213
   relational theory of, 216
   theory of, 19, 36, 111, 216, 218,
     247
structuralism, 22, 106, 230, 231
subject and resistance, 108, 109
subversion, 232
Surinam, 80, 82
Sweden, ix, 3, 22, 32, 214
teamwork, 8, 22, 38, 130, 144, 240
technisurfacing, 146
technocratic strategy (technocracy), vi,
     x, 123, 169-82
technological literacy, 179-80, 244
testing, 9, 19, 26, 143, 169, 171, 179,
     231, 237, 241, 244
   national, 4, 15-7, 46-9, 52-3, 55-8
textbook, 4, 5, 12, 20, 22, 47, 225, 234,
     241
Thatcherism, 83, 200
Toyota school, 130, 230
Turkey, 82
unemployment, 7, 17, 39-40, 50, 55,
     86, 129-32, 139, 158

United Kingdom (UK), ix-xii, 3-5, 11,
     16-7, 20, 22, 29, 39, 42, 47, 50,
     54, 56-7, 64, 71, 105, 131-2, 155,
     165, 196, 199, 202, 206, 218,
     221, 230, 234-6, 239, 241-2, 245-
     6
United States of America (US), iii, v,
     vii, viii, x, 3-5, 9-11, 15-8, 20, 22,
     25, 27-9, 33-6, 39, 42-3, 47, 50,
     52-6, 58-9, 64-6, 69, 73-4, 76, 78,
     80, 90, 94, 96, 105, 113, 117,
     121, 123, 153-5, 159, 161, 163,
     165, 169, 170, 172-3, 178, 180-1,
     184, 186-8, 190-1, 193-4, 200-1,
     206, 209, 215, 218, 224, 229-31,
     234-6, 238-9, 241-2, 244-5, 247
utopia, 6, 21, 25, 74-7, 79-80, 119,
     151-2, 189, 195, 232, 239, 242,
     245
welfare, v, 3, 5-6, 11, 22, 32, 49-50, 67,
     81, 83-100, 136, 147, 185, 212,
     239
Yugoslavia, 82